CANE RIPPLES

THE CHINESE IN GUYANA

by

Trev Sue-A-Quan, Ph.D.

Vancouver, British Columbia

Cane
Press

Published by

Cane Press
240 Woodstock Avenue E.
Vancouver, B.C. V5W 1N1

Other books by the author:
    Cane Reapers: Chinese Indentured Immigrants in Guyana
        First edition 1999
        Second revised edition 2003

National Library of Canada Cataloguing in Publication Data

Sue-A-Quan, Trev, 1943-
  Cane ripples : the Chinese in Guyana / by Trev Sue-A-Quan.

  ISBN 0-9733557-1-9

  1. Chinese--Guyana--Biography. 2. Chinese--Guyana--History. I.
Title.
F2391.C5S94 2003   988.1'004951   C2003-911094-X

Printed in Canada

Photo credits are shown in italics with the photos.

Crown copyright material is reproduced with the permission of the controller of HMSO and the Queen's Printer for Scotland.

Front cover: Kaieteur Falls – *Roy V. Wong*; Four generations of descendants of Lo Shee, from top to bottom: 1) Lo Shee, b. 1829 Kai Heng, China. *Andy Lee.* 2) George Lee, b. 1869 Ogle, East Coast Demerara. *Andy Lee.* 3) Katie Lee, b. 1897 Georgetown, Guyana. *M.R. Lam.* 4) Kenneth Lam, b. 1921 Vreed en Steyn, West Bank Demerara. *Peter Lam.*

Back cover: Transition in dress styles over the generations. Top: Phoebe Wong in traditional 19th century Chinese dress. *Patsy Layne.* Center: Josephine Wong-A-Wing wears a Victorian style dress of the early 20th century. *Sandra Wong-Moon.* Bottom: Pamela Sue-A-Quan, winner of the 1954 Miss British Guiana contest, in the evening dress she wore for the competition. *Pamela Whittle.*

FOREWORD

Dr. Trev Sue-A-Quan must be congratulated for compiling this important book. *Cane Ripples* is more than a collection of stories about the experience of the Chinese diaspora in Guyana. It uses oral histories, personal recollections, photographs, and archival materials to illuminate an important aspect of Guyana's complex history.

Since 1853, Chinese have been important contributors to all aspects of Guyanese life. Through *Cane Ripples* we are able to appreciate the ethnic diversity of our Chinese ancestors. We can see the names and the faces that influenced Guyana's social, economic, political, cultural, and scientific life. Contributors take us into their homes, share family histories, and tell us about the creation of some of Guyana's most successful institutions and enterprises such as Central High School, Tangs' Bakery, Lee Bros. Funeral parlor, Wing Lee Laundry, Ace Advertising Agency, and Sheila's Restaurant.

Cane Ripples is also a story about life in all regions of Guyana. Through the personal stories we find out about life in coastal and hinterland Guyana – Georgetown, villages on East Coast Demerara, East Bank Demerara, West Coast and West Bank Demerara, New Amsterdam, Pomeroon, and the Northwest District. The stories of residence in Georgetown tell us about the development of a Chinese enclave and its destruction by the Great Fire of 1913. The stories of the hinterland tell us about technological innovations in sawmilling, charcoal burning, and pork knocking.

Cane Ripples also permits us to explore the celebration of interracial solidarity in Guyana. The first Chinese women to immigrate to Guyana came in 1860; thus, from very early Chinese men married or established liaisons with other races in Guyana. Guyanese of Chinese ancestry have made a substantial contribution to the development of the professions in Guyana. Through *Cane Ripples* we find out about the obstacles that were overcome on the way to becoming nurses, doctors, dentists, pharmacists, and lawyers in colonial British Guiana. Guyanese of Chinese descent also made significant contributions to Guyana's political development. Stories about those efforts are also told in this book.

Some of these stories have spoken directly to me. I find David Foo's story about catching wild birds and training them to whistle in bird races especially intriguing. It not only reminds me of my childhood days, it reinforces a conclusion I had come to in 1995 when my family and I visited Singapore. We were fascinated by the place of caged birds in Chinese Singaporean society. In the mornings we awoke to the songs of these birds wafting throughout the Marina Mandarin Hotel. The experience made me think of Guyana and my "bird minding" days and caused me to conclude that our Chinese ancestors may have been responsible for the popularity of bird minding and racing in Guyana. David Foo's story supports my conclusion.

I grew up in Alberttown, Georgetown, during the 1950s and early 1960s. I would join other boys from the neighborhood to be "ball boys" for the tennis players at the Chinese Sports Club in Thomas Lands. In addition to retrieving the lawn tennis balls, we developed lasting friendships with many of the club members. One of them was Godfrey Chin, whose "nostalgia" in *Cane Ripples* was particularly poignant as it took me back to the Chinese Sports Club where we were "ball boys" and learned about fair play and savored the joy of seeing the underdog win.

Cane Ripples is an integrated work that expresses the joy and pains experienced by a vital sector of Guyanese society during the 20th century. It makes it clear that Guyana's complex history is about connections among all of its peoples. Dr. Trev Sue-A-Quan must be congratulated for a most valuable and accessible contribution.

Vibert C. Cambridge, Ph.D., Chair
Department of African American Studies
Ohio University
Athens, OH 45701

v

Contents

vi

Preface

The story of how Chinese came to Guyana during the 19th century was described in my earlier book *Cane Reapers: Chinese Indentured Immigrants in Guyana*. Since its publication, many readers have asked whether there would be a sequel. I had not given it any consideration when I embarked on writing *Cane Reapers*, but the interest expressed since then made me think about the possibility of presenting some further accounts of the lives of these Chinese migrants. In many respects the arrival of Chinese in Guyana was just the beginning of the journey, and up to the present time their experiences in a new homeland have largely been untold in any detail. This void in the knowledge about our ancestors led me to seek more information and some "ol' time stories." I asked Guyanese of Chinese ancestry, particularly those of the older generations, to describe their life experiences and those of their ancestors. The result has been a collection of personal accounts that give an insight into the various activities and interests of the Chinese who settled in Guyana – their work and home life, how they interacted with others, their involvement with local affairs, their ambitions, and what they managed to achieve.

These short stories describe the experiences of the Chinese from the 1860s to the 1960s and are presented in more or less chronological order so that a sense can be gained of the changes through the years. In May 1966, British Guiana became an independent country – Guyana. In this book, the name Guyana is used even for pre-independence times, except where the context requires otherwise. The transition to a Guyanese life-style is evident as the sequence of stories unfolds. But, at the same time, several Chinese customs and attitudes have persisted, particularly in family life and in the retention of a sense of being Chinese, with the latter feature expressing itself in different ways. The arrival of more recent immigrants from China, particularly in the period between the World Wars, helped to strengthen some of these aspects of "Chinese-ness" in the country.

As I collected the stories, I noticed that, besides being about the Chinese, the vast majority of them had a strong connection with water – for making rum, doing laundry, panning for gold, traveling by boat, living by the riverside, etc. The name Guyana is derived from the local

Amerindian language and means "land of many waters." I felt that the title *Cane Ripples* would be fitting as a sequel to *Cane Reapers*, by showing how the results of the toils of the early Chinese settlers have spread like ripples, not only within the Chinese community, but also reaching the nation at large, in the land of many waters.

In gathering the material for this book I have been greatly assisted by Andy Lee who has journeyed across Guyana and the world gaining information from archival records and from individuals. She was able to accumulate a veritable mountain of resources that has helped to resolve many uncertainties about family histories and enabled a clearer picture to be obtained about the Chinese in Guyana.

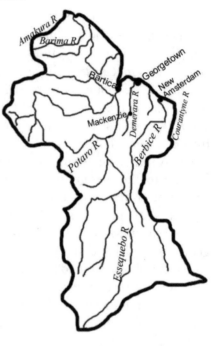

I am very grateful to all those who have told their stories, and undoubtedly there are other equally good tales that could also have been included, had the opportunity permitted. Indeed, there are several well-known individuals, families, and professions that do not appear in this collection. The intent was not to compile a Who's Who, but

Guyana – Land of Many Waters

rather to present more of a Who's What – showing various representative trades and occupations that the Chinese descendants undertook in Guyana. The choice of the accounts is a reflection of who was available and willing to share a good story than of a purposeful selection of certain individuals or families, or of trying to pursue a specific theme. The objective has been to give an overview of some of the different experiences that the Chinese have had in the country that became their home.

Trev Sue-A-Quan
Vancouver, Canada.

LAY OF THE LAND

Trev Sue-A-Quan

In the period between 1853 and 1879, there were 13,541 immigrants from China who landed in British Guiana, many of them obtained by deception and false promises. They were introduced to this distant colony to work on the sugar plantations following the emancipation of slaves of African origin in the British West Indies. The majority of black freedmen chose not to seek employment on the plantations, except for becoming casual workers whenever they wanted to earn some money for specific needs. With the significant reduction of manpower on the sugar plantations, laborers from other lands were sought. The Chinese were not the first group of workers – they were preceded by immigrants from India, who were imported in massive numbers, and also by Portuguese, many of whom were fleeing famine and adverse conditions in Madeira. All of these immigrants were obliged to work on the sugar plantations under indenture for a specified time, typically five years.

Once the term of indenture was served, the workers were permitted to remain in the colony, if they so chose, and many of the Indian, Portuguese and Chinese decided to stay. Each group adapted itself to the local scene and, generally speaking, the Indians took up agricultural occupations, while the Portuguese became the merchants and traders who dominated the middle economy. The administrators and people in power – primarily British – remained the sugar estate owners and they had no interest in setting up shops to serve the needs of the workers. This provided an opportunity for the Portuguese to flourish as shopkeepers and entrepreneurs. The Chinese, being relative latecomers, faced significant challenges and competition in getting themselves established in both the agricultural and the business fields. However, they managed to find ways to make a living, and eventually prosper, in the country that was their new home. By the time of World War II, the descendants of the 19th century settlers were joined by a number of "new" Chinese immigrants who arrived voluntarily to seek a better life in the New World. Even so, the number of Chinese in the country never exceeded 2% of the total population, but the economic and social contributions of the Chinese caused them to be regarded as one of the six races that make up the people of Guyana.[1] This tribute is a fitting recognition of the significant role that the Chinese have made to the country.

The transition from cane plantation workers into welcomed and respected members of the nation took several generations. When the Chinese first arrived in the colony, they were provided with accommodations on the plantations as part of the contractual deal, but these were the same shelters that had been used by the former African slaves. Called logies,[2] they were long narrow buildings that sometimes had two levels. The interior was divided into rooms separated by thin walls that could easily be scaled, each room being some nine or ten feet square, and accessible by a corridor that ran the length of the logie. On some plantations, as many as four people shared the same room. Near the logies there were communal sheds that served as kitchens. As one of the concessions, the immigrants were each given a small plot of land on which to grow vegetables.

For the immigrants, the sugar plantation was not just a place to work and rest – it influenced their lives in many ways. Some were given the names of the estate owners or managers, resulting in such Chinese names as Bridges, Hunter, and Stokes. A few plantation managers provided support to Chinese who, having completed their indenture, wanted to operate small shops on the estates. Even the physical layout of the plantations had an influence on the daily lives of the Chinese settlers, in particular through the use of the waterways, roads and rail lines that were arranged to best serve the plantations.

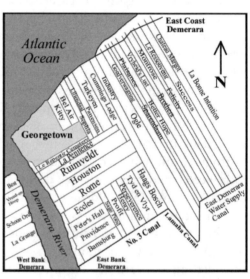

Sugar plantations, like these near Georgetown, were laid out in long narrow strips.

---

[1] The six races are African, Indian, Portuguese, Chinese, Amerindian, and European. The Portuguese are regarded as being different from Europeans because of the history of their arrival in Guyana as indentured laborers. For some analysts in more recent times, the people of Portuguese and European stock have been pooled together as "whites" and the sixth ethnic group has been assigned to those of mixed blood.
[2] Pronounced LOW-gee.

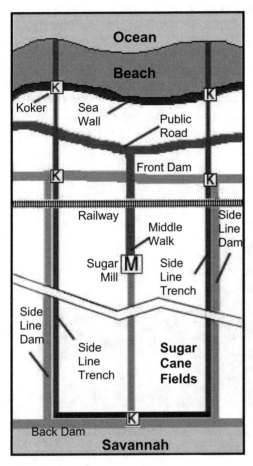

Layout of a typical sugar cane plantation. A network of punt trenches criss-crossing the fields provided the means for transporting the cane.

Sugar was the commodity that drove the colony's economy and the plantations were laid out to optimize the use of the land. The stretch of land along the Atlantic coast was very fertile and suitable for sugar cane cultivation. Typically, the plantations had a relatively narrow frontage, but extended for three or more miles inshore. But there were a few difficulties to be overcome. The first was that this very fertile area was below sea level and depended on an extensive flood-defense system, pioneered by Dutch colonists. Each plantation had a front dam with sluices, or kokers, which were opened to drain the plantation when the tide was low, and shut when the ocean tide rose. Guyana has two rainy seasons per year, and the downpours could be torrential at times, which could easily lead to disastrous flooding. This situation called for a "back dam," a line of dykes that prevented the cultivated fields from being washed away while, at the same time, retaining rainwater for irrigation purposes. To complete the enclosure of the plantation, there were side-line dams joining the front dam to the back dam. The elevated perimeter enabled each plantation to become a "walled entity" with independent control over the cane growing operations. In addition, a long "sea wall" that held the Atlantic Ocean at bay was built in the late 19th century to protect the coastal areas.

The plantation typically had a middle-walk dam dividing the area into two halves, and on this would be the main road leading to the sugar mill. This main road branched off from the Public Road that serviced all the plantations along the coastline. The houses for the plantation managers and workers were positioned close to, and on either side of, the main estate road. These facilities were near the front of the plantation, while at the back were the fields of cane, divided into sections by canals that provided a means of transport as well as water for irrigation. The network of canals enabled punts, loaded with sugar cane, to be hauled from the remotest part of the plantation to the mill. The sugar produced from the mill would be sent to Georgetown by the single railway line that traversed the district, cutting across the plantations near the Public Road.

Kokers controlled the flow of water past the Sea Wall and dams protecting the low-lying coastal areas of Guyana. *Roy V. Wong*

All these features on the plantation – housing, dams, canals, punts, main road, Public Road, mill, and railway – affected the Chinese not only when they worked as field laborers on the plantation, but also after they left, because they had to live with, or deal with, this infrastructure established for the growing of sugar. One of the great challenges facing the Chinese who had completed their indenture was what to do next to earn a living. Some remained on the sugar plantations, renewing for another period of indenture, while others sought to strike out on their own, particularly in shopkeeping. The Chinese opened shops on the plantation grounds, or on plots adjoining the Public Road, and provided daily-need goods and supplies for the workers on the plantation, who were mainly East Indians. Several Chinese headed to Georgetown to try their prospects there; others ventured to remote locations in the North-West District and the interior. Many others left the colony, some returning to China while others went to neighboring countries, including Trinidad, Surinam, French Guiana, St. Lucia, Jamaica and Panama.

The departure of Chinese for other countries was one of the concerns that was raised by O. Tye Kim,[3] a Chinese missionary from Singapore, who had arrived in British Guiana in July 1864. In January 1865, he presented a "Humble Petition" to the governor requesting that a tract of Crown land be granted to the establishment of a Chinese Christian settlement. O. Tye Kim indicated that he had found a suitable site at Camoonie Creek, which joins the Demerara River some 25 miles from Georgetown. William Des Voeux, a magistrate, claims himself to be the one who located that site.[4] This may not be a contradiction – perhaps O. Tye Kim gained the information from Des Voeux. In any event, the Chinese missionary was the one who pushed to get approval for the settlement. Some plantation owners raised objections, believing that the settlement would draw Chinese away from the plantations. However, Governor Francis Hincks and others in high office felt that it would be a benefit to those who did not want to continue doing plantation work. On 9 February 1865, the Court of Policy passed resolutions that permitted the establishment of a Chinese village on Crown land along the Demerara River, and approved a loan of $1,500 towards that purpose.

By coincidence, Admiral Sir James Hope arrived in the colony on 15 February 1865. He had headed a joint Anglo-French flotilla in 1859 that attempted to force its way to the Chinese capital to get the emperor to ratify the Treaty of Tientsin, which brought the Second Opium War to a close and extracted many concessions from China. He had also provided "important countenance and help" to J. Gardner Austin, who was in charge of recruiting Chinese for British Guiana. In 1861, Admiral Hope

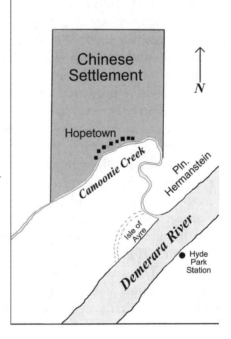

---

[3] Also called Wu Tai-kam in another dialect.
[4] G. William Des Voeux, G.C.M.G., *Experiences of a Demerara Magistrate 1863-1869*, Vincent Roth, editor, The Daily Chronicle Ltd., 1948.

participated in suppressing the Taiping Rebellion in central China thereby helping the emperor to retain his throne. With his experience in Chinese affairs, Admiral Hope was invited to visit the Chinese settlement at Camoonie Creek on 18 February 1865, accompanied by the governor and several dignitaries. A short meeting was held with O. Tye Kim and a few speeches given. The visit was concluded by the unanimous declaration that the Chinese village should be named Hopetown.

By the end of 1865, Hopetown had attracted some 170 Chinese settlers while, in the same period, about seven hundred free Chinese had signed up for another term of indenture on the plantations. Governor Hincks felt that he had made the right choice in supporting the scheme. He wrote: "That Hopetown will be a great colony, if Wu Tai-kam's life and health be spared, I have no doubt."[5] There was apparently no problem with O. Tye Kim's health. As it turned out, he was discovered to have been involved in an intimate affair with a local woman. This apparently was too much of a shame for him to bear, especially being the missionary espousing Christian principles among the Chinese. In July 1867, he made an escape from the colony, leaving via Essequibo and the North-West District.

Hopetown continued to grow and the 1871 census showed 567 Chinese men, women and children living there. By 1874, the number of residents reached about 800. While there was some cultivation of rice and vegetables, and the raising of poultry and livestock, the Chinese were mainly involved in the production of charcoal. The Chinese created a newfangled clay oven that was much more efficient than the open pits commonly in use up to that time. The timber and branches were stacked vertically in the enclosed ovens and a minimal amount of the wood was consumed in the burning process. The charcoal so produced was able to compete successfully with the output from the traditional pits, operated mainly by Portuguese manufacturers. The charcoal industry was a very lucrative one and provided employment and earnings for many Chinese in timber cutting, charcoal production, shipping and marketing.

Although Hopetown held out hope for becoming a center for Chinese development, it soon became evident that the lay of the land was not ideal. The area was susceptible to flooding and would have required the construction of extensive dikes to provide protection. In addition, the settlers found that a significant portion of the rice crop was being lost to birds and this discouraged them from growing rice. There was no long-term plan to cultivate other crops, such as coffee or fruit trees. Over the years, the population declined as those of the younger generation felt less

---

[5] Cecil Clementi, *The Chinese in British Guiana*, The Argosy, 1915.

inclined to be involved in agricultural occupations, choosing instead to migrate to the big city, Georgetown, or to have a go at starting up a small shop in the countryside. The other feature that put Hopetown at a disadvantage was its remoteness – it could take as much as six hours for boats to reach the settlement from Georgetown, since the journey was affected by the tide. By the beginning of the 20th century the population at Hopetown had dropped to about 200 people and it continued on this downward trend in subsequent years.

The place that gained from the decline of Hopetown was Georgetown. Besides their success in the charcoal business, the Chinese were making headway in a number of ventures – jewelry, tailoring, baking, cookshops, merchandising, etc. A Chinese Quarter emerged in the Lombard Street area and reached its peak of growth in 1913 when it was brought to an abrupt end by an enormous conflagration that consumed several blocks of the city. Later, another concentration of Chinese businesses sprung up a few blocks to the north, in the vicinity of America Street, although many Chinese entrepreneurs decided to disperse to different areas all across Georgetown.

Although it was the most populous city with educational and business opportunities, the capital city could not accommodate all the Chinese who would have liked to settle there, because there was too much competition from various entrepreneurs, including other Chinese. Several chose to open shops on the sugar plantations where their forefathers had worked as indentured laborers. Each plantation required several thousand workers, and in some locations more than one Chinese family set up shop on the same estate. This return to the plantation was a choice they made voluntarily to find a way to earn a living. Their circumstances this time were different, but they were still, as their stories relate, affected by the lay of the land.

ENTREPRENEURIAL SPIRIT

From the unpublished memoirs of James Chow

In 1978 James Chow, also known as James Ewing-Chow, completed his memoirs entitled *Mr. David and his Children* with the hope that readers "would be impressed by what God did for David." The son of Chinese immigrants who arrived as indentured laborers, David Ewing-Chow went through experiences that were typical of many other second generation Chinese, in that he took up shopkeeping as a livelihood, although his rise to financial fortunes was a relatively rapid one. By World War I the Ewing-Chow family had become well-known and prosperous in British Guiana. David's children – the third generation – continued to be prominent in the business world as well as through scholastic achievement in the fields of medicine, law, accountancy and pharmacy. James, the fourth of David's eleven children, became a lawyer as well as an Anglican priest and for a time was the parish priest for St. Saviour's Church in Georgetown, the Chinese church that had been founded in 1875 through the efforts of the local Chinese community.

James recorded the major events affecting his father's life, particularly the spiritual uplifting brought about by his conversion to Christianity during his teenage years. He describes the religious activities at Peter's Hall where a church was built from contributions of the local Chinese. When only a young lad, David had to learn to fend for himself following his father's death and his path to entrepreneurial success provides some insight into how the Chinese managed to make progress as businessmen in British Guiana in the late 19th century.

* * * * * * * *

On arrival, the pastor [who came on the same boat as David's father[1]] was sent to Peter's Hall, near the sugar estate there, but he could not stand up physically to the labour on the cane fields, and got ill. The overseers thought he was a malingerer, but soon found out that he was a

---

[1] In his book *The Chinese in British Guiana* published in 1915 Cecil Clementi indicates that Chau Luk-wu arrived on the *Dora* and was allotted to Peter's Hall estate, on the East Bank of the Demerara River. In actual fact, all the immigrants on the *Dora* were sent to estates in Berbice County. Archival records show that Chau Luk-wu was aboard the *Red Riding Hood,* which landed on 8 April 1860, five days after the *Dora*.

refined and educated man as he used to write letters for the other Chinese laborers to be sent to their families in Canton etc. . . .

He was then made a sort of teacher and advisor to the workers and that suited him, so that he was able to teach and preach to them about his Lord and Saviour, Jesus Christ; in the course of time he was able to get quite a number of converts. Through the help of his old pastor and [the] Baptist Church he was able to put up a church to seat about 120 people, and a house at the rear of the church with about four or five rooms and kitchen, with a large verandah. The house was built on high greenheart pillars and the wood for the house was of crabwood, which wood ants would not eat, because both greenheart and crabwood were very bitter.

The church went on expanding in [membership] and the workers on the estate saved enough money hoping to build another church and a house across the Demerara River, almost opposite Peter's Hall, as there were many Chinese workers at three of the largest estates there. . . . They therefore were able to build [the second] church near the Canal Bridge, that members from Peter's Hall could take their boats to attend service and leave them at the Canal Bridge, and walk to the church about 200 yards distant. Mr. Hoashoo,[2] a rich merchant helped considerably to put up the church, and years after he was buried there. They also put up a large building for the Elder or whoever was sent there to conduct services or stay there. . . . Adjoining the building was an enormous shed to have meals when baptism services were held for converts, who were baptized in a deep pond at the back of the church. Going to the rear of the church and baptismal pond was a long stretch of land with coconut and fruit trees, which was used for graves of deceased members. Now this church was on the West Bank of the Demerara River, whereas Peter's Hall was on the East Bank of the Demerara River.

At Peter's Hall the church [was] a long way [from] the river and as the river at low tide would recede about 50 yards, they built a bridge right up to the water (at low tide) so that baptisms could be held at low or high tide. Still later, another church on the west coast was built on land given by the Leonora Estate Company by the side of the main road, which branched off to the left. [It included] all the land from the bridge [and extended] several hundred yards up to the seashore. [At that site] the members followed the same pattern [used for] the various buildings at Peter's Hall (East Bank) and at the Canal West Bank Church. . . .

---

[2] Ho Shau, who became better known as John Ho-A-Shoo, immigrated in 1874 and made his fortune opening shops in the remote interior areas to provide supplies to the gold and silver prospectors as well as the lumbermen.

[At] the expiration of the contract[3] to work at the various estates, not many of the Chinese took advantage of returning to Canton,[4] but saved enough money to start groceries and stores on the estates or villages near the various estates, because they could speak "broken" English, and knew how to handle the coins and notes and calculate on their abacus, the change they would have to give to their customers. [They] also could understand that if they buy an article for ten dollars, they must sell that article for more than ten dollars, and believing that a quick cent profit was better than a slow dollar profit. On this principle, they succeeded in owning most of the shops on or about the various estates and the many villages, through which the sugar cane workers had to pass through, whereas the Portuguese stuck to their rum and liquor stores. . . .

David's father and mother worked on the few sugar estates near them, for which a man [was paid] three pennies per day, a woman got two pennies, and a child of 8 or 9, one penny a day. They were not lazy and around their house they grew all sorts of vegetables and fruits with the seeds they brought from China, which sprouted and grew quickly under the tropical sun and frequent rain, so that along with a few chickens to provide them with eggs and meat, they were able to get along quite well. They were then blessed with a girl first and afterward with a boy, David. David's mother was a herbalist and acupuncturist in China, [so she] was able to help out the Chinese workers, when they got ill and after they recovered they would show their gratitude by sending gifts, as she never would charge for her services. [In this way] they were able to save their earnings, living mostly on their garden products, eggs and chickens. When the children got to the Primary School and reached the ages of 8 and 11 years (David and his sister), [their] father became ill. . . . However, his illness was of a serious nature and despite all the help his wife could give, he died, leaving his two young children to be brought up by the mother, who did not fail them in any way in spite of her working in the cane fields, for she was by nature a strong muscular woman, only 5 ft. 3½ ins. in height.

In the Primary School was the School Teacher (head mistress) who did all she could for the children, especially for David who was clever in many ways and always willing to do extra "studies" work, so that he was able to progress and got to the 5th standard, always first in every grade of standard. His age was about 12.

---

[3] The contract of indenture required that the indentured immigrant work for five years on the allotted sugar estate. Some renewed for a second term of indenture.
[4] A sum of $50 was offered at the completion of the term of indenture to assist in a return passage to China.

His teacher's name was Miss Hewlings and [she and] the missionary Rev. D. Ewing (Anglican Church) were both fond of David, who was strong, healthy and fond of games – cricket, football and swimming – and used to build up his muscles with weights and boxing. Eventually the Rev. Ewing took a fancy to him, as he was good and studious in the Sunday School, and christened him, giving him the name of David Johnston Ewing-Chow, and as such he was registered in the church records.[5]

David's mother felt he was big enough to go out to work at one of the Chinese shops to learn the business, so she took him to a friend's shop [and there] he was employed especially as he could speak both English and Chinese and knew a little accounting which would be useful to his employer, who only spoke Chinese but very little English.

David then told Miss Hewlings that his mother had got him a job at a Chinese shop. Miss Hewlings said: "You have not yet got through to the sixth standard and that is a great pity." She suggested that as the shop opens at 6:15 in the morning, you could come to me at 5 - 5:15 and I shall teach you, especially in Arithmetic and English Literature and I feel sure you would be able to get through the whole course in five to six months, as I know you delight in studying, and further as you are keen on reading I'll lend you books on those subjects which ought to be of help to you in your future, but remember whatever you do, never forget God, who will help you in your problems. Then David thanked her and said: [I will come to you] every morning at 5 o'clock to continue my studies until I am through all the text books for the Sixth Standard, and I promise to read every book you lend me as quickly as I can to finish it, for I am usually a quick reader and retain in my head what I read. Within 5½ months, he had finished his course of studies, after which he thanked his Head Mistress for her kindness, which he hoped to return one of these days.[6]

Well, he worked at the shop and learnt all about buying and selling for nearly a year, during which time the shop-owner got a lot of new customers because David had a nice disposition and was pleased to see to their needs, not only [regarding] what they wanted to buy, but [also] advising them in their problems at home or in their work.

---

[5] This explains the origin of the official surname Ewing-Chow that David's children continued to use, although some descendants have resumed use of the Chinese surname Chow.

[6] Many years later, after Miss Hewlings had retired from teaching, James Chow found out that her pension was not correctly calculated. He took the matter up with the appropriate authorities and obtained for her an increased pension amount as well as a lump sum adjustment.

His sister was of age 17½ years according to Chinese custom,[7] [old enough] to be married, so a match-maker friend of his mother introduced a successful shop-owner named Mr. Kam to the daughter, and in due course [they] got married, and settled down resulting in three children – 2 boys and one girl. Unfortunately soon after the marriage the son-in-law was discovered to be an opium-smoker[8] and David's mother did not know it at the time of the engagement, so the business had to have an assistant and was not doing well.

It was then decided that David and his mother should go across the river to Anna Catherina village, where [the] son-in-law's shop was situated, not more than two miles from the Chinese Baptist Church at Leonora, not far from the Leonora sugar estate and Uitvlugt sugar estate. When David joined the shop, he was given a good salary, and the shop assistant was naturally dismissed.

As soon as David started his work at the shop, his brother-in-law got slack, and began to smoke more pipes than was usual so David had to take the train, cross the river ferry to do all the buying and introduced many new items, like clothing materials for the women and office necessities etc. [As a result] the business began to grow and make larger profits than was ever done. By David's going to the city so often – sometimes twice a week – to buy stock, he became quite well known to all the department stores and big groceries and especially the Chinese food stores in which they ran a little restaurant where David used to eat and meet many of the Chinese from the different sugar estates and villages.

This was when he came across Pastor Lau Fook, and some of his Church members, who introduced him to the Leonora Church Brethren. So every Sunday he would go to [the] Leonora Church by donkey cart or [on foot], or [else] cross by the first ferry boat to the city and then walk to Peter's Hall to hear Pastor Lau Fook. [He would then] eat at the Church, and after an early afternoon service, 4 p.m., would walk the 3½ - 4 miles back to the city to catch the ferry boat to Vreed-en-Hoop[9] and walk home the eight miles, singing and whistling hymns he had learned at the church. . . . He accepted Jesus Christ as His Saviour for "He is the Way, the Truth and the Life and no man cometh unto the Father, but by

[7] In Chinese tradition a child is reckoned to be one year at birth and thus would be a year older than calculated by Western custom.
[8] In British Guiana the sale and purchase of opium (in limited quantities) was legal up to the early years of the 20th century.
[9] Situated on the West Bank of the Demerara River, opposite the capital Georgetown, the Vreed-en-Hoop ferry stelling (dock) provided transportation access to estates and villages on West Coast Demerara (to the west) and West Bank Demerara (south).

Him." This decision he made known to the Pastor, Rev Lau Fook, at the first opportunity and asked [that] he be baptized at Peter's Hall Baptist Church, the Mother Church, at the forthcoming baptismal ceremony.

Before the Sunday on which he was to be baptized, he told his mother and sister and brother-in-law that he had decided to be baptized by Rev. Lau Fook. His mother was strongly against his accepting Jesus Christ as his Saviour, while the brother-in-law threatened that if he got baptized, he would have to leave his shop. In those days he wore a Chinese long gown in public, . . . and for this "special" occasion he had his gown washed and ironed ready for the Sunday morning. He got up at 4 a.m. although the shop [had] closed at 11 p.m. and, after cleaning up, he had returned to bed at or after 12 a.m. so he had a short sleep. But he got up with a happy heart, said a prayer and began to dress, after a wash, when he found his long gown missing. He knew at once that his mother wanted to stop him.

However, he took a couple [loaves] of bread and some cheese and a smoked herring. After a drink of water and munching happily a part of the bread and cheese, he began to walk the eight miles in the dark to the ferry, as he wanted to catch the first ferry boat at 6:30, which he did. As he got to the other side of the river, about 7 a.m., he walked merrily along the 3½ - 4 miles to the Peter's Hall Church, where he met the Pastor and some of the deacons and keen members, who were to help at the ceremony, and afterward to cook the Chinese feast that was to follow after the baptism. They looked at him with surprise, so he explained how he had washed his long gown to be ready in the morning, and that he awoke, dressed and found that his gown had disappeared so he left the house without the gown. So they all began to laugh, but someone supplied the "necessary" article. The pastor remarked "The Lord looks at one's heart, and not on one's clothes." How true can this remark be made to the "over-dressed" folks, male and female alike in our streets and churches today!!! Well, the baptism part took about 1½ hours accompanied with the usual hymns and the rite of submersion in the water, so by 11:15 all were happy as they took their seats in the church – the men on one side of the building and opposite to them the ladies on the other side. The rest of the service continued with an address by the pastor and prayer and those who were "born again" Christians took the Communion – the eating of the pieces of bread and drinking or sipping of the wine. . . . That was a glorious day for David.

When the service was terminated in the usual way with a suitable hymn, prayer and benediction, all then gathered under the pastor's house where tables were laid and the hot dishes and rice and soup were brought in then the pastor prayed, asking God's blessing on food and all, and expressing thanks to the Almighty for his mercies and goodness to them all. The evening service began early at 3 p.m. and ended at 4 p.m., giving time to those who had to cross the river boat to Vreed-en-Hoop, for folks on the West Coast, and for others to cross the river by boat or launch to the Canal (opposite Peter's Hall), who lived on the West Bank of the river. All traveling to the Churches was done by a donkey cart or by walking or a horse-wagon, which was of course expensive and everyone had to think of the future and save, especially the members who now had to keep up three churches and the traveling expenses of the pastor and elders,[10] who helped in conducting the services. . . .

Coming back to David, after his baptism he was filled with joy and sang praises and hymns all the way back home as he walked the 8 or 8½ mile stretch from the ferry, and got home late that Sunday. Not being a business day, the doors were all closed, so he made himself comfortable between some rice bags and went to sleep soundly after thanking God for his safe journey back. . . . No wonder he slept well, and woke up as usual early, as the light of day dawned on him.

When the shop was opened, his mother and brother-in-law, both of whom were not Christians, told him he must pack up his belongings, as they could not have him stay in the house, but David knew this was a test by God, so he said to himself, "He will see me through this trial." His brother-in-law paid him off in full, with an extra month's pay. David had saved all his salaries and deposited his money in the Post Office next to the railway station, so he said good-bye to his mother with a sigh and committed her to God's care, also the others.

On his way to the station he stopped in a shop owned by one of the members, had a few slices of bread and butter and a cup of coffee, told them nothing of what had happened at home, went to the Post Office and asked them to transfer his deposits to the General Post Office in Georgetown, which was done immediately in his presence. After that he went to the station and caught the first train for Georgetown[11] and met many of the Chinese shopkeepers and other friends, and chatted all the way until he got to Georgetown.

He prayed for guidance and the Lord put it in his heart to see the two Chinese store managers selling Chinese goods and medicines from China,

---

[10] The churches and pastors were supported by donations from the congregation.
[11] The train terminus was a Vreed-en-Hoop, from where the ferry would take passengers across the Demerara River to Georgetown.

one of them was Hoahing Stores,[12] and the other was Wo Lee & Co.[13] Along with their Chinese goods, [they] also had the restaurant or cook-shop in a section of the building and David used to frequent the cook-shop and eat there on his numerous visits to the city for the past two or three years. The owner of the Hoahing Stores had three big sons and a few daughters, while the owner of Wo Lee & Co. had only a wife and one daughter, so after much thought and prayer he was led to choose Wo Lee. Besides, he could have more chances to meet Chinese shopkeepers from all the estates and villages to <u>speak to them about Jesus Christ and he would be near Pastor Lau Fook and Peter's Hall Church.</u> So he approached the owner, as he felt also it was better to have one master rather than four masters at Hoahing & Co. [The owner of Wo Lee Co.] said you are the kind of young man I would like to have, because you are sincere and straight forward, so he was employed at a much better salary [than] his brother-in-law had paid him. There he worked and, as was the custom, he and his co-worker ate with the family, and slept in a room shared by his co-worker or assistant.

[There was a] slack period after breakfast, when shopkeepers [had] not [yet arrived in] the city [since] the two banks were opened at 9:00 a.m. for business. [Only then could they] deposit their week's cash sales, and then do their purchasing of their stocks, etc., David would take the opportunity of visiting all the big department stores and other shops to keep in touch with the managers and their staff and study the type of goods etc.

Also, he would pop in and see the tailoring department and observe how they cut [the cloth] and measured their customers and cut out paper patterns and stitched them together etc. etc. and what he saw stuck in his memory. Afterwards [he] took notes in his note-book; similarly he'd go to the jewelry shop and see how they used to melt the gold or silver coins and pour the molten mass into metal molds with various size of holes, and as the gold and silver came through the holes, the metal would harden into thin threads etc. as they dropped into an enamel basin of water, and these can then be formed into different shapes and turned into jewelry. He saw carpenters work in building a new house, saw how they laid the foundation to take the greenheart blocks, took mental notes of how the boards were laid on the pillars and on the pitch-pine boards above the pillar, the position of the windows and hinges to them, the

---

[12] Ho Hin, also known as Andrew Hunter Ho-A-Hing, arrived in British Guiana in 1862. He became established as a successful businessman in New Amsterdam, Berbice County, and then opened branch stores in Georgetown.

[13] Wo Lee opened for business in June 1879, dealing in Chinese and Japanese goods.

rafters etc. all of which he remembered and "noted" in his note-book for later use.

The same kind of observations he took in mentally as he passed into the kitchen, He saw "how they cooked rice," vegetables and meat and fish and what amount of salt, sugar, vinegar, bean sauce and oil were used in their different order, e.g. oil heated up, then the vegetables with salt, ginger or pepper, with a small amount of extra oil and water, so that the vegetables would remain green and crisp; in the case of meat, that is beef, the same process would be used, but the bean sauce would be mixed with sugar, a slight amount of water, a little salt, and thin slices of ginger, and "fried up" until it is slightly or half done, but never over done, or the meat hardens and so loses its lusciousness and flavour. Later, these experiences and observations played a great part in his future life, when he started out on his own and followed the notes to be able to help with the cooking in the church kitchen, after the morning service.

For a little over a year he worked for Wo Lee & Co. and sold some of the very herbs, ointments, and pills his mother used to treat the people with for different ailments. . . . He also sold groceries, like sugar, flour, rice (wholesale prices) and barrels of meat, so he had full knowledge of this kind of business, as he used to buy for his brother-in-law's shop and knew most of the prices, fluctuating now and then, depending on the scarcity of the stock, until new arrivals came.

He fully enjoyed his work, but God soon led him back to his mother and others of his family. It appears that his brother-in-law was losing in his shop business, because he did not give full attention to it and his hired assistant was not too capable and perhaps not too honest, coupled with the fact that he was becoming an opium addict, so he entreated his mother-in-law (David's mother) to write or send a message, to say his brother-in-law was sorry over his treatment and begged him to come back and be friends again, as he was not feeling at all well. What was David to do, but to put it to the Lord, and the Lord put it in his heart to resign his present job and return to his mother to whom he owed such a lot, so he decided to send in his resignation to his boss, who invited him to lunch with him whenever he came to the city on business.

That Sunday, he went to church as usual to tell the Pastor about his reconciliation with the family, who said he would be greatly missed especially as he possessed a strong and appealing voice and used to lead the singing of the hymns, along with a shy girl, Emily Leung, who sat opposite each other across the "Communion" table. David used to wonder why Miss Leung never seemed to want to look at him and why she was so shy.

At the end of the morning service the Pastor announced that he was led by the Lord to make David Chow (only 16 years old) (or Chow Loy) an elder of the Assembly and to take charge of the Leonora Chinese Baptist Church. He accepted on one condition: that he would be allowed to visit Peter's Hall Church every other week to keep in touch with Pastor Lau Fook, the other deacons, and brethren of the Canal West Bank Church, and by rotation of their visits to each church, all then would be encouraged and be filled with a new spirit to serve.

This was assented to, so [he returned] to Wo Lee to spend the last night there. The next morning with much regret on either side, the boss paid him what was due to him, along with a little more as a present. So saying "goodbye to all" he caught the first ferry boat, crossed the river, then entrained for Leonora station. When he arrived there, he went straight to his mother, who received him with joy and tears, as after all he was an only son, and her daughter had grown to be selfish, and thought only of herself. Well, he soon found out [about] the sad state of the thriving business he had left, and now it was up to him to build it up again, so his brother-in-law gave him a better salary than what he received at Wo Lee. To David's great disappointment he knew now why the business had deteriorated – his brother-in-law had become an opium addict, went from one pipe to another, as soon as he got over his sleep or drowsiness.

The result was [that] in a few months after David's arrival he got really ill, and the doctor could not help much, as he was an addict, and if he wanted to get well, he must fight against the habit. But he could not break the habit and got worse every day.

So he called out to David, "Will you pray for me to God and Jesus Christ, that I may give up this bad habit, and heal me, and I will promise not to touch the opium pipe, lamp and opium any more, if I get well." David then said, "Are you serious about your promise to God and me to stop smoking?" His answer was "Yes." He was lying propped up in bed. David then told him to shut his eyes, knelt beside him, prayed earnestly to God for his recovery and the breaking of the opium habit and asked in the name of Jesus Christ, His Son, to heal him entirely, and thanked the Lord for hearing him, and his appeal for the sick man.

That night Mr. Kam slept well, and woke up next morning feeling better but weak. He told them to put away his pipe, throw away the opium and lamp etc., which they did. The following day he was able to eat a little and the next day he felt so much better that he had a hearty breakfast, lunch and dinner and he knew he was really healed, and David knew God had heard and answered his prayer, so he thanked and praised God and His Son for the healing.

Well, business improved in the next five or six months, when David smelled that someone was burning opium, so he suspected that the offender had broken his promise to God and had started to resume the opium habit [so] that within a month or more he became seriously ill, and could eat with difficulty. Once again, he implored David to pray to God for him; although discouraged, he knelt beside the sick man's bed and prayed earnestly to the Lord for his recovery, but in the midst of the prayer someone came into the shop and shouted the sick man's nickname, "Hog's Head" who immediately replied, showing he was not listening to the prayer. David shortly after finished his prayer, felt that this time God would not answer his prayer. The next night he died and was buried the following day, leaving his wife and two sons, about 13 and 16 years.

Now there used to be a Chinese baker, Mr. Low, who used to play the cornet for the Salvation Army Meeting every Saturday night, not far from the shop, and in course of time got friendly with Mrs. Kam, David's sister. Six months after the husband's death, Mrs. Kam and Mr. Low got married quietly and complications followed as he of course lived with the whole family. The boys of course were very unhappy and much more so was the mother, but he helped to run the business; Mr. Low was trained as a baker, and used the rear of the house as a bakery, so "his bread" was a bit of an asset, at the expense of the shop, as he was not trained as a shopkeeper.

David at once decided to go on his own as soon as possible. As he used to pass through the village often, he saw an empty spot in the middle of the village with lots of houses owned and occupied by [Blacks] mostly and a few Indians. The empty spot was not looked after at all by the owner, but was full of bearing coconut [and] fruit trees, e.g. six of mangoes, two of oranges, several of guavas, many papaw, sour sop, and others. The place was more or less abandoned but it was about two acres, and could be extended further at the back to a creek, which was full of alligators, and not far from the land was a Scottish Church used once a Sunday, for a morning service, but was empty most of the time. He at once went to the black owner who had a large house and plenty of land, and asked him if he would like to sell that abandoned field he had. He promptly said, "Yes" and offered the place for $500, which David immediately bought and paid him the price, as soon as the legal part was put through.

The next step was to see a good master carpenter, a Mr. Griffith, who worked and built shops sometimes planned by David, as Mr. Hoashoo was a member of the Baptist Church, along with his wife and young family. In order not to waste time he had the abandoned place quickly cleaned of all weeds and grass burned and drains dug between the large trees.

The whole area was then surrounded by new and well-seasoned wooden palings leaving a large open space for the shop building and a large out-building for stocks with a large bedroom and plenty of room for a workshop, as he had an idea of opening a jewelry shop and a tailoring department at a later date. He had a large broad bridge built across the trench, which had potable water from the Canal Polder and creeks within a few weeks. He also had a large wooden vat to hold 4000 gallons of water, which could be caught from the zinc roof in pipes leading to the vat. At the back of the shopping area, he had two large and two small bedrooms, one sitting and dining room and pantry in the corridor leading to the kitchen. He made all arrangements to get the wood and timber and zinc sheets on the spot early with a watchman in a temporary hut, so that within four months the shop could be completed and [also the] out-buildings. They built an open-air veranda at the back yard with a shelter containing two small rooms for the carpenters and later for the [customers].

Whenever David went to buy things for the shop he would look up all the owners of the big wholesale dealers, the managers of the department stores, hardware stores etc. and hinted that he intended to open on his own soon, and they said if he did, he would be given all the credit he needed, as they had faith in him and always carried out his promises to pay promptly at the end of every week, when he brought his sales money to the bank.

This set his mind at rest, that when he knew for certain the two buildings would be completed with all their shelves etc. etc. and all the windows made strong with bolts and the front doors of the shops well fitted with bolts, top and bottom, as well as the front private door, fitted with locks and bolts of his own choice, he thanked the Lord. He had [been] training two half-bred dogs for the past month teaching them to eat only from him, and no one else and not to make friends with anyone except his folks, and then he confided in his mother and told her what he was going to do in the next week or two.

He asked the younger Kam (Hing Yow), his nephew, if he were happy with his new father. He said, "No" and his brother also was not too happy. "Well would you like to come with me as I intend to open a larger shop on new lines and if you like to come and be my help, I would like to take care of you and teach you all I know so that as you grow older, you could have your own shop too and get married!" Oh! The boy was so happy and thanked his uncle David, but after reflection, he said "What about my brother?" to which Uncle David replied, "He has his

mother to do his duty by her and help her and their little children (three
of them) until they are a little older, then he can get a job, but in the
meantime he must get all the shop experience he can, so that he would be
well fitted to manage a shop of his own, if he should save up the money
he gets." He said, "He gets no salary," so his Uncle David said "you must
tell your new father to give [him] a salary, [since] if he were to get a hired
assistant, he would have to give him a salary, feed him and give him a
bed." So he agreed to do that and later told Uncle David that he was
going to get a salary of $30.00 a month, which was a bit small, but his
uncle told him that after a few months' hard work, he could ask for a
raise and surely that would be granted.

The next two weeks saw David very busy in the shop and at leisure
hours he would go to the new building in preparation for its opening
[intending] to sleep there as soon as the stocks he ordered began to be
delivered and he got his nephew and mother to accompany him at times
and taught them how to decorate the place with the kinds of articles that
were brought. The grocery department was to be on one side of the shop
and the cloths, garments, etc. would be near the private door entrance on
the other side so that part must be clean at all times, but except for that,
the other things could be arranged in the same way as in the other shop.
This being done he told his brother-in-law and sister of what he was
going to do and they did not seem to mind, because it meant the saving
of David's salary and the feeding of two mouths, so everything went off
smoothly.

After a little publicity with the ringing of a bell to tell people, . . . the
shop [opened] on Friday morning, as Friday morning is always payday
for all [the estate] workers, so Friday and Saturday the business was brisk,
as everyone wanted to see what the new shop would sell and the amazing
display of toys, children's clothes, boy's and men's wear, new hardware
that had just arrived in the city, fresh items of various tinned meat and
fish etc. Business was active from morning till evening at 10:00 p.m.,
when the buying stopped or rather slackened with only the villagers to
serve, as the estate workers had a long way to cover to get home, for they
had come from 3 - 4 Sugar Estates to patronize the new shop, as they
knew Mr. David, as he [was] commonly called; who then announced the
shop would be closed at 10:30 p.m. sharp, as mother, son and nephew
were really tired. There was no stealing as David had two of his old
school friends posted on top of two barrels to keep an eye on suspicious
men and women and also to keep order. The shop was closed promptly,
then the two friends sat down to a cold supper of tinned meat, salmon,
sardines and cheese with hot tea or coffee, after which they chatted and
helped to put in order the disarray of articles etc. in their proper places

on the shelves. When the two friends left, mother, son and nephew [were] glad to have a quick wash-down and make for their respective beds; after posting one dog at the backdoor and one by the front gate, which was padlocked. . . .

During the week, business was better than David expected, but on Friday and Saturday there were buyers far and wide rushing to get to the newly opened shop, as rumors went around that the articles etc. displayed were of the latest fashion, so David had to call upon his old school friends to help, and sales were again brisk and steady, so they had to close the shop at 10:30 in order to give time for the buyers who had come from afar to get home at a reasonable hour, always remembering that walking was the only way to get home, unless they owned a donkey cart.

* * * * * * *

At this point several pages of James Chow's memoirs are missing which contain descriptions of David's business successes, his marriage to Emily Leung, the choir girl from Peter's Hall Church, as well as the birth of his children.

* * * * * * *

Father however saved all he could, as his family was getting larger and larger every one to **two** years.[14] One day on a visit to one of the sugar estate managers, he heard that the estate at Tuschen was in such financial trouble that it was to be sold. He approached the owners who said they were prepared to sell the factory, land and houses etc. at a certain figure, $30,000. He went with the consent of the owners to see the factory, the cane-fields which were about ready to be cut . . . and all the buildings for the manager, the overseers etc. Father calculated the cost of all the houses etc. that were to be sold and what amount they would get on the market. He knew he would make a large profit, so quickly went to the two banks and asked the managers whether they would loan him $20,000 and the managers said they would, so [with] the loan from the two banks ($10,000 each), together with what he had in both banks, he bought the estate and started to dismantle the factory, selling everything that could be sold there, while the houses with their land were quickly sold to the East Indians at good prices, as each house had a fair size of land to go with it. The sugar canes he knew he could sell to the next estate together with the mules and punts, as soon as the canes were ready to be cut, so he

---

[14] David and Emily had 11 children between 1887 and 1908.

went to the manager of the next estate who paid him a big price for the crop and punts etc., as he had no further expense at all with the planting and weeding [on the Tuschen estate] and within a few weeks his factory would be used grind their canes.

So with that purchase, he was able to repay the two banks and made a big profit, and was now worth over $60,000. He then looked out for other estates going on the rocks and there were eight to be sold, but who would buy? Father thought of some of his manager friends and his lawyer friend and an auctioneer, who agreed with his scheme, and they decided [to use] loans from the banks together with their cash to buy eight estates in all. No sooner had they bought and paid for these estates, the First Great War in 1914 broke out, and sugar [prices] went up and up, so the new owners now decided on no account to dismantle the factories at all, but to keep them running and they decided to take up larger amounts of new fields bordering the Canal Polder for planting new cane crops.

During the war years all sugar plantations and estates made a great deal of profit, for sugar that could get through the German raiders and "U" boats to Europe and America was a necessary article for food and sweets of all sorts, especially for the soldiers on active service and the Navy. Year after year hoarders of sugar throughout the world and especially United States of America would sell only limited quantities, so that prices would go up and up, with the result that enormous profits were made by the estates, and brokers did their part too in boosting up the prices by sending out hints that there was a shortage of sugar, whereas there was not at all any shortage.

Now of those eight estates Mr. David and his friends thought ahead so that after the first year of the war with Germany, they ordered new five mill-crushers and rollers to crush the canes, so that what came out of the mills was not only the juice but also the fibre or bagasse, almost dry, and these were fed back to the furnaces instead of having the expense of purchasing wood to heat their furnaces and boilers. After these rollers and other minor machinery and new parts were installed, their output of sugar was increased more than 25%.

Of course, labour demanded more and more wages, which was duly granted to the workers before the other estates did, for they understood more of the labour problems and met their demands in a more reasonable way, to the great annoyance of others. It was during this period of profit making that they declared 40% to 50% dividend on their $100.00 shares, so during the last three years or more of the war, the shareholders were amply rewarded for their $100 share was sold for $300 to $360 per share.

FIREWORKS

Excerpts from *Daily Argosy*

The Chinese started to open businesses in Georgetown in the late 1860s and by the beginning of the 20th century, one section of Georgetown became known as the Chinese Quarter because of their relatively high concentration there. As the year 1913 came to a close there was a festive atmosphere in the area, but it turned to gloom when disaster struck three days before Christmas. In literally a single blow, a large section of the Chinese business area was destroyed by fire. It was not the first great fire to devastate a large section of Georgetown, nor would it be the last. But the impact was severely felt among the Chinese community through the significant losses in property and lives.

* * * * * * * *

GREAT FIRE IN GEORGETOWN

Almost on the strike of half-past eight o'clock, citizens were startled by hearing a terrific explosion which was felt throughout the town. . . . It is rumoured that the disastrous explosion took place through the medium of a case of fireworks, but certainly the outbreak of fire, which ensued was both terrible in its intensity and the rapidity of its spread.

The burned out district is almost a square, being the properties in the Lombard Street lots from Hadfield Street with the exception of the B.G. Pawnbroking premises at the corner, to Harel Street on the one side and from Bugle Street to lot 9, beyond Schumaker Street on the other, and all the Water street lots up to and including the Demerara Company's premises.

It was one of the most congested areas in the town. The buildings were packed as closely to each other as was possible for them to be. Furthermore, the majority of the buildings were very old and in a somewhat dilapidated condition. This was particularly the case in regard to the buildings in and around the vicinity of Leopold Street.

GREAT EXPLOSION

A thud and then a terrible roar. The chair in which I sat rocked violently and the building shivered. Something terrible had happened. Almost instantly there came hysterical cries of "Fire," and in a few seconds the whole building was empty. "My God, the town's ablaze!" came a cry, then I realized that something really terrible had occurred. In Water Street as I raced along in the direction of the volumes of smoke that obliterated the azure blue heavens above the district of Charlestown, I noticed the storekeepers hastily barricading their premises. Their work was with difficulty accomplished for the stampede of people rushing helter-skelter towards the scene of the conflagration toppled many of the men over, shutters and all. Everybody, business men, clerks, policemen, traffickers, intermingled with a good sprinkling of the centipede fraternity were rushing in the one direction and the few cabs laden with ladies who had hastily left the breakfast table and were keen on witnessing the scene found difficulty in making progress. It was just nine o'clock and when I reached the Stabroek Market blood red flames were leaping high above the tallest buildings, whilst the ears were deafened by the crackling of burning timbers and falling debris. The whole block stretching from Mr. M. U. Hing's jewellery store in Lombard Street to Water Street was enveloped in flames and occasionally small explosions as the last vestige of Chin-a-Yong's premises were demolished, which later proved to be the origin of the blaze, told of the existence of a further store of fireworks. . . .

Bonded Goods Saved

For some time the Bonded Warehouse was threatened. A huge flame crossed Water Street and licked the white painted front as if, as a reminder, that "Its your turn next." Instantly a body of officials and labourers were to be seen rolling barrels of rum and other highly inflammable goods from the building into safety whist a strong jet of water from the *Vesta* deluged the building. His Excellency the Governor who, with the Hon. C. Clementi, the Government Secretary, had motored early to the scene, had secured an excellent point of vantage at the top of the clock tower over the Market and watched with the keenest interest the various stages of progress of the flames. He was frequently pointing in the direction of Lombard Street where at one time the flames which had by this time swept the thoroughfare, threatened the British Guiana Pawnbroking and Trading Company's building at the corner. Mr. Clementi was seen to leave the tower and take an active part in battling with the flames in Water Street as also did Captain Napier, His

Excellency's aide-de-camp. Though huge volumes of water were poured on to the smouldering woodwork, the building caught, but by a miracle the wind which veered in the direction of the city now had shifted and the building – one of the few in the area of the conflagration – was saved. It was at this time, that a glass case belonging to Mr. M. U. Hing was rescued from his burning building containing bangles, brooches and rings set with various precious stones. It has been got into the middle of the street and a crowd collected. There was a crash of glass, the case had been smashed in less time than it takes to write and the contents had been looted. The scene was a disgraceful one and the culprits had cleverly "worked" the oracle.

Dante's "Inferno"

In Water Street the flames had by this time swept as far as the Demerara Company's Warehouse and the dense black volumes of smoke lit up by incessant forks of blazing fire presented a realistic scene from Dante's "Inferno." . . . Women were as active as the men in their attempts to fight against the onrushing flames and when their futile energies had been exhausted they were seen rushing frenetically in all directions, bewailing their losses. Dr. Minett had by this time arrived with the ambulance of

the Public Hospital and did splendid work in dispatching the wounded to the institution for treatment. The bugles of the volunteers were now sounding throughout the city and in but a few minutes squads of well disciplined khaki clad men were taking up their various appointed positions to be ready if required. . . . The Mayor of Georgetown (the Hon. Francis Dias) was also amongst the throng and realizing that it was necessary for the Charlestown koker to be opened in order that the river water might be admitted for the use of the firemen who had taken up positions on the top of the premises of the Demerara Company and other buildings in the vicinity at once instructed that this should be done.

Kokers, such as this restored one on Camp Street, provided flood control for Georgetown. *Roy V. Wong*

From the Market Tower

From the Market Tower the scene was such that one seldom has an opportunity of witnessing. Looking down upon the burning mass of buildings it seemed inevitable that all the premises on the right hand side of Water Street from the Bonded Warehouse onwards were doomed. Huge flames stretched across the thoroughfare and the telephone cables, blazing and spluttering in mid-air snapped here and there and curled up like huge fiery serpents. The good work done by the *Vesta* and Sproston's tug boat *Cuyuni* was here seen. A tremendous jet of water rose from the rear of the Bonded Warehouse and fell like a silver streak through the dense black clouds of smoke from the direction of the *Vesta*, assisted by another volume of water, a little to the left, from the *Cuyuni*, the stream being concentrated upon the buildings to the right hand side of Water Street which were a mass of flames. . . . I descended the tower and proceeded along the forsaken Water Street. The stores had been closed and not a soul was to be seen.

Fire Swept Streets

When the fire reached the premises of Ho-a-Hing, which was very old, the buildings there burned like tinder, and the conflagration raged with the utmost violence. It was only at this stage that any serious attempt was made to demolish the buildings before the fire reached them, but it was obvious that this was to no purpose, as the blaze was then at its highest. The fire spread with great rapidity and vehemence in an eastern direction along Leopold Street to High Street, where it enveloped a three story building, the lower portion of which was a bakery and what was known as "The Rake Grocery," while the upper flats were let in tenement rooms. When the conflagration reached this building the water service was again none of the best, the jets being able to play no higher, and that none too effectually, than the second flat. An old building, the fire soon took complete possession of it, and at any moment it seemed likely to fall with a crash. Notwithstanding this, however, a few men, regardless of the danger, were busily engaged in helping themselves to the drinks on the shelves. . . .

All this time the fire was working its way down Water Street and at Schumaker Street, the "Iron Rod" rum shop which looks on to the extensive premises of the Demerara Co., Ltd., on becoming ignited readily spread the fire to these premises. Adjoining the rumshop was a large number of old rickety buildings, which once caught by the fire it was impossible to save, whilst in the buildings of the Demerara Co., Ltd., were 8,000 tons of sugar ready for shipment by this firm and Messrs.

Booker Brothers, McConnell & Co., Ltd. In little time these buildings were one mass of flame, as well as those adjoining the rumshop, and it was early apparent that their destruction was inevitable. From this street the fire sped with equal rapidity down to Harel Street, where taking possession of the International Pawnbrokery it again made its ravages onto High Street, destroying several buildings there and partially the premises of the Motor Garage and Service Company Ltd. Seriously threatened at this stage was the "four decker" known as "Dyer's Hotel," where, in the anticipation of further damage should the fire reach the building, a number of persons set themselves to work with utmost assiduity. Fortunately, the fire did not find its way to this building, but when the workers were told to suppress their activities much damage had already been done. On the other hand the branch of the London Electric Theatre, which was always in jeopardy, sustained some damage from the fire, but not to the extent which at one time appeared would be the case. Anticipating this danger the management of the Theatre early removed from the building all the equipments used there in connection with the nightly entertainments.

The Burning of the Demerara Company's Premises

The destruction which was caused in the area described was, however, of little importance by comparison with what was taking place at the Demerara Company's premises. With the large quantity of sugar stored there and this taking fire the adjoining property of Messrs. Pimenta and D'Oliveira was regarded to be in great danger of suffering the fate of the others. In the buildings of the Demerara Company, however, was included one of brick, and to this building must be accounted the fact that the ravages of the fire were at length arrested. . . .

The properties that have been destroyed and the businesses conducted in them are as follows:

Water Street (riverside lots): Bugle's sawmill and office, Psaila's stores, Lopes & Son office and sawmill, premises lately occupied by C. S. Chung, Bettencourt's sawmill, Demerara Company's buildings and office.

Water Street (East): Bugle's lumber store, coal store, Chin-a-Yong's back store, Tenement buildings, Opium and garage shop of Mrs. Simon, Salvation Army Shelter, Bettencourt's lumber shed, coal store, "Iron Rod" rumshop, cook shop, etc. etc.

Lombard Street - (West): M. U. Hing, Chin-a-Yong, the City Restaurant (late Wo Lee & Co), a dry goods store, Rebbitt's drug store, "Brass Castle" rum shop, the Non Pareil Store, Jeweller shop of J. H.

Loung, J. Madhoo's drug store, the Defiance Luncheon Room and part of the London Theatre.

Lombard Street (East): Clarke's jewellery establishment, A. F. Carew, S.U. Ming (jeweller), "People's" rum shop, Abel Maria DaSilva (hardware), Chin-a-Yong (retail), Ho-a-Hing (wholesale and retail), Fonseca (druggist), Ng-a-Fook (bakery), an unoccupied building recently occupied by Brodie and Raider, Chee-a-Tow's residence and three buildings connected therewith, three dry goods stores, and the International Pawnbrokery.

The Scene in High Street

As soon as the inhabitants of High Street, from Harel Street to Leopold Street, perceived that the flames, which had then been raging for 20 minutes, were threatening their quarter, all was pandemonium. Doors were thrown open, and willing hands lent aid in removing household effects to St. Philip's churchyard, then regarded by all as a haven of safety. One Portuguese man, who occupied a house a few yards away from Dyer's Hotel, losing all control of himself, indulged in weird gesticulations and antics, while he shouted himself hoarse in giving directions to those engaged in transporting to the churchyard his furniture, etc. At this moment too, numbers of barrels of petrol were rolled from the Motor Garage into the drain stretching along the northern side of the churchyard, their inflammable nature necessitating their removal. Under the direction of Sub-inspector Cresall some mule carts were procured in which to cart away the barrels. But regrettable to say, although dozens of stalwart young men stood around, few would make any respond to the Inspector's appeal for aid, and it was not until a corporal taking out his note book signified his intention of jotting down the names of those who rendered service, with a view to their ultimate reward, was the work carried forward. Away in the church, yard old tombs furnished timely dumping ground for such articles as looking glasses epergnes, ware, etc., whilst the walks were lined with the less venturesome of the onlookers. . . .

EYE WITNESSES' STORIES

As far as can be ascertained no one actually on the scene of the explosion is left alive to say what happened but one of the closest eye-witnesses of the tragedy was R.C. Jason, who lived next door to Chin-a-Yong's, above Wo Lee's old premises, occupied at the time by a Chinese man named Chung, as a cakeshop.

Jason states that he was sitting at his window looking over at Chin-a-Yong's when he heard a small explosion and then a greater one. He then saw the roof of Chin-a-Yong's lifted and the building immediately after collapse. He saw nobody and therefore all the employees were caught in a death-trap. This is a fairly accurate view to take of the situation, in view of the fact that when the debris could be searched fourteen charred bodies were counted, some burnt almost to cinders. Jason proceeds to relate that his house collapsed, the beams came tumbling about his ears and several of them on his wife, against whom he was thrown, and who was considerably battered. He managed to drag her out on to the street, when she was taken to the hospital, more dead than alive.

Beds Shot the Windows

Another eye witness of the first few moments of the fire stated that he was about fifty yards away when he heard the explosion and turning saw the roof blown into the air while beds were shot through the windows, one of them catching on to the trolley wire where it hung for some minutes.

As soon as it was seen that Chin-a-Yong's place was enveloped, Mr. M. U. Hing, who kept a largely-stocked jeweller's store on the north side of it, had his stock moved out. Before he had finished the place took fire. All this time, buildings on the other side of Lombard Street were blazing. These took fire through the second explosion, which came from the vault and shot blazing fragments far and wide.

The firemen now had their hands full. On both sides of the street, the fire was raging. Lengths of hose were run out and water, the volume of which had greatly improved, was played on the B.G. Pawnbroking and Trading Company's buildings, the property of the Hon. J. P. Santos, next to which, the Cornhill Grocery owned by Mr. J. W. Sam, a young Chineseman who not long ago started business, was blazing previously.

Huge columns of smoke rolled skywards from Sam's building and from Hing's and Chin-a-Yong's on opposite sides of the street, lighted up at every few moments by tongues of flame which spat, hissed, roared and fell back, when gathering fresh strength, they leapt up again, higher than before. They played around the Pawnbrokery which seems to bear a charmed existence, for though the flames which darted out here, there and everywhere in long, sinuous streaks, fanned it with their hot breath, it stands now intact except that the paint on its southern gable is slightly scorched. That this was not razed to the ground is due to the foresight of Inspector Craig, who with some helpers got into the place and kept streams of water playing on the walls. . . .

Cannonade of Kerosine Bottles

As the flames raged fiercely through Sam's grocery and Chin-a-Yong's and Hing's, there was a perfect cannonade, the effect of bottle after bottle of kerosine oil exploding and sending up fresh jets of light to make more awesome the terrible spectacle. . . .

The regular body of firemen was swelled by a number of civilians who rendered yeoman service. The fire still continued its onward rush, without any perceptible diminution in its rate. Hasty removable of furniture were made and firemen and civilians with axes attacked the buildings with the view, of course, of checking the progress of the fire, by leaving as little as possible for it to feed upon. . . .

It had not got on the one side as far as the "People's" rumshop. Then was seen one of the grandest sights of the whole conflagration. Explosions followed each other like the reports of a quick-firing gun, while as fast as they were heard, sparks of multi-coloured flame shot up to the sky. Try as they might, the firemen were unable to control the flames. On the west side of the street the fire had reached Rebbitts' drug shop which also aided immensely in its course of destruction. . . .

It was not quite obvious that the flames would reach much farther down and the cry went up as to why there was no attempt made to blow down houses in the way. Soon after the welcome sound of the bugle was heard calling out the Artillery, Militia and Volunteers and it was supposed that they had been summoned for this purpose. The Artillery arrived, but without any dynamite. They lent valuable assistance in the work of salvation and reduced to skeleton frames a number of houses in an incredibly short space of time.

SCENE OF DESOLATION

A representative of the "Daily Argosy" inspected the scene of desolation in Lombard Street shortly after one o'clock when the smouldering debris lay in bewildering confusion on each side of the thoroughfare. Charred human remains huddled up in the most ghastly positions lay in the attitudes in which the fire had overcome them a few hours earlier. Most of them appeared to be remains of Chinamen and on the site of Chin-a-Yong's shop, where the conflagration originated, were to be seen six bodies each of them incinerated. Identification was impossible and all that could be done was to collect the remains and note the spot at which they were found. A band of volunteer were safeguarding the ruins of Mr. M.U. Hing's store, and in the centre was seen Mr. Hing himself, disfigured with a black eye, his left hand swathed in bandages and walking with a limp. Mr. Hing had a miraculous escape from certain death as did also his assistants. The explosion took place next door at Chin-a-Yong's shop within a but a few feet of his office chair and the occurrence of the subsequent incidents were related to our representative by Mr. Hing, "I've had a wonderful escape," he exclaimed, upon being approached. "I was sitting at my desk attending to some accounts just beneath a plate glass window facing the direction of the Government building. Suddenly there was a terrific roar and my chair jumped, pitching me backwards whilst the glass window was shattered and falling inwards showered over me. I received a severe cut upon the crown of the head, and sustained a black eye, whilst in extricating myself from the broken glass I cut my left hand severely. I immediately shouted to an assistant to go out and see what had happened but he had hardly left when volumes of smoke came rushing in and then I noticed that all the show cases had been smashed, and a part of the front facing Lombard Street was lying in the roadway.

Daylight Robbery

"Then there was a rush to save the stock, and I am compelled to say that much of my property was plundered by the mob which collected. Excitement was high, and, suffering from my injuries, I could only partially assist in the salvage work, but I know at least one of my cases was rifled by the crowd."

"How much do you think you have lost, Mr. Hing?"

"About $30,000 or $40,000 worth of stock," he replied, "and," he added, "only about one-fifth of that was insured."

Mr. Hing was asked whether he had much valuable plate being repaired at the time of the explosion and replied in the affirmative. He added that a large and valuable quantity of silver cups,

M. U. HING,
MANUFACTURING JEWELLER,
30, CORNHILL STREET,
Opposite the Telephone Exchange.

A LARGE ASSORTMENT
OF
COLONIAL MADE JEWELLERY,
ALWAYS IN STOCK.

NUGGET JEWELLERY
A SPECIALITY,
COMPRISING :
BROOCHES, SCARF PINS,
BRACELETS,
PENDANTS, STUDS, EAR-RINGS,
HAT PINS,
AND
SOLID CHASED BANGLES.

ORDERS FOR
CHINESE HAIR PINS
AND
ORNAMENTS
of various designs
PROMPTLY ATTENDED TO.

Advertisement for M.U. Hing's store. *B.G. Almanac and Directory*, 1906

plate, rose bowls, etc., which he been repairing for the Hon. C. Clementi, Government Secretary, had been either lost or damaged, as well as a quantity of antique china which he had been entrusted with for repairing by Mr. Clementi, and all of which was smashed. He explained that the property had sustained damage in transit from England, and the honourable gentleman had instructed him to repair it. "When I had got two cases outside of the shop," he continued, "I ran back to save my daughter and get my books and papers. I was met by a large volume of fire which had by this time burnt through to the shop and my daughter ran out and it was impossible to recover the books. Meanwhile the smashing of the glass cases was heard from the street and I could see that I was losing everything." . . .

A SUDDEN HOLOCAUST

In all directions there were scenes of desolation. Crowds of the poorer class of Chinese, East Indians wandered helplessly about, many of them clutching some pitiful articles of furniture which they had managed to snatch from the flames. Others whose dwellings had not been touched by the fire hurried their little household effects into the roadway, and the lower part of High Street with its borders littered with a weird collection of furniture, was pathetically suggestive of the countless families, who last night were without a roof to shelter them. The back of the Public Buildings, too, was an improvised dumping ground for salvaged furniture, washstands, beds, tables, chairs, even monkeys and parrots, making a bizarre collection, incongruous to the dignity of the stately building, but quite in keeping with the weirdness and unreality of the tragic morning.

WHOLESALE LOOTING

While some members of the crowds which collected on the outskirts of the fire were engaged in the heroic task of trying to arrest its progress, a great number were at work looting all they could. The stocks of the rumshops suffered greatly in this respect, and several men, drunk almost to insensibility, were picked up all about the streets. Others helped themselves to provisions. One woman ran out of a shop with a bottle of currants in her hand and on being remonstrated with, declared: "Eh, eh, an' is wha. Ah help dem move out dey t'ings. Ah ent wo'th somet'in foh me trouble?" After which she went on her way devouring the fruit. Many were seen carrying away wearing apparel. One burly fellow declared that he was all right with boots for the Christmas. Someone standing near stated that the man had been seen to lift three boxes of boots and make away with them. Another, fortunately he was caught, had his shift filled with working shirts and a pair of boots. He has, of course taken to the Brickdam [Ed: Police Headquarters].

No description of the scenes of yesterday, would be complete without allusion to the good work of the Artillery, Militia and Volunteers. After the first hour they were called out and marched down under arms to the Brickdam. There they left their arms, and were marched out to relieve some of the police, some of whom were on duty the whole day. The Artillery first relieved the police and took their turn at 6 p.m. until 9 p.m. when the police again assumed duty. As office was on duty all night and last night Colonel De Rinzy, speaking to a "Daily Argosy" representative, paid a very warm tribute to the Artillery and Volunteers for their smart turn out and the efficient work they did in fighting the fire, preserving order and looking after the "gentlemen" who went "prospecting" as they put it. . . .

The Premises Destroyed

Asked as to the premises insured by his company, Mr. Bollers [B.G. Mutual] was good enough to provide the following list of owners of premises totally destroyed:

Mr. L. Psaila
M. J. Lopes & Son
Bettencourt's Saw Mills
Demerara Co., Ltd.
Estate of H. J. G. Paddenburg
Mr. Evan Wong
Mr. M. U. Hing
Chin-a-Yong & Co.
Mr. F. B. Edwards
Mr. D. L. Hutchinson
Mr. G. J. DeFreitas
Mr. Jose Rodrigues
Mr. C. A. Santos
Mr. G. Paddenburg
Mr. Man-Son-Hing
Mr. M. J. Lopes
Mr. Fung-Kee-Fung
Mr. Ho-a-Hing
Estate of Mr. Fonseca
Mr. Lee-a-Own
J. M. Teixeira & Co
Mr. J. V. Caetano

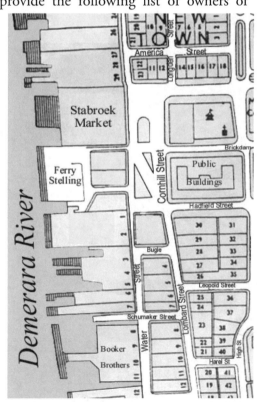

After the Chinese Quarter based in Lombard Street burned down, a new Chinatown later emerged in America Street.

The Motor Service & Garage Company, Limited
The Investment & Loans Association

"Many of these houses," added Mr. Bollers, "are jointly insured with us and the Hand-in-Hand and as we have not yet compared notes I cannot say the exact figure, but I should estimate that we are affected to the extent of 150,000 dollars."

TWENTY-THREE BODIES RECOVERED

Up to a late hour last night the number of bodies recovered from the debris totaled 23. Five were taken to the mortuary in the afternoon and remainder in the evening. The only body identified was that of Mr. John Tat whose remains had not been completely incinerated. The features were partly disfigured, but any doubt as to the identity of the remains was cleared away by the gold hunter watch and massive curb chain which easily identifiable. The remains were placed in a shell and conveyed to the mortuary.

Down by the Riverside

Elaine Fung-A-Ling
as told to Trev Sue-A-Quan

My grandfather was one of the early immigrants who came from China during the 19th century. Not much is known about him but he would have been a grown man when he arrived since he is shown to be 46 years old when he was baptized at St Saviour's Church on 8 April 1886, which was 20 to 26 years after the peak of the immigration program for Chinese. His name was Fung A Ling and became baptized as Job Fung-A-Ling. He was one of the fortunate Chinese immigrants in being able to find a wife – Rosa Chin-A-Kou. Grandfather Job became successful as the owner of a small sugar estate on Wakenaam Island, Essequibo as well as a merchant based in Georgetown by the time his first child, Alice, came along in 1887. The family was blessed with 4 children altogether and my father, Isaac Moses, was the youngest. He was born on 8 March 1898 and was known as Ike before being given the more formal name of Isaac Moses, which apparently was assigned to him by the missionary who was about to baptize Ike. In his adult years he also was popularly known as "I.M."

As the end of the 19th century approached Job Fung-A-Ling's fortunes took a turn for the worse when the price of sugar plummeted and the returns from the incidental products – vegetables and fruit, such as bananas, – were not enough to make a decent profit. Job's financial situation became bleak and he had to sell off the estate. In October 1898 Job died leaving behind a young family, with my father only seven months old, and his passing had a significant impact on the family. Alice had been a bright student at school and Rosa decided to send her to Edinburgh to study medicine. In 1916 Alice successfully completed her second year at university when she received the news that the family was unable to provide the necessary financial support for her to complete her medical degree. Alice then trained as a nurse and working first at the Public Hospital in Georgetown where she eventually became Assistant Matron. She subsequently was appointed Supervisor of Best Hospital, the sanatorium for tuberculosis patients at Vreed-en-Hoop, West Coast Demerara.

Alice Fung-A-Ling stands in front of the home provided by Best Sanatorium. The elevated main floor and windows with slats are typical modes of construction for buildings in Guyana. *Elaine Fung-A-Ling*

With the family's financial situation unchanged, Father could not continue on to higher education despite his good academic record at Queen's College, one of the leading secondary schools in the country. He turned his attention to becoming a draftsman and surveyor, training for which was available locally. The young man almost failed to make the grade after succumbing to influenza during the world pandemic of 1918. He became dreadfully ill and it took a long time before he regained his strength. Early in that year he married Margaret "Mag" Ng and later in the year became the father of Claude Fung-A-Ling. Father earned his qualifications just at the time that Alcoa (Aluminum Company of America), through its subsidiary, the Demerara Bauxite Company (Demba), was gearing up for a large scale operation to recover bauxite, the starting mineral for the production of aluminum. I.M. Fung-A-Ling began his career with Demba in 1918 and he served the company, and its subsequent parent company, Alcan (Aluminum Company of Canada) for 45 years.

Demba's base of operations was near Wismar, the furthest location up the Demerara River that was accessible by freighter. In earlier days Wismar and Christianburg (approximately a mile further downstream) were established when the forestry industry was flourishing. The villages remained as settlements with church and post office located at Wismar and the government offices, including the courthouse, at Christianburg, where a sawmill was once the center of activity for the area. The choice of the east bank for Mackenzie, where the bauxite plant was built, was because of its easier access to the rich bauxite deposits some 10 miles further upriver. The plant was completed in 1920 and consisted of ore cleaning and drying facilities to produce a better grade of bauxite plus buildings for storage and shipping, power generating plant, boiler house, machine shops, office and a laboratory. Later on an ice-making plant, called an icehouse, was built. To the south (the upriver direction) was a hospital with 67 beds and a dispensary. The area covered by Mackenzie stretched for a mile or more along the riverbank.[1]

The community that evolved at Mackenzie consisted of two separate groups, and separate they were in many ways. The expatriates brought in from the U.S. and later from England and Canada were provided with housing south of the Mackenzie plant at Watooka, named after the adjacent creek feeding the Demerara River. The housing was the best in the area and was designed to provide appropriate comfort for the managers, technical personnel and doctors who found themselves in the remote tropical jungle region of a little known country, far away from their own countries. Afternoon tea could be taken on the spacious and well-shaded verandahs. Various servants took care of the daily household chores and freed their employers to enjoy some leisure time. These expatriate white administrators and technical specialists kept to themselves and the location of Watooka itself added to their isolation.

The local staff for the plant were housed in more modest accommodations at Cockatara, just north (downstream) of the bauxite plant. This was where the hourly-paid workers of various ethnic origins – Blacks, Indians, and those of mixed blood – lived. The houses at Cockatara were of better standard than those available for workers on the sugar estates and much better than the motley dwellings that sprung up

---

[1] Deposits of aluminum oxide, or bauxite, had been known to exist along the upper part of the Demerara River since the late 19th century. No effort was made to extract the ore because of its relative remoteness as compared to the deposits found in other countries. There were also concerns about tropical diseases and insects as well as the lack of infrastructure including roads and power. In 1913 Edwin S. Fickes, in search for more resources for Alcoa, made a short trip to examine the bauxite deposits in more detail. He was sufficiently impressed by the quantity as well as the accessibility of the ore and he quietly enlisted the help of a prominent Georgetown lawyer, Joseph A. King, to obtain rights to the lands and mining privileges for Alcoa. Fickes then recommended that George B. Mackenzie, a Scottish-American expert in the company's bauxite operations, should go to Guyana to conduct further examinations and to secure those rights. Mackenzie's work in 1914 and 1915 led to the incorporation of Demba in September 1916, with Joseph King as the chairman. Mackenzie recommended that the preferred site for a bauxite processing plant be in the undeveloped jungle and mud on the east bank of the Demerara River, opposite the existing villages of Wismar and Christianburg. Unfortunately, George Mackenzie died at the height of his productive work and the place he had recommended for the plant was later named after him.

on the other side of the river at Wismar and Christianburg. My father and his family, which included my grandmother, were the only Chinese at Cockatara and we were provided a two-bedroom house a little distance from the river but after Father had been employed for a few years he was promoted to a managerial position in the company when it became difficult to get expatriates to work at Mackenzie. We were then allotted the best house in Cockatara, the one down by the riverside. In all the years of service neither my father nor any other local employee of importance to the company was offered the option of living at Watooka. However, after WWII key local employees were offered housing at Watooka.

The Fung-A-Ling's home down by the riverside. The covered verandah had mesh screens to keep out the insects. *Elaine Fung-A-Ling*

I remember swimming in the Demerara River. At this location in the river's long path the water was clear and cool but stained reddish brown from the vegetation of the forests through which the river coursed. Our family employed an Amerindian girl named Ivy to assist with household tasks and take care of us children and she used to take us to the river to swim, sometimes with one of us clinging to her back. Before we ventured deep into the water she led us in a native traditional custom and that was to have us bend over and clap our cupped hands below the surface of the water. This would produce a significant noise that traveled through the water and it was intended to scare away any dangerous fish lurking nearby. I do not know if this really worked in practice although admittedly I did not have any unfortunate encounters with the marine life. However, we were very aware that there were pirai (piranha) in the river so we would faithfully clap our hands with much vigor every time we went into the water. The flesh-eating pirai gained considerable respect in the local community especially when news arrived of some animal coming to a tearful end as it tried to cross the river, leaving behind a skeleton to bear witness to the ferocity of the pirai armed with razor-sharp teeth and considerable appetites. We also were very wary of the River Monster, named Massacouraman, which the adults talked about from time to time. I suppose it may have been a local version of the Yeti and I was only too happy that my underwater clapping persuaded it to leave us alone.[2] We sometimes swam and played among the huge runaway logs that drifted down the river and became beached near our house. These logs were even used to make a private swimming pool of sorts by placing two logs pointing to the river and another log or two set at right angles to form a rectangular enclosure where we could play in the water. Several years later the company dredged the river so as to accommodate bigger vessels at the loading docks and the excavated sand was dumped near our house so that our river frontage became a lovely swimming beach.

My elder brother Claude, who was a year and a half older than myself, was a bright little fellow and at the age of five was awarded a medal for his excellent schoolwork. In contrast, I just hated going to school, a one-room schoolhouse not far away up the main road, so much so that I had to be ported over in a wheelbarrow by my uncle. At age eight I was sent off to Georgetown with my brother Claude to attend primary school and we were placed in the kindly care of Elizabeth Lou-Hing. She became my second mother and I called her "A-Yipo," great-aunt. When my sister Bonnie was old enough to start school she joined us in the downriver journey to Georgetown. Just before the school year began Mother would carry out the annual ritual of making sure that our insides were cleaned out; she gave us strong doses of awful-tasting purgative medicine, which she insisted was to take care of any worms inside us. Sometimes Mother took us in tow on the trip to Georgetown but mostly we were dispatched on our own. On those occasions Mother would pack a picnic basket for the long ride and we would hardly be settled in on the boat than Bonnie would exclaim: "Let's see what's in the

---

[2] According to Amerindian legend Massacouraman is a large ugly hairy ape-like beast with huge red eyes and long sharp nails on its hands and feet. It lives in black deep water and damp dark forests and feeds on red meat. Adults would tell children that this creature would come and get them if they behaved badly.

basket." Although the *R.H. Carr*[3] departed at 8:00 a.m. we never knew what time it would arrive because of the tide and also the stops to pick up and drop off mail and passengers at points along the way. We would try to amuse ourselves as best we could by running around the main section of the upper deck and visiting the bridge. There the captain let us see how he steered the vessel and pulled on the throttle to change speed and direction. Once in a while, to our delight, the captain would let us place our hands on the wheel and let us imagine that we were in control of operations. But one thing that was a real irritant to our young spirits was the lack of access to the bow section on the upper deck, which would have been a wonderful place for us to play and allow us to see what was ahead of the vessel. However, the upper level bow area was reserved for the expatriates and others of importance.

The *R.H. Carr* had two levels, the lower one being the crowded second class section and the upper one being the first class section, complete with dining room, where we could relax in deckchairs or sit on fixed benches along the side rails and enjoy the view and cooling breeze as the boat made its way along the river.

On the lower level were the engine room (fascinating to look down and see the shining wheels and pistons smoothly turning), post office, benches for the second class passengers, and, towards the bow, open space for the animals and produce. There was always a high level of activity, more so when the vessel journeyed upriver and made frequent stops to take aboard people and goods. The captain of the *R.H. Carr* would send off a few sharp blasts with the horn as the boat approached the rendezvous point. The vessel would stop in midstream while miscellaneous watercraft headed out from shore with intended passengers who would scramble aboard and then pay their fare to the purser. They included vendors with baskets of fruit, vegetables, eggs and poultry. On occasion a pig would be among the items brought on board to go to

---

[3] In 1921 Alcoa appointed Ralph Hamilton Carr, a tall British gentleman with staidly deportment, complete with monocle, to be managing director of Demba. He made significant contributions to the development of the Mackenzie community but died suddenly in November 1926. He was memorialized by the naming of the motor vessel that provided communication service between Wismar and Georgetown as *R.H. Carr*. The vessel made trips to Georgetown on Mondays, Wednesdays and Fridays and the upriver journey on Tuesdays, Thursdays and Saturdays. The 65-mile trip would take 8 to 9 hours because even at that long distance away from the ocean the tide significantly affected the flow of the river. *R.H. Carr* was operated by Sprostons Limited, a company founded in 1850 by Hugh Sprostons, a retired English sea captain. Sprostons Ltd. was involved in shipping, ship repairs, boilers and machinery, timber trading, and other activities. The recession after 1918 left the company in a difficult financial situation and it was bought out by Alcoa which was then in the process of expanding its operations at Mackenzie.

market. Bound by its feet with ropes, the fidgeting animal would squeal its objections as several people manhandled it aboard ship. Even more interesting was the loading of cattle. With their horns tethered to the vendors' small boats the cows were guided along swimming in the water. A sling was lowered to haul the bulky animals up to the open gate on the ship's side. When cattle had to be unloaded at an intermediate stop they would be led to the opening and pushed overboard. Fortunately, the second-class level was not far removed from the water so the animals did not fall any great distance. Someone in the boat that had come out to meet the *R.H. Carr* would then attach a tether to the horns to lead them ashore. This was the Demerara River version of taking the bull by the horns.

When the steamer arrived at Wismar the vendors would scurry off with baskets balanced on their heads to pick a choice spot on the roadside at which to set up "shop." They spread out their blanket, canvas sheet or cloth and proceeded to arrange their items for sale in neat piles. Five mangoes, four set out in a tight square pattern with the fifth one perched on the top of them, would be available for 8 cents. In comparably stacked neat piles might be yams, cassavas, tannias, okras, green beans, star apples, pineapples, bananas, coconuts, bunches of green plantains and many other items. The chickens were kept off the "display counter" and lay in a basket with feet bound together, their tongues hanging from open beaks. The pigs and cattle were dragged off to the local butcher and all the way to the end the pigs would squeal their protests. The open market place with their colorful items and beckoning vendors was a place that we frequented because of the wider selection of fresh goods for sale and the more attractive prices compared to the company store.

The store operated by the bauxite company, located in Cockatara, was called the "ration store." It carried general goods such as cloth, thread, hats, cooking oil, butter, flour, rice, sugar, kerosene, matches, rum, etc. and also some fresh vegetables grown on the company's farm set up in the wide clearing behind the plant that also served as a mosquito barrier. The ration store was the main supplier of daily-use items for all company employees, including the expatriates. The system of purchase required no exchange of money. Each employee was given a little booklet in which the items of need were written down. The booklet would then be presented to the store operator and the cost of the items written down in it. At regular intervals the company's accountant would receive the booklet and deduct the amount due from the employee's fortnightly wages or monthly salary. It was a convenient system for the expatriates who only needed to write down their needs and then have their servants go and pick up the items from the store and take them back by donkey cart. Our family purchased most supplies from the ration store but would occasionally shop across the river at the Chinese-owned shops and, particularly on Fridays, we would pick up our cuts of meat previously ordered from the butcher. Perhaps the item most regularly bought by us from the ration store was fresh red snapper brought by steamer from Georgetown and kept on ice produced in the Company's icehouse.

The "ration store" at Cockatara. Fresh fish and ice were sold from the small, attached hut (center). The small, motorized launch (with canopy) was used to transport employees and equipment upriver to the exploration sites for bauxite. The flat-bottomed ballahoos in the foreground were popular for conveying goods. *Elaine Fung-A-Ling.*

A small river steamer plied between Wismar and Mackenzie, a distance of some 200 yards. It carried goods and passengers but it was not always available at the time required. For the expatriates there was a launch for whenever they ventured away from the company town but of course it was reserved for company executives and senior personnel. On just one occasion was our family given the privilege of using the launch. It was when Mother's mother died. She had requested that she be buried alongside other Chinese in the Le Repentir Cemetery just south of Georgetown because she felt that she would be all alone if she were to be interred near Mackenzie. The company offered to help and had her coffin placed above the canopy covering the middle section of the boat. The launch then made a slow journey downriver to take her to her final resting place.

Ferryboats were the typical means of transportation across the Demerara River between Mackenzie and Wismar. Passengers were required to paddle themselves. *Elaine Fung-A-Ling.*

For the local folks the main means of transport across the river was by private "ferryboat," essentially a river taxi. These boats were owned and operated by individual entrepreneurs and boarding took place at improvised landings consisting of three large logs strapped together. (Demba later built ramps and provided sheds for the waiting passengers.) The boats could carry a dozen passengers, or a few more, and were utilized primarily by the mineworkers commuting to and from work. Passengers were required to power the boat using paddles provided by the owner, the captain, who sat at the stern steering the boat. The fare was four cents per person for the crossing and if a passenger decided not to paddle the fare would be eight cents. Most of the commuters had their favorite captain and boat. On many an occasion there would be a rush of workers at the end of the workday running to and scrambling into their boats, then paddling furiously in a race with other boats to get home first.

Our family also had a preferred captain, Bennett, and Mother secured his services on a weekly retainer basis so that we did not have to search for fares every time we boarded. Whenever we could we would put in an advance request when we needed ferry service. Actually, favoritism was also practiced in reverse because a captain would sometimes refuse to take a hopeful passenger if he didn't take a liking to that person. It may have been because on a previous trip the traveler turned out to be a more of a passive passenger than earnest paddler, thereby getting away with four cents worth of payment and throwing the captain's schedule (if there were one) off track. Mother went across every Sunday to attend church, where she was also involved with the Dorcas Society, essentially a sewing club crafting articles for St. Aidan's Church annual bazaar to raise funds for charity. On special religious days such as at Easter Sunday we had to go across for the 5:00 a.m. mass and our faithful captain would be there to ferry us across the river. It was still before daybreak and the boat carried a kerosene lamp perched on a pole at the stern. It was quite a dream-like ride to be on the river in the semi-darkness, quietly cutting through the thin layer of cool morning mist that lightly floated on the surface of the water. Then there were other times when we were on one bank of the river when the ferryboats were on the other, particularly in the middle of the day. With hands cupped to our mouths we would shout "boat, boat" at the top of our lungs hoping that our chorus would stir a captain from his siesta. Sometimes there would be only two or three of us and if the tide was not in our favor it would take quite an effort to get the boat across.

I remember once when the non-response to the call "boat, boat" and "Bennett, Bennett" almost caused a disaster. My younger brother Whitty, who was not yet old enough to go to school with us three older ones, remained at home with Mother. It was mid-afternoon, when ferry traffic was almost nil, and he needed to cross the river to attend his cub meeting at St. Aidan's Church in Wismar. He made the usual call but not one boat pushed off from the other side. Next to the landing was a small gully across which stretched a large plumrose tree that provided shade for passengers waiting for a boat. The tree was laden with luscious fragrant plums and Whitty tried to jump across the gully to get at the plums but his little legs were not up to the task and, to make matters worse, it was a spring tide and the river was at its highest and so too was the gully which flowed into the river. He landed in the water in the middle of the gully and was being carried to the river. Fortunately, a waiting passenger was able to grab him and pull him out before he was swept away. He was taken home none the worse physically for the mishap but Mother immediately cancelled Bennett's retainer. However, Bennett was our favorite boat captain and a short time later he was reinstated.

The mineworkers using the ferryboats disembarked at Cockatara and walked a short distance to the train. The main terminus for the rail line was actually at a roundhouse at Mackenzie but a rail spur was laid out to Cockatara to transport workers as well as to take goods going to the ration store. At 6:00 a.m. the whistle at the plant would pierce the morning silence and the steam train then chugged its way along the 10 to 12 miles of narrow gauge track that took the workers to the bauxite mines. The train made another journey three hours later to take food to the workers. This was called the "breakfast train" but in essence it carried the lunches prepared by wives or servants. The food was packed in circular stacking metal trays held in place by U-shaped prongs that threaded through the loops on opposite ends of each tray. A set of three or four stacked trays was commonly called a "carrier." At midmorning the womenfolk could be seen balancing large wooden boards on their heads, each bearing six or more carriers. Although the boards had rimmed edges to prevent the carriers from sliding off, it took considerable agility to keep the boards properly balanced, especially when the women were late for the train and had to hurry. The carriers were well marked with the names of the owners and some were wrapped in a towel or cloth for identification as well as to retain warmth. The breakfast train was intended to enable the workers to get a hot meal but it is hard to say how hot the carriers were by the time they arrived in their owners' hands. In this regard Father was enabled the privilege of having his carrier placed near the locomotive engine.

The "breakfast train" transported people, breakfasts, and bauxite between Mackenzie and the mine site. The person second from the left holds a food carrier popularly used for meals. Fourth from the left is I.M. Fung-A-Ling. *Elaine Fung-A-Ling.*

Working as superintendent of the Three Friends open-pit mine at Akyma was just one of Father's different appointments with Demba. He started off in the office doing drafting work. His duties also included surveying which took him into the field, or, more appropriately, the jungle. He was later put in charge of explorations and this would sometimes keep him away for weeks because it was necessary to clear away the trees, bushes and vines before setting up the machinery and then doing the drilling.

My father told us of one incident when he was out on an exploratory trip with Dr. E.C. Harder, a senior geologist from Canada. Dr. Harder had a dignified manner and worked in a careful and unhurried manner. He was one of the high-ranked members among the expatriates and even in the remote wilderness his tent was set up away from the rest of the group. On one outing the exploration party was walking along a trampled path in the jungle when grunting sounds

Camps were set up in the jungle when teams went out to explore for bauxite. *Elaine Fung-A-Ling.*

were heard. The locals quickly realized that wild boars were heading their way, and the men took off in a flash for safety. Father urged Dr. Harder to hurry and although his pace may have increased, it was only an incrementally change. Father grabbed his arm and had to haul him away from the approaching wild beasts that were well known for their long tusks and vicious nature.

I.M. Fung-A-Ling and companions show off two wild pigs that they shot during a hunting trip. *Elaine Fung-A-Ling.*

Our family was quite familiar with the local wildlife and Father would join others on hunting trips for wild pigs, birds and other game. As a youth, Claude would occasionally take my younger sister Bonnie and me venturing up the creeks in our corrial in search of prey. The creeks were always challenging and mysterious places to explore because we were going into unknown territory and the dark narrow creeks brought out the adventurous spirit in us. But when we went tracking along a narrow trail he would sometimes ask us to wait and there we two girls would sit back to back with our eyes searching for any unwelcome intruder from the jungle. Sometimes we would notice a cocorite palm from which the nuts had ripened and fallen to the ground. Claude would then find a nearby tree in which to set up a blind, in fact just a small ledge. Seated on this makeshift perch he would wait until dark with helmet, mosquito netting, flashlight and his .22 rifle. It was at night that the labba[4] and acouri[5] would show up in search of the nuts and Claude would turn on his flashlight thus freezing the animals and then fire his rifle to bag himself a prize. Father and Mother took part in preparing the animal for the pot, using ample amounts of boiling water to help them in getting the hair removed by scraping. The labba did not provide a large amount of meat but the family did delight in having a meat dish for a change because we more frequently ate fish, much of which we caught ourselves with the water essentially at our doorstep down by the riverside. We would also buy snapper on ice at the company store, although the purchasing was done in a separate shed that was set apart so that the odors wafting through the busier ration store would be reduced.

I.M. Fung-A-Ling with a camoudi. *Elaine Fung-A-Ling*

Father liked to go fishing and he made himself a long spear with trident-like prongs. At nighttime during low tide he would go out in the corrial to the edge of the mudflats where the river bed dropped off sharply and there he would wait quietly with spear at the ready for suitable fish to come by. The glint in their eyes as they came to the surface revealed their presence. It was not unusual to see a snake swim past. On one occasion he looked in the water and saw his reflection moving but then he thought to himself I'm not moving my head. It was in fact a large water camoudi[6] staring back at him. Unfortunately his spearing techniques were not of the same caliber as his drafting ability and many a time he came back empty

---

[4] The labba looks like a giant sized hamster and its meat is a delicacy in Guyana. A popular Guyanese saying: If you eat labba and drink creek water, you will return to Guyana.

[5] Also known as agouti, this member of the rodent family can be up to two feet long.

[6] Otherwise called the anaconda. Belonging to the constrictor family of snakes the camoudi is a good swimmer and capable of growing to several metres in length.

handed from his fishing outings. However he relied more on the more conventional fishing rod and hook to bring home a dinner dish for the family. He also knew a better way of catching fish. At a few locations there were small bay-like indentations in the riverbank created by swirling eddies. There Father would set up a fish pen, which was in fact a flexible gate made of sticks tied together. As the tide came in some leftover food would be thrown into the enclosure to act as fish bait and when the tide crested the gate would be closed quietly thus trapping the fish. There would be a variety of fish caught in the fish pens and we relished the patwa and sunfish while being careful in handling any pirai that we had caught.

As youths we did not have many toys and had to make our own gadgets to amuse ourselves. The courriah tree produced the ideal object to make a spinning top. The courriah tree had many spikes on its trunk and very difficult or rather impossible to climb. We had to wait until the fruit dropped to the ground. The thick skin would be removed and the flesh eaten. This left a hard round nut somewhat larger than a golf ball. After piercing through the nut we would insert a spindle and wind a length of string on the top portion of the shaft. We could then launch the top and watch it go spinning across the floor or ground. In addition a couple holes were punched into the top and these produced a whistling sound as it whirled on its way.

Claude Fung-A-Ling helped in the construction of the railway bridge across the Demerara River, from where he would go diving. *Elaine Fung-A-Ling*

When Claude was a young man he was employed by Demba and he would go diving off a railway bridge that he had helped to build across the Demerara River. The bridge was needed to take the bauxite from the new Hope mine, opened up on the west side of the river, to the processing plant. During his lunch break Claude would often take a quick dip in the river. One day he was about to go on such a cooling swim but he first thought that he would test the temperature of the water with his foot. He had barely dipped his toes into the river when he felt a tug on his toe accompanied by a sharp pain. He lifted his foot and saw blood spurting from a missing big toe. Apparently some workers had been washing out their lunch carriers nearby and the food remains had attracted some fish, pirai included. The fish were eagerly awaiting the next morsel when Claude's toe came dangling in the water. Hopping about in great pain, he scurried off to get medical attention. As it turned out the pirai had managed to mangle off a portion of flesh below his big toe. After this incident he knew better that to try to go swimming close to where other fish food was being offered to the pirai, but he still did not lose interest in taking a cooling plunge into the Demerara River. In our family we did have a few stories about the big one that got away but in Claude's case he bore evidence with his somewhat smaller big toe. I suppose that from the pirai's perspective it really was the big one that got away.

Although there was running water piped to the homes in Cockatara, this was non-potable and used for washing and flushing the toilet. Drinking water was obtained from barrels or a vat that collected rainwater running off from the roofs of the houses. From time to time a government inspector would come by to check the quality of the water and to add a few small-sized fish in order to take care of any mosquito larvae. The rainy seasons came twice per year and the accumulated water had to serve our needs until the rains came again. As a little innocent child Claude once opened up the tap on our vat and delighted at the gushing water pouring out freely. I suppose our parents considered him more of a brat for that incident.

My sister Bonnie was the cute little girl who became the darling of the expatriates particularly Dr. Romitti, the surgeon recruited from Italy. He just loved baby Bonnie and when Mother asked him to pierce her ears he admitted that it was something not within his surgical experience but he went ahead with the request, and successfully performed the job. He and the physician

Baby Bonnie Fung-A-Ling.
Elaine Fung-A-Ling

Dr. Giglioli, another Italian, took care of the patients at the company hospital – one of the few places where rank and skin color did not affect the treatment provided. Dr. Giglioli became known locally for his skill and expertise. Indeed, when Walter Lou-Hing, one of A-Yipo's sons, contracted tuberculosis in 1932 Mother suggested that he go to Mackenzie to be checked out by Dr. Giglioli and I was asked to accompany him on the trip upriver. Unfortunately his condition was beyond recovery and he was taken to spend his remaining days at Best Hospital where Aunt Alice Fung-A-Ling was the Matron.

In the early days of the company's operations there were a few local girls employed as secretaries but after a loss in working time caused by pregnancy, a policy of having male secretaries was introduced. This continued up through the 1930s. When I completed high school at the beginning of WWII my father asked the company if employment could be offered and thus I became the first female secretary in a long while. When this experiment proved a success the company employed other females as secretaries and another contributing factor was the difficulty in finding male secretaries. The manager, chief engineer and accountant had personal secretaries and the remaining expatriates made use of a secretarial pool, all the secretaries in the pool being Guyanese girls. One of the secretaries was Lawrence "Larry" Ho, who was employed with my father's help. Larry was a competent secretary and was given the responsibility of administering the typing pool. Larry later opened up his own secretarial school in Georgetown.

Larry Ho was one of the Chinese who came in the wake of my father's pioneering experience. For quite a few years our family had been the only Chinese family settled in the area but then a few came to make their home in the area. The Lee-Ting family opened a grocery in Wismar and other new immigrants from China followed. The shops opened six days a week and on Sundays the high-pitched wail of Chinese opera could be heard across the river. There were ongoing visits to the courts in Christianburg by Frederick O. Low, the first Guyanese lawyer of Chinese descent. David Foo, one of whose responsibilities in the civil service was taking the census, was also at Christianburg. As the bauxite operations expanded the population of the company town and the nearby villages grew and a few more Chinese families migrated to the Mackenzie area. Augustus "Gus" Kwok became the dispenser when Akyma became a small settlement with a local health clinic and ration store. William Li and his wife Ethel, a niece of F.O. Low, were hired to operate the ration store. Some of these later arrivals came through the influence of my father, either through direct recommendation or else through the fine example that he had set. The Chinese were not numerous in the community but they shared similar experiences in the company town down by the riverside.

Mixed Marriage

Barney Singh

The story that follows was adapted from material prepared for presentation to the Toronto Kaieteur Lyons on the occasion of the celebration of United Nations Day on 25 October 1994.

* * * * * * * *

I invite you to eavesdrop on a conversation between a father and a son that <u>very likely</u> took place many years ago, in 1927:

"Baap, I decide to get married."

"Is time. I bin after you a lang time now. I had a good, good match fuh you, but you say you want to mek you own match. Is who daughter?"

"Is no nobody you know. Is a Chinee gal me gun marry."

"Oh beta, what you trying to do to me? Dem got so much nice, nice Coolie gal and is Chinee you want to marry?"

"Me mind mek up Baap, and nutten' can stop me."

"Is how come you mind mek up so hot and sweaty?"

"Is not hot and sweaty. Me know she a lang time now. Me bin ah meet she everyday in the afternoon when me riding me bicycle home from wuk."

"But we don' know nutten 'bout she and she family."

"Is not she family ah marrying. She is a good gal, and me tink you gun like she and everything gun be alright."

"Me hope you know what you doin'. You know Chinee does eat poke and ahwee chatri don't have nutten to do wid hag."

"Me and she talk about everything and we 'gree she will never cook poke and cow and give me. Me sure we can wuk out everything to satisfy you and everybody else."

I leave it to you to imagine the discussion and dialogue among the members of the Chinese family when the young lady announced her intention to marry an East Indian, someone of a different race and religion. I am happy to report that the young man and woman did marry and the optimism about things working out to satisfy all parties was not wishful thinking. These two young persons of different cultural, racial and religious backgrounds shared a marriage of over 61 years. In their years together, they respected each other's religious beliefs and practices. They did more – they actively promoted, participated and celebrated each other's beliefs, practices and festivals. By all accounts, this marriage was a success.

I am the eldest offspring of this union, and I have been happy to share this bit of personal history. I believe that something like this conversation must have taken place between my grandfather and my father. It was a time when our mostly immigrant population had little knowledge of the customs of people from lands other than their own. People were thrown together in the melting pot of the colonial era and had to overcome ignorance of the customs of other races and suspicions about beliefs and practices. Yet these two, and a few others like themselves, took the bold step of inter-racial marriage.

It takes little imagination to realize the adjustments in habits, outlook and behaviour this young couple had to make to avoid a clash of cultures as they journeyed along to make a happy home and household. The greatest adjustment was in the matter of food, food preparation, and table manners.

I will share with you how this very tricky matter was resolved. Neither my father nor mother required the other to forsake his or her customary foods – my Chinese mother would continue to eat beef and pork while these meats would never be prepared for my father. Fortunately, father did eat meat, except for beef and pork, and so there was always enough other meats – chicken, duck, turkey (all grown at home), mutton and goat to satisfy most meat requirements.

In the beginning, beef and pork would be prepared and eaten when my father was away from home. Care was always taken to avoid contamination by the utensils used in preparing these dishes. Father's food would remain "kosher" or "halal" at all times. I observed the commitment and trust that existed between my parents that the right thing would be done at all times. Later these dishes were prepared when my father was at home but were not brought to table when the whole family including my father dined together. Much later my father would say, "I know you have prepared your own stuff, why not bring it to table and enjoy it." This was a magnanimous gesture in saying that all the family members – and there was always a lot of family around – were entitled to enjoy their food in his presence, and he did not wish to stand in their way. He was confident that care had been taken to satisfy his requirements.

Today, in Toronto, we look around at our large Chinese population and observe their dining habits in our many Chinese restaurants. My father did not have this opportunity. You can imagine his discomfort during his first visit to my mother's large Chinese family. Here they were, sitting around, serving themselves piecemeal from the serving platters on the table, using chopsticks or forks on a continuous basis to transfer small portions to their individual bowls. The atmosphere is noisy and the food eaten with great gusto. It must have been like being in another world.

Compare this with my father's family. Following the tradition of rural India, a plateful of food would be dished from the pot on to individual plates and eaten with their hands. We can imagine these ancestors of mine remarking "Eating with knives and forks and chopsticks! What's wrong with their hands?"

The melding of these two cultures was not lost on the children. In the matter of food, I follow my mother, my younger brother follows my father, while my youngest brother, as far as I know, is undeclared. I really do not know his eating preference and it is unimportant. My household, with a Portuguese wife, follows the practice of taking great care to avoid "contamination" when serving mixed foods at family gatherings. The tradition of respecting cultures continues.

Growing up in a mixed marriage home provided unique experiences for my two brothers and me. We routinely ate foods of both cultures without a thought about whether it was Chinese or Indian. My mother's curiosity and talent for cooking made her an excellent cook of Indian foods. We ate curries of various kinds regularly. Vegetables were called by their Hindi names—alu, jingee, nainwah, bora, baegan, bhagee[1] etc. Our enjoyment of a meal of "dhal bhat"(dhal and rice) was heightened by various types of chokas[2] such as alu, baegan or coconut. The last was especially delightful. Our gustatory experience was made more enjoyable by the ever-present spicy or fruit-based chutneys, and achars (made with chunky pieces of various fruits, such as mango, lime, or blingbling, otherwise known as souree). These delights were usually prepared at home.

Our curries were prepared from various spices such as coriander, cumin, jeera, cardamun, tumeric(dye) which made up what is generally

---

[1] Alu (potato), jingee (a variety of long squash with a fluted skin), nainwah (similar to zucchini), bora (long beans), baegan (eggplant), and bhagee (spinach) are terms that became familiar to most Guyanese.

[2] Chokas are side dishes prepared to enhance repetitive meals such as dhal bhat; they add variety to the monotony of the same meal eaten day after day; the rural Indian had limited means and were ingenious to provide variety by these simple dishes.

known as the massala. There was different massalas for various dishes. The spices were ground on a flat indented stone base referred to as a sill, with a handheld horizontal stone using a unique wrist action to grind the spices into a curry paste. This Indian traditional way, handed down from generation to generation and still used in the villages today, was used in our kitchen.

My father maintained that the traditional way of freshly ground spices was the only way to make a good curry. When curry powder – which would reduce the housewife's work – came on the market, my father claimed he would be able to tell the difference between powder and paste. He was probably right, as the early curry powders were not very good. But gradually the blends and qualities improved to the point of being just as good as the freshly ground paste. My mother wanted to change to save herself the drudgery of making fresh curry paste every time but was faced with my father's bias.

My mother introduced a small quantity of curry powder to the freshly ground paste and got no unfavourable reaction from my father. The proportion of powder to paste was gradually increased until the day when it was all curry powder. My father still enjoyed his curry believing it was being prepared in the traditional way. When a favourable moment was chosen to reveal this game of deception, my father was gracious enough to acknowledge that there was no need to go back to the old way of drudgery when a good enough substitute was available. Apart from being a family joke, this became a family lesson on how to be gracious when your certitude is demolished. Very few households in Guyana prepare curry in the traditional way any longer.

While Indian cuisine predominated, we were exposed to the delights of Chinese cooking. My mother had grown up with her grandmother, a first generation Chinese who was an importer and a retailer of Chinese foodstuff in the Stabroek market. My mother had a good knowledge of Chinese foodstuffs and how to prepare the dishes from these ingredients. My Chinese family soon recognized the wanyee mushroom growing on fallen logs of the courida trees, or "crab bush," that grew on the foreshore beyond the sea dam. These were harvested, dried and used in our Chinese dishes. Our non-Chinese villagers – our Chinese family was the only one in the village of Best – referred to these mushrooms as "rat ears" and rarely ate them. At other times, my family harvested bamboo shoots, which the other villagers did not recognize as edible.

My father's introduction to Chinese cooking was gradual and he grew to enjoy many of the dishes. Our wonton and other soups were always prepared with chicken as beef and pork were taboo. Our dishes were enriched with funsee, foochuk, wanyee, kimchim, ginger and other ingredients. Squash was an important vegetable with many others common to both Indian and Chinese cooking. Chow mein and low mein were household favourites and have transcended their Chinese origin to become staples of Guyanese cooking.

Apart from the western sweets of cakes, buns and the like, we benefited from both of our heritage cultures. From the Indian side we enjoyed bara, jalabee, peera, gulgula mohan bhog;[3] and from the Chinese side we had the delights of towsa (Chinee cake), rice cake, isinglass etc. It was the best of the many cultures of our society.

Our experience with religion was very enlightened. My mother's family was Hakka and very likely became Christians before they left China. My father was Hindu and remained one throughout his life. My brothers and I were baptized in the Anglican faith and our religious teaching was gained principally from attending the Anglican school, the only one in the village.

Christian festivals such as Easter and Christmas were celebrated as well as the Hindu festivals of Divali, or Festival of Lights, and Pagwah. There was respect for the faiths of each parent and every assistance was given for the other partner to remain faithful to his or her beliefs. My father was a leader of his faith in our village and would sometimes dress in his kurta and dhoti[4] for festivals. When my grandparents died the rituals for the departed were observed including the shaving of the head and the churkee, a small dime-sized clump of hair left on the head. I carried out these rituals for my father when he died in Canada.

In matters of faith there was no argument, one was as good as the other if you live by its teachings. The good Christian is indistinguishable from the good Hindu except for the rituals practised. We had the best of both worlds and have grown up with a great degree of tolerance for things that are different. Mixed marriages, both racially and religiously, predominate in the descendents of our family. One grandson is a Catholic priest.

Our language was enriched from both cultures, but less so from the Chinese. Apart from the names for foodstuff and a few for showing relationships like Popo (mother's mother), Apac (father's elder brother), Koko (elder brother), Asow (elder brother's wife), not many Chinese terms that were in constant use. The Hindu terms were used with greater frequency and so my grandparents were Ahja and Ahjee (paternal

---

[3] Various sweets made with different combinations of milk, flour, split peas flour and sugar to form smooth fudge squares, crispy curlicues, and crumbly balls.
[4] The kurta, a light-coloured collarless shirt, is typically worn over the white, billowing trousers, or dhoti.

grandfather and grandmother) to me, while they were Nana and Nanee (maternal grandfather and grandmother) to some of my cousins. My cousins referred to my parents as Mamoo and Mamee (meaning uncle who is my mother's brother and his wife) or as Chacha and Chachee (uncle who is my father's brother and his wife, respectively). While the Chinese system was just as detailed and elaborate as the Indian one, it was in declining use in our family due to the anglicizing of customs. This was indeed a loss as the English system of aunt and uncle is very imprecise as to the exact relationships.

I am grateful for my parents' example of tolerance and respect for customs that were different, and people who are different. As we reflect on the ideals of the United Nations, in today's troubled world, a world that is facing what seems to be insurmountable conflicts let us dedicate ourselves to the ideals of peace, harmony, respect and better understanding.

We, who share a Guyanese heritage, know from experience that people of different races, culture and religions can live together in harmony and peace. We have done it successfully and can be great role models as we face forces from many sides that are threatening to divide people who happen to have different backgrounds.

Bearing Fruit

Frederick "Joe" Pierre
as told to Trev Sue-A-Quan

The North-West District of Guyana is different in many respects from the rest of the coastal areas bordering the Atlantic Ocean. The soil there is primarily pegasse which is peat-like material, spongy in nature and although rich in nutrients is able to sustain cultivation of cash crops for only a few years. Not far inland from the coastline are hills making the place economically unattractive for sugar plantations but suitable for citrus and other permanent crops. As a result the sugar barons steered clear of this region and the North-West District (called North-West, or NWD, in local terminology) became a remote and relatively isolated place, even though it forms a part of Essequibo County, the largest of the three counties of Guyana.

NWD would have become a forgotten place but for the discovery of gold in the region in the 1850s which stirred up interest in uncovering El Dorado, or another place that could match the riches of the legendary treasure trove. The district borders on Venezuela and it became a place of interest for setting up various governmental agencies to establish national presence and administration. Morawhanna itself started as a collection of shacks, huts and houses along the waterfront of the Barima River. It was not the most appealing nor the most advanced location in Guyana yet it was here that the Chan-A-Sue family members established themselves and became recognized and well-respected in the area.

Chan A-sue, an immigrant from China, became known as Joseph Ignatius Chan-A-Sue and he married Maria Wong, bearing four children, a boy followed by three girls, born between 1889 and 1902. The eldest, Emmanuel, had 9 children of his own while one of his sisters, Mathilda, married Philbert Pierre and raised a family of 6 children. The surname Pierre is believed to be derived from a Frenchman named Pierre Dubois who may have changed his name to become less noticeable in the colony of British Guiana. Another of Emmanuel's sisters, Cecilia, married Julius Pierre, the son of Philbert by his first marriage, and they had three children, including Frederick who became popularly known as Joe Pierre. Joe's mother died when he was a small child and Joe was brought up by his grandmother, Maria Chan-A-Sue, and her daughter, Mathilda Pierre, at the Pierre family plantation at Wanaina, on the Koriabo River, a tributary of the Aruka River. Between the Chan-A-Sue and the Pierre branches of the Chan-A-Sue family a wealth of experience was gained in growing fruits in the North-West District.

* * * * * * *

In the early days the North-West District could be reached only by boat. The vessels would have to travel along many rivers, one such route being along the Orinoco, Amakura and Barima rivers in order to get to Mora Passage. This journey would take a day and a half. Morawhanna was a settlement at the very narrow Mora Passage joining the Barima River to the Waini River and accessible only by small boats. But it was the traffic along these narrow waterways that contributed to the erosion that opened up a route for larger boats. The first steamer to make the journey to Morawhanna was early in the 20th century after the settlement of the border dispute with Venezuela in 1899. It was barely a navigable passage because people standing on either side of the boat could reach out and touch the branches of the trees on shore. This was the time that Morawhanna became the initial capital of the district. The steamer service marked the beginning of a communication link between the district and the nation's capital, Georgetown.

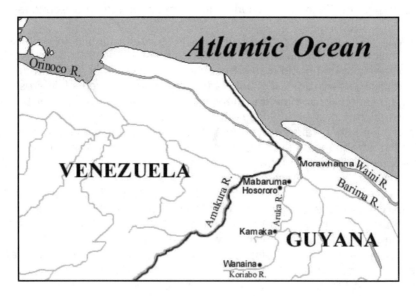

Grandmother Maria Chan-A-Sue opened the first general store in Morawhanna. The store supplied a variety of goods for the people in the district and Maria had to take out a licence for dry goods, another for malt liquor, a third for tobacco and yet others for patent medicines, hardware, etc. In addition she ran a rum shop and a bakery. The baking was done by Mr. D'Abreu, who was very skilled at his craft and produced delicious pastries and cakes. In those days yeast wasn't used. Instead, a portion of the soft dough from one day's baking would be set aside and

left overnight under a moistened cloth. This was used as the starting
material for making the next day's bread by mixing it with the newly
prepared batch of dough. The residual yeast in the old dough was
sufficient to make the fresh bread rise nicely. The bakery was not a large
operation but it was a busy place providing all the bread and baked goods
for the North-West District.

Among the people coming to the shop were gold diggers and
lumbermen who came into Morawhanna from the remote regions. One
of their important requirements was oil for cooking food at the camps,
but a glass bottle could easily break during their arduous trip, so many of
them purchased a large slab of belly pork fat from which they could cut
off a piece to create the oil for cooking. These gold prospectors, or pork-
knockers as they were called locally, would go off for weeks at a time and
then make their appearance in the shop to stock up with supplies before
taking off on their next expedition. There were a number of Venezuelans
who came by boat bringing large amounts of salted morocut[1] and they
would barter the fish for sugar, condensed milk, rice and other foodstuffs
as well as clothing. Because the prices for goods were lower than in
Venezuela these salt fish traders would come into town every two weeks
at the same time that the steamer arrived from Georgetown. When they
joined those who came from upriver as well as local residents the
mingling crowds in Morawhanna created a carnival atmosphere until the
steamer departed the area a couple days later. The steamer would set out
from Georgetown on a Monday and came first to Morawhanna the
following day at about noon to discharge the cargo destined for that
location, including supplies for the Chan-A-Sue shop. The next day the
vessel then proceeded further up the Aruka River to the Kamaka stelling
(dock) and returned to Morawhanna on Thursday to load up with local
produce and goods bound for Georgetown. Over the years Morawhanna
grew in size with the establishment of various institutions – church,
school, government offices, hospital and police station.

The river was the lifeline of the town but it also was the cause of its
decline because by the late 1920s the riverbanks became so eroded that
water encroached into the town. The government decided to move its
administrative offices to Mabaruma hill some five miles away and across
the river from Morawhanna. But there were still some residents who
persisted in staying in Morawhanna because the place had become a part
of their lifestyle and it remained the main port of call for the area.

---

[1] Belonging to the pirai (piranha) family, the morocut is much larger in size and has a
vegetarian diet. It lives in the rivers of the North-West District.

Emmanuel "Sonny" Chan-A-Sue, the son of Emmanuel, opened a general store in Mabaruma and was responsible for supplying goods for the hospital, government offices and police station. The police station was the only place where there was a phone and it was a hand cranked magneto model connected to similar phones at the police station in Morawhanna and also at the caretaker's house near the Kamaka steamer stelling on the Aruka River. The primary use for the phone was for medical emergencies and if there were such a need on the Aruka River or its tributaries the phone would be cranked to request that the ambulance be sent from Mabaruma to the Kamaka stelling. In similar fashion a call from the Morawhanna station would result in the ambulance being dispatched to the stelling on the other side of the river across from Morawhanna.

Sonny Chan-A-Sue had a small herd of cattle, maybe a bull and about a dozen or so dairy cows. There were other livestock on the farm as well – mules, donkeys, sheep and pigs. The animals were given free rein to roam around the large 500-acre lot, although they preferred to forage in the 300 acres of grassland rather than venture into the other 200 acres of forest. They feasted on the paragrass as well as the fruits from the guava and lime trees that grew wild on the property. An East Indian fellow by the name of Ramasar was employed to care for and milk the cows and was provided with free accommodations as part of the working arrangement. The milk was collected in cans and sold as raw milk. There was no facility to pasteurize the milk; instead the buyers would have to scald the milk themselves. The main consumer for the milk was the local hospital a mile or so away from the dairy farm, and a few government officials would also buy milk. Each day Ramasar took the cans of milk on a donkey cart and brought back the empty cans from the hospital. They would then be cleaned out with boiling water in readiness for the next batch of milk. These galvanized milk cans were also the means of carrying the milk to the government officials in which case a certified dipper, also made of galvanized metal, was used to measure out milk by the pint. The dipper had a long handle attached to the side of the cylindrical cup allowing the seller to reach deep down into the milk can.

One day Sonny received a complaint from the hospital that the milk was not up to standard – it seemed to be diluted. This was a real concern for Sonny because he had no way to test for adulteration and he felt that Ramasar was trustworthy and not likely to be responsible. However shortly thereafter some folks from the neighborhood told Sonny that they noticed his milkman was stopping at a particular house on his delivery route. Sonny figured that his worker might have some answers in this matter and he asked Ramasar what he knew about the changed quality of the milk. When the milkman realized that he had been caught he confessed that he had been going to his girlfriend's house to provide her with some milk after which he would top up the milk can with water before making the regular delivery to the hospital. The man was remorseful about his on-the-way activities and Sonny decided to retain him now that the situation was clarified and could be corrected.

A few months later another problem arose with the milk. This time it was noticed that the cows were not producing as much milk as expected and the hospital was concerned about the reduced supply. There was no obvious reason for the shortage and Ramasar was asked about the matter. He declared that he was not the cause and he himself was worried about this drop in production, especially coming so closely on the heels of the diluted milk incident. Ramasar decided to take the initiative in doing some investigation. He reckoned that someone was secretly milking the herd during the night and so he went out to check on the cows while they were tied up to the guava trees overnight. He took along his sturdy stick, which he normally used for rapping the trees to gain the attention of the cattle when he was herding them, but this time he was prepared to use it to deal with the nocturnal intruder. He treaded cautiously as he looked for the thief and then he caught sight of the culprit. His eyes opened wider at what he was seeing – the large 500-pound Berkshire boar sucking the milk from the cows. The pigs normally mingled with the cattle during the day and they were good companions but here was the boar taking advantage of their friendship by gorging itself on a hearty helping of fresh milk as they cozily lay next to each other. Since several cows had become low milk producers it was apparent that the boar was making the rounds among the various cows to enjoy its midnight feast. Ramasar never imagined that he would encounter a non-human consumer of the milk and in order to convince his boss he ran over to summon Sonny to witness what was going on. Sonny liked the Berkshire pigs because with only minimal care they could grow to a hefty size and this particular boar was being fattened for Christmas dinner. However this self-indulgent method of pigging out which jeopardized the milk supply for the hospital patients was the last straw. The next day a special enclosure was built to isolate the boar and the effect of the solitary confinement was that milk production immediately returned to its normal level.

Guava and lime trees grew naturally on the property and no care was provided for them. In some places the guava bushes were so thick that they became impenetrable to vehicles as well as humans. The branches were sturdy and would bend rather than break. This proved to be dangerous for any vehicle trying to drive over the guava bushes because the branches could snap back and hit the fan with enough force to bend the blades, which would then smash into the radiator. There was no ready market for the guavas and, except for the small amount consumed by the family and neighbors, the guavas were mainly fodder for the cattle and other animals. The limes, however, were valuable assets and Emmanuel Sr. planted some 300 acres of lime trees. Some of the lime trees were 40 feet across at the lower branches and bore hundreds of limes. Emmanuel came to an agreement in which he rented out the lime fields to an overseer, Mr. Sampson, who had set up a steam boiler and engine to process the limes. Samson employed some 50 women to pick up the limes that had dropped to the ground. The operations went on for 364 days a year since the lime trees would bear fruit continuously. The workers were not allowed to hit the ripe limes from the trees with sticks because that could bring down the blossoms and young limes and in any case there were enough ripe limes on the ground to keep the workers busy. The limes were loaded on a Ford truck that Samson had purchased. The Ford was an old model with the gas tank on the hood and the filling spout just in front of the windshield. The gasoline flowed to the carburetor by gravity. On many an occasion the truck would stall and come to a dead stop when going uphill because the flow of fuel was cut off. The truck had wooden spoke wheels and a hand crank had to be used to start the motor. It was this old Ford truck that took the limes to the processing factory where they were dumped into a huge pile.

The women workers extracted the lime oil manually using an ecuelling device. This was a one-inch deep round pan with a 6-inch collecting tube attached vertically to the bottom, near the rim. The bottom surface of the ecuelling machine was covered with short sharp copper pins.[2] Each woman worker would sit astride a bench next to the pile of limes with an ecuelling machine in front of her such that the collecting tube stuck through a hole in the bench. By rolling the lime on the pins the oil glands were punctured and lime oil would be extracted from the skin. When enough lime oil collected in the tube the liquid would be poured into a 26-oz bottle. The full bottle was fitted with a wine cork and for each bottle the women were paid 5 shillings. After this initial oil-extraction process the limes were tossed into a chute that conveyed them to a steam-powered press. The juice from this pulping process was pumped into storage vats and steam would be passed through the liquid to extract additional oil, which floated off to a collecting pan. The lime oil was shipped to Booker's Drug Store in Georgetown for the

---

[2] Ecuelling is derived from a French term écuelle a piquer meaning a bowl for pricking.

production of Limacol, the popular Guyanese astringent lotion, known by the promotional slogan "the freshness of a breeze in a bottle," as well as becoming an export item for the manufacture of essences and fragrances. The leftover juice from the pulping operation went to waste while the residual pulp was tossed aside and became feed material for the cows and sheep that wandered by. In fact the animals were aware of this abundant supply of edibles and were frequent visitors to the lime processing facility.

Much of the pioneering effort in agriculture in the North-West region was done by Emmanuel's brother-in-law, Philbert Pierre, who owned a 249-acre plantation at Wanaina. Philbert cultivated a variety of trees and plants – coconut, coffee, cocoa, banana, rubber, cinnamon, nutmeg, lime, grapefruit, orange, citron – some of them as experimental ventures. While growing crops and trees that would provide returns within a few years, he also planted some teak trees that required 30 years before they could be harvested. The teak trees grew well locally and after many years reached a size of some 16 to 20 inches in diameter. The seeds from the teak tree dropped to the ground and sprouted very easily resulting in a small forest of teak. A quicker return could be obtained from a tree known as the Congo pump. This produced a softwood that made an excellent brown paper commonly used for wrapping groceries and making paper bags. Attempts to grow the Congo pump from seed were in vain but the trees would spring up naturally in an area cleared from the forest by burning. Apparently the seeds needed to pass through the digestive system of toucans or bats in order to get started and in 10 years the trees were large enough to produce an economically worthwhile harvest. Philbert also tried his hand at growing rubber trees. These grew well in the local environment and their seeds would be spread afar when the seed casing exploded so that a group of younger rubber trees eventually sprung up near to the mature ones. The rubber from the plantation was limited in quantity but still made a valuable contribution to the war effort for World War II while keeping some businesses in Georgetown viable. The invention of synthetic rubber during the war years then significantly reduced the interest in Philbert's small rubber operations.

The Pierre plantation had a number of fruit trees. There was a variety of banana called the Cayenne banana and the fruit would be almost a foot long and an inch and a half across. The bunches were not easy to carry and this may have contributed to its lack of popularity. The best tasting kind was the "apple banana,"[3] a very sweet variety. Another tasty

[3] Also known as the 'Silk' variety of banana, common in the tropics.

variety was the cocorite banana that was the size of a fig and had a yellowish flesh. These bananas were also the favorite of the canaries and blue sackis.[4] This was different from the cocorite palm that produced a bunch of nuts with tasty kernels, favored by the saki winkis (squirrel monkeys). We did not lack for delicious fruits because there were other fruit trees including sapodillas and star apples.[5] Even the soursop fruit,[6] which could grow to about 10 pounds, was nice to eat with some condensed milk and nutmeg. Philbert put a lot of effort to growing citrus trees. The citron trees produced a fruit that was a foot long and very thick. There was not a great demand for citron in those days and the ripe fruit would fall to the ground and roll down the hill. But on occasion the family would collect one or two, remove the inside so as to leave the peel, which would then be soaked in a thick sugar syrup and left to dry in the sun. The resulting candied citron was a delight to eat and was probably better than the commercially produced product available in stores today, packaged in small bottles and costing a significant amount. Philbert put his attention to the citrus fruits, grapefruits and oranges, and had to contend with bark rot, which appeared as a discoloration of the tree trunks and would eventually kill the tree. Philbert believed that insects were responsible and he tried cutting a shallow trench around the base of each tree, which he then filled with coal tar but these moats did not solve the problem. Only the sour oranges appeared to be immune from the disease and this provided a method for overcoming the disease.[7]

Sonny Chan-A-Sue decided to start his own orange grove near his shop at Mabaruma. Sonny began initially with 100 acres converted into an orange tree orchard and later this was expanded to about 200 acres. There was a nearby government agricultural unit, the Hosororo Experimental Station, that grew citrus fruit seedlings and from here local planters could order as many as they wished to start their groves. There was no charge for these seedlings since the intent was to promote the economy for the nation. Sonny chose the Ruby and Valencia varieties that not only gave more juice but also ripened later in the season. He benefited from the efforts of the government experimental station where sour Seville orange trees were being cultivated. When the trees were about two feet in height the tops were cut off leaving the roots and trunk.

---

[4] A bird some 6 inches long with a silver-blue body and dark blue wings.
[5] Sapodillas are round in shape with a brown skin and 2 to 4 inches across. Star apples belong to the same family as the sapodilla and the seed pattern exhibits a distinctive star shape when the fruit is cut.
[6] The soursop has a definite sour taste that gives the fruit its name and it has a skin covered with short spikes.
[7] Bark rot, also known as foot rot, is caused by a fungus.

Grafts from other species of citrus fruit trees were then budded to the Seville orange rootstock and the grafted variety would continue to grow on the new host. There were several advantages with this approach, the important one being that the Seville trees were immune to bark rot. At the same time the thorny branches inherent in the Seville tree were avoided and the grafted trees came into fruit much faster than if they were grown from seed. It was possible for different varieties to be grafted onto the same Seville host, and this was called "crown grafting." The Seville tree rootstocks were also used for growing grapefruits and Sonny also opened up some 100 acres for grapefruit cultivation. For oranges, the trees were planted 25 feet apart while the grapefruit trees were spaced 40 feet to allow a vehicle to get through. The trees bore fruit in four years, and five years later the branches on adjacent trees would be touching. Sonny was able to promote their growth by setting up mobile pigpens that he shifted from one location to another. The pigs were fed with fruits and vegetables and they left behind their natural fertilizer.

The orange trees bore fruit once per year, with the exception of the Navel variety, which produced oranges all year round. When the white orange and grapefruit blossoms came out there would be thousands of humming birds flocking to the trees to gather nectar, pollinating the flowers in turn. It was an amazing sight to behold these birds of variegated colors ranging in size from a bumblebee to a small sparrow, all busily flitting from tree to tree. A few months later the fruits would appear, first as pea-sized balls then rapidly growing into green globes that were left to ripen on the tree. One or two employees would pick the oranges from the trees and pack them into wooden crates or barrels to be sold to the hucksters who came on the steamer once every two weeks. Sonny grew two varieties – Marsh, a very acidic grapefruit, and Surinam, which was very sweet and came in pink and white varieties.

Pears[8] were also grown on the estate and the pear trees grew to an impressive size, much higher than the house. The pears were left to ripen on the tree and were picked when they started to turn from dark green to a light green/yellow color or rose-colored. The branches of the pear trees were fragile, unlike the guava trees, so it was not safe to go climbing the pear trees to get the fruit. The pears high up in the tree were picked using a "fruit picker." This consisted of a long pole at the end of which was a basket and above this a levered blade that could be swung by pulling the attached cord. The fruit picker was also used to trim high branches of the trees. Sonny also grew grafted pear trees that were smaller in size but bore fruit much earlier. There were two varieties of pear tree, the less preferred

---

[8] Pear was the local term used for the avocado.

one being the "bottleneck" pear that bore fruit throughout the year. These pears were not so tasty and were left to drop on the ground where the labba would come by to feast on them. The more popular variety had a round shape and was available over a long fruiting season. They were sold at 50 cents per 100 and they were not the size of a cricket ball (or baseball) but rather as large as a grapefruit or a small papaya. An average sized pear would weigh about two pounds and pears close to the size of a soccer ball were not uncommon. As for papayas, they would be among the first kinds of plants to grow naturally in an area cleared from the forest. The papaya trees would spring up from the seeds carried in the droppings of birds and animals and unless the area was already designated for planting specific trees or crops they were allowed to grow in the wild. Peppers were the other plants that grew quickly from seeds deposited by the passing birds and capable of growing into sturdy trees that a child could climb. If the land were left long enough the Congo pump trees would take over the site.

Before the land was put to the cultivation of permanent crops it was used to grow root vegetables such as cassava, tannia, eddo, yam and sweet potato. The cassava trees, which could grow to more than a metre in height, were of two varieties, sweet and bitter cassava, although the tubers were fairly similar in appearance. One difference, however, was that the brown skin of the sweet cassava could be easily peeled. By making a knife cut along the length of the piece of cassava the skin could be pried loose from the white tuberous flesh. The skin of the bitter cassava on the other hand had to be scrapped off. There was another very big difference between the sweet and bitter cassava. The sweet variety could be treated much like other root vegetables such as eddoes and yams and some popular local dishes were prepared using a mixture of these different tubers. With the bitter cassava, it was necessary to pay great attention to make it into an edible product because it was poisonous.[9] The skill in utilizing bitter cassava was mastered by the local Amerindian people who were capable of producing several useful products from it. After scraping the skin away the cassava would be grated and pressed in a matapee. This was a tube some six feet long made from fibers of the mocru plant interwoven to make a lattice-like stocking. (Mocru was typically used in criss-cross pattern to make baskets and ornaments.) The matapee would be hung from a tree or high beam in a camp and when filled with the grated cassava would take on the appearance of a snake that had just

---

[9] Bitter cassava contains hydrocyanic (also known as prussic) acid, and in fact the acid was the material that gives the cassava its bitter taste. On heating the acid breaks down into harmless products.

ingested a large meal. A long pole was stuck through a loop at the bottom tip of the matapee and the end of the pole fixed to the nearby trunk of the tree or post to act as a pivot point. The person would sit on the other end of the pole causing the matapee to be stretched into a thinner tube thereby squeezing the juice out of the cassava. The liquid flowing from the matapee would drip into collecting basins or buckets.

Juice is extracted from bitter cassava using a matapee, and then converted into casreep. *Marva Hawksworth*

The cassava juice would be left to sit overnight and this resulted in a powdery, white sediment topped by a clear liquid. The liquid would be poured off and the remaining solid powder dried in the sun to produce starch that was used for laundry purposes. The liquid at this stage was a potent poison and if it were to be drunk by humans or cattle the result would be a suffocating death in short order. Even so this liquid was the starting material for a popular sauce called casreep.[10] It was made by boiling the liquid for an extended period until it turned into a thick concentrate. This was the seasoning for pepperpot, a local dish prepared with various cuts of meat, including ox tails, pig trotters and ears stewed in the casreep with, of course, liberal amounts of pepper. The cassava pulp remaining in matapee was also converted into another popular staple, cassava bread, made by spreading the pulp on a large round metal plate and baking it into a thin giant white wafer some 30 inches across.

---

[10] Also spelt 'casareep,' this sauce had a consistency almost like molasses.

This was one of the staples in the diet of the local Amerindians. The bitter cassava produced two crops a year and the Amerindians came by to pull up the large tubers that Sonny sold for 4 cents a pound. Sonny would then buy cassava bread from them at 4 cents a piece, as well the casreep they made.

Emmanuel Chan-A-Sue, Sr. opened up 500 acres of land to plant coffee trees at the Aruka plantation, a mile or so from the Kamaka stelling. The *Liberica* variety was the one that was best suited to the soil and grew well, with the ability to reach ten feet or more in height. During the season when the white blossoms came into bloom a large number of humming birds flocked to drink their fill of nectar. The coffee trees were also a place where wild pigeons by the thousand made their roost. They would be away during the day in search of food and as the sun started to set they came flocking in to find a suitable perch for the night. If the family felt like pigeon for dinner, a single blast from a shotgun would bring down a few to go to the pot.

The fruit from the coffee trees, or coffee cherries, sprouted in bunches on the branches and became brilliant red when ripe. Pickers of East Indian origin came from the sugar cane plantations on contract to do the picking of the coffee cherries. The picking and processing operations went on for 24 hours to prepare the fresh crop for market. The cherries were first sent to a pulper, made by the Crossley Company, which removed the tough skin. The main parts of the machine were two bumpy or pimpled disks than spun in opposite directions. The cherries were caught between the disks and the skin rubbed off by the abrasive action of the bumps. The skin was saved to become fertilizer. With the skin removed the coffee cherry took on the appearance of a skinned grape with a pulp that was sweet in flavor, so much so that many of the people and children around enjoyed sucking the pulp. However, this pulp was not utilized in the subsequent processing and was removed by washing and raking the cherries in a trough. This exposed the coffee bean itself, which was put out to dry in the sun. If rain came covers had to be rolled out to protect the beans from becoming wet. At this stage the beans retained a hard covering or hull, with a toughness almost like that of a fingernail. This was removed by another machine with rotating disks and left the coffee bean as the final product. The beans were dried again and then graded, the broken bits becoming lower grade coffee. The beans were then sold at four cents per pound.

On the Pierre plantation coconut trees grew plentifully along the dams and between the lime trees. Although the water from young coconuts was a delight to drink the coconuts were usually left on the tree to ripen and fall to the ground. The coconuts were gathered and split open to expose the white meat inside. This was scraped out and then grated. The resulting particles of coconut meat were placed in a trough to which water was added. When left overnight the coconut fat would float to the top and be skimmed off. The next step would be to boil the fat to purify it. This process took some skill because the longer the fat was boiled the browner was the color but this produced an oil that could last much longer on the shelf without going rancid. By contrast a lightly boiled fat would result in a higher yield of processed oil but the quality would not be as good.

Cocoa plants were grown on the Pierre estate although not in numerous amounts. The cocoa pods grew off the trunk of the tree and took on different colors – red, yellow, deep orange – and were of varying size. After they were picked the pods were split open with a cutlass and the hull used for vegetation. The cocoa seeds were put into boxes and covered with a jute bag to make them sweat, i.e. to ferment. The seeds were then dried in the sun and sold to the huskers. For family use the cocoa seeds were parched in an oven resulting in beans that could be easily shelled, rather like a peanut. The cocoa beans were then ground up in a mill rather like a sausage-making machine that extruded a soft thick tube of cocoa, coming out almost like toothpaste squeezed from its tube. These soft fat tubes of cocoa were run onto trough-like indentations in a board. The board had perpendicular markings six inches apart to guide the knife used for cutting the cocoa into uniform sticks. The cocoa sticks were boiled to make a chocolate and to that milk and sugar were added and given mostly to the children.

Before the cocoa plants grew sufficiently to sustain themselves it was necessary to provide a covering to give shade to the seedlings and young plants. The dwarf banana was planted to provide the shade. These grew quickly and their long wide leaves created a large shaded area below. These banana plants were of little use other than serving as protectors for the cocoa plants because the dwarf bananas were not as tasty as compared to other bananas available. They became food for the yaworie.[11] Even so the family was able to make use of them by putting the ripe dwarf bananas into covered glass jars. After five days or so the liquid was poured off and used as vinegar. In this way it can be said that even the less appetizing or seemingly useless things available in those days were utilized in a productive way. The Chan-A-Sue family's choice of settling in North-West District truly bore fruit.

---

[11] Local name for the common opossum.

WHEELING ALONG

Gladys Kissoon, née Lee
as told to Trev Sue-A-Quan

Gladys Lee's maternal great-grandparents were immigrants during the 1860s when the majority of Chinese indentured laborers arrived to work on the sugar plantations.

* * * * * * *

It was a nice day for a ride – sunny and bright, with little traffic on the Public Road going through Providence, East Bank Demerara. Gladys had tried before, but for some reason she just couldn't get the hang of riding a bicycle. Maybe it was the road, made of burnt earth, packed down by heavy rollers, but still susceptible to erosion by passing traffic and rain. So unless the surface was recently refinished the road would be uneven, with loose dirt and particles strewn over the surface. This presented an even greater challenge to the young lady who was having enough difficulty maintaining her balance. Even with Sherlock running alongside, holding on the back of the saddle to give her stability, the bike would wobble its way along and the riding lesson would come to a halt with only minimal progress. But Sherlock did not feel resentful about this situation; in fact, he was happy to have a good reason to visit the girl that he was courting. Gladys thought that riding a bicycle was such an easy thing to do, seeing just about the whole of the population of Guyana wheeling themselves merrily along. However, in practice, the bicycle beneath her would just not cooperate, no matter what she tried, and despite the number of lessons. It was so much different than riding in a carriage.

Gladys could recall the days of her youth when she rode in the family's carriage to and from school. She made that journey four times a day because she also came home at lunchtime and returned for the afternoon session at school. The carriage had a pair of wide cushioned seats facing each other and was usually driven by one of the employees at her parents' shop at Schoon Ord, West Bank Demerara. The driver sat on his own bench-seat high above from where he had a clear view of the road and the horse. Gladys did not have to worry about losing her balance or getting wet from the rain since the carriage had curtains that could be drawn, as well as a retractable cloth top – the forerunner to the convertible car. Nevertheless she was not altogether pleased to be making the journey to school, because she really disliked school.

To the tiny schoolchildren, the schoolmaster seemed to be a grouchy giant, who was quick at the draw with his cane. He had little tolerance for lack of discipline and gave nicknames to those boys who caught his attention as being mischief-makers. "19 Tom jackass," he would shout. It was even worse on those days when he arrived in an irritable mood. He would then rip into the boys with the wild cane for even minor infractions. Perhaps it may have been a disagreement with his wife that made him cross, but the backsides of the boys suffered the consequences. The school, located in Goed Fortuin, was run by the Anglican Church and drew children from the district – Versailles, Pouderoyen, Vreed-en-Hoop.[1] It appeared that the schoolmaster held more firmly to the tenet "spare the rod and spoil the child" than to any consideration of turning the other cheek. There was nothing that Gladys liked about the school – not the teacher, not the subjects, not the punishment – and when she saw that the 4th Standard textbook was the same as the one used in 3rd Standard, she decided she did not want to go back. That was the last of the carriage rides to school.

Much more enjoyable were the rides on Sundays to St. Swithin's Church in Vreed-en-Hoop, and the pleasure outings. On occasion the family would pile into the carriage and start out in the morning to Beterverwagting, a village on the East Coast Demerara. This meant taking the ferry across to Georgetown and then heading off on the East Coast Public Road. Popularly known as BV, the village was where Gladys' grandmother lived. In fact, Gladys was born in BV in 1907 when her mother went there for the birth of her baby. The carriage journey to visit her grandmother was a long one and sometimes bumpy depending on the conditions of the road. On one occasion the Lee family nearly ended up in the water when the horse stepped onto a large wooden bridge that spanned a drainage trench. Perhaps the horse was startled by

---

[1] Along the west bank of the Demerara were Vreed-en-Hoop (meaning peace and hope), Klein Pouderoyen (pronounced Poe-DRYNE), Malgre Tout, Versailles (Ver-SALES), Goed Fortuin, Schoon Ord (Skoon-ORD), La Grange (sounding like "Gran" as in "granny"), and others. The names reflect the Dutch and French presence before the British gained possession of the territory.

the sudden change in sound as its hooves struck the planks; it started to rear up and kick, jostling the passengers inside the carriage. There were no railings on either side of the bridge and the driver wrestled to bring the horse under control. For a moment the carriage headed for the edge but fortunately the horse settled down in time and the Lees remained unharmed. The family found out that the subsequent carriage to cross the bridge carried a bride and it was felt that they saved her, because they were affected by the incident that would otherwise be fated for the bride.

Gladys' parents had two shops at Schoon Ord, one in the estate and one on the West Bank Public Road. Both shops sold similar products, and the customers for one shop were mainly those living on the estate while the roadside shop catered to passers-by. The shops were called salt goods shops because the primary product was salt fish that Gladys' father would buy every Thursday, in anticipation of payday for the estate workers on Friday. The salt fish came packed in 50-pound cases and delivered by dray cart. Gladys helped to cut up the fish and make parcels of one-pound, half-pound, quarter-pound weight, and penny cut. Sometimes a customer would buy goods and then plead, "Please fuh piece o' salt fish," and a piece would be given. Another salty item was Palm Tree butter that came in large tins. This butter was popular when eaten with bread. For those customers who did not bring a container with them the prevailing practice was to wrap the butter in a sheet of brown paper. The salt butter was also the starting ingredient for making cakes in the Lee household, but before it was blended with the flour, the butter had to be washed to remove the salt. It took many basins of water and a lot of physical effort to stir the butter and crush it sufficiently to extract the salt. The cakes came out tasting just fine.

The shop sold the "usual" types of goods – flour, rice, sugar, potatoes, split peas, smoked herring, canned fish, spices, cooking oil, kerosene, etc. and there was a limited selection of cloth fabrics. In addition there was tobacco, sold either in tins or as cigarettes that were individually rolled by the Lee family. Another product was gange, a form of cannabis, which could be sold legally.[2] The gange was weighed with a small balance, such as would be used for weighing gold, and sold in small paper packets. The

---

[2] The sale of opium and cannabis, in the form of bhang and gange (GAN-juh), was legal up to the time of World War I. There were restrictions on the amount that could be sold to an individual in a single day. A popular Guyanese folk song, called "Gange money," tells of a person begging for a shilling to buy gange, the pleas first being ones of flattery and compassion, and then changing to derision and cursing.

customers for gange were mostly East Indians, who made up the majority of the population in the area.

When Gladys was in her early teens, her mother sold one of the shops at Schoon Ord and the family moved to a house in La Grange, another sugar estate a short distance further south along the Demerara River. Behind this house were several acres of land extending to the waterfront. There were long rows of elevated earthen beds in which crops and fruit trees were grown. Between the rows were water ditches for irrigation, and that was where rice was planted. In the beds were plantains or bananas and at the base of these plants, root crops such as cassava or eddoes were planted. In this way the spaces above and below the earth were turned into productive use. However, this method could not be used for coconut trees because their root systems prevented other crops from growing there. The farm was not organized in a systematic way with a certain section devoted to a single crop; instead, plantain and banana suckers[3] were pressed into the beds at whatever spot was convenient. The planting and reaping of the various food products was done by hired hands. Wielding grass knives, the workers waded through the ditches to cut the rice stalks. These were then threshed to separate the rice grains, or paddy, which would be taken to the rice miller. To produce white rice, the paddy would be first dried in the sun, while brown rice was obtained by steaming the paddy before drying the grains. The harvested rice and food crops were more than enough to satisfy the needs of the family and any extra amounts would be sold to the field workers or to those people who found out about the availability.

For a while the Lee family had a couple cows that were kept in a cowshed on the farm. They were fed with paragrass that grew in the beds that were not yet cultivated. A man was hired to take care of the cows – cutting the paragrass, feeding and milking the cows, and cleaning the shed. The milk was then given to the Lee family for personal consumption and any excess would be sold in the shop. Of course, it was not a big dairy setup – maybe three to six gallons could be obtained each day – but it had some big consequences when the cowhand decided to sell off some milk to the road repair workers. The work crew had come to the area to lay a new surface of burnt red earth on the public road and the cowhand saw an opportunity to milk the Lee family of some money. He would sell some of the milk to the thirsty workers and then top up the

---

[3] Plantains and bananas do not produce seeds for reproduction. New plants are started from a sucker, an offshoot from the root of the mother plant

milk jug with water. The crafty fellow was not able to do this for a long time, however, because the regular customers to the shop caught him in the act and reported to the Lee family. The problem loomed that if the Sanitary Inspector were to test the milk in the shop and find it diluted, there would be fines imposed. The cows were promptly sold.

Shopkeeping was hard work. Gladys' father had to leave early in the morning to catch the ferry to Georgetown where he had a job as wharfinger[4] at Sandbach Parker. After returning home at 5:30 to 6:00 p.m. he had to help out in running the shop until it closed at about 8:00 or 8:30. There were few amenities to reduce the labor-intensive tasks. At Schoon Ord at that time the Lee family had no phone, radio, nor electricity. Kerosene lamps provided light at night and the glass chimneys had to be cleaned every day because of the tendency for the lamp to generate soot when the wick was set too high in an attempt to get a brighter light from a larger flame. The wick of each lamp also had to be trimmed to remove the charred portion at the top. Some of the lamps had clamps attached to them so that they could be hung on the wall. The kerosene vapor lamps that produced a bright glow were not yet available.

One day, Gladys' father was approached by another shopkeeper, who owned two shops at Providence, East Bank Demerara, one of which he wanted to sell. Mr. Lee was given a lot of sweet talk[5] about the shop. Gladys was sent for two to three days to see the state of the shop and the business, and it appeared to be a viable proposition. So the family moved from the west bank to the east bank, but the business was not as good as it appeared. Unbeknownst to the new owners, the former owner had taken away the accounts of the good customers and Gladys' father had bought over those of the delinquent debtors. Issuing credit was an ongoing practice in running a shop but the customers remaining on the books would try to pull some tricks. Instead of paying for their new purchases plus a portion of the debt, they would ask that they be allowed to purchase more goods on credit and then pay a portion of the outstanding debt. The amount of indebtedness would thereby increase. The shop at Providence was not a prosperous one and was eventually sold.

It was at Providence, however, that Gladys got to know Sherlock Kissoon. He worked for the Sanitary Inspector's office and one of his

[4] The wharfinger (war-FIN-jer) was in charge of the goods in stock and delivered the purchased items to the customer after payment was made to the cashier.
[5] Depending on the context, this Guyanese expression could mean flattery, persuasion, praise, or embellishment.

duties was to take a sample of the butter and performs tests to see that it was not adulterated. Shopkeepers were sometimes caught adding margarine to the butter; they both were of the same color and texture but the margarine was much cheaper. Sherlock lived at Diamond, a few sugar estates further up the east bank of the Demerara River, and after work he started to come by and just hang around. Later, having apparently seen enough for his conviction, he asked Gladys' mother if he could visit, meaning that he wanted to be able to meet with Gladys. The Kissoon family was already known to the Lees, and Sherlock's maternal great-grandfather was an immigrant from China so no objections were raised to the young man's intentions.

Bridges in the middle of a major road were not uncommon. This drawbridge on the East Bank Road at Diamond allowed punts to get from one part of the estate to the other. At the end of the line is a public bus with its high-sided roof carrier. *Crown copyright material.*

Not long after, Sherlock went into business for himself. He bought a 14-seat bus (with the brand name Don Juan), which he used to provide passenger service between Grove (just beyond Diamond) and Georgetown. Starting out early in the morning the bus would head out to Georgetown picking up people who stood by the roadside waving for the bus to stop. The busiest times were when the passengers set out for work in the morning, and again when they returned home at the end of the workday. During these busy times it was not unusual for the bus driver to stop for additional passengers, i.e. more than the permitted limit of 14, hoping that the police would not stop the bus, or else would be kind enough to let the bus proceed after being inundated by pleas from the passengers that they were late for work, or would miss the start of school, or had to go to the hospital, or needed to get to the market in time. Normally, the police would turn a blind eye to the overloading situation unless they happened to notice that the springs of the bus were almost touching the ground. But those who did get stopped by the police were fined; even so, it was well worth the risk of taking on the extra fares. The bus went back and forth during the day and it was at the off-peak times that the market sellers and hucksters traveled. Each would typically port a large basket on the head and carry a bulging cloth bag (or even two) filled with goods – fruits, vegetables, provisions, fish, poultry, crabs, and more. The baskets and parcels would be loaded on top of the bus where there was a railing around the perimeter that prevented the articles from falling off. Sometimes there would be so much stuff piled on top the bus that the driver was unable to take on any more goods-carrying passengers even though there may have been seats available. The consumable products were destined for the small markets in the countryside.

Roadside vendors, like these at Rose Hall, Berbice, were a common sight in the countryside. Large, round woven baskets (at the feet of the lady at the center) were popularly used for carrying goods. *Crown copyright material.*

Sherlock loved going to the pictures – the silent black-and-white movies of the day. On Sunday mornings he would stop at the Lee's shop in Providence and make arrangements for a date with Gladys for the evening show. Setting out half an hour before the movie was scheduled to begin, they would be in Georgetown until 10 o'clock, and then had to drive along the unlit country road to get back. Sherlock would park the bus on the road, because there was no way to turn off, and escort Gladys to her door before continuing on to his home further along the way. Quite frequently they would go to the matinée screening which would get them home before it got too late at night. If Sherlock found out about an interesting movie during midweek, when the bus traffic was busy, he would arrange for another driver to run the route, and he and Gladys would become passengers. Then, at the end of the movie, the driver would return to collect them and take them home. If they passed any paying passengers on the way, the bus would stop to pick them up.

On those days that Sherlock did not go to see a movie he would sit around and chat at the Lee's house, although the conversation would be with Gladys' mother because her father did as much talking as the black-and-white movies Sherlock liked to see, and mostly sat there fanning himself. When there was no conversation in the making, Sherlock would just hang out, or "lime" around.

Gladys lived through two world wars as well as the Great Depression but never encountered any difficulties or shortages of goods and supplies. The only time that shortages became evident was in the 1960s during the period of civil unrest in Guyana. By then, she and Sherlock were married with grown children. Sherlock had to join up with other families to buy cooking oil and other items in bulk from wholesale importers because the retailers were out of stock. To get bread, he had to show up at Tangs' Bakery at a certain time, when the bread was fresh out of the oven. But these kinds of difficulties did not occur during the war years. In fact, the establishment of the Air Base by the Americans during Word War II created an employment opportunity for Sherlock who became a chauffeur for the U.S. staff and soldiers.

It was not long after the war was over that Gladys rode on a bicycle – but she was sitting on the cross-bar holding her baby while the baby's older brother sat on the carrier above the rear wheel, and Sherlock pedaled the bicycle, wheeling along in Georgetown.

Path to Education

Compiled by Trev Sue-A-Quan

One of the prominent Guyanese of Chinese descent was Joseph Clement Luck, better known as J.C. Luck, founder and principal of Central High School in Georgetown. J.C. himself was part of a large family of twelve children born to Lok Kim-hee, an immigrant who arrived from China in 1879. As a local-born second generation Chinese, J.C. Luck experienced the transition that the majority of the Chinese settlers went through – manual labourers – shopkeepers – educated professionals. However the path to education was not a straight and easy one and he reached his goals through perseverance, dedication and plain hard work. His children became successful in a variety of professions: law, medicine, surveying, teaching and business.

This account has been compiled from the recollections of various Luck family members including the children, grandchildren, nieces and nephews of J.C. Luck, as well as from archival records.

* * * * * * *

Luck A-fat was the Chinese name of the seventh child born to Lok Kim-hee and his wife Annie, who was also known as Maisie. The baby boy was born on 28 August 1896 at Dunoon, some 50 odd miles from Georgetown on the west bank of the Demerara River, and he was later christened, Joseph Clement Luck. Dunoon was a small village yet big enough to boast a local post office. Lok Kim-hee opened up a small shop to provide groceries and daily supplies to the local residents. Maisie took an active part in running the family shop and, in addition, she kept cows, sheep and goats. In the dead of night when she heard the animals moving about and making noise in the pasture, she would come out blowing a conch shell to scare the tigers away. She blew furiously until the eyes disappeared in the distance and the animals quieted down. Now and then she would find a carcass in the morning. Maisie also undertook to do the weekly outing on the river in a boat laden with goods. She would stop at various locations at the river bank, blow her shell, and the people nearby would come to shop – a proper shop it was too, with hand-held scales for weighing flour, sugar, etc. and measuring cups for oil and kerosene. Some customers also came from a distance away to the shop at Dunoon and

Lok Kim-hee set up a logie where these visitors could spend the night and get a rest from their long journey. The shop was just a small business and the Lok family was not a particularly prosperous one.

The Chinese have traditionally had great respect for the benefits and status from being educated and when J.C. showed promise in academic studies, his father sent him to Georgetown to attend Queen's College.[1] Lok Kim-hee died when J.C. was in his early teens and J.C. had to take on odd jobs to pay for his tuition. While in Georgetown he boarded with other Chinese students at one of the lower level of "Colonna House,"[2] which was then owned by David Ewing-Chow. At that time the Ewing-Chow and the Ho-A-Shoo families were two prominent and wealthy Chinese families in Georgetown and had their own carriages for transportation – a distinctly visible display of their affluence. They were willing and more than able to help Chinese families they felt deserving of assistance, even if in little ways such as giving away silk clothes that they no longer wanted. J.C. was a good student and was accredited with several passes at the Senior Cambridge examinations.

The Lok family fortunes were not sufficient to send J.C. away for higher education and so he remained in the colony and tried his hand at various activities to make a living, including the civil service, farming, shopkeeping, gold-digging and rice milling but his reputation in British Guiana eventually came from education, through the founding of a school. J.C. was 21 years old when he married Clara Fung, daughter of Isaac "G.P." Fung-Teen-Yong, a proprietor of cocoa estates in Essequibo. J.C.'s father-in-law also owned a cocoa plantation at Hanover which was not far from Hopetown, the Chinese settlement that was established in 1865 at Camoonie Creek on the opposite (west) bank of the Demerara River. The civil service job did not provide enough for J.C.'s growing family and he undertook the management of the Hanover plantation. Actually, the word "plantation" makes it sound like a huge operation but the Hanover plantation, though not large compared to the sugar plantations that formed the mainstay of the colony's economy, was still a sizeable area. J.C. dug a trench so that punts could get access to the cocoa trees. That one trench alone was enough to serve the plantation. Workers

---

[1] Queen's College was established in 1844 as a secondary school for boys. Tuition was $80 per annum and the entrance fee $25. By the end of the century it had gained much respect both in the colony and the Commonwealth since the school utilized standards set by examination boards of Oxford and Cambridge.

[2] This large two-storied building had been where several government administrative offices were located including the Government Secretary, Colonial Treasurer, Attorney General and Customs Office. Early in the 20th century it was regarded as an old house and had become known as being haunted. David Ewing-Chow's Christian faith dispelled his fear of ghosts and he bought "Colonna House" for $6,000.

came in their corrials and canoes to take care of the plants, and to pick and prepare the cocoa for shipment to Georgetown. The cocoa pods were cut across the width to split open the hard shell. The cocoa beans were coated with a pulp that had a sweet and "fainty" taste. The workers took the beans to the "dragalay,"[3] in which they were dried by air circulation. The cocoa beans could then be ground up and extruded into sticks, used for making a cocoa drink. If the ground cocoa were heated up, it would produce a layer of white cocoa fat, also called cocoa butter, which was commonly used to rub on the skin to remove latta (dark spots or discolorations) as well as to ease soreness.

The house at Hanover was a spacious one with two stories and a verandah facing the river. But it was a rather isolated location with no roads serving the area. The Demerara River was the lifeline for the family. A boat had to be sent out to meet the steamer *R.H. Carr* in order to get mail and goods. The river was also the means for the doctor to make his rounds. If anyone needed medical attention, a white flag would be hoisted by the river's edge to serve as a signal that the doctor was required. It had to be put up on those occasions when any of the children suffered from malaria, and the Hanover area was a haven for mosquitoes. The attacks of fever and ague would come on as night approached and sometimes the sick child had to be cradled in the bosom of the maid to become comfortable enough to fall to sleep.

Besides managing the cocoa plantation, J.C. partitioned a section of the house and opened a shop to provide general merchandise for the workers. Even so, these efforts did not bring any significant riches and he soon tried starting a sawmill. The name might have been "sawmill" but, in reality, it consisted of a couple men pulling a saw between them to make planks from timber. J.C. used these boards to make three punts that he rented to people transporting timber downriver. Typically the punts were filled with various goods and the logs were tied to the outside of the punt.[4] There were a few men in charge of the punts and they used long oars to propel them along. J.C. also built a launch, one with the motor mounted in the center of the boat and a tent-like canvas cover above deck. This launch was used to take the family on trips to Georgetown. Another of J.C.'s hand-made boats (most likely of his own

---

[3] A shed with its roof supported on a frame with wheels.
[4] Several varieties of local timber, particularly greenheart and mora, are denser than water and cannot be floated down the river. Tying the logs to the boat allowed the water to provide buoyancy for the heavy timbers and thus a punt of shallower draft could be used. Logs that were longer than the punt could also be transported in this manner.

design) had such a square appearance that it seemed that it was hardly seaworthy, but it did float and accomplished the tasks assigned.

A boat designed and built by J.C. Luck. *M.R. Lam.*

For a short period J.C. went off to the goldfields in the Bartica area.[5] He did not have much luck at gold-prospecting and he went back to Hanover none the richer for his efforts. He then decided to open up a school. In fact this was just a shed near the house and the pupils consisted of the children of the workers on the plantation who paddled their own canoes to get to school. J.C. hired a teacher to provide some basic education skills for the children in English and mathematics.

Sometime about 1929 J.C. moved the family to Georgetown. By this time there were seven children in the family and the first three were already at or approaching secondary school level but did not have proper schooling. J.C. could not afford to enroll them all in the prestigious government schools and so he started up his own school at his house on Smyth Street. A few other boys and girls who were in a similar financial situation were enrolled to make up the school compliment of 35 children. It was common knowledge that the school was a "poor man's school" and it almost made J.C. a poor man because he did not pressure the parents to pay if they had hardship in coming up with the school fees. J.C. had to take out loans during the vacation period to pay the teachers. If all the pupils had paid their fees, J.C. would have been a lot better off financially.

After a couple years or so, J.C. joined up with Modern High School run by Mr. Ramphal on Charlotte Street. However the joint effort did not last long and J.C. started up his own school as an independent operation further along on Charlotte Street. J.C. named it Central High School and there were about 100 students enrolled. Word was getting around about the school and the need for expansion prompted J.C. to move the school to yet another address on Charlotte Street. The appeal of an affordable school for the growing population of children created a business opportunity for J.C. in the field of education and he later

---

[5] Bartica is at the junction of two large rivers, the Essequibo and the Mazaruni, and served as a gateway to the gold-bearing interior regions of Guyana.

bought from J.T. Chung a lot at Smyth Street a little way further along and on the opposite (west) side from where he had originally started up his small school in 1929.

Central High School relocated to 91 Smyth Street in the mid-1930s. *Jane Chin.*

J.C. set about building his school and he himself put his carpentry skills to work in making the benches and desks for the students. His wife Clara provided the much-needed support for his ambition, even to the extent of holding up the ladder as he climbed to the top. He taught Latin and Mathematics to some of the classes and employed a number of teachers including his nephew Albert "Cowie" Luck to teach Mathematics, Brentnall Adams for history, while English was taught by A.P. Alleyne, later to become Speaker of the House of Guyana's Parliament in the 1960s. J.C. realized that the school would become recognized only if the students were of sufficiently high caliber in their scholastic achievement. He opened the school during the night for students to come and do their homework in an "educational" environment. There they were able to consult with the teachers who made their time available for tutoring. There were also enrichment and tutoring sessions for keen students and these programs helped to pull up the standard of the participating students.

The staff at Central High School during the 1950s. J.C. Luck stands in the center of the middle row. Vice-Principal Brentnall Adams stands at J.C. Luck's left side. *Jane Chin.*

Over the years Central High School gained the reputation of being a good educational institution and when the students won honors in examinations equal to the best that were achieved by pupils in the other prominent schools, CHS became recognized as one of the top schools in the country. J.C. also managed to pull off a coup of sorts in 1935, the Silver Jubilee Year for King George V. It was announced that special Jubilee awards would be given for scholastic achievement. J.C. enrolled his son Eton at Central High School (although he had been accepted at Queen's College) along with Forbes Burnham, the future Prime Minister and President of Guyana. L.F.S. Burnham was a keen student, his forte being in the arts subjects more so than in Mathematics, and this is how he got his nickname Odo.[6] Harry Annamanthadoo[7] was also one of the competitors. When the examination results were released, Eton Luck came out with top honors and Forbes Burnham was the second best student. J.C. and Eton Luck were obviously delighted with the outcome although Forbes Burnham may not have been as pleased to end up with a

---

[6] Odo, the Bishop of Bayeau, was a half-brother of William the Conqueror (William I, King of England, r: 1066-1087). Odo commissioned the Bayeaux tapestry, a famous 11th century embroidery depicting the Norman conquest, with titles in Latin.
[7] Harry Annamanthadoo became a professor of surgery and Dean of the Faculty of Medicine at the University of the West Indies, Jamaica. He was later knighted by Queen Elizabeth II.

set of books as consolation prize. When he rose to high political office he would make mention of his concerns about "privileged students."

Pupils at Central High School writing their examinations. *M.R. Lam*

J.C. had achieved a great deal in founding a school that rose to prominence and his name has become recognized in that capacity. He provided educational opportunities for thousands of students and thus gained fame and respect in the country through his contributions to education. J.C. paid more attention to the scholastic side of the operations and, because of his continued tendency to turn a blind eye to those in financial hardship, the revenue aspect did not improve until his children were grown and started to take on the management of the school in a more businesslike fashion. There were times when one chicken had to be shared in the Luck household – among ten children, two parents and the cook. At Christmas time J.C. would buy a pound of apples and, sitting at the head of the table, he would carefully cut them into little pieces so that each one in the family could have a taste. In one year the best he could offer his children were two grapes and a couple walnuts placed in each of their Christmas stockings.

The family's riches could not be counted in material things but by their educational achievements. Through all this J.C. took the time to improve his own educational level by taking correspondence courses with the University of London and in 1947, he was awarded a B.A. degree. In both his personal achievement as well as in his career choice, the path to education was not a straight one but it was one that was eventually crowned with success.

* * * * * * * *

J.C. Luck and the Luck family have essentially been private individuals and even though J.C. became a prominent and well-respected person because of his success with Central High School, the family chose to stay out of the limelight. A greater understanding of J.C. as a person and his dedication to education can be gained through the observations of those he affected. The following nuggets are fitting tributes to him and his role in their lives.

Memories of J.C. Luck
Barney Singh, CHS Student 1939-45, later a teacher at CHS.

My contact with J.C. began in September 1939 when I attended Central High School as a twelve-year-old. CHS was in a growth stage being only ten years old with an attendance of about 270 to 300 pupils. The school had outgrown the accommodation of the main building and expansion with the building of new structures was in progress. The building construction was undertaken by Mr. Luck himself to keep the costs down. He undertook these works during the August school holidays. On one occasion the opening of school was delayed for two weeks to permit the completion of a major new building. Mr. Luck also made the desks and benches as well as the desks for the masters. The masters' desks would have been Mr. Luck's own design.

We students were inspired by the industry of our principal, a Jack-of-all trades. We were sure that this was the only way that new buildings could be erected and still keep the school fees at the level of $3.16 per month. The $3.00 represented the school fees and the sixteen cents was a levy for sports activities. At the time Central had a very successful cricket team that competed with the other "private" high schools in the city – Modern High, Modern Educational Institute and Progressive High. Many other high schools, such as Enterprise and Washington, were just starting. Mr. A. P. Alleyne the former vice-principal of Central had just left to start Washington High.

One of the teaching methods at Central was a competitive system described as "take down." It was used in language classes as well as for subjects like History, Geography, Geometry, etc. Classes started out with questions about the assigned homework, which was an oral exercise. The students seated in rows were regarded as forming a continuous line. A student, let us assume it was you, was asked a question about the subject, e.g. a translation in a language class. By answering correctly you maintained your position, and the student next to you was asked another question. If you did not know the answer, or responded incorrectly, the same question passed to the person next in line and so on until someone produced the right answer and then that person moved up into your place. Hence the name "take down." There was constant shuffling of students during this period. If you got the first answer wrong and moved down a place you were asked another question, and the take down process was repeated. If you missed three questions in succession, you went to the bottom of the line and faced a significant challenge in working your way up because frequently there was not enough time during the class to get questions coming your way. The environment was competitive and very open. Some people stayed at the top most of the time and others at the bottom. Take down was generally followed by a period of instruction and discussion and then homework would be set for the next session.

The school prepared students for the University of Cambridge Local Examination Syndicate certificates at the Junior and Senior levels, usually at ages 15 and 17, respectively. Students doing well at the senior level qualified for exemption for the University of London Matriculation, which was important for any student wishing to pursue an external degree from the University of London. A certain number of students qualified for matriculation exemption each year.

In 1941, I found myself with 35 other students in the scholarship class preparing for the Junior Cambridge exam. The students were the most highly competitive and gifted that I have ever encountered. Forty percent of the students were underage for that level of study and qualified for a government prize for passing while underage. Two scholarships for boys to attend Queen's College, and one for girls to attend Bishops[8] were awarded colony-wide. The two boys' scholarships were won by students in my class and in the following year one boy and a girl in that class won scholarships. I felt proud to be part of a school system that was successful in open competition with the other high schools at the time.

---

[8] Bishops' High School was founded in 1870 as an educational institution for girls and became a prestigious school in the country.

In 1942 I completed my senior year and since this was during WW II, we had to wait until June of 1943 for the results to get back to Guyana from Britain. Central was turning out people like myself, who were not yet 16 years old but then had no chance of further education unless transferred to Queen's, Saints[9] or Bishops. Some students, including myself, hung around the school while waiting for results of their examinations. However, some students from the 1940 and 1941 senior classes had decided to pursue studies for the Higher School certificate through individual studies. They were assisted by staff members at CHS without having the benefit of regularly organized classes. So, in 1943, Mr. Luck organized a 6th form for instruction for the Higher School Certificate exam with a group of seven students. Since the fees were still only $3.00 per month, this class was being run at a financial loss. Wishing to pursue higher education I had applied to Queen's for the September term.

I was accepted for the September term of 1943 but along with several others was informed, just days before the start of the term, that there was a change of policy and the sixth form would now be available only for students already at Queen's. So it was the sixth form for me at Central in 1944 where we had a class of 11. Most of the graduates of this class went on to university in various disciplines. The starting of a sixth form was a bold venture for several reasons. The school was not staffed with university graduates. No one had a degree of any kind except for a short while in 1943 when Eton Luck, J.C.'s son, was on staff before taking a teaching appointment in Grenada. Without exception no staff had an education beyond the matriculation level and several were only at the senior level. Our choice of subjects, which did not include science or mathematics, was an adventure in learning for both the staff and the students. It can best be described as a tutorial system with lots of discussion. We were learning on our own and sharing at the same time.

After I severed my connection with Central at the end of 1945, I continued to follow developments with interest. The absence of science was one of the things that was rectified shortly after I left. Once again, J.C. had to reach into his pockets and provide equipment and employ graduates from Queen's to provide the necessary instruction. As mentioned earlier students were very successful over the years in winning the government junior scholarships and moving on to Queen's. This robbed the school of some of its best students. So when his son Donald won a junior scholarship, it was refused and he stayed on to study at

---

[9] St. Stanislaus College was started by a Catholic priest in 1866 as a school for boys and became another of the prestigious local high schools.

Central and eventually won the Guiana Scholarship in competition with the other well-established schools.

During these years I found Mr. Luck to be interested in providing low cost but good education. For the five years spent there, I consider that the $180.00 my parents paid for my education was the best bargain anywhere. I am aware that many parents did not pay their fees on time but J.C. never asked any one to leave because of the non-payment of fees. In fact, a classmate and friend of mine admitted later that when he left Central he owed one whole year of fees, which he paid off with the earnings from his first job.

Mention must also be made of Mrs. Luck for her contribution. She provided the eatables for the morning break. It is my opinion that her seizing the opportunity to contribute to the economy of the home had a lot to do with J.C. keeping the fees at a low level and making education affordable to so many people. With the family living on the premises, early students like myself felt like part of the Luck family. We associated with and watched the young ones grow up and had many interactions with the older members who either taught or had something to do with activities of the school.

Where did the teachers come from for this growing school? Former students provided most of the teachers for the school. For many of us it was a stepping-stone to our future. Although many started teaching, only a few stayed on to make teaching at Central a career. And so it was when in 1945 I was asked to join the staff even before the results of the higher school were out. It is true that you really begin to understand a subject when you are required to teach it. The learning experience during my year of teaching at Central was significant in my development.

Mr. Luck provided experiences for development beyond the class-room. One of these was the scout troop. The Scout Master, Ivan Smith-Green,[10] was a former student who could only afford to attend up to the junior grade and had to leave to go out in the work force. Mr. Luck provided opportunity for this leader to finish his senior and then employed him as a master for many years. This was an act of humanity to bring out the best in people and to let them develop their potential. The groundsman[11] for the sports field was a former friend of J.C. He provided a home for this man and his wife and child on the premises and the boy was eligible for attendance at the school free of charge.

---

[10] Ivan Smith-Green became the head of Personnel Department at Bookers, a large conglomerate of stores in Guyana.
[11] The person in charge of maintaining the playing fields in good order.

Getting to know the country beyond the confines of Georgetown was another of his wise decisions. School trips were planned for students to the Wismar/Mackenzie area during one August holiday and another trip to the Essequibo coast the following year. These were educational and broadening experiences from which the students benefited greatly. These were activities that required planning for billeting, food and travel for mixed boys and girls and must have taken up a lot of time and energies.

He did introduce cultural activities during my time. Madam Alice Fraser-Denny who had returned from the States after a musical teaching career was engaged in an after-hour activity to introduce studies in the study of music. At one stage a grand piano was acquired and placed in the school with access to those who had music training. The students, like myself, remembered being entertained by some of our colleagues who had the talent to play the piano.

Mr. Luck recognized the need for a library and so he started one with access limited to students of the upper levels. All of this was done out of the low school fees being charged. It should be remembered that my high school education took place during the war when textbooks and other books were difficult to obtain. When students encountered difficulties getting textbooks he started a book store. Of course this was a commercial enterprise, which provided additional income, employment for family members and served the needs of his students as well as those of other schools.

As mentioned earlier, sports was considered important and J.C. was able to use his connection with St. Philip's Church, where he was a warden, to obtain a playing field for the school on church property, at the corner of D'Urban and Smyth streets. On another occasion he acquired gym equipment, gym rings, punching ball and bag, and parallel bars for use of the school. All of this from the 16 cents levy for sports.

A very quaint custom was the respect that had to be shown to the female students. Boys were not permitted to refer to the girls by their personal names. The girls were Miss Luck or Miss Gittens but never Stella or Joyce. It worked. Why? I do not know. It did not prevent the normal romances expected in a mixed school. I have no idea where J.C. got this idea and for how long it survived.

J.C. Luck as an educator and a builder
Wilfred G. Hoppie, CHS Student 1935-38. CHS Teacher 1950-74.

I entered Central High School in 1935 and was placed in Form I on the bottom flat of a three-storey building. The principal and his family occupied the top flat. There was a smaller building and a garage in the compound. The garage was sometimes used as a workshop for making desks and benches to accommodate the large influx of students. At those times we were amused to see our principal not in his usual teaching outfit but in carpenter's apparel. His assistants were two or three students from our form; I was nearly always one. We also learned that our principal was a carpenter and boat builder by trade, and that for measuring, carpenters use 8ths, 16ths, and 32nds and not 10ths as we did in class.

When I was leaving school, J.C. had started to make changes to the building in which he lived. A few of us gave a hand breaking bricks, fetching board, etc. While he was teaching, J.C. had hired a carpenter, but he made sure that he remained foreman of the job.

When I returned as a teacher in 1950, J.C. was just completing the corridor on the top flat. His attention the turned to completing a portion of the "small school," as it was called then, and almost without a break he turned to building a sports pavilion on Thomas Lands. The method was the same – the teachers and students helped to remove debris from the land while J.C. and his crew worked on the building. The janitor of the school was the painter. Finally he turned to constructing an auditorium to improve the level of fine arts in the school. As the auditorium and pavilion were not used for their designed purpose until after 3 p.m., the principal held classes in them, thus making CHS the largest secondary school then.

Central High School – School Motto: Cogito Ergo Sum
Hector Lachmansingh, CHS Student 1948-53.

Starting out in High School is a major event for most children. To move from a small rural Primary School and attend one of the largest High Schools in Guyana, when I was twelve years old, filled me with apprehension. Would the city boys and girls make fun of my country accent? Would they be friendly? Would I be able to compete with them? These were some of the questions that bothered me when I accompanied my brother Clement on my first day at Central High School in May 1948. My fears were dispelled within a few weeks as I settled down quite nicely in my Home Room class – "Remove B." Mr. Collins, my form teacher, taught most of the subjects and I quickly took a liking to Latin. I worked hard because there was a fair bit of competition in my class. I got a perfect mark in Latin for a few terms and was second in overall class average for three consecutive terms. I had no trouble making a number of friends and was happy to be at Central High School.

My brothers Clement and Reuben and I paid our school fees quarterly and got a reduction for being from the same family. Once I was called down to the office when I was late with my fees. It was embarrassing. All students wore a school uniform; boys wore khaki pants, a blue shirt and a CHS tie. Girls wore a dark blue tunic, a white blouse and a Panama hat. Girls were addressed as Miss and boys by their last name. Most students rode their bicycles to school; some boys rode long distances and towed brothers and sisters on the cross bar.[12] My brothers and I walked. Other students traveled by steamer (ferry), train or bus. One of my classmates, who traveled by train, left home at 5 a.m. and returned at 6 p.m. Some students were very poor and had very little lunch. They hung around Dean's Cake Shop and bought a small lemonade and a bun for five cents. We had no cafeteria or lockers at our school.

The Luck family occupied an apartment at the front of the second (top) level of the school on Smyth Street. The ground level was occupied by the lower forms; the first level by Forms 3 and 4 and the second level by Forms 5 and 6. The roof of the building was covered with zinc sheets without insulation below them. There were no fans or air conditioning and I always felt drowsy during the afternoon classes. The grounds of the school were very small and were surrounded by a fence made with zinc sheets. There was no playing field on the property. The boys played cricket or soccer after school in a field close to St. Philip's Church. Girls did not play any sports.

The school operated with the help of a Prefect System. Prefects wore a special CHS tie. They supervised the halls and classrooms until our teachers arrived. They also manned the school gate and gave detentions for late arrivals and discipline infractions. As far as I remember, they conducted themselves well and we never questioned their authority. I was fortunate to graduate from Central High School without receiving a detention or the strap. I was just lucky. On one occasion, when I was twelve years old, I was sent to Mr. Munroe, a senior teacher, for not completing my homework. I was in tears and Mr. Munroe spared me the strap but gave me a warning. I learned my lesson. In retrospect, I feel that the Prefect System was very successful and was necessary for such a large school with limited space and facilities.

For a while I was the Desk Champ in Table Tennis. We played on a long narrow desk and used two books on edge as the net and our Latin text as our racquet. Subsequently we went to Compton Sanmogan's home in D'Urban Street to play on his table and use racquets. We played

---

[12] It was permitted for a "passenger" to sit on the horizontal bar connecting the handlebar strut to the saddle pole on the bicycle (men's model).

cricket next to Clinton Choo-Kang's home on Hadfield Street, at King's ground near the Sea Wall, and also at St. Philip's ground.

Most students left High School at the end of Form 5. Some joined the Civil Service. Others got jobs as teachers or became clerks in stores or with corporations. Job opportunities were very limited. I remained in school and went into Form 6 where I spent two years studying for the Higher School Certificate Examination. Those were two wonderful years during which long lasting friendships were cemented. We were a good class and worked hard with our studies. I remember getting up at 3 a.m. to study because I found that time quiet and cool. Some of us supplemented our studies by taking correspondence courses from Wolseley Hall in England. The subjects I took in my examinations were English Literature, Latin, English History, European History, and a general paper comprising of English and French. I wore long pants for the first time when I wrote my final exam in December 1953 and received some teasing from Mrs. Griffith, our neighbor.

I was ecstatic when exam results were published in *The Daily Chronicle* and I had passed. I rushed around to many of my relatives and gave them the good news. Our class had done very well. Hard work had paid off. I was seventeen at the time. Three of my friends – Arthur Chang Yen, Harry Jainarine and Neisha Khadir – were only sixteen. We were too young to enter the Civil Service; the age for entry was eighteen.

Our teachers deserve a lot of credit for our success. One teacher whom I admired was our principal, Mr. J.C. Luck. He was involved in school administration but covered classes in Latin and English when teachers were absent. He spent most of the class period entertaining us with jokes and his many experiences. The work that he covered was done so well and made so simple that I wished that he had been a regular teacher. To improve his academic credentials, J.C. took correspondence courses from England. A few years later, Mr. Luck, the Principal, and his Vice-Principal, Mr. Adams, earned their B.A. degrees simultaneously. It was a reason to celebrate. I was told that the students were given a week of holidays. This was quite an achievement for two middle-aged men at a time when there was no post secondary institution in Guyana. It was also a period when less than five percent of the students from primary school attended High School.

Old J.C. had many children all of whom went on to be successful. His two sons, Donald and Stanley, did some supply teaching[13] when they were on vacation from the University of The West Indies in Jamaica. They were medical students. We liked and admired Donald because he

---

[13] Substitute for an absent teacher.

was a very good teacher and had a very good sense of humor. Another son, Rudy, also taught for a while. He was interested in Economics and Politics and after becoming a lawyer, entered the political arena. For a while he was a Member of Parliament. Mrs. Stella Low, J.C.'s daughter, and her husband were teachers at Central High. Mrs. Viola Lam, another daughter, and her husband later ran the school bookshop.[14]

Bobby Moore, a senior student and Head Prefect was an inspiration to me. At the time he did a fair bit of extra-curricular duties and public speaking. I remember attending a few evening lectures given by him. One was on the career of Robert Clive, the British statesman. It was an excellent presentation. A few months later I wrote an English History exam and to my surprise there was a question on the career of Robert Clive. It was a breeze for me. Bobby later became Guyana's High Commissioner to Canada.

I have often wondered why so many students were successful in Guyana in spite of the poor facilities in our schools. There is no simple answer. However, one major reason is the desire/motivation on the part of the students. We realized that an education was the key to suitable employment. There was the choice between being a laborer/cane cutter and being a civil servant/teacher/clerk. The job market was very limited. Also we showed a lot of respect for our teachers. They had received no teacher training and many did not have a good academic background – most were at Grade 12 or Grade 13 level.[15] They never encouraged open discussion in the classroom. During my years at CHS only three teachers had degrees. However, what they lacked in training was compensated by dedication and perseverance. We did our homework or paid the penalty. There were no excuses or after school jobs to prevent us from doing homework. School was our number one priority.

Keeping in Touch with the Student Body (In the Beginning)
Stella Low, née Luck, seventh child of J.C. Luck, teacher and Headmistress at CHS.

J.C. was a man of vision. He introduced an intercom system with telephones in each room and also a public address system with loud speakers, which were state of the art for that time. It was possible to address the entire student body simultaneously.

---

[14] Central Book Shop was started and operated by J.C.'s eldest daughter Yvonne and her husband Claude Woon-Sam in the 1950s. Ken and Viola Lam took over in December 1962 after the Woon-Sams moved to England.

[15] The final year in high school according to the North American grade system.

Keeping in Touch with the Student Body (At the End)
Hector Lachmansingh, CHS Student 1948-53.

Rudy Insanally, Minister of Foreign Affairs for Guyana, and I were friends and classmates at Central. He told me he used to make announcements on the P.A. and on one occasion he was "set up" by a few of his friends. It was raining heavily at lunchtime and he announced when cars were up front to pick up certain students. He announced that a donkey cart had arrived to pick up Lennox Perry. Lennox Perry was a prefect and was not well liked because he was very strict and tough on the Juniors. Rudy related that J.C. was not amused and he, Rudy, was on the receiving end of a few strokes.

Fish at the Door
Peter Lam, grandson of J.C. Luck, CHS student 1966-71.

When J.C. went to search for gold, he lived in a house at Goshen, opposite Bartica, so close to the river that the water would flood into the yard at high tide. J.C. cleverly built a fence to enclose the yard thereby forming a safe and private swimming area for his children whenever they came there for a visit. He also attached a long rope to the gate, which was purposely left open as the water rose in the yard. At high tide J.C. would pull the gate shut and after the water receded he would gather in the stranded fish and make a delicious meal.

Trekking Religiously
Rita Graham, née Cheong, CHS student 1953-58.

I remember that J.C. was small in stature, however carried a presence. He did insist that the whole school attend church services at St. Philips, most likely for Ash Wednesday. The whole school walked over to St. Philips, which must have been quite a sight as each class had about 35 to 40 children and there must have been at least 1000 students at the time.

Sundays at Hanover
Yvonne Woon-Sam, née Luck, eldest child of J.C. Luck, teacher at CHS.

One lasting memory is Sundays in Hanover – my mother in the hammock with her hymnbook, singing, and Dad sitting on the floor nearby with his mandolin and all of us children around them. Those were the days.

Cruising Down The River
Desmond Luck, grandnephew of J.C. Luck, CHS student 1948-55.

It's interesting about J.C.'s origins at Hanover down the Demerara River. Once every few years he would organize a family picnic for all the family, immediate as well as peripheral members. He would charter a diesel-engine boat to hold maybe 40 people and then take them all to Hanover. I attended one of these picnics and I have to tell you, it was an absolute blast. There are great sandy beaches down the river where you can wade out a hundred feet from shore and still be only chest high in water; and the food was great. I was only 15 years old, but that remains one of my most vivid memories.

J.C. Luck "Uncle Joe"
Amy Thompson (née Tang) – Niece of J.C. Luck

J.C. Luck was our mother's brother and our beloved "Uncle Joe." J.C. and my mother Clara, fondly known as "Tilley," were very close. He allowed my three sisters and I to attend his Central High School free of charge because he saw that our financial foundation was not that secure. In addition, he provided the textbooks and paid the examination fees whenever my parents could not afford to do so. Being his nieces did not provide us with any special privileges, in fact he was sterner with his own children and us than with the other students.

Yes, J.C. was a man of vision. He encouraged the reading of good books written by the "masters." This was evidenced by the books (*Julius Caesar*, *She Stoops to Conquer*, *The Rape of the Lock*, to name a few) that were introduced and taught in the Literature classes. There were annual plays to provide active realization of these works. One such play, *Christmas Carol*, was directed and produced by our Literature teacher, E.O. Caleb. The main character, Scrooge, was played by Bobby Moore, whose performance merited an Oscar if there were such an award at the school. He got an outpouring of congratulations from all who saw the play – students, teachers, parents, friends and guests.

J.C. saw the need for an early start in education and extended his school to provide a kindergarten and primary education section. His eldest daughter, Yvonne Woon-Sam, was in charge and the rest of the teaching staff was taken from those students who had passed their Junior and Senior Cambridge exams and G.C.E. "O" Level and were awaiting employment opportunities in the Government and private sector services. Yours truly was one of those teachers.

J.C. was a very good and caring person. He had the gift of imparting his knowledge in an affable and simple way, as a result of which we all enjoyed it, when he filled in during a teacher's absence. He taught us not only about academics but also about real life qualities, among these to be caring and kind, honest, courteous and respectful always.

Tall Tales
Godfrey Chin, CHS student 1948-55.

We loved/admired our principal – his teaching was a delight, never about schoolwork, but always "tall" tales of his rascality. He admitted to us how he liked to "pull" at the girls and this is no exaggeration. Imagine the awe at his tales, which left us in greater admiration of this 5-ft. giant. When he felt we needed some bucking up in the sixth form, he gave us free lessons at night.

J.C. (60+) Takes Piano Lessons
Jane Chin, nee Luck, tenth child of J.C. Luck.

Mr. Dummett, the piano teacher, came home every week to give my father, "The Old Man," piano lessons. What prompted him in his later years to begin taking piano lessons, no one remembers. What cannot be forgotten is the hell through which he put Mr. Dummett. Why this, why that, why write notes on 5 lines and 4 spaces and create confusion when the addition of a few more lines would accommodate all the notes and confuse no one. Never mind he put Mr. Dummett to sleep. . . .

By dint of perseverance and his unwavering belief that one could do anything to which one puts one's mind (try telling him you COULDN'T do X/Y/Z: "Not at all. No such thing. You haven't put your mind to it." Such was the swift and stern reply), he succeeded in playing his favorite pieces: the *Blue Danube Waltz* and Schumann's *The Happy Farmer*, surpassing son Rudy's signature tune, *On the Navajo Trail.*

J.C.'s Community School
Beverly Ramcharan, nee Luck, grandniece of J.C. Luck.

I remember being co-opted by J.C. (or my father "Cowie") to teach adults in the evening. I remember doing math with them so I think it was some kind of community scheme that J.C. had, to raise the educational level of the community. I do not think anyone was charged for this.

J.C. has always been a role model for me especially when I have these crazy desires to learn something new at this late stage of my life, e.g.

clarinet and oboe lessons after 60, renew my acquaintance with the French language after 45 years, etc. I truly believe that he could do whatever he put his hand to. That is why he has always been someone I admired. Nothing would faze him out. He would give it a try, and see how it all panned out.

J.C. Luck. *Andy Lee.*

Outdoorsman

Leonard Ten-Pow
in conversation with Trev Sue-A-Quan

According to family accounts, Ho Ten Pow came from China when he was a young lad, brought over to Guyana by his mother. In adulthood he had two children with his first wife in the late 1880s, while twelve others were raised by his second spouse, Charlotte Tanner Lam. It was a large household, and Lenny Ten-Pow, the last of the children of Ho Ten Pow, was born in 1918, by which time the eldest ones were already adults.

The conversation was conducted in Guyanese dialect, peppered with informal slang that adds nice color to the recounting. The switching of tense between past and present is common in such dialogue, and highlights the ongoing nature of the actions.

* * * * * * *

[Trev]: Tell me first of all where you were born.

[Lenny]: In West Coast Demerara – Blankenburg. After Blankenburg there is Den Amstel, Fellowship, Hague, Catherina, Leonora, and Stewartville.

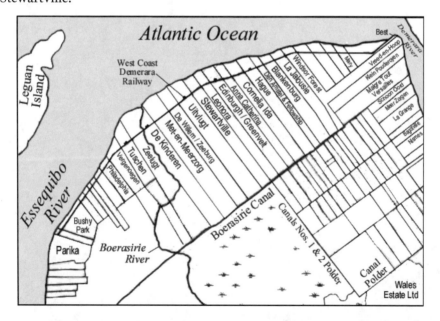

[T]: You are the last one in a big Ten-Pow clan, and you must have lived in a large house, right?

[L]: Yes, the old man[1] had a big house with several rooms. It was a long house, and on one side the old man had his writing table there and a door; then there was a long table, and at the back of that was a pantry. Behind all this was the kitchen. All along the right side of the house were bedrooms, his own is the first, then four or five other rooms. We had an outhouse right down in the back of a long yard. It was perched over a trench that drained out in the ocean. The outhouse had two doors, and each door took you to two seats, so four seats in all. The seat is a plank with holes cut in it and you would sit down there, or stoop down, whatever you wanted to do.

[T]: So you had to double up. What about the bedrooms? How many children in each bedroom?

[L]: Three or four in a room. We didn't have bunks; there were big beds. If you go to one room and catch row[2] with one of them, you just go in the next room.

[T]: What sort of business was your father doing?

[L]: The old man had a bakery, grocery store, cloth store, and a wine store. The main one was the bakery; it supplied bread to all the shops, so many miles away on one side, so many miles on the other side. We had a donkey cart with barrels to deliver the bread; count out the bread, put it in barrels, give the man a list – so and so shop wants so many loaves of this, and so many loaves of that. He wrote it in the book and off the cart would go, from shop to shop.

[T]: How many Chinese families were there in Blankenburg, in your time?

[L]: There was a man named Yhap; he had two children. As a little boy, I used to pass their shop. They used to make something I liked – pow. You go and buy cent pow, and you get two.[3] So on the way home you buy pow, and would be eating on the road go down home.[4]

[T]: With such a big family, did you eat together or in shifts? What was the routine?

[L]: For me, I used to get up in the morning, go and bathe, wash my face, brush my teeth, eat breakfast and go to school. But the others had to

---

[1] The terms "old man" and "old lady" were used in some families to refer to a person's parents.
[2] Have a quarrel with someone.
[3] Pow is a steamed bun with meat and vegetable filling. One cent's worth could buy two pows.
[4] While on the way home.

go to work – go to the bakery to help. At breakfast, most of us would be together, only[5] the people in the shop – one of them had to get up and go sell in the shop – but we all ate together. There was a long table but no chairs, just long benches on two sides. The old man would be at the head, the old lady would sit near to him, and I'd be near to him on the other side – the small fry. I had a privileged place.

School was only a five-minute walk away, quite near. One of my brothers used to teach at the school, at one time. The majority of children were Black, Indian, with just a few Chinese. It was an Anglican church-school, and the church was next door to the school. So once a week we would go marching over to the church, and they'd talk rot, rubbish, and then we'd march over to the school.

Everybody went home for lunch. Midday meal was always heavy, the big one. They knew when we were coming from school so the food would be ready on the table. We had big platters of food, two or three, whatever was cooked. Everybody would go and dip for himself, but the old man got to dip first. He used to pick up his chopsticks and take out whatever meat he wanted, put it in his plate, and take out the choice meat and put it in my plate. He was a chopsticks man, but none of us used chopsticks. I would get the duck head – I love it. I love the chicken head and the bum. When we ate chicken, there would be two or three chickens cooked because there were plenty of us, you know. We ate mostly local style food, but on Saturday and Sunday we got Chinese cooking. My mother would cook that, and once a month or so, he would go in the kitchen and cook.

[T]: Did they have you helping . . . making foo foo, or things like that?

[L]: They used to get me to pound the thing. We had servants and they know to cook metagee, foo foo[6] and 'ting.[7] They had a lot of work to do, because there were plenty of pots to cook, and they would call on us to pound the foo foo. I didn't mind doing it.

[T]: How come they were picking on the lil' one? What about your other brothers?

[L]: The big ones own way,[8] they ain't getting them to do nothin'. You can't go calling them to work in the kitchen, they ain't taking that.

---

[5] Except for.

[6] Metagee and foo foo are two popular local dishes; the former is made with provisions (such as cassava, plaintain, potato) cooked with pig tails and salted meat in a coconut broth; the latter is prepared by pounding moistened plantain or cassava into dough-like consistency using a mortar and pestle.

[7] Other things.

[8] Would have their own way with things.

[T]: But I guess when it's time to play, they would show up.

[L]: Yeah. We used to play ball in the back yard. Black fellows used to come, and we'd play together. We used to have big cricket matches in the back yard, a big yard.

[T]: Did any of the brothers like to pair up, or have favorite brothers?

[L]: All of them went their own way, really, but I think George, Edwin, Edgar . . . the three of them were nearly the same size. Well, George and Edgar used to pair up. Edwin was . . . he was a gentleman, he was a schoolteacher and he was a different chap altogether – he wasn't rough and tough like the others.

[T]: Besides cricket, what else did you do?

[L]: We went catching fish with cast-net at the back there. Whoever picked up the cast-net, I would go with him. My brothers would cast the net – they were bigger than me – but I would always go, they don't have to ask me . . . I liked the outdoors. The drainage trench was here, and you had to go further down, half an hour or so, and there was an irrigation canal for the cane fields. You throw the net and catch hassar, and with the hassar you get a couple patwa, a couple houri.[9] I would help to take them out, and put them in the basket. Then we'd take them home and the servants would clean them, salt them up and do whatever.

I used to go to catch crabs on the mud shore. You put your hand in the hole, and pull them out. If they bite, it's not severe. You just leave your hand there, don't move, and he would let go, and then you pull out your hand. Sometimes he'd bite you and when you pull it out you're left with the tengle[10] on your hand. So you shake off the mud, and bite it off. Professional people, who used to catch and sell crabs, they would tell you that if the sun is this way, the crab would have its back that way. I never had experience with it, the professionals just say[11] that the crab would turn its belly towards the sun, so you could know how to go behind the back, pull him up.

I loved shooting. The bigger boys, they had two rifles, and whenever they went to town they would buy a box of bullets . . . and then leave the rifles in the corner, and the bullets on the dressing table in the bedroom. And I would go and steal a half a dozen or so. When they were not around, I used to take the rifle and go off to shoot. It was dangerous, very dangerous, because I didn't have the experience, but I loved shooting. I used to practice to shoot, practicing on birds. If the birds are flying low,

---

[9] The hassar belongs to the catfish family and has hard armour-like exterior scales, or scutes; the patwa is a variety of tilapia; the houri is a tasty but very bony fish.

[10] Ten-guh-LAY, a local term for the crab's claw or pincer.

[11] Would mention.

to shoot low with a rifle is very dangerous, in a populated place. Even in the back area there were people there too, not just you alone walking down there. People went there to cut grass for the cows and so on. Very dangerous, but fortunately I never got into trouble with that. But I always would take the bullets and go and shoot. There was a bird called the spur-wing. Then you had chow, which is also a water bird – it fed by the water. You had parrot; you had crane, gaulin, all those sea birds. By the rice field, you'd see them feeding.

[T]: If you shot a bird, did you take it home?

[L]: Nah, you can't take it home, because they would know you t'ief the gun and go and shoot birds.

[T]: But they know anyway, because you were taking the bullets.

[L]: They don't count them. I used to go with one or two black boys. In the shops, there were 8-ounce Capstan tobacco tins, and we would get one of these tins, and I'd go in the shop and put some salt butter . . . that much in the bottom . . . and take the rifle, and go and shoot birds. After shooting a bird, we would go down to the trench water, peel it, take off the skin, take out the belly, catch a fire and fry it in the tin. We took matches to make a lil' fire, then take a stick and hang the cup over the fire. The bird tasted sweet when you fried it in butter. Sweet, man. We took only one can. It was hard to get three, four, five birds. Some days it would be just one; sometimes you get none. When I think about it, those were good days.

In the yard there was a cherry tree and a couple orange trees. When the cherries were bearing, we would climb up and sit down and eat a bellyful of cherries. When the orange trees bear fruit, we pick the ripe ones and eat them. My big brothers apparently weren't fussy about the oranges, the cherries and so – they never bothered. It was myself, and two other brothers before me.[12] We used to go up with two other black friends and skylark,[13] and pick cherries and eat.

[T]: Did you ever help in the shop?

[L]: Nah, nah. Well, the old man got enough children. When I grew bigger, and three, four of us brothers sat down, and somebody came in for cent salt fish, or cent flour, they'd chase me to go and sell. "Get up, get up and go and sell." I learned that way. But if the people wanted a big order, then they would get up and serve.

[T]: At least they shared the work and didn't pass on the burden of dealing with the big buyers.

---

[12] The brothers just older than myself.

[13] Fool around or take things easy with nothing much to do.

[L]: Yes, at least they were considerate that way. One day, my big brother got sick with typhoid and that was something I'm glad he didn't pass on. We shared the same bed and he started to get a high fever and became delirious. The old man put out a white flag to signal for the doctor. The white flag is for the district doctor, the government doctor. The red flag is for the private doctor, like Dr. Foo. When the doctor came, he said my brother's got a problem. He gave him medicine, but he didn't send him to hospital. He gave him medicine and he got better.

[T]: Did the family do anything as a big group?

[L]: The big gathering (for those who were living at home) was at Christmas, because the old man would bake cakes for all his customers. And that was a big thing because he got to fold up[14] each cake nicely. Everybody had to chime in to wrap it up and send it out with the delivery boy. It was a whole cake for each customer, about a two-pound cake – lots o' cake, lots o' cake. Well, that was a big thing because everybody had to join in to help – to mix up the batter, with buckets and buckets of sugar and butter and so on. It was a fruit cake, and the old man would buy the fruits from Georgetown – raisins, currants, prunes, cherries, and all sorts of things – to put in. We got chickens,[15] so we had eggs from the chickens, and got butter from the shop. That is the time that everybody got to come together and help out. Apart from that we didn't have any big gathering.

[T]: Well the family by itself was quite a gathering. You must have been consuming a lot of supplies. Did you eat meat regularly?

[L]: We were eating meat every day, every day. We had a lot o' chickens, we had a lot o' pigs in the yard. I used to love it when they slaughtered a pig. When we were going to kill a big pig we would collect orders from the shops where we delivered bread. We told them we would kill this big fat pig, and ask how many pounds they wanted. We then wrote it up – five pounds, two pounds, whatever they ordered. We used to kill a pig on a Friday night, and on Saturday morning it was cut up and sent out to the customers who had ordered. We used to catch the blood to make black pudding.

[T]: Who would be holding down the pig?

[L]: A black fellow. He'd catch it, and tie it down. Get the foot and the mouth, and he would get help to put it on this table and then he would stick it; he had this long knife and he'd stick it, and I used to hold the basin there to catch the blood. The pig made a lot of noise – squealing. But they tied it down; held it down. It would kick up, but it

---

[14] He had to wrap up each cake as a present.
[15] Raised our own chickens.

was dying. It was a cruel way to kill it, but that's how we did it in those days – we didn't know any better. When he was done, he got a fire started to heat two cans of water. He threw the hot water, and scraped the pig to get it white and nice. All the hair would come off. I used to love to be 'round them. And this is in the night, you know. They do it in the night, eight o'clock, nine o'clock, because the man was working. When he came from work and was finished making dinner, then he'd come over. There were one or two people who used to specialize in that – go around slaughtering pigs for people. Our family would use up most of the pig. If the pig was going to be 200 pounds, we'd put a hundred pounds for sale.

[T]: How often did you kill pigs?

[L]: Depends on when we got them. When one became big enough, we then killed it. We raised pigs, we had pens right 'round the fence.[16] We had 25 to 30 head at a time. There was plenty of food to eat from the bakery, you know. You get stale bread from the bakery. You get mash rice from the rice factory, called boosie, and some fellows used to come and feed the pigs. The old man used to buy provisions[17] from the farmers. When they came and couldn't sell, they would bring the leftover provisions and sell them cheap to him. He would buy it, cut it up and give it to the pigs. I used to go and help feed the pigs and wash them down.

[T]: The pigs would get little piglets, I suppose.

[L]: Nah, nah, nah, we didn't breed the pigs. We never used to breed pigs. We would buy lil' ones. A man used to come down from the East Coast, walking with these pigs on his back. The man had them in a bag, a cloth bag. The old man would buy five, six of them, and push them in the pen.

[T]: Oh, buy a pig in a poke.

[L]: Real pig in the poke. There also was a place not far away with a lot o' pigs – wild. They were domestic pigs, but they were not in pens, they were let loose on the estate. We would go over and if a pig had a litter, we would bargain with the owner to buy the litter. Sometimes there would be eight or ten little pigs. So whenever we saw that the pigs had little ones, we would go over with a bag, and buy the whole lot. The old man put them in the pens. He raised them 'till they got big, and then slaughtered them.

[T]: Did you ever roast a pig?

---

[16] In the fenced perimeter of the yard.

[17] Root tubers and vegetables.

[L]: Nah. We'd cut it up. The old man would make dried pork. He used to cut the pork into long strips, season them up with the Chinese powder[18] and put them on a string and hang them up in the sun. The pig's head was used to make pepperpot. The cook would make a big pot o' pepperpot with the snout and ears, and pig's feet, too. But the old man used to take the fine guts[19] and make chook[20] – lovely, lovely. The other parts, like liver, and heart, we would use also – put some in the chook. Nothing went to waste. We also made black pudding.[21]

[T]: So what other animals did you have in the yard?

[L]: We had some cows, but only to get milk. I tried to do the milking – once or twice. Mostly we got Indian chaps to look after the cows. We kept several donkeys to haul the bread cart, but we had only one cart. But what we had mainly were the chickens and the pigs.

[T]: You mentioned the Christmas cake. Was there any other time that you celebrated any other festival, say Chinese New Year?

[L]: Well, . . . no celebration, but the old man used to buy Chinese things and we all shared them. For Chinese New Year he would buy kai en chee[22] and all those Chinese sweets to put on the table and everybody would sit down and eat. We used to go and take two, and walk away with one. No big celebration.

Harvest time was another time that the old man used to bake harvest bread and give to the Church and wholesale customers. Bake as much as a donkey cart full, a big amount. Two or three brothers used to compete to make the nicest bread to give to the Church for free. After the Sunday service, they would have the bread for sale on Monday and then people would tell you whose bread got the most money. They collected all sort o' things – rice, paddy, fruits – anything you got, you would round up. Everybody used to give. I can't remember what month that used to be. I got a feeling it might be harvest time for the rice cutters, because a lot of people used to get long rice plants and plat them up and make different decorations.[23]

[T]: So your father was a Christian.

---

[18] A powdered mixture of several spices, including clove, cinnamon, and anise, typically used for seasoning meat before roasting.
[19] Small intestines.
[20] Chinese style rice porridge, or congee.
[21] A sausage-like creation made with a mixture of rice and blood, stuffed and cooked in cleaned intestines, called casings, or runners.
[22] Preserved Chinese fruits.
[23] The long rice stalks were woven into different shapes – circles, fantails, crosses, etc.

[L]: My father? He wasn't a Christian. But my mother, she would always want to go to church. When I went to church, there would be three of us brothers, the lil' ones, with my mother – my father don't go. He went once. She got him to go one evening, to evening mass. And he sat down . . . and took out a cigarette. She jabbed him, and gave him one good look.[24] He said, "What happen?" "You can't smoke!" He put it back. When he came out, he said, "Damn fool, me ain't goin' back dey." He said the man that turn the collar upside down, the parson with the vest, is the biggest vagabond, don't worry 'bout him.[25]

Opposite where we lived was another church. Whenever a funeral came passing by we had to close up the shop. You would hear the church bell ringing: bang-bang . . . bang-bang, then you know a funeral was coming, and you go and close up the shop, don't make the jumbee[26] come in the shop. I don't know the reason why they closed, but they closed up, all the shops. After they passed you open up again.[27] There was a trench on the other side of the road and people had to cross this trench to get to the church. One day, there was a funeral and the hearse – one that was pulled by a horse – stopped on the road in front of the church. The people were carrying the coffin over the bridge . . . and the bridge broke down. The whole lot of them fell into the water, the living and the dead; and the water pulling,[28] going out to the ocean. The old man sat down there and he ain't saying one word. I think that was a Saturday. Next Monday morning he called a fellow that used to do carpentry work and he said, go and measure that trench and see how long the timber should be. Then he went to town and he bought two lengths of timber, and he built back the bridge.

[T]: So at least he was generous . . .

[L]: He would always do that. But he never went in the church. He ain't even like the parson.[29] But he just figured, well, it's a thing that must be doing some good, so buy the 'ting and give them.

[T]: Was he Hakka or Punti?

[L]: Hakka, I think we are Hakka. He never mentioned anything about the family history; he don't talk. My father? I don't think my father had five minutes o' conversation with anybody in the world. If you go sit down and talk to him, he'd say, uh, yeah, no. That's it – he hardly

---

[24] Stared at him disapprovingly.

[25] Pay no attention to him.

[26] Spirits or ghosts.

[27] The practice of shutting the shop for a passing funeral procession was a common local custom, as a mark of respect.

[28] A strong current of flowing water.

[29] Had no liking for the parson.

talked. He could sit down the whole day without saying a word to anybody. But he had a brother who was on the ship when they were coming over. This boy was with his mother too, and was about the same age so they used to play together on the ship. And my father's mother adopted that boy. He changed his name to Ho Ten Pow, like my father. He was living on the West Bank and he would come down, say, once every two months or something like that, and he and my father would sit down and talk in Chinese. That's the only time I would hear him talking. A very quiet chap, he loved to be by himself.

[T]: Except when he was running shop and he had to talk with . . .

[L]: Well, he got to trade, that's a different thing. He would always go to town, do the shopping. He went himself every Tuesday. The suppliers would post the goods, to come by the train. He had a man with a donkey cart, an Indian chap, he used to go and collect the shipment from the railway station, and bring it in and load it in the shop. Sometimes he would bring thirty, forty bags of flour. The station had a bond[30] to take all these goods. The train people had to take it off and put it in the bond.[31] And then the man in charge of the station would hand over whatever belonged to Ten Pow. This was at Hague station – by donkey cart, about 15 minutes away. Blankenburg had only a little platform, but Hague had a station with a bond and everything. My father had accounts with Bookers, Sandbach Parker, J.P. Santos. They would always take credit,[32] and every month he'd pay them.

[T]: Your father, did he wear a Chinese outfit?

[L]: Chinese, always Chinese. Yes, this baggy silky thing, and it was buttoned up across with some gold buttons.[33] Every week they had to take out the buttons and send the outfit to the laundry, and he'd put on another one. He had several of these jackets, some silky things, but always a dark color, a dark thing. Inside here he had a pocket and he could push his hand under this flap. There were buttons along the side too, gold buttons. That was my mother's job – to take them off and put them back on the other one. People used to come every week for the laundry. You know how much clothes we send out to wash? And they got to sit down there, count them out piece by piece in front of my mother. Then she would write it down, so many pieces. When they came back . . . they would spend a week to wash it . . . she got to check every piece. The

---

[30] A secure storage place, typically a locked shed.

[31] Employees of the railway company were responsible for unloading the train and storing the goods.

[32] Provided goods, charged on a credit account.

[33] A line of buttons across the chest and side.

laundry people were mostly black, and I imagine all o' them were church people, like my mother.

My father would wear slippers, always leather slippers. And you can stand in the shop and he'd be coming up from till down at the back,[34] clip-clop, clip-clop – it's the old man coming. It was a big leather thing, always hitting on the floorboard; you didn't have carpets. Plop-plup, plop-plup, coming down. If we were doing anything wrong, we got to stop doing it, the old man coming. For instance, we used to make our own spinning tops, and he didn't like that. He'd say, you goin' to bore out you eye. We used to get a knot from the guava tree to make the top (jamoon tree would also made a good top). You got a knot from a branch and, with a knife, you shaped it. You scrape it down, and you strip it, and you sand it, and sand it, and then you bore a hole and you knock it easy, easy – push a nail through it and sharpen the point. There's another top that you can make from a yellow fruit with a big seed, and that one used to sing. Well, the old man didn't mind that one. But he never liked the one we made out o' wood, with a nail inside. You would spin your top there, and I'd spin mine and put it on top yours. If my top started boring into your top, it would break. So whenever he saw us with a top like this he would take it, go in the shop, put it on the meat board, whack it hard with the saltfish axe and break it. But all these things were home made. We didn't know anything about buying toys, we had to make our own toys.

[T]: Well, you knew how to entertain yourselves. Tell me about school life.

[L]: I would get up 6 o'clock, 7 o'clock, whenever I woke up. School started at half past eight, I think, and the school was nearby. I used to wear short pants, and yachting shoes, but no socks. Only when you go to church you got to wear socks, no other time.

The school is one big open thing. In each class there must have been 15 to 20 students. Every class had a couple desks, and you'd sit down there. That's it – we didn't have classrooms. Not even the headmaster had a room . . . he had a platform. He had a desk, and he had his wild cane, and a bell, and that's all he had. And he had two presses[35] where he put some things. Number one, he had quinine tablets. Malaria used to tear tail[36] down there, so everybody would get one quinine. Had to drink this damn thing, bitter like hell. Every week you got one; and if you had fever, you got two. Then he had some of his private books there, books

---

[34] Far away, at the back of the house.
[35] Cupboards.
[36] To be rampant.

for the school, and so on. And his wild cane – his stock o' wild cane was used mostly on boys.

We had homework and we would be doing it by gas light.[37] My father had a gas lamp, and you had to pump it up. We didn't have electricity down there. As soon as you finished your homework, you went to bed. Is licks[38] next morning if you don't carry your homework. But the old lady would see that you do your homework first. Then you go to bed . . . maybe about 8 o'clock. Because we boys were active the whole day, we were tired when the night came, you know.

I went all the way to sixth standard at that school. Then I left there and I went to Central.[39]

[T]: But you preferred the outdoors. Did you ever go to the canefields?

[L]: Nah, personally I didn't go, but I used to suck the sugar cane. The village boys used to go and pull off a couple from the punt. They had just cut it[40] and would be carrying it to the factory. Indian boys, black boys – they just skylarking; they'd say, punt passing, we goin' collect some cane. They'd jump on the punt, pull out a couple and throw them on the road, jump off and come home with cane. I never did that myself, but they would bring more than they could eat, and we'd go out and sit down and eat it. I enjoyed eating it, sucking the cane.

[T]: So what other outdoor experiences you have?

[L]: I went in the goldfields, I went in the diamond fields. That would take a year to tell you.

[T]: Well, tell me a few stories.

[L]: My brother, George, always went in the goldfields, diamond fields. Henry used to go too, but they wouldn't accept that I could go with them – I was too young, or too stupid, or whatever. But I really wanted to go, I like the outdoors. I asked George several times, he'd say, no, I ain't carrying you with me. George was courting, and I know his girlfriend. So I rode[41] from Blankenburg to Windsor Forest to where she lived – she was a seamstress – and I said: "A-kam, how you dey? How you do? I want to ask you a favor, A-kam, you do it for me?" She say, "Wha' you want?" I said, "Ask George to carry me in the bush with him." I came home and I saw him ready to go to town. I knew that when he came back from town he would go to visit her. I went to sleep. Next

---

[37] A lamp that burned vaporized kerosene, producing a bright light.
[38] A caning.
[39] Central High School, in Georgetown.
[40] The cane had just been harvested.
[41] Rode a bicycle.

morning, when we were having breakfast, he said, get ready we going to town. I said, "Me?" He said, "Yes, you want to go in the bush?" I answered, "Oh yes, I want to do that." So he carried me into town to buy some clothing and canvas shoes. I was so happy, man; yes, man! That is how I went in the bush the first time. Man, I love it.

We went to Parika with the train, caught the boat from Parika to Bartica, stayed the night, and he sent up a lot of rations. He saw to it that all the rations are all right. Then we took the boat going up in the Puruni. He used to go steady[42] and he would stay there often, but this was my first time. This boat had to go up some rapids . . . and the poor boat, the engine ain't going.[43] They were paddling and paddling and they ain't making any headway. So my brother George sat down near to me. He can't swim, but I could swim. He said, if the boat sink, hold on to a bag o' flour and that would float you – you would come to the shore some way. I said OK, but I think I coulda swim it. And we were going up in this thing . . . this thing was frightening. The water was coming down and the boat ain't moving. So the captain had to tell the bow man to jump off and carry the rope on to the rock. And that is how we got up. Two people there, pulling the boat up. There were about fifteen to twenty of us in the boat.

George had five or six men with him, black men working with him. They had to put all this flour and rice and 'ting on their backs, and walk in this trail here, up and down hill, in and out creeks. I said to myself, "Lenny, what you doing here?" But I couldn't turn back. So I went there and we worked in the diamond field. We worked in the tributaries of the Puruni River. I learnt by seeing what they were doing. You had to sink holes to look for an indication. There is one kind of indication for gold, and a different indication for diamonds. You had to dig holes with a shovel, and if the indication was good, you then opened a pit, a big pit, 20 by 20,[44] or something like that, whatever we could manage. We set up a tom – that's a board on which you throw the gravel, so as to it wash down, and a man standing down here would catch the small particles – the sand with the diamonds – in a sieve, and sieve it out.

It was a good experience. The best part of it was that George had a gun and I had permission to go shooting in the afternoon. So I loved that. We had a double-barreled shotgun then. Anything we came across we would shoot, like acouri, deer, monkey, baboon, anything. We ate

---

[42] Frequently.

[43] Not powerful enough to move the boat forward.

[44] Twenty feet square.

acouri. If I shot a monkey or baboon, the fellas ate it. This trip lasted for three months. We carried rations to last three months.

[T]: Wait, wait a minute. Five men walking with enough on their backs to last three months?

[L]: No, no, no. They went to the site and first they built the logie. You had to cut down trees and build a logie – it would take a day to build. It's just a shelter to keep the rain off, that's all. Then they would go back to the waterside to bring the rest. They had to make three or four trips, each of them. Everybody had a hammock, hanging up in the logie. I had mosquito netting but not everybody. My sister-in-law made a mosquito netting for me, because she had made one for him, so she did one for me too. We used to always have a big fire going outside the camp.

[T]: So who's doing the cooking for you?

[L]: Well, we had one fellow who used to do the cooking, but everybody used to fall in and help. But it was one fellow chiefly – that was his job. Tarbuck was his name.

[T]: When you needed to use a bathroom, did you have to dig a hole, or just go creekside?

[L]: No, you had to go in the hill and find a tacooba[45] and you made the best of it. Sit down on a big log, a big tree that had fallen, and do your business there. Or you can take a shovel and dig a hole, if you don't have a tacooba.

[T]: Wait, you walked with paper, or did you use a leaf, or something?

[L]: I think we used leaves. Where are you going to get toilet paper, ha, ha, ha? When you were finished there, you walked down in the creek, say. Near where you're working, the water was flowing, so you would go in the creek and you could bathe.

[T]: The first time you went out, did you have any good find?

[L]: Yes, my brother brought down a dinner plate o' diamonds, but in those days, a carat of diamond was only two dollars.[46] It was his expedition, so he would buy all the food and 'ting – the rations – and pay the workers, and everybody was supposed to get a part of the find. He would take it to Georgetown, to diamond merchants there, mostly Jews.

On one outing we were coming down from the back to go to town, and George had his dog. He got it as a little pup and after a few months it had grown big . . . but the dog was afraid of water. So we were coming out this day, and we had to pass a little dry creek, only a foot of water in

---

[45] An Amerindian word for either the heartwood of a tree, or else a fallen log.
[46] Small diamonds were of little value. Prospectors struck it rich only by finding large diamonds.

it. And this dog wouldn't come across, he wanted George to lift him up and take him across the creek. But George walked ahead, and I walked ahead too. We left him there, standing on the bank on the other side crying, and a tiger just came and picked him up and went off with him. We didn't know that there was a tiger there, hanging around. If we had known, we would have picked him up and brought him across. It was too bad.

I went with Henry on other occasions. Well, he was a better brother to go with – he's more down to earth. George is more of a bossy chap, he's the top guy, he would boss you around, whereas Henry, he don't care a damn. And Henry loved shooting too, just like me. After he started the work going in the morning in the pit, he would take the gun and go out shooting.

[T]: The gold expedition, is that any different from looking for diamonds?

[L]: Yes. With diamonds, you can get rich suddenly . . . you get a couple big diamonds and you were rich. Whereas with gold, you had to go gradually, find a vein and follow it, and you suddenly might get some gold ore, but you wouldn't get fabulously rich, but nice. One day we said, let's get some of this gravel here, and in that thick gravel I got a nugget, a gold nugget. How did it get there? I still ask people that question, they can't tell me. They said, maybe a powis[47] ate it . . . found it some place else and passed by here and dropped it. That's what some people told me, but I don't know.

We would use quicksilver[48] to hold the gold and in the afternoon we used to burn out the quicksilver. That's dangerous stuff, but in those days we didn't know that. But it hasn't kill me up to now, ha, ha, ha. You have the tom and cant it like that,[49] with the water coming in at the top, and you got a man with a hoe, bringing the gravel down, and you got a tom iron, a piece of iron with holes in it, like a screen. The big stones you throw to one side, and the fine gravel drops through, and lower down is a little box with the quicksilver. Well, gold is heavy so it sinks down and the quicksilver would hold it there.[50] So in the afternoon we would go and clear this quicksilver, squeeze it out in a cloth, and whatever was left we carried up to the camp to burn it. The quicksilver and the gold would become a lump, and if you put it in the pot, and made a fire below, the quicksilver would burn away, disappear. You don't know where it went,

---

[47] A large game bird found in Guyana.
[48] Mercury, a poisonous substance.
[49] Set up at a sloping angle.
[50] The gold particles would form an amalgam with mercury.

but it was gone. We used to buy the quicksilver from Bookers, and this thing was heavy. When you bought two pounds you could hardly fill up a witch-hazel bottle.[51] We would buy maybe two pounds at a time. You can't buy much – it was a lot of money for it. At home, we would play with it. If it got into the crease[52] you never could pick it out; you can't pick it out.

[T]: You sure lived a dangerous life.

[L]: Well, we didn't get rich, but we didn't poison ourselves either. And for me, it was enjoyable, because I love the outdoors.

---

[51] Witch-hazel was sold as a medicated ointment in small, but thick-walled, glass bottles, just over an inch in diameter.

[52] In small spaces where the sections of the floorboards were joined.

DRY GOODS SHOP

Ruby Sue-A-Quan, née Lou-Hing
as told to Trev Sue-A-Quan

Edward Lou-Hing was born in 1876, the younger of two children born to an immigrant from China who had arrived in Guyana in the latter half of the 19th century. At an early age, Sarah and Edward became orphaned and they were raised by a black couple in Leguan, an island in the Essequibo River. In 1899, Edward married Elizabeth En-tong Woon-Sam who became known as Aunt En because of her Chinese name. She was the granddaughter of an immigrant who had arrived in 1860 and whose trade in China was noted as "grog seller" in the immigration records.

* * * * * * * *

Edward Lou-Hing
Roderick Sue-A-Quan

Edward and Elizabeth Lou-Hing were the parents of six children by 1908 and they decided to open a shop in Uitvlugt, a village in West Coast Demerara. There was some degree of prosperity and Edward later expanded his business by building a new and larger shop that offered a variety of groceries, hardware items and liquor. The family then grew to eleven children, the last ones being twin boys born in 1915. As was common among the Chinese families, it was an ambition to have their children obtain a good education, and when Clarice, the sixth child, gained a scholarship from her primary school, Edward and his wife made the decision to send their children to school in the capital, Georgetown. Thus, in 1919, Elizabeth headed off to the city with the children while Edward continued to manage the shop in the countryside. However, the loss of family members to assist in operating the shop, together with the added rent required for the home in Georgetown, became too much of a physical and financial strain for Edward. A few years later he sold off the Uitvlugt shop and bought a much smaller shop in La Bonne Intention (LBI) some seven miles from Georgetown in East Coast Demerara. Not only was this closer to Georgetown, but there was no longer a need to use the ferry to cross the Demerara River.

La Bonne Intention estate, showing: (1) Plantation managers' quarters. (2) Lou-Hing's dry goods shop. (3) Hindu temple. (4) Middle walk trench. (5) Estate road. (6) Workers' housing. (7) Outhouses poised over the drainage trench. *Booker Bros. McConnell, Ltd.*

The Lou-Hing family's shop was reached by crossing a wooden bridge over the punt trench that ran alongside the estate road. The bridge continued as a ramp that connected to the platform, or gallery, that formed the frontage of the shop. Although known as a "dry goods shop" a portion of the premises was a liquor shop, or "rum shop" in local parlance, but the two sections of the business were kept apart by a dividing wall and accessible by two separate entrances. A single serving counter extended through both the dry goods and rum shop sections, with some 15 feet of length on the dry side and eight feet on the "wet" side. Immediately behind this commercial section of the building were the living quarters consisting of a sitting room containing a small sofa and a Berbice chair (a wooden lounge chair with swing-out arm extensions on which the feet could be propped), a kitchen area with a small dining table and two or three chairs, and a bedroom. There was just enough space to fit two brass poster beds head to head, one being for

Edward and his wife Elizabeth, who was able to join him since the children had since become grown and were working. The other bed was for their daughter, Ruby, who assisted in running the shop until she got married. Besides these few rooms there was a small area, offset between the kitchen and bedroom, assigned as the bathroom but this was merely an unlit closet-like room where the family members could have a sponge bath with the aid of a bucket or two of water. Additional ablution, of the face and hands, was achieved by using a jug of water and a basin sitting on the ledge outside one of the two bedroom windows. The whole building stood on supporting pillars of stone so as to keep the house sufficiently elevated, away from potential flooding. Standing in the backyard of the shop was the toilet, a basic outhouse where pieces of brown paper or newspaper were pressed into sanitary service. Also in the backyard was an enormous vat collecting rainwater channeled there by

Ruby Lou-Hing
Roderick Sue-A-Quan

gutters on the fringes of the sloping galvanized tin roof that covered the main building. The two rainy seasons that occurred annually were the times that water accumulated in the vat to serve the ongoing needs throughout the year.

Water was a necessary part of the rum making operations, beginning with the bottle-washing operation. The clear glass bottles came in two sizes, pint and half-pint, and some were recycled bottles that were returned by the customers for a refund of one cent per bottle. Using washing soda, soap and long thin brushes, each bottle was washed individually by hand. If any residual material remained stubbornly attached to the inside of the bottle, a marble or two would be inserted to improve the scrubbing action. The bottles were then rinsed and stacked upside-down in a barrel to drip dry. This sometimes required some delicate balancing of the bottles one on the other until a sufficient number of bottles were in place to pack them tightly together. Rum was made from "high wine" obtained from the sugar estate and delivered by donkey cart. High wine was produced from the distillation of fermented cane extracts, typically molasses, and would be between 90 to 95% alcohol, or 163 to 167% proof, at the point of production. Casks of high wine of about 140% proof were then sold to rum manufacturers. Edward had about four large casks in his shop, one being of high wine and the others of rum which was made by diluting the high wine to the desired strength of about 80% proof and letting it mature in the wooden casks for an extended period, the aging process being necessary to bring out the full rum flavor. It was important to carefully measure the strength of the rum because over-proof rum would represent an unnecessary loss of high wine and consequent reduction of profit. On the other hand, any watering down of the rum could be subject to significant penalty by the government inspector who came by on occasion with his own hydrometer to make sure that the correct blend was being prepared for sale. One of the casks contained "white rum" which did not contain any additives while another cask held "colored rum" prepared by adding caramel or other coloring agent, to produce dark rum, which was the more popular product.

Bottling of the rum was sort of a small-scale assembly-line process. Sitting on a low stool, Edward would draw the rum directly from the tap on the cask using a funnel to guide the liquid into the bottle. The bottle would be placed on the ground and as the rum reached the required level in the neck of the bottle he would, with his right hand, shift the tip of the funnel to the next bottle, held in his left hand such that the tops of the two bottles were touching. In this way the filling operation continued without interruption with no need to shut off the tap, and with minimal loss of rum. As one bottle was being filled the just-filled bottle would be placed in the receiving area – another part of the floor, an arm's length away. His assistant would take each full bottle and insert a cork which would then be struck with a "beater," a thick paddle about 4 x 5 inches with a short handle. The corked bottle would be upturned to check for any leaks, in which case the bottle was set aside for cork-replacing treatment. The top inch of each well-corked bottle was then dipped in a pot of molten red seal poised atop a small kerosene burner. The seal was a material similar to that used in days of old to seal letters and documents. Right after removing the bottle the seal would solidify into a thin shiny red cap. The sealed bottles were then ready for labeling. The paste for the labels was a thick starch gel, rather like heavy porridge in consistency. A small dab of starch picked up on the back of the right-side edge of the label would be transferred to the bottle. Leaving a smudge of paste on the bottle the label would be positioned such that the non-pasted left edge lay over the smudge and the starch remaining on the right edge would hold down that end. A towel was used to remove any excess starch as well as to smooth the label or adjust the alignment on the bottle. The bottles of rum were then stored on the shelves on the wall behind the counter ready for the customers' arrival.

The customers were primarily Indian laborers, as well as some black workers, who received their weekly wages each Friday, and several of them headed for the rum shop after that. Friday and Saturday were thus the busiest days of the week. The imbibers came in and typically asked for a shot of rum that would be measured by a schnapps glass and poured into a drinking glass. Many would ask for some bitters to add to their drinks – Angostura bitters, a few drops of which altered the rum flavor to their taste. They stood around in the shop, or on the gallery where a bench was available for their use, where they could easily obtain a refill. Some purchased a full bottle and went to the nearby shed in the yard. Heineken beer and Guinness stout, both at room temperature, were also available for sale but these foreign and expensive brews were much slower sellers that the local liquor. On some occasions the drinkers became tipsy, or really intoxicated, but there were not any brawls or physical conflicts although the volume of the voices would become significantly elevated and the language being used would usually not be heard in polite company. The drinking glasses left behind had to be collected, and an Indian deaf/mute sometimes used to help with this. He would come by and provide his services for a few weeks at a time and then disappear for a while. Communication with him was done using signs and gestures, and it was not a problem because he could be instructed to help with gardening and washing the exterior of the shop. The water for washing the glasses came from a tap above the sink at the far end of the counter, but the supply tank had to be regularly replenished by fetching buckets of water from the vat.

By law, shops had to be closed on Sundays and the sale of liquor was strictly prohibited, with the threat of heavy fines for the offender. Although the doors were shuttered on the Sabbath, there would be the occasional person who came knocking to plead for some consideration . . . and a bottle of the good stuff. Edward would not deny their entreaties, while making sure that there were no strangers in the vicinity with an authoritative demeanor. Some of these off-hour purchasers would ask for an item or two from the dry goods store, such as flour or potatoes, in an attempt to cast a degree of humanitarianism on the proceedings, and then add the request for the desired liquid as a closing remark.

The dry goods shop opened six days a week from the crack of dawn until about 9:00 p.m. On the slack days, Monday to Thursday, the shop would close early, at about 8:00 p.m. However it was not unusual for the shop to open even beyond 9:00 on Fridays and Saturdays, particularly the liquor section. Operation during the evening hours was facilitated by two light bulbs hanging from the ceiling in the dry goods section and a single bulb in the rum shop, the electricity being supplied from the sugar factory. The early morning opening was necessary to provide breakfast snacks for the workers who were heading off to work. The main item purchased was small loaf of bread that was oval in shape with each end stretched into a point. The customer would buy one or two and then resume his walk to work while munching on the bread wrapped in brown paper. There was also a variety of other items such as tarts, turnovers, large sweet biscuits, coconut buns and small cakes, but these were less popular than the pointed bread. These fresh goods were replenished daily by a delivery van belonging to the bakery in the nearby village of Beterverwagting.

The products sold at the dry goods store were mainly daily-life items that did not require refrigeration. Below the counter were a number of cubicles that held the flour, sugar, salt, corn flour, rice, split peas, black eye peas, channa, sago, barley, onions, garlic, etc., that the plantation workers needed. Some of the high-demand items, such as sugar and flour, were pre-packaged by Edward in one- or two-pound packets. The commonly used type of sugar was brown sugar, although a more refined "yellow crystal" sugar was also sold. There were no ready-made paper bags – the correctly weighed amount of each product would be placed at the center of a brown paper sheet. The far and near edges were then brought together and folded over to form a closed seam. One of the open ends of the just-formed paper tube would be folded over to seal that end. The packet could then be stood on end and the top folded in to produce an enclosed paper container. For items sold in small quantities, including spices, black peppercorns, cloves and curry, the packaging consisted of paper cones. These were made from smaller triangular bits of paper that were rolled into a conical shape. The point of the cone would be twisted to seal the bottom and hold the cone in shape. When filled with product, the paper at the top of the cone would be folded in to seal the contents. Several empty cones, small and large, were stacked below the counter in readiness for duty. Edward also prepared several tiny packets containing a pinch of turmeric, or else a small quantity of Cow's Brand baking soda, one of which would be given with each purchase of a two-pound packet of flour.

Products of a few pounds or less were weighed on a scale having tilting balance pans each suspended by three light chains similar to that held up by the legendary blindfolded Justice. Shiny brass weights, down to half an ounce, were used with this balance. Spices and purchases made in small quantities, such as curry powder and cloves, were measured out in this scale. There was also a heavier-duty scale with a large deep oval pan to hold the goods and this was counterbalanced by weights placed on a small round platform at the other end. This scale also had a sliding weight running along a graduated horizontal bar which allowed the weighing of fractional amounts of a few ounces. Edward also kept another "Justice" scale for weighing salted fish, locally called "salt fish," a very popular food for the Indian customers. The salt fish was cod and came in crates, imported from Canada and Europe. Edward kept a pile of newspapers specifically for wrapping the salt fish. Alongside the salt fish were barrels of salt beef and pigs' tails, or more familiarly "pig-tails," these items being preferred by the black population. The saline solution in which the beef and tails were packed acted as a preservative, but the dry salt fish would turn pink if it remained unsold for a long time in the tropical heat.

Cheese, butter, and lard were also sold in the shop. The cheese was imported from Holland and looked like a thick disk with rounded edges and came encased in red wax. It was commonly called "Dutch head cheese." There were two kinds of butter, Cow and Girl fresh butter and Palm Tree salted butter. They came in large tins and had to be dipped with a scoop. These items were very much in demand by the customers and as a result there was not a problem with spoilage. Even though they were liable to become soft and oily, the butter would be sold wrapped in the same versatile brown paper. Since it was not a long distance away the product would still be intact when the customer arrived home. There it would be used that very day or else transferred to a metal or porcelain container. Most of the customers brought shopping baskets to carry away their purchases, but some would have a large cloth in which everything was tightly wrapped and then the bundle delicately balanced on the head. Identification of the goods, which were all wrapped in brown paper, was done by feeling the parcel, with flour being softer to the touch than granular sugar or beady peas, while the butter would make itself evident. Only canned goods such as sardines and corned beef had labels. The items in high demand were the ones needed for cooking curries and highly spiced Indian foods. Curry powder was supplied in large tins and sold in Edward's brown paper funnels as were masala, jira and turmeric. Ginger came in a dried state. Peppercorns and nutmeg came in their original whole state and needed to be ground or grated at home. Loose tealeaves, coffee beans and cocoa powder were also available in the shop and there was no choice about the kind of tea or coffee because there was only one variety of each beverage ingredient available.

Some goods were sold by volume even though they were solids, including barley, sago, split peas and rice, because of their granular nature. In this way, it was common practice to measure out a pint of peas or a gallon of rice. The measuring containers in these cases were government-certified vessels, the one for rice having the shape of a conical can with a pouring lip and handle. The rice would be poured into containers brought by the customer, sometimes a cloth bag, basin or tin can. Two kinds of rice were available, brown and white, the former being more popular with the Indian customers. Rice was purchased from wholesale dealers in Georgetown and packaged in large jute bags. The shopping expedition in the capital was Elizabeth's responsibility and done on Tuesday when the shop was not busy. She left early in the morning

and walked for about 20 minutes to the railway station not quite a mile away. The LBI station was a simple wooden platform with a hut from which the attendant sold tickets through a purchasing window. In Georgetown, Elizabeth would go to the various wholesalers to order rice, potatoes, onions, garlic, flour, salt fish, etc. She collected the receipts and headed home by which time it would be close to sunset. On Thursday, the dray cart belonging to the estate would be dispatched on one of the twice-weekly journeys to town on official business, and the driver would stop by the shop to pick up the receipts from Elizabeth. There was a standing arrangement

Elizabeth Lou-Hing
Roderick Sue-A-Quan

with the estate management by which the goods could be brought back to the shop on the dray cart. Comprised of a long flat platform on four large rubber wheels the dray cart was drawn by a mule and rumbled its way along the road at leisurely pace. It would be late in the afternoon before the cart returned with the purchased goods for the Lou-Hing shop. On some occasions the driver of the cart would be accompanied by an assistant who helped him with loading and unloading, but perhaps the assistant of greatest value was the large tarpaulin that had to be deployed in rainy weather. The arrival of the goods completed the purchasing loop that Elizabeth initiated a few days earlier. The process was even more remarkable because Elizabeth was not literate.

Because the vast majority of the customers were Indian they would frequently ask for items in Hindi, and Edward and Elizabeth became familiar with the key words used in shopping and daily life. With their heavy accent the exchange in the English language would sound almost like an Asian dialogue: wan pong bajra (a pound of barley), too pang piaz (onions), foe pong alu (potatoes), and so on. In this way the shopkeepers accumulated a varied Hindi vocabulary – baegan (eggplant), chai (tea), kapra (cloth), pani (water), murghi (chicken) etc. Some customers were also capable of using expressive body language when they asked for purchases on credit accompanied by pleas of "massa, please massa," or "missi, good missi," while giving every assurance that the debt would be settled at the next payday. Edward kept a debtors' ledger and a number of the customers would pay only a quarter or a half of the outstanding debt. In this way a revolving or deferred account was effectively set up and Edward became the loan officer for these persons. However, this was the way that business was conducted so as to retain customer loyalty. Only on a few occasions were delinquent customers denied because of the accumulation of excessive debt.

Coconut oil was a popular product with the Indians. It was used not only for cooking but also as hair oil as well as body oil that imparted a glistening look to the user. In addition to edible items, the shop offered candles, kerosene, lanterns, cigarettes and matches, made of wood and packed in a small box with a slide-out tray. The kerosene was sold in the same clear bottles used for rum, or else poured into containers brought by the customers. The cigarettes were made by Edward, with each cigarette rolled with an appropriate amount of Capstan tobacco and stored in a wooden box from where they were sold individually. The shop also had a couple bolts of cloth, one white and the other printed cotton, the pattern being the one that Elizabeth considered suitable during her Georgetown expedition. The cloth was measured out against the yardstick fastened to the counter and sold at eight cents per yard. A small selection of ribbons was also available and the Indian customers were very adept at making their clothes from white cotton trimmed with ribbon. Some reels of thread, mainly white plus occasional colored ones, were part of the sales inventory. The shop stocked a few cans of Menin's baby powder as well as some bath soap. Bay rum, used as a liniment, was also sold and some desperate customers would attempt to use it as a drink, much to their detriment. There was no demand for toothbrushes and tooth powder, because it was the local habit to use the twig of a bush that formed bristles when the end was chewed. Other utilitarian goods on sale included galvanized pails, washing soda, soap, "soft grease" and Rickett's Blue, the last two items being specifically for the laundering of clothes. Cutlasses, the main working implement for the cane field workers, were also available and Edward carried a limited stock, one type having a straight blade and the other with a curved end.

The living quarters were scrubbed once a week, and the hired cook, who was usually a black woman from the area, would help with this chore. Using soap and a bucket of water with added washing soda, she would use a scraper to work on the white pine floors. The scraper was a piece of flat sheet metal some 3 x 5 inches in size with one of the long ends folded back to form a blunt handle of sorts. The cook would spend some two to three hours on her hands and knees getting the floor clean.

She also did other housework, including scrubbing the pots and pans with ashes and soap. But the main duty of the cook was to prepare meals for the family on the wood-burning stove. One of the food preparation chores was picking rice. The rice grains were placed on a sifter, a woven basket tray with an elevated back rim and tapered sides. Standing outdoors, the cook would toss the rice into the air so that the wind would blow away the bits of chaff that remained after the rice-milling process. The grains were then spread out on the sifter so that the broken bits and discolored rice grains could be picked out by hand.

The dishes prepared by the cook were usually rice plus a stew, casserole or similar creation, using primarily local foods. The cook came six times a week plus two Sundays a month, and was paid a wage of four to five dollars a month. Her daily routine would end with the preparation of dinner at 5:00 p.m. On the days that she did not appear, and usually without advance warning, the family would have to scramble around to get the tasks completed. The Lou-Hings enjoyed curry and metagee. Because of the need for someone to tend the shop the family could not eat together. The dining rotation started with Edward, then Elizabeth, and lastly Ruby. Once a week there would be okra and crab soup with foo-foo. If Elizabeth wanted Chinese food she would have to teach the cook the way to prepare it. Such Chinese dishes would typically have either dried mushrooms, bean curd strips (foo chook), bean thread noodles (funcee), bat ears (wanyee – a black mushroom looking like a wrinkled leaf, hence the nickname), dried shrimp, mostly prepared with soy sauce.

For a while Elizabeth raised some chickens, sheep and a couple pigs to supplement the diet, as well as putting some for sale. The sheep were cooped up under the house at night and let out to roam around during the day while the chickens found themselves a roost in the large tree in the yard. The pigsty was close to the outhouse and they both produced comparable odors. Eventually Elizabeth changed from animal management into garden cultivation. She managed to secure a large plot of land from the estate and laid out a number of rectangular raised beds surrounded by irrigation ditches. She would put on her rubber boots to go to the garden where she grew eggplant, okra and peppers, with some of the produce being sold in the shop. These, and bananas sold at one cent each, were among the few fresh produce items available for sale. The irrigation ditches served another purpose, and that was as a storage area for hassar. On occasion, individual sellers would come by with freshly-caught hassar strung up through their gills,[1] and Elizabeth would buy the whole lot, use a few for the day's meal, and put the unused ones into the ditches to live for a few more days until they ended up in the pot.

Throughout his life Edward was a healthy person and never in need of medical services. However, it appeared that he would come down with a headache every Monday morning with regularity. For this he would retire to the Berbice chair and lie there with a handkerchief soaked with Limacol on his forehead for a couple hours, and he would be fine after that. He did not have any recreational activities but would read the newspapers, which then ended up as wrappings for the salt fish. On rare occasions a picnic outing was organized for family and friends. Edward would request the use of a punt from the estate manager as well as an estate employee to guide the mule that pulled the punt. The picnickers, maybe ten to a dozen people, would head off to the punt trench and climb into the waiting punt. Off they would go by slow punt to the back dam where the water was much deeper and cleaner, and there the revelers would swim and relax. The picnic offerings were cooked beforehand – curry, pepperpot, metagee, or cook-up rice.[2]

The people attending these picnics were primarily Chinese relatives and friends from Georgetown who found the outing to the back dam to be a "different" experience from city activities. For them it was "a day in the country." Along with local-styled foods, the picnic in the outdoors reflected the influence of the popular practices on the Chinese families. By this period, the clothes, language and foods had become westernized. However, the traditional Chinese custom of respect for the elders was retained, and expressed itself in the use of Chinese titles in addressing others. Gong Gong (grandfather), and Popo (grandmother) were used to such an extent that in some families the younger ones would know their grandmother only as Popo, and not know her full name. Chay Chay and Ko Ko were required prefixes in calling out to an elder sister or brother, respectively. These forms of address persisted even among those who were several generations removed from the original immigrants from China. Thus, the terms "Uncle" and "Auntie" – expressed in either the English or Chinese version – would be used by children and adults alike when speaking or referring anyone who was older, whether or not that person was a true relative.

---

[1] A portion of the hassar's gills has evolved to provide air-breathing capability, so that the fish can survive out of water for a reasonable time.
[2] Cook-up rice is popular local rice dish containing black-eye peas and various cuts of meat.

The customs of other ethnic groups were also recognized and respected by the Chinese. Two examples were the major Hindu festivals known locally as Pagwah Day and Tadjah Festival. In addition, there were two public holidays per year (one being in celebration of Queen Victoria's birthday, although she had long departed from the world) at which time Elizabeth Lou-Hing would organize a gala celebration. Prior to these holidays she had pamphlets printed that offered the prize of a bottle of rum to the winners of three events – a foot race, a boat race and climbing a greasy pole. These advertisements were distributed to the customers and in the nearby villages. The result would be a large crowd of participants and spectators in festive mood. The road race started near the railway and ended outside the shop, convenient enough for the exhausted but exalted winner to easily retrieve his prize. The boat race was held in the punt trench outside the shop using small flat-bottomed boats capable of carrying six paddlers. The finish line was once again at the bridge of the shop where the winning team, wet on the outside, could then wet their insides with the liquid prize. The third attraction was the source of greatest amusement as, one after another, the courageous individuals tried to clamber up the pole that had been liberally lubricated with black grease. The crowd would shout its encouragement as the competitor made vertical progress and then burst out in laughter as the sliding body headed for Earth, courtesy of unkind gravity. Eventually the participants would rub off enough of the grease such that one daring entrant would be capable of reaching the heights that would gain him the coveted prize. Meanwhile, Elizabeth would be joined by her twin sons, Harvey and Clyde, who came from Georgetown for the holiday to deal with the rush of customers. In fine enterprising fashion she had created an activity that drew in swarms of people, and the few bottles of rum offered as trophies were more than compensated by the purchases made in the shop by those who thirsted for sports and spirits.

These holidays were the only times that Mondays were busy with sales. Normally it was during the slack period between Monday and Thursday that Edward and his family prepared the goods for sale. They would be busy washing bottles, filling bottles of rum as well as bottling other liquids – coconut oil poured from tins, vinegar from demi-johns and kerosene from tall cans. Then there was the task of slicing the long corks in half with a diagonal cut so as to obtain a tapered end to facilitate insertion into the bottles. Other duties included wrapping one- and two-pound parcels of sugar and flour, making cigarettes, preparing paper funnels. It was an almost never-ending list of tasks to be completed but that was the nature of the business of running a small dry goods shop in the countryside. The 1930s was not a prosperous period and the income generated from the shop was not great. This was also the time that their eldest son Wilfred, known as Fred, decided to become a doctor, after having some exposure to the medical profession through a job at Georgetown hospital. Edward and Elizabeth continued as best as they could to generate the funds needed for his medical training in the United States, and the other children (and even cousins) were asked to contribute whatever pennies they could spare toward his education. It was a hard tough life but one that they all endured to achieve the ambition of having at least one educated person in the family.

Baker's Man

Donald Tang
as told to Trev Sue-A-Quan

Tang A-chi arrived in Guyana on 13 April 1861 aboard the *Red Riding Hood* and was allotted to Plantation Caledonia in Essequibo as an indentured field laborer. He had five sons, the fourth-born being Reuben Charles Tang, born in 1876. R.C. Tang married Sarah Lam and operated a general store in Essequibo. They had six children, the boys being Peter, Simeon and Donald, who all became prominent businessmen in Georgetown.

* * * * * * *

Tangs' Bakery was started in the mid-1920s as an enterprise spearheaded by Simeon Tang with the assistance of his eldest brother Peter, and their widowed mother. The bakery, located at Leopold and George streets, was formerly owned by the Fung family but was bought over by the Tangs. Simeon had been working before as a bookkeeper for Garnett & Co. but the family made a decision to venture out on their own in the bakery business. Peter was then becoming established at his own business – Tang's Drug Store – and provided the main financial support. Even before he was a teenager, Donald, the youngest brother, helped in running the bakery. His first assignment, after arriving at 5 a.m., was to sign in the employees as they reported for the day shift. He sat at a desk and checked off their names and noted the time of arrival on the timesheet for employees. Then he had to go off to school. Over the years he went to Dolphin's School and then to St. Stanislaus College.

In the beginning, the bakery employed 57 people, divided into a day shift and a night shift. As the number of customers for the bakery's goods grew, the number of workers expanded to some 200. In practice, the baking operations began with the night shift. Simeon would be the one checking them in as they arrived between 4 and 6 p.m. The making of the dough that would become bread, and preparation of the ingredients for cakes and pies, were the important jobs for the night shift workers. There were large machines available for mixing and kneading the dough, which then had to be left for four hours to rise. There was still a lot of manual work involved – weighing the correct amount of dough that was then paced in individual baking pans to produce loaf bread, sandwich loaves and other types of bread. These preparations continued until the day shift took over.

The day shift began about 6 a.m. although some employees reported earlier depending on the nature of the tasks for which they were responsible. At one time, during the early period of the Tangs' involvement with the bakery, the day shift began at 4:30 a.m. However, the workers went on strike and the starting hour for the day shift was moved back to the later hour. But the bread making process could not be altered to suit the shift schedule and so the night shift had to take over some of the work formerly done by the day shift.

As Donald grew to manhood he took on more responsibilities in running the bakery. He learned to roll the dough to make different kinds of bread, and with a quick turn of the wrist, was able to turn out breads of a specific shape. One of the customers' favorites was the penny loaf that was tapered to a nipple at each end. "Antigua" was the name given to larger versions of the penny loaf, varying up to six cents in price. Platted loaves were another item requiring some dexterity. The three-plait loaves consisted of three strands that were platted in a manner similar to braiding hair. Larger plait loaves had two double strands on the bottom and three strands on top. These breads were popular in homes whereas large sandwich loaves would be needed by hotels to make toast.

There were boys as well as men working in the bakery, the boys taking on the less demanding tasks such as moving the baking pans to the desired locations, greasing them, and later delivering the bread to customers. The delivery of bread required a large number of boys, especially for the morning session when the bread and pastries had to arrive at various restaurants, cookshops, cakeshops, hotels and merchandising outlets in time for the early-rising customers to get breakfast. Deliveries also had to be made in time to catch the morning train and ferry that took the baked goods to the countryside. The clients were scattered all over the city and meant that a few hundred boys would be involved distributing bread. The bicycle was the main means of transport in the early days, and each had a large, square wicker basket mounted above the front wheel. The loaves of bread would be counted and stacked in the basket, then covered with a flour bag as the young cyclists wheeled their way across town, starting at about 6 a.m. Of course, a close accounting had to be kept of what bread went to what place. Later, vans were bought to do the delivery. The boys would sometimes be as young a 10 years of age when they joined Tangs' Bakery and, perhaps at age 15, would be assigned to other tasks, such as rolling dough, if they wanted to continue doing bakery work.

The day shift typically ended at noon but there was still a lot more work to be done. All the equipment had to be thoroughly washed and working surfaces cleaned. If there were any residual dough that became mixed with fresh dough the result would be the formation of "rope," and the dough would have to be discarded. Boys working on the afternoon shift did the cleaning and the home deliveries. The orders that were earlier placed by phone would be recorded and the required items packed into the wicker baskets. The boys were responsible for delivery only and the collection of payment was done by a couple clerks who went around with their accounting records in hand. Some of the families would also come by to the bakery to pay monthly, or sometimes weekly.

The shops and retail outlets for baked goods earned 20% of the price of the items. Any bread that was left over unsold would be picked up by the delivery boys a day or two later and brought back to the bakery for full credit. In those days no preservatives were used in making the bread. The unused bread then became the starting ingredients for other baked goods. One such item was Scotch buns, familiarly called "bull stones," in which the old bread was dried, ground up, and mixed with sugar and lard. A ball of this mixture would be covered with a piece of fresh dough to produce a round bun. The secret to success was the three holes pierced into the Scotch bun to let it 'breathe' and prevent it from disintegrating or exploding. Chester was another item made with a moist mixture of crumbled bread, sugar and lard. The rectangular pans of chester would be left overnight to allow a little fermentation, and then baked. Chester was also called "crepe sole." Yet another product utilizing wet stale bread required the addition of molasses to produce a sweet, black filling. This was placed in a large baking pan and covered with a piecrust. The resulting "queen cake' was a rich-tasting delicacy. Perhaps if Marie Antoinette knew of this recipe, her call to let them eat cake might not have caused her to lose her head. One other popular item with the masses was bread pudding, where once again the starting material was stale bread, but usually as slices.

Tangs' bakery produced a number of pastries and cakes, and the larger number of employees in the cake department reflected the greater amount of labor needed to make these products. The filling for pinetarts had to be made from fresh pineapples. The pinetarts could be recognized by their distinctive triangular shape. Guava tarts, on the other hand, were round. Chinese black-bean cakes, or towsa, were made with thin layers of very flaky pastry, and traditionally bore a few dots at the center, made with red food coloring. "White eye," made with dough sweetened with white sugar, took the shape of a dome. Then there were coconut tarts, sweet hearts, lemon biscuits and other puddings and pies.

The cake section also produced items with a salty flavor, such as meat pies, commonly called patties, cheese pies, cheese rolls and cheese straws. Edam cheese from Holland was bought from Resaul Maraj or Amalgamated Groceries, and came in large, thick circular discs coated with red wax. It was called Dutch-head cheese. Baked pastries, sweet and salt, were sold from a small counter at the front of the bakery, where soft drinks were also available. Many schoolchildren from the neighborhood would come by for a quick lunch, or a snack after school.

On occasion there were products made without using flour as an ingredient. Cassava pone, for example, was made with grated cassava. However this was made at the customer's request, perhaps for a social gathering or party.

In addition to baking for their business customers, the Tang brothers also baked for individuals who brought their cakes, pastries and buns that were too large or too numerous to fit into an oven at home. A typical request would be to bake a black cake (a traditional cake made with molasses and a lot of fruits and liquor) that was popular as a wedding cake, or as a festive cake, particularly at Christmas. At a later time the cake section at Tangs' even undertook the icing of cakes.

There were two ovens in the bakery, one having revolving racks. Each pan of dough was placed on the rack as it came past the oven door. The pan would then be conveyed up and into the oven for baking and by the time two rotations of the rack were completed the bread would be cooked and ready for removal. The second oven was a conventional oven requiring a peel to insert and remove the pans. The peel had a flat spade-like end, looking rather like a broad oar with an extra-long handle, which allowed the items to be placed deep in the oven.

Before the ovens were lit, the ashes from the previous baking were cleaned out. The ovens were then fired up using "ton wood," long big pieces of wallaba that were cut it up into small sections. This was done by the employees on the premises, using a saw. The wallaba was brought by a supplier of firewood, one such person being Sam Low who had a grant in the forest. Sam Low would deliver the wood by dray cart. The firing of the ovens required some skill because it was the amount of wallaba stoked into the furnace that determined the temperature of the oven – too much wood would cause the bread to burn. When the day's baking was done, a heap of ashes remained and was removed after it had cooled off. The man in charge cleaned out the ashes with long-handled shovels and piled them up in the yard. This material did not go to waste because the townsfolk would come by to take some away to add to their gardens or use as a scrubbing agent for blackened pots and pans. It was an excellent fertilizer that also killed slugs.

Tangs' Bakery was one of several bakeries in Georgetown, some others being Mansell's, Haly's and Harlequin's. Most of the breads and cakes made by these competitors were similar, but Tangs' was the first to introduce butterflaps in Guyana. It happened by chance when a cricket team from Trinidad was visiting Guyana sometime about 1934. Among the players was a person named Crichlow, who happened to be a baker in his non-cricketing life. Because of Donald's interest in sport he managed to meet with the touring baker and learnt about butterflaps being made in Trinidad. This consisted of a small, circular piece of dough that was first buttered and then opposite edges folded over to the center like flaps. Two holes (like eyes) were punched to release any buildup of gas within the butterflap during baking. This product became very popular with customers.

Another item with "sporting" connections was the tennis roll. These were made by every baker in town and its name is said to be derived from the fact that it is made by rolling up the dough into a ball, the size of which was comparable to that of a tennis ball. In making the tennis roll, the dough had to be kneaded for a longer time to compact it into a tighter texture.

For a while Tangs' Bakery obtained its supply of flour from local importers, Resaul Maraj being one of them. The bags of flour were delivered by dray cart every two days or so. Later, because of the large quantities being used, the Tang brothers found it more economical to import directly from Canada. Purchase orders were placed through direct correspondence, and when the flour arrived and had cleared Customs, the Tangs' Bakery van would go to the wharf to pick up the 300 to 500 bags of flour in each shipment. At Christmas time, up to 1000 bags would be required to meet the increased demand for breads and cakes. The shipments included stocks of more highly refined flour, called "super flour," that was needed for making cakes. At the bakery the bags of flour were taken up by mechanical lift to the storeroom, essentially a loft high above the work area.

Of those working on each shift, some 12 or 13 (a baker's dozen) would be assigned to make bread while the remaining would be in the cake department. Exactly who would be working in which department would be determined by the level of skill of the individual and by prevailing needs. Some of the bakers rose up the ranks while others were hired, based on prior experience. One such person was named Linton, and he was like an uncut jewel that needed to be refined. There was much strong and truly unrefined language exchanged between the Tang brothers and Linton, but he learned to do the work in Tang style and became a skilled foreman of the shift.

Tangs' Bakery operated seven days a week and Donald became familiar with every aspect of the operations, even going out to collect payments for home deliveries. It was hard and hot work and he had to learn to love the bakery. He felt that he didn't have enough time to play tennis, his favorite sport. However, it provided a good livelihood and Tangs' Bakery became one of the well-liked bakeries in Georgetown.

Hand Laundry

Ada Akai
as told to Trev Sue-A-Quan

Ada Akai gained her Bachelor's degree in geography at Leicester University. She returned to Guyana and taught at Queen's College, where she eventually became Deputy Head. She also taught at University of Guyana and took a major role in curriculum development for this as well as for other Caribbean universities.

* * * * * * * *

My father was one of the new Chinese immigrants who came in the early years of the 20th century to Guyana. The term "new" is a comparative one taken in contrast with the community of "old" Chinese descended from the indentured laborers who had arrived in the mid-19th century. By the turn of the century these descendants had become established in the colony mainly as shopkeepers, traders and owners of small businesses. Their success in these occupations was an encouragement for the new Chinese immigrants, some of them relatives or fellow villagers invited by members of the old Chinese community to come to help them in their business operations. Others decided to embark on a journey to Guyana in hopes of obtaining a better life. Typically the new Chinese, who came to be called "Hong Kong Chinese," worked for the local Chinese businesses before venturing out to set up their own enterprises.

I cannot recall where my father worked when he first arrived in Guyana, only that he operated a laundry in New Amsterdam, the second largest city in Guyana and the capital of Berbice County. This laundry was the business with which I became familiar as a youth since it was located on the lower level of our home and we children were often required to lend a hand in its operation. The name of the establishment was Wing Lee Laundry and that has always been a mystery to me because the family name has no association with either Wing or Lee. I suppose he must have acquired the laundry from a previous Chinese operator and continued using the business name. A wooden plaque with the name

WING LEE LAUNDRY hung prominently above the door of the business.

The Akai family with seven of nine children. Ada Akai, the eldest, is on the right. *Irene Akai.*

Wing Lee Laundry was by no means a big establishment. In the reception area there was room for only four or five people to stand although one of them could sit on the solitary seat specially made by my father for the comfort of his customers. With my father on one side of the counter and the customer seated on the other side a conversation would ensue that passed the time away. It always was a complete amazement to me that Father could carry on a dialogue so extensively in his halting English and that the customer remained for so long to exchange in the banter. There were some who apparently came by just for a chat, including a large, strong fellow of African origin who would sometimes bring along a turtle or two for our dinner and on occasion leave a shirt to be laundered.

The laundry opened for business at 8:00 a.m. and would remain open until well after sundown, frequently until 9:00 p.m. during the busy days. The customer would typically bring in the items to be laundered in a paper bag. (The brown bag was one of those ubiquitous items that Guyanese folks used for carrying a variety of things.) Father would issue a claim ticket that he made himself by cutting sheets of blank paper into small-sized bits on which he inscribed the name of the laundry. He then wrote on the claim ticket a notation in Chinese to identify the owner who could pick up the finished laundry in a week. This was the first step in the laundry operations. Father would then bring out his inkstone and, with a bit of water added, use a small stone rod to rub the inkstone gently with an easy circular motion to produce a black ink of moderate consistency – not too watery and not too thick. He took up his Chinese calligraphy brush and wrote an appropriate identification mark on the label (or unexposed corner) of the item to be laundered. Only he knew the meaning of the secret codes that he put on those labels and I would not be surprised if he assigned Chinese names to his various customers or else used a suitable adjective or two that described their features. I knew that Indian ink had the reputation of being permanent but Father's Chinese ink was really something else and stood up well to the rigors of the washing process. The colored clothes would be separated from the whites and placed in baskets awaiting washing day.

Two days a week were normally assigned as washing days. Work began at 7:00 or 8:00 in the morning and normally the washing could be all done by noon although there would be busy days when work stretched into the afternoon. The baskets of dirty clothes would be taken outside where, along the side of the house, there was a long scrubbing table. It was made of concrete with a flat wooden platform about four feet wide fitted on the top. On the outer edges were small gutters to take the wastewater to the drain. Above the table was a tap that supplied the water for the operation. The water flowed into a bucket in which the scrubbing brushes would be dipped so as to slop water on the garment being washed. A few hired hands, usually black women from the city, did the scrubbing work. One of the employees – we called her Nana – also helped with household chores and became a close friend and companion. She was fed by my mother who would typically have food on hand for a number of guests if they were to appear without notice. Nana and the others would use a piece of soap cut from a long bar made specifically for washing clothes. Although washboards with their rows of ridges on the surface were commonly used in households, we did not use them, relying purely on muscle power and the scrubbing brush. The scrubbed clothes were next dipped in a bucket of fresh water and rung by hand to remove as much water as possible. They were put into baskets to be taken to the clothes lines strung up in the back yard. On rainy days there would be a rush of people scrambling to gather in the clothes, then they had to wait for a later opportunity to take the clothes out to be hung up to dry.

The cleaning of the white clothes required a different method of approach. Outdoors, not far from the scrubbing table, my father had built an oven out of concrete. It was cylindrical in shape about 18 inches high on which a drum could be mounted. On one side of the cylinder was an opening where pieces of cut wood or charcoal could be inserted to fire up the oven. The wood originated from up the Berbice River and would be delivered by donkey cart to the parapet outside our house. From there we fetched the wood and stacked the pieces against the side of the house ready for use in stoking the oven. Into the drum went the dirty white clothes and soap added. Father would stand above the bubbling drum wielding a long wooden pole to provide the agitation needed to get the clothes clean, and sometimes he had to struggle to get the clothes turned around. When he felt that a certain item had become clean he would use the same wand to lift the garment out of the drum and deftly drop it into cold clean water contained in a wooden half-cask. It was a hot and tiring task that literally was sweat work. The whites were also dipped in "blue" which was solution of Rickett's Blue that imparted a whiter finish to the clothes. This product came as packet of small, square slabs each about a quarter of an inch thick. A slab of Blue would be put into a cloth pouch and dipped into a bucket of fresh water. The blue seeped out much like tea from a teabag and it took a trained eye to determine when the correct hue of blueness was reached. On some occasions a gentle squeeze of the pouch was needed to attain the desired degree of blue tinge in the water.

If the clothes needed to be starched they would be dipped in starch water before being put out to dry. The starch was produced from bitter cassava and sold in the market by the pint although on occasion a traveling vendor would come by offering starch for sale. The starch was basically a powder but with some lumps in it. The starch was put in a bowl with a little bit of cold water and the lumps crushed and stirred to make a smooth paste. My mother would add a small bit of "soft grease" to make the ironing process smoother. Although it had the appearance of a candle, the soft grease was, as the name implies, a pliable wax and in our minds it was much more than was described by the two parts of the name. Rather, it was a commodity made for the laundry process and was more commonly called "sof-grease" and regarded as a specific item of utility in a comparable way that "toothpaste" would typically be envisioned as an oral hygiene product rather than a paste for teeth (or a tooth, as the case may be). To the thick mixture of starch and soft grease boiling water was added to produce a clear starch solution of desired strength. This then went into the "starch bucket" in which the items to be starched were dipped. For handkerchiefs the starch solution had to be mild whereas for collars a thicker consistency was required to obtain a stiff almost board-like finish. The technique of preparing the correct starch solution was one that was acquired by experience.

Ironing was also carried out twice a week but on different days from when washing was done. The mainstay of the ironing process was the furnace, another creation of my father. Like the oven used for washing the furnace consisted of a cylindrical concrete base some 18 inches high topped by a thick flat iron plate. The furnace was located in the kitchen area right behind the wall separating the shop from the private section of the premises. Ironing days were a time of considerable heat stress when both the furnace and the kitchen stove, also fired with wood, were going full blast. Some 7 or 8 irons were placed on the furnace to be heated. The irons were old fashioned with an almost triangular shape similar to than of a modern iron, only with a smaller working surface and much heavier, being made of solid black iron. The wooden handle on each iron was elevated some eight inches from the hot surface presumably to keep the handle as well as the hand a respectable distance from the heat. The ironing was done on two tables some 4 feet wide and mounted along the walls. On each table, a padding, made up of an old blanket topped by a large cotton sheet, was used to provide the soft smooth surface needed for the ironing process. Prior to the actual ironing step the baskets of dry clothes that were stored under the pressing tables were pulled out and the laundry items prepared by sprinkling them with water and rolling them up into bundles that took on the appearance of loaves of unbaked bread. In this way the moisture would permeate the garment to produce a consistent level of dampness. The bundles were left to sit for a couple hours or so while the furnace was being fired. With insufficient moisture the ironing process would not go smoothly and produced a "rough dry" finish.

The person doing the ironing would pick up one of the hot irons and put the free hand a few inches away from the hot surface to test the amount of heat being radiated. The iron was then rubbed on a piece of cloth lying on the pressing table so as to remove any particles of dirt adhering to the surface. These cloth pieces would be discarded after they had accumulated their quota of dirt. Another very important piece of fabric was the "pressing cloth" which was a section taken from a white cotton sheet and measured some 36 inches by 24 inches. This would be moistened and placed on the garment to produce a steaming effect during the ironing of some of the articles, particularly to obtain a knife-edge crease on a pair of trousers. The pressing cloth was also used for the first few strokes of the hot iron to gauge the temperature and smoothness of the iron. If the iron did not glide well it would be upturned and a dab of sof-grease placed on the hot surface and distributed evenly by a few passes on the pressing cloth. When the quantity of steam rising from the ironing strokes diminished and the iron glided less smoothly over the fabric the worker knew it was time to switch to a new hot iron. For shirts the cuffs were ironed first then the attached collars followed by the body. The shirt was then buttoned, folded neatly such that it appeared to be a brand-new purchase from the box and set aside to be wrapped with the other items belonging to the owner.

The ironing of trousers followed a set sequence. The garment would be held up with the back of the trousers toward the ironer who would shake it a bit to displace any folds or crumples. By placing it forward onto the pressing table the worker was first able to iron the back hip panels. The trousers were then turned over and the front hip panels ironed. The trousers were then lifted up, rearranged to a side-view orientation and laid out on the pressing table. The upper leg of the trousers was turned back to lie over the just-pressed hip panels and the lower leg set straight by lining up the seams on the outer and inner sides of the pant leg. A few tugs and hand caresses would be employed to smooth out the leg of the trousers, after which the pressing cloth was put in place to achieve the desired long straight crease. The garment would then be turned over to allow the outside of the same leg to be pressed and the whole process would be repeated for the other leg of the trousers. The finished piece would be examined to see that all parts were properly ironed, and, if need be, the hip panels were given a touch-up pressing with caution exercised not to disturb the beautiful creases on the pant legs. The pressed clothes would be stacked up and my father then sorted them according to the customer name, wrapping the finished collection in paper tied up with string. On the outside he wrote a notation in Chinese together with the payment to be collected. The parcels were stored on shelves on the wall behind the counter, the lightest ones in one section and the big bundles in another.

With operations going full swing ironing day was filled with a variety of sounds – the "thump" of the hot iron hitting the pressing table, the "hiss" of the steam rising from the pressing cloth, the "clank" of the iron being returned to the furnace, the "clunk" of the furnace being stoked with wood and the ongoing chatter of the workers. Along with these came the smell of wool wafting through the air that mingled with the aroma of the dishes my mother was busily preparing. On an ordinary day the ironing went on until 6:00 or even 8:00 p.m. but there were times when ironing carried on to 9:00 or 10:00 p.m. because of a heavy workload. On those days the counter was also pressed into service as an additional ironing surface.

There would be an unusually high demand for laundry services following Pagwah Day.[1] There would of course be some enthusiastic revelers going around with basins or buckets filled with abhir anointing others with much more than a sprinkle of the red dye. The result was that many people would become drenched from head to foot with the ruby liquid. In addition it was the Hindu custom for white clothing to be worn on this festive day and the sugar plantation owners and managers drew no exception in this case, coming out in their white flannels and suits which, at the end of the day, were transformed into various shades of pink and red. Invariably, on the next day, our laundry would have a number of drivers, or work-gang foremen on the sugar estates, come by with a load of off-color clothes that required restoration to their original pristine white state.

The estate owners and managers were among our regular customers because of their need for neatly pressed shirts, trousers and suits although they did employ washer-women to take care of underclothing, dresses and everyday items. When the time came to pick up the laundry the claim ticket would be handed over and my father would be able to identify the appropriate parcel. Sometimes when we children were around he would point out a specific parcel and tell us to "bring that one." Not having been tutored in Chinese we were always amazed by his ability to recognize which parcels belonged to which customer but that was Father's secret. The charge for laundry services was a few cents per item and my father calculated the total in his head although he was adept with using an abacus, which I suppose he used for calculating grander totals such as the receipts for the day or week. The money received for the finished laundry went into a drawer below the counter. If someone came by without a claim receipt it was not difficult to find the correct parcel after the owner described the kind of items involved. This was where the sorting of the parcels on the shelves based on size came in handy. The customer was always forewarned that uncollected items would be sold off for the benefit of the laundry. Whenever it appeared that a parcel was lingering on the shelf it would be shifted to the top shelf. After a few months my father would remove the parcel and sell the contents. Presumably the owner died or moved away forgetting his clothes but in reality such incidents of unclaimed laundry were rare.

---

[1] This is a Hindu religious holiday that takes place in March, the exact date depending on the lunar cycle. Celebrating the triumph of good over evil, the main activity during Pagwah Day is the sprinkling of a red dye. The herbal dye, called abhir (or abeer), would be carried about in bowls and deep dishes and handfuls of the dye would be cast at persons nearby in a mutual splashing ritual.

Ada Akai with four of her brothers at their home in New
Amsterdam. *Irene Akai.*

The laundry was a part of our home and a part of our life. We
children were involved in the operations from fetching wood to handing
over the packets of finished laundry. We endured the rigors and
discipline necessary for the laundry operations. On occasion a well-
known person would stop by and we would peer through the holes in the
wall between the shelves and try to listen in as Father engaged in
conversation. But my father was also conscious of the need to give us a
good education so our schoolwork was given priority. But even in this
respect the laundry played a part because the pressing tables were also the
place where we did our homework.

Bee Queen

Alice Singh, née Loo, and Arif Rayman

On 21 May 1885, John Cheong, aged 22, married 17-year-old Eliza Fung Fo-kyan at All Saints Anglican Church, New Amsterdam, Berbice. Family accounts indicate that Eliza was a girl of five when she arrived in British Guiana. By the time she died in 1962, at the age of 95, she had shared the experiences of five generations of Chinese settlers in the colony. Recollections of her life have been provided by her niece, Alice Singh, daughter of John Cheong's sister, Louisa, and by Arif Rayman, Eliza's great-grandson.

The Cheong family clan is fairly representative of the way the Chinese have become integrated with other races in Guyanese society. In three generations the Cheongs have formed inter-racial unions with people of various ethnic origins who make up the majority of Guyana's population. Marriages with other Chinese have been predominant, in association with surnames such as Chu, Loo, Kum, Seow, Hing, Lee, Ting-A-Kee, Kong, Low, Chee, Phang-Hing, and Leung. Unions with people of African, Indian, Amerindian and Portuguese origin, among others, have also occurred resulting in descendants bearing the names Van Couten, Prabhu-Das, Denny, Singh, Saunders, Rayman, Joseph, Wellington, Maloney, and Laurent. This racial mixing has continued through subsequent generations, resulting in people with Chinese roots who have a range of complexions, and surnames that would hardly be recognized as Chinese.

* * * * * *

Not long after they were married, Eliza and John moved to 8 Croal Street in Georgetown where they lived with John's parents, Cheong Ling-shim, and his wife, Lean Shee. Ling-shim was a merchant and, with Lean Shee, carried on business in the Stabroek Market, with imports from China being among the commodities. John's younger siblings and some of their offspring made up the extended family household, which was a "typical" Chinese home, as far as customs and relations with others were concerned. They were willing hosts to relatives and friends from out of town, and especially for children who were sent to Georgetown for their education. John and Eliza had five children of their own but only one, Augustus Joseph, often referred to as A.J. Cheong or simply as A.J., born in 1888, survived to adulthood. John Cheong progressed in the business world and became a Commission Agent. He was well respected in the Chinese community.

Eliza Cheong was well aware that her husband had fathered children with other women, who were not of Chinese origin, but that did not bother her. Somehow, she accepted the past Chinese tradition of a husband, and especially a successful one, having subsidiary wives. Perhaps this attitude was acquired by living at the Chinese settlement at Hopetown, on Camoonie Creek, where old customs prevailed. Eliza knew that she was the number one wife, queen of the household, and that was good enough; she treated all her husband's children as one family. There was no bickering over the matter and harmony prevailed among the children when they gathered together. Testimony of how well Eliza achieved this harmony is exemplified by the fact that Mrs. Winnifred Van Couten, the last surviving daughter of her husband John Cheong, who lives in Aruba, is a revered aunt of her great-grandsons living in Canada and the UK.

In the late 19th century, a few successful Chinese sought membership in the English-styled Masonic Lodges but while they were congratulated for their interest in masonry, they were directed to seek membership in the Mount Olive Lodge, an organization primarily serving the mulatto community. They did so, and in 1892 John Cheong was the first Chinese initiated into the Mount Olive Lodge. He later became Master of the Mount Olive Lodge in 1901. The Chinese found that their applications for membership were taking a long time for processing while the mulattoes were quickly accepted.

The Chinese decided to start their own lodge and the Silent Temple Lodge, aptly named to represent the Chinese characteristics of silence and circumspection, came into being. A warrant was issued in September 1907 and the lodge was constituted in January 1908 with John Cheong as its first Master. The founding members were John Cheong, Commission Agent; Benjamin Hunter Ho-A-Hing, businessman; John Augustus Too-Chung, accountant; Evan Wong, businessman; Job Wong, businessman; Manuel U. Hing, jeweller; and Joseph Mason Hunter (brother of Benjamin Ho-A-Hing), mercantile clerk.

A.J. Cheong followed in his father's footsteps. He submitted his petition to join the Silent Temple Lodge in 1915 and was installed as the Worshipful Master in 1924. The Lodge was dedicated to performing charitable work, and made donations to charitable organizations, offered scholarships to needy and deserving students, and provided funds for disaster relief.

A.J. Cheong joined the civil service and became a surveyor working mostly in the interior of British Guiana. He rose swiftly in the service and at the time of his application for membership in the Lodge he was stationed in Morawhanna in the North West District. He was promoted deputy head of the British Guiana/Brazil Boundary Commission and died in the Rupununi in 1934 while still engaged in demarcating the boundary between the two countries. When A.J.'s first wife, Olivia Rodrigues, died in 1916 she left a young daughter, Dorothy, popularly known as Doots, in the care of her grandmother Eliza. It was a close relationship that continued until Eliza, or Popo in the Chinese form of address, died in 1962. A.J. was married a second time to Laura Hing, the daughter of his father's friend Manuel U. Hing, one of the founders of the Silent Temple Lodge, and had four children from this second union.

On one occasion when A.J. Cheong was working in the interior, Eliza satisfied her curiosity and spirit of adventure by joining her son on one of his expeditions, in order to visit Kaieteur Falls. But it was not to be, as she took ill with blackwater fever at Tumatumari and had to be rushed back to Georgetown for urgent treatment. What A.J.'s mother did not achieve, his daughter Doots did in 1943 when she visited Kaieteur Falls with a party of relatives. It was very touching to see the Amerindians at the Tukeit encampment, at the foot of the falls, gather with curiosity and reverence to "view" Doots when word got around that she was Papa Cheong's daughter. It was obvious to those of us looking on that he had been a great influence in their lives and was much loved.

Doots had a genuine love for the interior and when, in the fifties, an opportunity presented itself to acquire a business interest at Issano in the Mazaruni with one of Popo's nephews (her sister's son), she took it. She used the opportunity to lead several trips to Kaieteur and other places of interest in the interior. One of A.J.'s sons, Tony, and also his grandson, Gary Farouk Rayman, followed in his footsteps and became surveyors in the Department of Lands and Mines. They both subsequently worked as surveyors in the Bahamas and helped in the development of those islands.

Eliza was widowed in 1913 and succeeded to the matriarchy of the Cheong family when her mother-in-law, Lean Shee, a widow since 1910, died in 1917. Shortly thereafter she moved out of the city to West Coast Demerara. After a short stay at Vreed-en-Hoop, the terminus of the Demerara River ferry, she settled in the adjoining village of Best. The house at Best became a home for her granddaughter Doots, her niece Olga, and a haven for the siblings of her husband John and their many children. Many came, lived and went on their way.

Popo was small in stature but strong physically and mentally. She was self-taught and self-reliant in many respects. She became well known for the apiary of about two-dozen wooden beehives she established soon after she moved into the village. She was a skilled beekeeper and performed all the tasks necessary to maintain the hives and the health of the bees. We do know that she did not receive any training from the agriculture extension department and can only assume that she acquired and developed her skills while living in the community of Camoonie Creek.

Popo Eliza Cheong in front of a tamarind tree. *Alice Singh*

Honey extraction day was a time of great excitement for all the kids in the family. Popo would be decked out with a hat from which a protective mesh was draped, over her neck and shoulders and with the smoker[1] in hand she would send a few puffs of smoke into the hive to stun the bees. She would then reach into the hive and remove the racks holding the honeycombs and take them over to the extractor. Everyone would stare in wonder at the sight of the bees that alighted on Popo's hands without stinging her. She did admit to being stung a few times but seemed to have developed an immunity from stings and at the same time had no dread for the fearful stings.

At the extractor, the outer layer of wax that sealed the honey in the combs was sliced off to open up the cells now dripping with honey. The racks were placed in the cages of the extractor, four at a time and the handle of the extractor turned, with each child wanting a chance at the handle and the reward of a piece of the sliced honey comb, filled with honey. This would be squeezed or sucked with great delight and relish. Some of the wax from this operation would be retained for making little wax toys. The centrifugal force of rotation forced the honey out of the combs and it drained to the bottom of the drum. When sufficient honey had collected, the stopcock was opened and the honey was drained into demijohns for bottling at a later stage. The frame, now empty of honey, would be returned to the hive and a new set of four brought for extraction. There was constant activity between hives and extractor. When the extractor was brought out from storage it had to be inspected carefully because on one occasion yawories had found it a wonderful place to make a nest for young ones.

While bottling time was an occasion of great activity, it was not as exciting as extraction day. The demijohns would be emptied into containers and, by the use of funnels, cleaned bottles would be filled,

---

[1] A special can for generating smoke, with a bellows that delivered puffs of smoke.

corked and the tops dipped into molten sealing wax. Labels were pasted to the bottles and the product was ready for market. This cottage industry involved a lot of activities like washing, filling, corking and labeling of bottles as well as the preparation of paste and hot sealing wax. The usual outlets for the honey were mostly drug stores and some groceries. The extraction and bottling operations involved the whole family, young and old, but the more difficult and skillful activities were performed only by Popo.

When the honeycombs on the frames were exhausted, the wax on each frame had to be renewed. A layer of wafer-thin wax was purchased and was placed on the wooden frame strung with about four slender wires by Popo. She was skilled in replacing the wires, plus all other activities involving beekeeping, such as dealing with swarms. When the bees swarmed and nested on a nearby tree, Popo would get her long stick with a mesh net attached to the end of it. She would gather the bees, making sure that she trapped the queen bee, and take them over to an empty hive that awaited a new colony. The bees obtained an ample supply of pollen from the flowers on the pigeon-pea plants, grown by the villagers to supplement their income, and from the courida trees growing on the foreshore, generally referred to as the crab bush. The roots of these trees, like those of the mangrove, anchored the soil and minimized the eroding effect of the ocean waves.

The wax from the beekeeping operation was treated and used for many purposes. The wax was placed in a special glass box that allowed the sun to both bleach and melt it. When the molten wax was sufficiently bleached – sometimes golden in color or nearly white if bleached long enough – it was poured into moulds creating blocks of golden or white beeswax. The beeswax came in useful for greasing the end of a length of thread so that it could easily pass through the eye of a needle. Another use was to grease flat irons while ironing clothes, as well as to coat the irons before putting them away so as to prevent them from going rusty in the high tropical humidity. Almost every household would have a piece of wax available that would come in handy as a sealing agent, a rub for insect bites, scratches and bruises, and a lubricant for the moving parts of toys and machines.

Popo owned a donkey and cart and on Fridays would drive – or more often would have one of her younger relations drive – to the grocery at Vreed-en-Hoop to buy the weekly rations such as rice, flour, oil, etc. On Saturdays, Popo would go on the cart to the market at Pouderoyen. Some of the villagers would ask her to take goods to the market for them, which she willingly did as a good neighbor since the cart was rarely fully laden. These were happy occasions for the younger kids to go the market, which was two miles away. Travel was leisurely and a good time was had by all.

In the church record for her wedding, Eliza had signed her name with an X because she did not receive an education in English, and was illiterate. Her great-grandchildren would read her the comic strips from newspapers, magazines and comic books and she would be able to relate the story back to others accurately, as if she were reading the text. With tutoring from the younger generation, she learned to sign her name so that she was able to affix her signature to documents. Learning new skills was a life long process for Popo.

Her niece Alice lived with Popo because Alice's mother had died when she was just two years old. She was the last of some fourteen children born to Louisa, and so her father Alexander Loo-Chan-Nam put her in the care of her aunt. From time to time, especially during vacations, Alice would return to Leonora where her father ran a grocery with help from Alice's older brothers. When she was there, Alice helped with some of the easier tasks, such as preparing the onions for sale by peeling off the flaking outer skins. She also made little packets of baking soda, a necessary ingredient in the making of roti, that were then inserted into the folds of a two-pound parcels of flour, as a bonus for the customer

As the shop at Leonora was separated from Georgetown by the Demerara River, Alexander or a representative of the family would make purchases from wholesale suppliers in town, and make arrangements for delivery via ferry and train. He might perhaps stop by at Kon-Sue's shop for a snack of Chinese delicacies such as towsa or icing-glass and have a chat before heading back to the West Coast. The purchases were delivered to the ferry and then were transferred to the goods train and sent to the Leonora railway station where it was stored in the bond until collected. The waybills for the goods would be given to the regular deliveryman who would set out with a dray cart to collect the goods for the Loo shop and his other clients. The customer's copy of the waybill would be checked with the copy of the waybill attached to the shipment indicating the nature of the consignment, purchaser and destination. Over time, this procedure became routine for the shopkeepers, the deliverymen and the stationmasters. Alice enjoyed the times she spent at Leonora, but it was with Popo that she grew up, and received her primary and secondary education, the latter at Bishop's High School. She became a teacher, married and raised two children.

Popo was of Hakka origin and throughout her life she wore the traditional black or dark blue smock and trousers of the Hakkas. She made these garments, including the buttons, herself. The button making was interesting to the younger generation who were exposed to what it was like back in China. Starting with narrow strips of cloth, she would wind each tightly around to make the knob of the cloth button that would be inserted into the loop, which she also made from pieces of cloth. She used a hand-cranked Jones sewing machine to make her clothes, complete with embroidered edges. She was a familiar sight in a community where she was the only one dressed in the garb in which she was most comfortable.

Popo's lifestyle, providing for members of the extended family, was possible through a generous allowance from her only son. With his untimely death in 1934, and the marriage of her granddaughter shortly thereafter, it was no longer possible to provide a home for the extended family. In spite of these circumstances she continued to provide a home for Alice and another nephew for whom she felt responsible. You look after those who are in need, was her motto. In 1937, Doots and her growing family became the principal members of the Best household and continued to be so until 1942 when the family made a short move to Vreed-en-Hoop to live in the property of Doots' husband Ayube Rayman. It was in this new home that Popo was to spend the last twenty years of her life – with Doots and her six great grandsons of whom Arif was the fifth born.

When the family moved to Vreed-en-Hoop, the property at Best was rented to a nephew who had lived there in his younger days. Popo kept her bees on the property and she and one of her young great grandsons would often be seen walking the mile along the Best public road or tamarind dam, to visit the beehives and to look after the fruit trees. Caring for fruit trees was a passion of Popo. She could not bear to see bird vine, so called because it was spread by birds cleaning their beaks on trees and leaving the seeds, strangling the growth of trees. While in her eighties Popo fell out of a tree trying to rid it of bird vine and she had to curtail this activity as she broke her arm.

The household ate mainly local foods based on ground provisions but also enjoyed curries and the occasional Chinese meal. Since there was no shop in the village selling the Chinese ingredients, purchasing these items was done whenever someone went to Georgetown and stopped by the Chinese goods shops owned by Woon-Foo or Kon-Sue. The farm was able to provide most of the food supplies for the family.

In addition, Arif, her young great-grandson and his other brothers would sometimes go to the beach to look for buck crabs among the courida trees. He had the knack of putting his hand deep into a crab hole to pull the resident crustacean from its hiding place, the trick being to feel for, and grasp, the back of the crab. Of course, it was not always that the prey was suitably positioned, and Arif would swing his body around while lying on the muddy foreshore with his hand still in the hole. The crab would try to swing its body also, and Arif would sometimes trace a complete circle on the ground as he maneuvered himself to outmaneuver the crab. If the crab encountered a few fingers probing around within reach of its claw it would clamp down on the intruder, and Arif would find himself with a new attachment on his digit. The crab would then completely drop its offensive weapon so that Arif would be left with a crabless claw locked on his finger in a vice-like grip that seemed to be stiffened even more by rigor mortis. Arif's only solution would be to knock the claw against a tree to try and break off this appendage. Fortunately, the buck crab's claw was not as sharp, and its seizure not as severe, as that of another local crab, the sheriga, to which a hand should definitely not be offered.

As far as food supplies were concerned, there was hardly a need to go to shop for meat and vegetables. In the yard, Popo planted and cared for all manner of vegetables. In addition, there were a number of feathered stock kept in the fowl pen – chickens, ducks, turkeys and even powis (acquired on one of Doots' travels in the interior). There was a pond in the yard, not so much for the ducks but rather as a source of fresh water for the livestock and for irrigation, because rainwater had to be stored to last through the dry season. Sometimes an alligator would be found in the pond, having made its way from the side canals that served the former sugar estate. This was really an unwelcome visitor and would be shot. Intrusions by alligators or snakes were almost a weekly occurrence, but they did not end up on the dinner plate.

There were also some 20-odd sheep that Arif and his father tended. There was not enough grass on the property and the sheep were let out to graze near the railway line or by the foreshore. Later in the evening they had to be herded back to the yard. After a period of time the shepherds found that they didn't have enough time to take proper care of the animals and they were sold off one by one. A few of them died, and there were also several losses to the neighbors' dogs when they came on a marauding search for food, and the helpless sheep became suitable targets. There was a huge ram among the flock that Arif would sometimes ride. But it was this ram that was the undoing of Popo. One day it butted her and knocked her off her feet. Up to the day before, she was still energetic, wielding an axe to split the wallaba logs that she bought for firewood from the traveling salesman. However, after this encounter with the big ram her activities noticeably declined.

When Popo died in 1962, she had lived a life of 95 years that had begun in China; experienced a new beginning in a new country of British Guiana, including life at the Hopetown Chinese settlement at Camoonie

Creek; marriage in the county of Berbice; upward mobility of her family in the Chinese community of Georgetown; and the changing times that accompanied general growth and development of British Guiana during more than the first half of the 20th century. She had outlived her husband and sons and every one of her and her husband's generations. Intermarriage and integration of the races of her new homeland was the order of the day and she welcomed into her family relatives who comprised all the races making up the colony of British Guiana.

Many of her descendents have achieved prominence in various professions in different countries. In the UK her grandsons Percy (Bunny) is a doctor and Keith is an engineer while their brother Tony is a land surveyor, like their father, in the Bahamas. Her great-grandsons Derek and Colin are engineers in Canada and Gary a land surveyor in the USA while other brothers hold teaching, administration and business positions. Many of the younger generation are university graduates filling a variety of professional roles in the changing global job market. But her legacy is not in the achievements of her descendents but in the way she went about fulfilling her matriarchal role as advisor, counselor and leader by example. She was not ostentatious, although she stood out in her traditional Chinese garb, but could always be counted on to give consolation and advice when necessary. She believed that being active resulted in a long and healthy life and that sitting about too much resulted in one being fat, lazy and unhealthy. She lived her life according to these beliefs. She helped those in need without being asked and imprinted in the younger generation her example of looking out for others. This is her lasting legacy to those of us who have been lucky enough to share her life.

Rice Milling

Marlene Crawford, née Kwok

My parents, Alexander and Albertha Kwok, lived at Mahaica, East Coast Demerara, about 26 miles from Georgetown.[1] At first there was just my brother and myself, a second brother having died in infancy, but twelve years later, after a few stillbirths, my three younger sisters were born. We lived in a house that my father built with three bedrooms and a living room with a front and a back gallery. There was also an outhouse in the backyard. We lived in a side street off the Public Road halfway between the Mahaica Railway Station and the Market. The railway station no longer exists since the railway system was discontinued several years ago!

Mahaica is a flourishing township on the left bank of the Mahaica River, near its mouth. About 7,000 persons now live in Mahaica, mostly East Indians and Blacks (in a ratio of 60%-40%) and with a few Chinese, Portuguese, Amerindians and Mixed. The main crops grown are rice, coconuts and cash crops of green vegetables such as boulanger,[2] packchoy, and bora which are sold wholesale to vendors in Georgetown. Mangoes and cassava are also grown to supply the local market. Most of the people in Mahaica are self-employed. Some have small poultry farms of about 1,000-1,500 birds and some also mind a few cows and pigs, but most are small peasant farmers.

Mahaica always had its own Post Office, Police Station, market, Health Center and stelling. There are now also four lumberyards, three dispensaries, three gas stations, three schools, five Chinese restaurants, several churches of all denominations, many rum shops, cloth and grocery stores, and one rice mill. There used to be seven rice mills in my father's time but their owners have now all died or emigrated and the rice farmers now sell their paddy to the Government Mill in Mahaicony.

---

[1] Alexander's paternal grandparents arrived in 1863 aboard the *Ganges*. They had five children and James, the fifth child, became the father of Alexander who was born in 1905.

[2] Also called aubergine and eggplant.

The East Coast Public Road from Georgetown to Mahaica was made of red burnt brick at that time. In order to obtain this red brick, large mounds of earth were collected and burnt on the foreshore. The earth became hard and red when burnt and had to be pounded and crushed by hand. This gravel was then used to pave the road to make it an all-weather road.[3] Of course, whenever vehicles drove along the road, there was a huge cloud of dust trailing behind them!

Front view of the Kwok's house at Mahaica. The coconut trees are in the neighbour's yard. *Marlene Kwok Crawford.*

My father was a rice miller and bought the property with a rice factory in the mid-1930s. The main factory building housed his office, the rice mill and a very large storage bond that was used to store the bags of paddy when it was bought. Paddy is the threshed unmilled rice with the husk on. The entire ground at the southern side of the building was concrete and was used as a drying area for the paddy, and there was a boiler room attached to the eastern side that contained a boiler and two huge concrete tanks. Wallaba wood was used for fuel and was bought from a local lumberyard and stored nearby in the yard.

My father did not grow his own paddy but, instead, he bought it from the many rice farmers in the area. There were about 500 acres of land under rice cultivation in Mahaica all owned by East Indian peasant farmers. Each rice farmer owned 1-10 acres of land and besides rice, would also grow cash crops and have a few coconut and fruit trees. Paddy was bought twice a year during the Spring Crop and the Big Crop. The farmers on donkey carts brought it in jute bags to the factory until very late at night, often after midnight. After it was weighed, it was stored in the bond. Crop-harvest time was the busiest time of the year at the Rice Mill. The farmers were paid, I think, whenever my father was paid for the rice he had to mill and sell to the Rice Marketing Board. Milling went on

---

[3] Most of the Atlantic coastal area of Guyana can become a quagmire in the rainy seasons. The red earth roads in the countryside served as the arterial connections between the population centers.

continuously throughout the year as my father always bought enough paddy to be able to do so.

Rice farmers preparing their harvest for shipment to the rice mill. *Crown copyright material.*

My father was the sole manager of the business and employed several workers, both male and female, to do all the manual work it entailed. Since he only milled brown rice, it meant that the paddy had to be put into the two concrete tanks to steep in boiling water. The water was fetched in buckets from the drainage trench in front of our house. The paddy was left to soak and cool for a few days. It then had to be spread out on the concrete ground and left to dry completely in the sun before being raked in by a donkey into the storage area in the factory. It was later fed into the mill by a female worker, to be milled into rice. White rice does not require the paddy to be steeped before it is milled and is the preferred rice used by the Chinese in Guyana, but at that time brown rice was popularly used in Guyana by everyone else, and also for export. The mill was probably powered by diesel or gas oil.

In the mill the rice was bagged off separately from the boosie (paddy husk) and "broken" rice, placed in 180-pound jute bags, and sent in hired trucks to the Rice Marketing Board in Georgetown to be sold. All rice had to be sold through the RMB and could not be bought directly from the factory. At the RMB, the rice was graded for quality as Super, No. 1, No. 2, etc. according to its sheen and the amount of whole rice grains per bag. The boosie and "broken" rice was also bagged off and could be sold separately to anyone, typically for animal or poultry feed.

My paternal grandfather had died before I was born, but as far as I can remember, my paternal grandmother and her daughter carried on a grocery store at Lusignan, a sugar estate on the East Coast Demerara. Her sister and her husband also lived with them and he helped my aunt in the business. Before going to Mahaica, my father used to help an older brother at his own rice factory at Beterverwagting, the village next to Lusignan, nine miles from Georgetown. This no doubt influenced him to set up on his own factory when he had the opportunity to do so in Mahaica. He was helped by his mother financially but his brother did not help in any way – financially, by expertise or in construction.

Bertha and Alexander Kwok in their living room. The hats were used on special occasions, e.g. attending church services. *Marlene Kwok Crawford.*

My father was well respected as an astute businessman by everyone in the village and my mother took good care of the home and family. She had a maid who came six days a week to help her generally e.g. going to the market, sweeping and cleaning the house, plucking poultry, peeling vegetables, but my mother cooked all the meals for the family. We ate mostly the local Creole food such as mince balls, curry, stews of all kind, soup, cook-up rice, pepperpot, etc, Of course, she also cooked chow mein, and on Sundays, we usually ate Chinese roast pork and baked chicken. Other Chinese dishes were cooked on special occasions. She also sewed things like curtains and cushion covers on a Singer treadle sewing machine and did any mending that was necessary, but our dresses were sewn by a dressmaker. There was neither electricity nor running water in homes at Mahaica at that time so we used a Coleman gas lamp and various kerosene lamps for lighting the house. The gas lamp had to be pumped up by hand and was hung from the ceiling in the living room. It gave off a bright light that illuminated the front and back galleries as well as the kitchen. Small kerosene lamps were used in the bedrooms. The gas lamp was lit as soon as it became dark by either of my parents, and was shut off also by either one of them when they were ready to go to bed.

Back view of the Kwok's house. The rice was dried on the concrete pad in the foreground. The iron vat stored rainwater for drinking and cooking. Bags of paddy were stacked in the enclosed shed on the left.
Marlene Kwok Crawford.

For domestic use, trench water had to be fetched in buckets by the maid and stored in barrels in the kitchen and bathroom. Rainwater was caught and stored in a large iron vat and was used for drinking purposes. The water was put into an earthenware goblet to keep it cool and ice was bought every day from an "iceman" who purchased blocks of ice from the ice factory in Georgetown. The ice had to be broken up by using an ice pick and it was then put into two large Thermos flasks, ready for use when needed. An oblong iron Dover stove (3'x 2'x 2') was used for cooking and baking (using wallaba wood for fuel). The pots were placed over holes on top of the stove and there was a chimney leading from the stove that took the smoke out of the kitchen into the open air. Clothes that did not need to be ironed were washed by the maid in a large galvanized tub in the kitchen and were scrubbed on a scrubbing board. A washerwoman came to collect the dirty clothes that needed to be ironed on Saturday and returned them, washed, ironed, and neatly folded on a wooden tray, on the following Saturday.

Everyone in the village knew my family but we only mixed socially, visiting and chatting with a few other families, e.g. the proprietors of the grocery store, the bakery and the haberdashery. We did not take part in any of the village activities e.g. Pagwah, dances or sports but my mother sometimes took us to the Anglican Church on Sundays. We attended the nearby village school by walking to it until we had to attend High School in Georgetown as our parents believed their children should get a good education. We did not visit other parts of Guyana much although we always went to spend the Christmas holidays at Lusignan where there was always a lot of good food to eat and drink and we were all happy to be together as a family. My father also took me to see the famous Kaieteur Falls before I left to study in Scotland. It was a truly marvelous sight to see as it has sheer single vertical drop of 741 feet.[4] It is on the Potaro River, 50 miles up on the left bank of the Essequibo River, the longest river in Guyana. When we attended school in Georgetown, we stayed at first with three sets of cousins and an uncle before my father bought a property in Bourda and my maternal grandparents came down to town to live there and look after us. We only went home to Mahaica on weekends and during the school holidays, traveling first class by train. At the train station we then hired a horse-drawn cab to take us home.

---

[4] Kaieteur Falls, named after Kai, a legendary Amerindian chief, was seen by Europeans for the first time in 1870. It is acknowledged as an awe-inspiring natural wonder because of the height of the free-falling water (5 times greater than Niagara Falls) as well as its breadth. In 1935 a higher waterfall was discovered in Venezuela by Jimmy Angel but the Angel Falls is considerably narrower in width.

Comings

Ulex Hugh, née Phang
as told to Trev Sue-A-Quan

Ulex Phang was born in 1922 to William A. Phang, well-known merchant in the North-West District and Member of the Legislative Council, and his wife, Beatrice Too-Chung. Beatrice was the granddaughter of immigrant Chinese, her paternal grandfather, To Cheung, having arrived as a 10-year-old boy with his mother aboard the *Ganges* in 1863, while her maternal grandfather, Ng A-kwong, was a passenger on the *Sevilla*, which landed in British Guiana in 1865.

Ng A-kwong had seven children, three boys and four girls. One of the girls, Mary, became the mother of Beatrice Too-Chung (born in 1900), and her sister, Angeline, known as Moy, married Matthew Wong, and took up a career as a nurse and midwife. Angeline was well-known among the Chinese community and popularly addressed as Aunt Moy or Nurse Wong. She had three children of her own and, in her professional capacity, brought numerous babies into the world, including those of her grand-niece Ulex.

Training and accreditation as a sicknurse were usually obtained locally. Some chemists and druggists also became qualified as sicknurses so as to enhance their ability to recognize and take care of minor illnesses while they dispensed medications. Additional training was required to become a registered nurse, usually through the Public General Hospital, Georgetown, and some of the nurses went on to gain further accreditation as midwives. Nurse Angeline "Moy" Wong was one of these.

* * * * * * * *

Angeline was the fifth child of immigrant Ng A-kwong and she was born in 1894. She gained her qualifications as a nurse and specialized in midwifery. For a while she lived in Grove, East Bank Demerara, but later took up residence in North Road in Georgetown. This was a convenient and central location for her to get about to attend her clients in the city because she used a bicycle as her mode of transportation. She would strap her bag – a large black bag usually associated with doctors of bygone days – to the carrier above the back wheel of her bicycle, and off she would go.

Nurse Wong was a person of medium build and went about her duties in a calm and professional manner. She wore a white uniform with brown trim that nurses regularly used and which was well suited to her sense of duty and authority. Although she was qualified to provide general nursing services, she became known as the person with expertise in delivering babies. Expectant mothers would usually have their doctors monitor the progress of their pregnancies and if there were no unusual indications the babies would frequently be delivered at home with the help of a midwife. In the months prior to the birth, Nurse Wong would also be regularly consulted to check that everything was in order, and to have a general chat about what should be expected. She was both industrious and informative in her work. When Ulex Hugh was approaching full term with her pregnancies she also paid visits to Aunt Moy to get confirmation that things were progressing as expected. Then, when the contractions began, Ulex would advise her husband Alvin to "Go and get Auntie."

Nurse Wong was an independent type of person, and worked on her own in bringing the baby into the world, although other persons would be outside the room, helping to fetch hot water, basins, towels, and other necessities. In her calm fashion she advised when pushing should be done and provided counsel about the progress of the birthing process. Relatives of the mother-to-be would wait outside the room in various states of expectation, or anxiety, for word, delivered either by Nurse Wong or by the baby's own declaration of his or her arrival. It was not that others were consciously prevented from being present during the birthing, but rather that it was customary for the husbands and others to stay out of the way – in essence they themselves considered it none of their business.

Nurse Wong would cut the umbilical cord and then clean and dry the newborn. A mild solution of boric acid would be used to flush the baby's eyes and serve as an anti-septic. She would then present the new family member to the mother. She might also be asked to dispose of the afterbirth, typically burying it. The navel string, the last physical connection with the mother, would be treated with some reverence by some families, and, when it shriveled and dropped of, would not be allowed to lie around, and might be saved among the family's collection of treasures or be buried in an appropriate, and sometimes secret, location. It would be said that improper care of the navel string would cause the child to develop bellyache.

Post-natal checks were also done by Nurse Wong – she even took a week of her leave from work to spend time with the Hugh family when one of Ulex's babies was born. It was this kind of care and attention that made her popular with those she attended. For some families she would be the person reporting the birth to the registrar, in which case she had to carefully note the relevant names and details for the child and the parents.

As far as bearing children, Ulex was a good example of how smoothly things could go, because all of her six children came into the world within two hours of the onset of labor pains. Only on one occasion was there something unusual, and that was when Aunt Moy was called when she was attending another patient and was feeling unwell from all her exhausting duties. The midwife serving Wales estate was brought in as a backup. But Ulex was well experienced in the procedures, this occasion being the arrival of her sixth child, and the birthing went along without difficulty.

Nurse Wong worked for the hospital administration and was paid accordingly, but she would also be paid for those services that she provided on a private basis. At one point, in 1945, she told Ulex that she would be going to Trinidad for a visit and perhaps may not be returning. However, for whatever reason, this did not materialize and she resumed her duties in Georgetown. Later she was appointed to Leonora, West Coast Demerara, and remained there as nurse and midwife until she retired.

Goings

By Michaele Low-A-Chee, née Young
as told to Trev Sue-A-Quan

In 1861, Li A-ying, a 22-year old shoemaker from Hoi Ping, China, arrived in British Guiana, and was allotted to Plantation La Jalousie, West Coast Demerara. He married Joykee, an immigrant from India, and had three children, the youngest being Samuel Edwin Lee, who was born in 1877. Samuel and his wife Emily raised a family of 12 children, 8 girls and 4 boys, with Michaele, his granddaughter, being the child of Cataline and her husband Joseph Young.

Samuel E. Lee was the founder of the Lee Brothers Funeral Parlor, and the family business became well-known in Guyana. He was not the only Chinese in this line of business; Theophilus Milton "T.M." Chee-A-Tow (1882-1963) was another person who owned a funeral parlor, complete with livery stables, but he did not continue in this business for very long.

* * * * * * *

Like the majority of the second generation Chinese, Samuel E. Lee was a shopkeeper. He ran a shop in Vreed-en-Hoop that sold groceries and other daily-need goods. But he decided to give that up and, in the 1930s, moved his family to Georgetown where he went into business as a mortician. Actually, it was not Samuel himself that operated the new venture, because it was started as a partnership for his four sons, Harry, Ralph, Edwin, and Benjamin, and called Lee Brothers Funeral Parlor. It was located at Regent and Albert Streets. Harry worked for Sprostons Ltd., and was a civil engineer so he did not participate in the ongoing management of the funeral parlor. It was left to the other three, with Ralph taking the lead, while Edwin and Benjamin were in charge of the office management. The business began to prosper as the Lee Bros. name became known.

In the 1940s, the funeral parlor was moved to a new location, at 218 Camp & Lamaha Sts. It was a huge place with the business operations set up on the ground floor while Samuel E. Lee and his wife resided above, along with some of his children. Up to about the early 1950s the hearses were horse-drawn, by one or sometimes two horses, and the driver, dressed all in black, sat on a high seat at the front end of the hearse. He wore a tall hat somewhat like a top hat, and carried a long whip that he would insert upright in a holder at his side while he took hold of the reins. The whip was hardly used because there was no hurry in a funeral procession but it was part of the traditional equipment carried by hearse drivers. The horses were kept in a stable at another location and an Indian employee was hired to take care of feeding, grooming and exercising them. One place that he took them for an outing was the sandy beach beyond the Sea Wall, and on occasion Michaele and her brother were allowed to ride on the horses as they trotted along while the handler ran alongside with tethers in hand.

The horses eventually gave way to motorized hearses. This transition was introduced through Ralph's initiative. A brand-new hearse with its modern accoutrements was very expensive to buy and import. During a visit to North America, Ralph saw that American-made station wagons were very large and this gave him an idea. He bought an old one and shipped it to Georgetown. He had it totally revamped to make it into a hearse, with sliding trays to allow a corpse or casket to be easily inserted or removed, black curtains along the side windows, and an elevated railing on the roof to hold the wreaths and flowers. With the success of the first experiment Ralph repeated the procedure and was thus able to get a fleet of motorized hearses.

Ralph Lee was the entrepreneur, the one who kept on thinking of ways to improve the business. He traveled to North America to see the things that were done abroad for funeral arrangements and interments, and he was very down to earth, so to speak. He would bring back pictures of floral arrangements and wreaths and buy a limited number of caskets to be shipped to Georgetown. Then the staff at Lee Bros. Funeral Parlor would examine the design and workmanship of the caskets and re-create them at the workshop. While abroad, Ralph also learnt the skill of engraving stone and marble headstones and taught Joseph Young, his brother-in-law.

Cataline Lee and Joseph Young were married in Trinidad, and after the birth of their son, decided to return to Guyana in 1944. The Lee brothers were then in need of a hands-on manager for the funeral parlor business and Joseph was felt to be the ideal person, thereby keeping matters within the family. The Young family took up residence above the funeral parlor. Joseph was an easy-going, non-complaining type of person and he learnt the trade, becoming involved with essentially every aspect of the process for committing the body to the grave. He would be the one to answer when a phone call came from relatives of a deceased person. The call would come at any time of the day or night. If it were after normal business hours he had to go to the bedroom of his father-in-law,

Samuel, where there was a hole in the floor that allowed him to haul the black telephone up from the office immediately below, using a pulley system. This was the only phone on the premises and the hole in the floor saved him from the necessity of going downstairs to answer it. Then Joseph would take the hearse, go off to collect the body, and bring it back to be stored in the freezer. If he needed help he would call on one of the employees on the way. The family of the deceased would typically arrive the next morning to make funeral arrangements.

The body had to be cleaned and made presentable by applying make-up. This was a skill that Ralph learnt abroad and taught to Joseph. The cosmetics, as well as the tools needed to apply them, were all brought back by Ralph. The casket selected by the family of the dead person would be prepared with a cloth lining made by a seamstress working for Lee Bros. The cloth was folded so as to give a billowy and fluffed-up appearance. Joseph would help to staple this into place. The caskets were made from scratch by a crew of carpenters utilizing the available woods that there were, stacked up in large piles in the workshop area. Because the burial could be in a matter of a day or two, there were a few caskets already finished, so many of pine, so many of cedar, and so on. If a prominent or wealthy family wanted one of the imported caskets, then that would be sold because the carpenters would already have knowledge of how to make a similar one.

There was an ongoing need for caskets and this required a full-time team of carpenters working Mondays to Fridays. The wood had to be cut, planned, sanded and carved. Joseph would finish off by staining and polishing the casket. In some cases the burial had to be delayed to allow family and friends from abroad enough time to arrive, perhaps a week or so. Again, Ralph called on knowledge gained in North America about embalming to keep the body from decomposing. When the technique was the tried for the first time at Camp & Lamaha Streets the whole place smelled of formaldehyde.

There was a sandbox in the yard, literally a huge box with sand, and trucks would come every so often to dump a fresh lot. The sand was used for covering graves, and for making headstones and other decorative items, such as flower holders. The sandbox was open to the elements, getting wet from rain, and drying out when the sun came out. When Michaele's cousins came for visit, and the adults were upstairs chatting at night, the children would be outside playing and would dive into the sandbox, jumping and throwing sand at each other. Michaele's mother did not like it because the children entered the house with sand in their clothes and she kept repeating that they would get chiggers from the sand. She would say: don't play in the sandbox, because you goin' to get chiggers with your shoes off.[1]

Lee Brothers Funeral Parlor provided "full-service" funeral arrangements, from collection of the body to interment. This was based on the premise that a grieving family might not necessarily know the necessary procedures. Thus, the Lees took care of the formal documents that had to be competed to officially record the death. They prepared the death announcements that were broadcast at a fixed time on the radio, preceded by a solemn dirge that allowed listeners to either turn up or turn off their radios as was their wont. Obituaries to be printed in the newspapers were sent out. Arrangements for the funeral service, whether it be at the funeral parlor or at a church or temple were planned in the Lee Bros. office. The plot at the cemetery had to be booked and inspected, gravediggers arranged, and the headstone selected. Floral arrangements, however, were not done by the funeral parlor, although there was a book of floral designs and wreaths from which the client could chose a suitable arrangement and have it prepared by a florist.

At Lee Brothers Funeral Parlor, there were two rooms available for holding funeral gatherings, laid out in suitable fashion. For example, for those of the Christian faith there would be an altar with a shiny chrome-plated cross and another smaller cross placed on the casket, but these items would be absent for a non-Christian funeral. The sounds of mourning and weeping could be heard, along with expressions of dismay, "Oh, why you got to go and leave me all alone." The caskets did not have hinged covers and the full-length body of the deceased would be visible. A lid to the casket, a single piece, would be attached when the departure for the cemetery was about to begin. If there were insufficient pallbearers among the mourning family and friends, employees at Lee Bros., including Joseph Young, would act in that capacity. In some cases the family would request to have the cortege go past the former residence of the deceased, or even for a drive to the Sea Wall, as felt befitting the habits or interests of the dead person. The death of a prominent or wealthy person would usually bring out an extremely long procession of cars that would require a police escort to direct traffic.

Cataline did not take part in any of the activities of the mortuary business except perhaps to make a cloth that hung over the high table that served as an altar in the funeral parlor. In fact she was rather afraid that her husband would bring ghosts into the house with him, especially when he returned in the dead of night. She would constantly remind him

---

[1] A tiny mite that burrows into the skin and deposits eggs, resulting in an irritating rash.

to enter the house walking backwards to prevent the spirits from coming in. She kept her slippers turned upside down outside the bedroom to prevent ghosts from following him. Frequently, she would be troubled by nightmares causing her to wake Joseph, and then curse and shout at the apparitions that she imagined before her, telling the ghosts to get out.

There were some townspeople who would spread a rumor that, late at night (and perhaps at midnight), they had seen people dressed in white, floating above ground, sailing by in the vicinity of the funeral parlor. It sounded like the stereotypical depiction of a ghost, and others were unable to confirm such sightings. Actually, the front of the funeral parlor was set up to be a showroom to promote the products, like any other business. Here, behind the large glass window would be purple-lined fancy casket, and over there, a simple model or an elaborately carved casket could be viewed. Perhaps the displays may have stirred the imaginations of passers-by into seeing things.

There were a few competing funeral businesses in Georgetown, including Sebastiani's, Lyken's and Merryman's, but Lee Bros. and Sebastiani's were the two top ones. Lee Bros. was located at one of the busiest intersections in town. Camp Street led all the way to the Sea Wall. It was a beautiful boulevard and right down the middle was a double row of large flamboyant trees[2] that formed a canopy over a central walkway. When the flowers were in bloom the street would be a blaze of brilliant red. Children, including Michaele, used the walkway as a playground, hide-and-seek being a popular game. In the rainy season the walkway would become flooded but this did not deter the children. Michaele enjoyed wading though the calf-high water, sloshing her way home from school, kicking up waves and getting thoroughly wet. These episodes would be greeted by her mother with some dismay. "She would tear into my skin, as we used to say, asking why I didn't take my yachtings off. Then I would tell her 'and walk barefoot? You prefer me to walk barefoot?'"

For the Lee family members, dealing with death did not carry any sinister or ghoulish implications – it was just another way of doing business. It was also quite a viable business, because people were always dying.

---

[2] Poinciana trees.

GHOST STORY

Neville Luck, as told to Trev Sue-A-Quan

John Philip Luck is the fifth child of immigrant Lok Kim-hee, and an elder brother of J.C. Luck, the more recognized name among the Luck clan members. Born in 1891, John Phillip's whole life was connected with the Demerara River.

* * * * * * * *

Daddy was born in Warrida,[1] grew up there, and went to school in that area also. Warrida wasn't a village or settlement – just a series of houses, and not many either, along the riverbank. From his house the nearest people could be reached by a five-minute ride in a canoe or ballahoo – that would be the next-door neighbor. The house at Warrida was elevated off the ground, on pillars about three feet high. This was intended to keep the house above any flood tide. There were two bedrooms, and we also had a bathroom, or more correctly, a place where we used to bathe. Water was fetched from the river and stored in three buckets in the bathroom. We used a calabash to dip water from theses buckets for our bath. The house was some 20 yards or so from the landing where ballahoos could tie up.

At the front of the house was a small shop with a counter. People would come and eat whatever Daddy had bought in Georgetown. He used to bring a lot of cakes, cookies, drinks and candies. These items were bought for maybe three or four cents apiece and sold at the shop for 10 cents. But it was a convenient place to come because the shoppers would otherwise have to go all the way to Stabroek Market in Georgetown.[2] I remember when I was only about five years or so, Mummy was at the back doing something, and there was a jar of candies on the counter looking very tempting. I decided to enjoy myself with two candies and

---

[1] Warrida was located on the east bank of the Demerara River some halfway between Georgetown and Mackenie.

[2] Before becoming a British colony, Guyana was a Dutch possession with its capital named Stabroek. This name was changed to Georgetown by the British but 'Stabroek' lived on as the largest public market located near the wharves along the Demerara River.

stuck my hand into the jar. Just then I heard the sound of Mummy's slippers – slip-slop, slip-slop – and realized that she was coming back. I pulled my hand out as fast as I could, but the mouth of the glass jar had been chipped. The sharp edge cut into my forearm and made a nasty gash. I was caught red-handed – with blood. Mummy had to help patch me up; she put on a bandage with some medicine. From then on, I would never forget that – pushing my hand in the jar – and I have a permanent scar to remind me.

When I was born in 1930, Daddy owned a grant[3] on the opposite side of the river where he felled timber for shipment to Georgetown. It formerly belonged to Peter Ho, with whom Daddy had formed a partnership of sorts. When Peter Ho retired, Daddy bought over the grant. It was quite a large area and was valuable not only for its size but also for the bountiful timber resources on it. The forest contained wallaba, a hardwood tree that made an excellent fuel. There would be about 20 people working to cut down the trees, haul the logs to the waterside, saw the logs, and load the punt. There were two trucks to transport the logs to the landing where the punts awaited, but otherwise the work was all done by manual labor using axes and saws.

When the trees were felled the branches had to be cut off to leave only the trunk. If the log was too long for the punt it had to be sawed to fit. Sometimes a few long logs would be tied together and strapped to the outside of the punt. The tree branches were stripped of leaves and put into a chamber where they were burned to produce charcoal. It took some skill to know when to take out the charcoal or else it would burn down completely to ash. When the wood appeared sufficiently blackened and charred through, it was pulled aside. This was not a big operation, but charcoal was a valuable product. The charcoal was stacked in the middle of the punt where it would be protected from rain by the canvas erected like a canopy over the center section. It was important to keep the charcoal dry or else it would end up as mush and difficult to unload.

When the punt was fully loaded, some ten men would take it downriver to Georgetown, floating with the current and guided by the oars that the men manipulated. But this transporting step did not begin as soon as the punt was ready. The workers had to wait until the river current was favorable. If the current changed when midway on the journey, the punt had to be parked at the side of river until the next outflow current resumed. This might take five or six hours. Sometimes a steamer might come passing by and the people on it would wave their

---

[3] Timber-bearing sites required permits from the government to be logged. These were known as grants.

hands, and there was nothing the punters could do but watch them go by as they waited with the punt tied up to the trees on shore. Because of this dependency on the river current, the shipping would sometimes be done during the night. Two or three lanterns were hung on the punt so that it remained visible to other traffic, especially if the punt had to be parked in the middle of the night. Normally the punt would be guided so as to hug the riverbank where the water was calmer, thereby staying out of the busy lanes where motorized boats traveled. But this required that the men work their oars to prevent the punt from hitting the riverbank. When the punt reached its destination in Georgetown, it had to be unloaded, and then the men had to bring it back to the grant. However, less expenditure of effort was needed during the return journey because the punt would be empty. Nevertheless the whole shipping process took a lot of time and energy.

While these operations were going on, Daddy owned a speedy motorized launch, named *Ghost*, which he drove up and down the river for business and pleasure. He used it to haul supplies and food for the workers at the grant. A hut was set up at the grant and acted as a kind of shop where the people could buy goods. The workers at the grant were mainly Blacks, supervised by a foreman who directed the operations. These employees were paid every week and Daddy kept an account for each of them. They would make a list of things they wanted Daddy to buy for them from Georgetown, and the cost of the items would be deducted from their weekly earnings. Sometimes a person would over-run his account and Daddy would tell him that he could have the requested goods – not now, but next time when payday came around again. So it was not very often that Daddy had to take a lot of money with him to pay the employees, although some did request cash payment if they planned to go to Georgetown themselves. Daddy kept a logbook of the accounts, and he was a good bookkeeper.

When I was a young boy, Daddy took me, and maybe my younger brother Alan as well, across to the grant to experience a bit of the life there. We slept in tents and had to hang up nets to keep the mosquitoes from attacking us. Then we were so cold we had to have extra blankets. In the morning, Daddy woke us up early to have breakfast. There was no cook. We had to eat bread with some sardines from a tin. There were no eggs to eat because we didn't have a frying pan. We much preferred to be back at the shop, sleeping in our own beds, and having a nice hot breakfast. I don't know how the laborers used to get by – it was a real tough life. To make a fire they probably would get wood from the forest, cut it up in small pieces to burn, and most likely they brought their own frying pan from town.

The *Ghost*, if unloaded, could carry about ten people, and when Daddy was not transporting goods he would provide a personal ferry service to the public. A trip might take an hour, or an hour and a half, compared to a whole day if they were to go by the launches and steamers that plied the river once a day. He enjoyed driving the launch and the passenger traffic provided some additional earnings. However, he did not have a regular schedule and the availability of the passenger service was dependent on what his activities were. He might stay overnight at Georgetown, for example, and if a passenger needed a ride back, that person too would have to spend the night there. When the boat was taking food and goods he might have room for only one or two people.

One day, when my elder sister Jean was about three years old, Daddy took her out on the river aboard the *Ghost*. The boat was not laden with goods and so it was light and ran swiftly over the water. Daddy then made a sharp turn and the boat began to flip. He immediately shut off power to the engine as he felt the *Ghost* turning over. He was thrown out of the boat and started swimming to shore. He was a good swimmer and was not injured by the accident. But it was when he was heading for land that he suddenly remembered that Jean was with him. He looked around while treading water but could

see no sign of her. In a panic he headed back towards the overturned *Ghost* and that was when he heard some crying in the distance. He swam over in the direction of the sound and as he got closer he saw his daughter floating on a large lily leaf. If it were not for her cries he would not have known where to find her. Somehow or other she managed to end up on the lily leaf, and exactly how that came about remains a mystery.

Large water lilies, like these at the Botanical Gardens, grew naturally in the creeks and streams feeding the main rivers. *M.R. Lam.*

When we were of school age, Jean, Alan, and I attended the Anglican school downriver from Warrida. In the morning we had to get up in time to have a bath, get dressed, and eat some breakfast. We never wore yachtings,[4] and went barefoot to school. We were taken to school by ballahoo, steered by a man who started his journey further upstream by

---

[4] Rubber-soled canvas shoes, called yachtings, were commonly worn by children.

picking up two children. Our house was the next stop, and three of us got aboard. Another two children were collected at a subsequent house, and this was all that the ballahoo could carry. With the man steering from the back, we had to paddle our own ballahoo to get to school. Normally it would take about ten minutes to paddle there. However, we had to make the trip when there was no opposing current, or it would take much longer. So we had to know when the current was running and adjust our departure accordingly. The same thing applied for the return journey. Although school would end at 3 o'clock we sometimes had to wait to maybe 5 or 6 o'clock to get a favorable current to get home.

Our school was a real one – it even had a bell. The school had about 25 pupils who arrived by ballahoo. It was a building big enough to hold maybe three or four classes, plus rooms allotted to the schoolmaster and two teachers. Whether they were certified as teachers is hard to say but they knew enough to teach us what we needed to learn. The schoolmaster was a strict fellow, and had a wild cane.[5] He was the only one who could beat you, but the teachers would complain to him: Neville did so and so. . . . Then he would call you before him. If it was a serious offense he would probably beat you, if not he would tell you what to do or what not to do. We used to sit in different sections, for instance, Jean would be in a higher section than I was. Then I was in a more advanced section than the one Alan attended. You could hear what the other person was teaching in the other classes.

All our work was done on slates; it was only later, when we moved to Georgetown, that we were exposed to exercise books. Each slate was about 8 inches by 10 inches and had a wooden frame around the edge. We wrote with a slate pencil, essentially another piece of slate that was shaped into a round, thin, pointed implement with a paper label wrapped around it. It was as long as a regular pen, enough to be comfortably held, but it would inevitably break so you ended up keeping a half and writing with the other half. When that became too short to hold, you threw that piece away and used the other half. We used a wet cloth to wipe the slate clean when the work assignment was finished. We did not have our own textbooks. All the books we used remained at the school and the teacher would write on your slate: Question 1, Question 2, Question 3 etc. and that became your homework. The questions were written at the top part of the slate and you would write the answers below. If the front side became filled and you needed to write more, you would turn the slate over to continue on the other side. We schoolchildren had to be careful

---

[5] The word 'cane' would usually mean sugar cane, but the term 'wild cane' was known by all to refer to the implement for enforcing discipline at school.

with the slates because they could break easily. More likely than not the slates would not be replaced by the annoyed parents, and writing then had to be done across the crack(s). It was only if the slate became badly shattered that a new one would be bought. It was not uncommon for a child to have a slate with a missing piece in the corner, especially since the wooden frame could easily come away from the slate, by chance or otherwise. In the hands of little children all these possibilities existed.

During lunch break, we would eat sandwiches, or some other thing that Mummy made and packed for us. But the time we would really get hungry would be in the afternoon when we had to wait for a favorable river current. We would be ready to come home but the current might be bad and we weren't strong enough to paddle against the tide.

When the rainy season came we would put on plastic coats with hoods. Not much water would accumulate during the short ride to school, but the boat did have a calabash for bailing. I remember when it was drizzling and there was homework on the slate, I had to be careful. I had to put the slate inside the plastic coat or else I would be in trouble with the teacher. Some children used the rain as an excuse for homework that went missing from the slate but after a while the teacher no longer took that as an excuse.

We went to the local school to about 5th Standard and then we moved to Georgetown after Daddy bought a house there for the family so that we children could continue our education. I was about eight years old at the time and attended Central High School. Daddy continued to stay at Warrida to run the shop and manage the grant, but he kept coming and going between Georgetown and Warrida to take care of the wood business in town.

The punt arriving from the grant would tie up near the koker in the southern part of Georgetown. Daddy would hire a donkey cart to move the logs to the wood shop, some three hundred yards away. Several workers were paid to do the heavy work of unloading the punt and then sawing the logs into one-foot lengths. The short pieces would then be sawed lengthwise into quarters. This was very hard work and eventually Daddy installed an electric circular bench saw, about 14 to 16 inches in diameter. This cut down the labor intensity considerably. I don't know if this was what had cut off the thumb of his right hand, only that Daddy had four fingers and could not grip your hand in a handshake. One of the drivers at the grant, named Hilton, was later brought to the wood shop to manage operations. The workers also had to unload the charcoal from the punt. The charcoal was shoveled into large bags, looking rather like rice bags but stronger. This had to be done with some care otherwise the charcoal would become pulverized. The chopped-up wood and charcoal were sold as fuel to businesses and households, including places such as Tangs' Bakery. The customers paid the transportation charge on top of the price for the fuel. There were several others in the wood fuel business and because it was "just wood" the competition was fierce. Mummy would always tell Daddy that it was one of the hardest kinds of work with the least pay.

Daddy continued to ride the *Ghost* up and down the river for about five more years, but time plus wear and tear took their toll on the boat, and the cost for repairs began to mount. So Daddy decided to sell off the grant and move permanently to Georgetown to join the rest of his family. However, he continued to operate the wood shop for his livelihood, and the supply of logs from the grant kept coming. For a long time the boat was his workhorse as well as his hobbyhorse, but now the *Ghost* had given up the ghost.

Dental Practice

Jerome "Jerry" Manson-Hing
as told to Trev Sue-A-Quan

In the field of health care delivery, dentistry was not as popular a choice as medicine among the Chinese in Guyana. However, the need for qualified dentists in the country provided a career opportunity for promising scholars. After the first few Chinese returned to set up their dental practice, it created a ripple effect that caused others of Chinese descent to follow in their wake. Before WWII, the few Chinese dentists in Guyana included James Fung (registered in 1926), Leslie Evan-Wong (1935), Reginald Fung (1937), and Denis Evan-Wong (1938). Jerry Manson-Hing, was one who followed soon after. He was born in 1920, and is the grandson of Mun Sun-hing, an immigrant aboard the *Mystery* in 1861. His maternal grandfather, To Cheung, arrived as a boy on the *Ganges* in 1863.

* * * * * * * *

I cannot say that there was a specific event or person causing me to be interested in dentistry. There were a couple Chinese dentists practicing in Georgetown, including James Fung, and by the time I needed to think seriously about a career choice, Leslie Evan-Wong returned from abroad. I suppose they had some influence on me as role models, but I think it was mainly because there was a need for dentists locally that prompted me to pursue this profession.

Northwestern University, in Evanston, a suburb of Chicago, was considered one of the top schools for dentistry, and I applied there and was accepted. I enrolled in 1938. There were two others from Guyana with me in dental school that year – Orin Dummett, and Cheddi Jagan. Both of them had been at Howard University and then transferred to Northwestern. Then there were Ronald Lovell, Denis Evan-Wong and Arnold Lee, who started in different years. Another student of dentistry was Ping-chi Kwong[1] – he was ahead of me and completed his studies before I did.

---

[1] P.C. Kwong was a student from Tianjin, China. When he completed his studies, China was embroiled with a war with Japan and this prevented him from returning home. Some of his fellow students who were from Guyana persuaded him to go to

I graduated in 1941 and went back to Guyana immediately aboard the *Lady Drake*. That ship was sunk the following year by a German submarine. I had brought back various pieces of equipment to set up my office, but when I arrived in Georgetown I was not permitted to register as a dental practitioner. I was not yet 21 years of age and barred from registering because, in the event of any lawsuit, a minor could not be sued. Later on, my brother Roy faced the same situation after he gained his degree before he was 21. We were quite young among the boys in our classes at Queen's College, although I recall that the youngest during my time was Forbes Burnham.

In December 1941, I was permitted to register to practice dentistry. I was then asked to be the dentist for the South Caribbean Forces and the Canadian Veteran Army. This was a contingent of some 70 soldiers sent down to Guyana to guard the bauxite ships as they traveled on the Demerara River to Mackenzie. Aluminum was a much-needed material, especially for making aircraft, and that is why bauxite was considered valuable enough to warrant safeguarding. When the bauxite ships arrived in Georgetown from abroad, the soldiers would board them and provide military escort to Mackenzie and back. They would see that no sabotage took place on the ship. They then disembarked and awaited the arrival of the next ship while they were stationed in Georgetown. I managed to become the dentist for the soldiers through meeting Colonel Hooker when we both were on the *Lady Drake* traveling from Boston. Colonel Hooker was the head of the South Caribbean Forces and had some difficulty finding a dentist locally before he asked for my services. I was the army dentist for about two years.

I set up in private practice in Georgetown and did the regular kinds of dental procedures, nothing unusual. In subsequent years, dentistry became very attractive career choice for up-and-coming students, and Northwestern, because of its reputation, was receiving a lot of applications for entry, more than it could accept. The university decided to appoint P.C. Kwong, Captain Nobbs,[2] and myself, as local screeners on its behalf. Whenever an application was received, Northwestern would send it to us so that we could evaluate the applicant's academic record and interests, and verify that the information provided was accurate. Only two students were being accepted from Guyana each year, and we were entrusted with the duty of choosing those with the best potential. In one year we recommended Talim and David Ewing-Chow to

---

Guyana. P.C. Kwong set up his dental practice in Georgetown and married a local girl, Helen Wong.

[2] Headmaster of Queen's College.

Northwestern, and that was the same year that my brother Roy decided to apply, although he was relatively young. With the quota for Northwestern already filled, I told Roy to apply to Tufts University, in Boston, where a former professor of mine had transferred. Among those that we approved to attend Northwestern University were Neville Fung-A-Fat and Delbert Sue-A-Quan.

In 1962, I was again looking the military in the mouth because the British soldiers, who were brought in to quell the civil disturbances, had engaged my services. I later worked for Demerara Bauxite Company (Demba) after the soldiers returned to Britain. It was not a full time commitment and I was required to go up to Mackenzie only on occasion, usually one weekend per month.

Besides being involved with my dental practice, I was very active in various sports, mainly cricket and hockey, although I also played soccer for BGCC.[3] I was a member of the BGCC cricket team playing Case Cup cricket, and was selected to be on the team to play against the Leeward and Windward Islands. I was an opening bowler – a medium pace bowler. I was also on the cricket teams for GCC[4] and Chinese Sports Club (CSC), in different years, playing Wight Cup cricket.

Field hockey was my other passion, and I played on left wing, representing GCC and CSC (which later became Cosmos Sports Club). There was no real conflict with the cricket schedule because hockey was usually played during the week and would take a couple hours of time, whereas cricket could be prolonged over several days and was usually played on weekends. In hockey, I represented Guyana for a tour to Surinam. Vincie Luck was also a member of that team. Some years later, Maurice Chee-A-Tow introduced me to the game of golf. We played at the Lusignan Golf Course, mainly for recreation, following the return of the expatriates.

Another area in which I was active was in the Lions Club. A man named DeNegri came over from Surinam to get a local branch of the club started. He looked around for people that he felt would form a good nucleus to get the organization going. Cecil DeCaries became the president and I was the secretary. There were about twenty-one of us in the founding group and we would meet at the Tower Hotel, talk, and go home. But this was accomplishing nothing, and so Cecil and I came up with the idea to initiate a project to build some bus stop shelters in various parts of Georgetown. We had to come up with various ways of raising money, because, unlike some other clubs, the members of the

---

[3] British Guiana Cricket Club.
[4] Georgetown Cricket Club.

Lions Club were not required to make donations out of their own pocket
– unless they were willing, of course. Instead, we got some companies to
donate cement and timber and we organized various fund-raising events,
such as fairs and bazaars, with many of our wives chipping in to help. It
wasn't so easy, and it took us a while before we were able to accumulate
sufficient funds to cover the labor costs for constructing the bus stops.
Eventually, we got fourteen bus stop shelters erected and this was the first
project that carried the Lions Club stamp. The club membership grew
significantly for a while, but our activities started to decline after the
country's social relations and economic outlook faltered and several
prominent members in the Lions Club left Guyana.

Several professionals had left the country, including Dr. Talim, and
there was a shortage of dental practitioners. When Forbes Burnham was
Prime Minister, a school was established to teach dental nursing in
Georgetown. I taught there for three years. The program was funded by
Pan-American World Health, or PAHO, an agency of the World Health
Organization (WHO). The instructors were required to go on study
tours to Trinidad, St. Lucia, Jamaica, and Mexico to learn what was
being done at training schools already established in those countries. I
remained in Guyana for a dozen years after independence, working in my
dental practice until my five children emigrated from Guyana.

Chinese Merchant

Phoebe Wong, née Kon Sue

In the year 1923, a young Hakka man, Ngui Kon Sue, left his home village Ngu Fu in Bo-an County to travel to Guyana (then British Guiana) to seek his fortune. His father and elder brother had already gone to Jamaica, but because immigration there was now restricted, he decided to try his luck in Guyana where other clan members had settled. There he found work with an uncle who owned a Chinese goods shop. It was customary among the Chinese to help their newly arrived members to find employment and settle down in the community. After a number of years Ngui Kon Sue was able to start his own business. He was now in a position to send for his wife Ngui Chung You Moi. They had been married in China and, as was customary, she had moved from her own village to live with her husband's family in his village.

On her arrival in Georgetown, their first home was in quarters in the back of the shop, and it was there that three of their five children were born. The shop sold traditional Chinese goods such as foo chuk (tan colored dried bean curd in two varieties – stick and sheet), fancee or vermicelli (translucent mung bean threads), toong koo (Chinese mushrooms), wan yee (cloud ears), and mook gnee (wood ears) – two kinds of black tree fungus. In addition there were cans of lychees, water chestnuts and bamboo shoots, plus an assortment of salted vegetables: chuk shun (salted radish strips), chet choy (pickled radishes), and chin choy (salted turnips). There were also dried scallops and dried oysters and preserved fruits like kai en chee, chan pei moi, wah moi (a highly salted plum), as well as a small fruit with a tiny seed. The sauces included soy sauce or Chinese casareep, as it was called locally, brown bean sauce or mein shee, lam yew (salted red bean curd), teow shee (salted black beans), ham ha (a shrimp paste with a pungent smell), and oyster sauce.

The shop also carried a number of goods with medicinal attributes like dried red dates, lily bulbs, wolfberries, ching bo leung, star anise, dong quai bulbs, etc., as well as Tiger Balm[1] for colds and aches, ship yun

---

[1] An aromatic liniment that would be rubbed on the chest and neck to alleviate discomfort from colds.

dan (a powder in a little bottle for fever), pak a dan would be used for colds (this was flat and thin and could broken off and sucked like candy). Another favorite for colds and aches was ee yow, a packet of tiny silver balls was the treatment for tummy aches.

In addition to foodstuffs Kon Sue's also carried Chinese teas, silks, fans, inkpads, ink sticks and brushes, jade pieces, and woven straw mats. Although the products available were varied, the shop catered to a niche market because, apart from the small Chinese community, the goods were not familiar to non-Chinese in those days.

In order to widen his clientele, Kon Sue had a section of his shop set aside for the sale of local snacks and soft drinks – crab backs, Chinese cakes,[2] pine tarts, patties, star cakes[3] and other pastries. But the hot sellers were isinglass and custard blocks.[4] The isinglass was made from agar agar, a natural edible seaweed, and was very cooling and refreshing; this was complimented by the custard blocks. These items were so popular that for years afterwards many people remembered having enjoyed them in Kon Sue's shop.

The location of the shop at 21 America Street was very convenient for customers to leave their early purchases there. At the end of the day they picked them up before going to board the ferry, train or bus on the way home, so in a way the shop became a depot and last stop for many out-of-town customers. Ngui Kon Sue was a friendly, caring and trustworthy person who could be relied on to sort out messages and packages for everyone. He also encouraged and advised those who were interested in trying out new products, as he was a good cook himself. Many times he would visit a home to show the person how to use certain Chinese goods or demonstrate a cooking technique like deboning a duck. Many of these people were the local born Chinese, whose ancestors had arrived in Guyana many generations ago. They spoke no Chinese but still enjoyed Chinese foods. They could have been descendents of the Hakka families who had settled in Hopetown in the Camoonie Creek. This was the source every Christmas of the Yen Loong Ban – a large Chinese New Year cake made of rice flour, wrapped and steamed in banana leaves. They could be bought whole or in sections at Kon Sue's shop.

Kon Sue was very civic minded. He supported the Chinese Association and worked many years on the committee. He was also a founding member of the Chinese Sports Club, and supported them

---

[2] Made with flaky pastry, this small, round cake, called towsa, contained a filling of black bean paste.
[3] A hard-crusted cake with a flower petal layout, stuffed with brown sugar.
[4] Frozen cubes made with custard powder, milk, eggs, and sugar.

financially. Each year could be seen at the Chinatown Fair helping at the gate or supervising. He was later made a life member. He firmly believed that young people should take part in sports and outdoor activities. He himself rode a bicycle for the greater part of his life. First he used to tow his daughter to kindergarten every day, then his son as well, on the bar of the men's bike. He visited his friends that way and his pastime was riding to the Sea Wall or Promenade Gardens.[5] He continued to commute from home to business on his bicycle even after he had bought a car – which was used mostly by his children.

When Bettancourts, the owner of the premises at 21 America Street, decided to renovate the property, Ngui Kon Sue moved to the corner of 9 America and Longden streets, which was only a few doors away. There he continued his Chinese goods business until the Japanese invaded China and it became increasingly difficult to obtain shipments from China. He decided to switch from Chinese goods to selling provisions – sugar, flour, potatoes, onions, cooking oil, etc. – on a wholesale basis. The wholesale provision business turned out to be more successful than the more specialized Chinese goods. He retained many of his old customers who had shops in the country and gained other new customers as well. Kon Sue imported some of the provisions directly and also purchased from large-scale importers thereby becoming a distributor. He employed a sales clerk named Mr. Gopie who would write the bills and receipts. He himself kept a record in Chinese and at the end of the day he and Mr. Gopie would reconcile the accounts. He also employed a porter named Gerald who was very strong and could easily lift and stack the bags of sugar and flour. Another employee was Chandoo who was in charge of the donkey cart, which was used to transport supplies between the shop and the bond or warehouse and to make small deliveries around town.

When the shop was moved, Ngui Kon Sue had to find new premises as well for his family. He rented the former offices of De Freitas' sawmills on Water Street for sleeping quarters and used the lower level as a warehouse. Because there were no cooking facilities on the premises, he built a Chinese fireplace in the back of 9 America Street and so was able to provide meals for his family. His wife cooked and raised the growing family. This fireplace was a replica of the one in his home in the village in China. Made of bricks and concrete, there were two openings – a large one for the wok, and a second one for a regular pot. It was a wood-burning fireplace. For the odd times when he wanted to bake, he had a box oven – a wooden box lined with zinc, and a coal pot provided the

---

[5] A large garden in the center of Georgetown, laid out in Victorian style.

heat. The two older children, Phoebe and Lynton, were taken to St. Joseph's High School in a hansom cab.

In 1945, a great fire consumed the main business section of Georgetown. As the fire raged and continued to spread Kon Sue took his family to Popo Lam's house for the night. Victoria Lam, or Popo Lam, as she was called by many, was a good friend and godmother of his children. She was a kind hearted woman and a strong pillar of the local Chinese community. With five growing children, it was time to move into more permanent quarters so Ngui Kon Sue bought a property at 11 Charles Street. It was like a small housing compound. At the front was a large two-storey house, which was rented to Mr. Samuel Loquan[6] and his family. (Samuel Loquan and Alfred Too Chung were two people who had helped a great deal when Ngui Kon Sue was a newcomer in Guyana.) The cottage beside it was occupied by his family; this cottage was enlarged and once more a Chinese fireplace was built in the kitchen to accommodate his wok. The other three cottages at the back were rented to the Wong, Cho Yee and Bristol families and there was still a big enough yard for his children and the neighbors' children to play.

Needing more help at the business, Kon Sue decided to send for his nephews in China. In this way he was able to give the same opportunity to other clan members as he had been given. They worked for a while in his business until they could venture out on their own. In 1950, Ngui Kon Sue moved his family to 17 Brickdam. This was a large and centrally located property, closer to his shop and large enough to furnish supplementary storage for his growing business. Once again he built a Chinese fireplace in the kitchen and enlarged the house.

He now branched out into the agency business, becoming the sole distributor for Ajinomoto[7] and Sno-Cone machines.[8] His second son, Carlton, and two younger daughters, Eileen and Maureen, each spent some time in the business. With their help he and his wife were now able to travel and enjoy holidays. At this time he also began to stock Chinese goods again as the demand for these were growing.

He was a man of vision and worked steadily to achieve his vision. He was also a caring and compassionate man and adhered to the concept of respect for elders and honoring of ancestors. He sponsored his mother from China so that she could meet again all the male members of the family who had emigrated to the various Caribbean countries. He

---

[6] Samuel Loquan operated a photo studio in Georgetown.
[7] Monosodium glutamate crystals used as a flavor enhancer in foods.
[8] The crushed ice from this machine would be placed in a conical holder and bathed with syrup.

insisted that his children be educated and encouraged them in various careers. He believed in equal opportunity for his daughters as well as his sons. His eldest daughter became a teacher and his elder son a dentist.

Throughout his endeavors, he was supported by his wife, a true Hakka woman who worked tirelessly in the background running the home and, later on, cultivating a garden. She also supervised the operation of the warehouse when it was part of the Brickdam property. Kon Sue was well known in the community, especially among the local born Chinese. Throughout the country Ngui Kon Sue and Kon Sue's shop are well remembered.

Best Little Whorehouse

Godfrey W. Chin

When the Chinese arrived in British Guiana during the 19th century as indentured laborers, only 15% of them were women. Godfrey Chin's great-grandparents were among these travelers to a distant shore. Many of them left China under duress of war – the Chinese had fought with the Europeans (primarily the British and French) in the Opium Wars, with the Americans able to claim some of the spoils of war. Not long after, China was embroiled in a tremendous civil conflict, the Taiping Rebellion, which claimed some twenty million lives.

In the 20th century, war and the shortage of women played out in a completely different fashion; this time the Europeans were slaughtering one another, while American soldiers found themselves posted to the tropical mainland of South America – British Guiana. Their need for R&R (rest and recreation) offered interesting possibilities to those who had an enterprising inclination, and some Chinese were able to seize the day and capitalize on the night.

* * * * * * * *

This one was not in Texas,[1] but in Georgetown, at Wellington & South Road, opposite the Catholic Guild Club. I am not ashamed to admit now that at age seven years, in 1944, I frequented that "whorehouse" – certainly not as a customer, but as a favorite nephew, eager to visit at every opportunity as the "hostesses" adored me and granted me bountiful favors. Now don't jump to conclusions with your "dirty mind." This is not about porno or child abuse – the favors were "jills"[2] for pocket money, and chewing gum that the paying customers doled out lavishly to their favorite hostesses, who in turn spoiled me rotten!

My uncle Bobby owned this large house and it was tenanted by a host of Mistress Moms who managed this oasis – so I had privileges. This was during the Second World War – before Pearl Harbor – when the U.S. policy towards the Allies was "Aid short of war." America supplied

---

[1] "The Best Little Whorehouse in Texas" is a musical drama that was first presented in 1977. It is based on an establishment called the Chicken Ranch because, in the days of the Depression, the clients were allowed to pay for services with poultry.

[2] Pennies (i.e. two-cent pieces)

armaments – ships, tanks, guns and ammunition in exchange for land in the British Colonies where Overseas Bases could be built. The U.S. Seabees were then assigned to build an American Base – 25 miles inland along the Demerara River at Atkinson Field, and the Americans had landed.

Of course they had every entertainment facility provided at the "Base" – a small cinema, a huge swimming pool, baseball fields . . . but the one thing missing was the same that Rogers & Hammerstein sailors longed for in the Broadway show "South Pacific." The Yanks had everything . . . but GIRLS. The nearest village outside Atkinson Field was Soesdyke. There, the sparse families now went to bed earlier than their chickens, 'cause the "Yanks were around!" Their call to action: "Neighba, neighba, do hide your daughters!" The G.I.'s, eager for action, were only too glad to undertake the two-hour dirt track trip to Georgetown, the capital city 25 miles away. The local cinemas – Empire, Metropole, and the newly constructed Astor – were not the targets; neither was their goal the several rum-shops, with names to challenge any macho male: Russian Bear, Demerara Ice-House, Houston's, John Bull, Fighting Cock, Jumbie Jack! They were seeking the weekend all-night ribaldries with girls: booze . . . dancing-girls . . . bacchanalian orgies at "Moms," their favorite watering hole! On my visits, during the day after school, the young ravishing hostesses were a mélange – a pot-pourri of the six nations of the colony ranging in complexion from black to white, and every shade in between . . . take your pick!

The hospitality operations were run by a buxom lady named Waveney Baird, whose heart was as big as the chest that enclosed it. On her days off she would take a bunch of us kids to go kite flying at the Sea Wall, with the trunk of the car stuffed with a lot of delectable goodies. She and Uncle Bobby made sure that the retinue of girls was able to provide the needed services that gave the house a certain repute. But business was business, and Uncle Bobby did not let his three daughters come even close to being hassled. One of my best friends got a sound cut-ass after his actions during an outing to the Sea Wall were thought to have gone too far.

I was too young and innocent to understand what these giggling, kind, friendly girls – often skimpily clad – were doing in my uncle's mansion with several rooms. However I welcomed and cherished the wide variety of tight hugs . . . and the gifts of jills, chewing gum, and foreign chocolates.

I remember my favorite hugger, giving me a special white two-inch egg – which was very light. She warned me never to drop it. For days I cradled my gift . . . until it bounced out of my hand – ping, pong. Hell, it was the first table tennis ball I had seen! I did note a well-stocked bar on the second floor as my father, who was an electrical linesman at the Base, helped his brother on weekends as barman, to cope with the "full-house."

Of course, at home at 115 Regent Street, I recall my Mom complaining that while his weekend work brought in a few needed Yankee dollars, he was earning them in a "house of sin." Coincidentally, I had another uncle who owned the "Idle Hour" at Tembledora – off the U.S. Base at Chagaramus, Trinidad – who catered also for the "Yanks on leave." A young Francisco Slinger in his teen years hung around that bar, and in 1956 composed "Jean & Dinah" – hustling for the Yankee dollar on the Gaza Strip.[3] We now know him as The Calypso King of the World – The Mighty Sparrow!

After the War, and the Yanks left, the local patronage was insufficient to keep open the "Best Little Whorehouse" in town. The building was replaced by Lall's Embroidery Business, and the whorehouse moved to smaller premises on Alexander Street, Kitty, but by the early sixties it went out of business.

After "Mom" moved her operations to Alexander Street, and as I reached manhood, I would sometimes pay her a visit, not for business but for pleasure . . . of a spiritual nature. She was as kind and respectful as ever. My experiences at the "Little Whorehouse" taught me valuable lessons in life . . . not to judge a book by the cover, and, most of all, don't point fingers! Prejudice, bigotry, racial discrimination, etc. were eliminated from my psyche.

---

[3] Words from the popular calypso include: "Jean and Dinah, Rosita and Clementina / 'round the corner courting / bet your life is something they're selling . . ." The Gaza Strip at the lower end of Wrightson Road in Port-of-Spain, Trinidad derived this nickname from the similarly-named area in the Middle East. The residents in the shantytown in Trinidad were poor, and frequent conflicts would erupt because of economic and social frustrations, with the police having to intervene to maintain peace and order.

The swimming pool at the Base became a popular recreational place for locals after WWII. *M.R. Lam.*

The aprons and runways of former U.S. Base at Atkinson Field became an excellent racing track for motorcycles in later years. *M.R. Lam*

BROADCASTING ACE

Vivian Lee
as told to Trev Sue-A-Quan

On 24 August 2002 Vivian Lee was one of 36 recipients of the Wordsworth McAndrew Award, in recognition for his outstanding contribution to Guyana's culture and heritage. The presentation was made by The Guyana Folk Festival in New York.

* * * * * * * *

My father came from China when he was quite young. He was probably born in the late 1890s. He told me that he had intended to go to Trinidad but somehow or other he ended up in Guyana. He mentioned something about "wrong" and "ship," but whether he really meant a problem with the ship or that he took the wrong ship, I'm not sure. I think he had heard that prospects were good in Trinidad and he was apparently an adventurous man to be traveling on his own to a foreign country. His name was Lee Yew and he came from a place south of Canton. After he arrived in Guyana he worked for some shopkeepers on the East Coast – in Beterverwagting, I believe – and later became a shopkeeper himself. He next went into the laundry business in George-town. I think he was baptized in the Catholic religion with the name John. I understand that when he got married my mother thought that his name was too complicated (maybe because it sounded like "Lee, you") so the family name was shortened to Lee. She also interpreted his name as William so that he was legally known as William John Lee.

My mother's name was Adelaide DeFreitas. She was working at the London Cinema (now Plaza) on Camp Street when she got to know my father. My parents were living in Albertown when I was born on 27 August 1919. My mother liked the name Vivian since there were a few well-known men with that name, like Vivian Dias, Vivian Woolford, and so on. So the full name chosen for me was Vivian John Lee. The friend who was given the assignment of registering my birth (and apparently, also, the guy recording the name) couldn't spell Vivian so he only wrote down "John." I didn't realize that I was "John Lee" until many years later when I wanted to apply for a passport and I was told that my name was not Vivian. Then I had to make a special application at the registry to have "Vivian" inserted.

I started primary school at St. Angela's on Church Street. It was run by the Catholic Church. Then I attended St. Mary's Roman Catholic School and St. Stanislaus College where I got my Senior Cambridge Certificate. After leaving school, my first job was with Andrew "Chunnie" James[1] at BG Pawnbrokery, at Hadfield and Lombard streets, at $4 a week. I had answered an ad in the paper for the job and I worked there for about two years. I was a clerk taking pledges for the goods coming in. At that time I was playing football and one thing that used to annoy me was when stocktaking took place, every month or whenever, when we had to go through every item in the place and record it. I wanted to go and play football at 5:00 o'clock, and there I would be – helping them with that job. That was a little bit of an annoyance for me but I had to tolerate it because I was getting the magnificent sum of $4 a week, which I needed, and which could have bought a pair of shoes in those days.

I was only five or six when we moved to the corner of North Road and Camp Street. My family then moved to 108 Regent Street, and finally to 49 Robb & King Streets. My father was always a laundryman with no chance to become a millionaire at all . . . and he wasn't a very thrifty guy. My mother was the one saving pennies. When I was offered a job in the Civil Service she was very happy, because she, like many others locally, felt that there were four or so careers worthy of merit – become a lawyer, become a doctor, work with Bookers,[2] or work for the Civil Service. Well, of course, I didn't have money to go to any university or anything more than secondary school. So my objective was to get into Bookers. I had applied there and to other stores too, like Sandbach Parker,[3] and then the Civil Service came through with the job offer.

I think the very first place I worked at was the Price Control Office with a Mr. William Macnie, an Englishman. We would go around to

---

[1] 'Chunnie' James (1915-2000) is the grandson of Chinese immigrants who arrived in the 1860s. Chunnie's father, Henry James, became successful through his pawn broking business. Chunnie continued the business, and later opened Auto Supplies, another prosperous enterprise.

[2] The Booker family owned sugar plantations from the early part of the 19th century and branched out into a variety of businesses, including the wholesale, retail, engineering and service sectors. By the 1930s Booker Brothers was the largest private business enterprise in Guyana.

[3] Samuel Sandbach and his partner Philip Tinne owned plantations in Guyana in the 19th century. Sandbach Tinne & Co. joined with McInroy Parker's company and became established in shipping and merchandising.

check whether bakeries were selling bread less than the legal weight. Then I was transferred to the Audit Department and later on to the law courts where I was a clerk, along with Ken Lam, with whom I established a lifelong friendship. Finally, I worked at the District Commissioner's Office on the East Coast. The D.C. at the time was Mr. Walter Green. Lawrence Yhap, who himself later became District Commissioner, was a colleague in the same office.

My last job was as Distillery Officer on the East Coast. I used to go and inspect the liquor storage tanks, test the strength with a hydrometer and give out certificates. One thing scared me though – I had heard stories about an officer falling into a vat and dying during a cleaning inspection. These were really huge vats; we had to climb a ladder to get to the top. The fumes coming from the vats were powerful and I made sure I didn't go near the edge. When the liquor was drawn off we would measure it and issue a certificate for them to pay duty on it. This liquor from the distillery – high wine – was highly over-proof, and had to be diluted and aged before it became rum.

I didn't like the Civil Service because it was mainly work by rote, repetitive tasks. It left nothing for one's imagination and initiative, especially at the lower levels. I probably would have had to wait a few more years for a promotion. That is one reason for my dissatisfaction. The next thing is that promotion was based on years of service. There might be a dumb guy as your superior and it was because he had more years of service than you that they automatically placed him higher than you. I had occasion to meet people like that, so that browned me off. It was only when I was Distillery Officer that I felt some satisfaction with my job. I liked being outdoors and not having to sit down in the office every day at routine tasks. And I learnt to drive at that time. The guy who used to drive me around – we had a car for the office – would let me drive and I remember learning on the two strips of pavement on the East Coast road.[4]

---

[4] The public roads in the countryside were made with burnt earth that was red in color. But the red earth tended to crumble and be blown away with the passage of traffic during dry weather, and sections of the road were liable to be eroded when the rainy seasons came. This resulted in a very uneven road surface and it was not uncommon for cars to weave all over the road in an attempt to avoid potholes and craters. To alleviate these problems two strips of concrete, each a foot or so wide, were laid a car-width apart on the road to provide a smooth weather-proof surface for the vehicles. In a way it bore a resemblance to a railroad track. The drivers of cars coming from opposite directions had to make their own decisions when to veer off from the concrete strips and usually drove such that at least the right wheels of the vehicle remained on track. (Traffic kept to the left in Guyana.)

After working in the Civil Service for four or five years I took a holiday to Barbados. This was granted to me following an accident at football in which my cheekbone got broken. I had a great time there making new Bajan friends but not long after I returned I submitted my resignation – I had had enough. My mother was unhappy with my decision. It meant the loss not only of reasonable pay and security but also of benefits. We got three months holiday every four years, and unless you killed the governor, or did some other nonsense, you had a job for life. But I had made up my mind . . . I just felt that I was wasting my time and wanted to do something better.

It was not long after World War II ended and I had a friend, Leon DaSilva, who had served as a merchant marine for the Americans and later became a U.S. citizen. He became a handyman in charge of a building in New York and he invited me to visit him. So I packed my bags and went off. Now I didn't have money to go by plane so I went on one of the "Lady Boats," I believe the *Lady Nelson.*[5] Going along with me were two fellows about my age, one was Joe Bacchus, the weight lifter, and the other was Monty Harper. We had a pretty nice time. We were down at the bottom, the lowest deck, but we used to go up on the upper decks because they didn't worry about us young guys. I always remember one thing remarkable about the trip – we were coming in to New York and the sun was shining. It was just like the day before, when we were OK, but this morning we woke up and went upstairs and felt as cold as never before. We were wearing the same clothes and the sun was shining the same way but we wondered why we were so cold – we were not accustomed to this change of weather. That was my first encounter with Autumn. It must have been around October.

I stayed with my friend who used to paint houses. I learned to paint, and to do many little odds and ends, fitting in with his work as a handyman. One day, by chance, I met a lady, a Guyanese, who had been living there 40 years but I think she was in her 50s. She suffered from arthritis and didn't like the cold. So I was telling her that my father had a laundry and that I would like to study dry cleaning and go back and improve his business. She said that she too would like to go back to Guyana eventually. She arranged to lend me money to go to a dry cleaning school in Virginia. She had a sister in Guyana, and it was agreed

---

[5] In 1925 the Canadian government agreed to provide passenger, cargo and mail service between Canada and the Caribbean. Five "Lady" boats were built – *Lady Nelson, Lady Drake, Lady Hawkins, Lady Rodney*, and *Lady Somers*. During the war the ships requisitioned for service and three were sunk. The *Lady Nelson* and *Lady Rodney* returned to their regular routes in the summer of 1947.

that my mother would pay her sister for the American funds lent to me for my tuition, board and lodging. The arrangement was OK – until halfway through my course the lady told me it couldn't work anymore because my mother had stopped giving her sister the money. I wrote my mother right away and she replied that that was not true. My mother knew that I depended on this and if she didn't do her bit then I would starve or probably stop my courses. But whatever I had to say, the lady insisted that it was my mother's fault. Well, I couldn't argue with her. Apparently her husband, an American fellow, was not in agreement and believed, in effect, that his wife was stashing away money for herself in Guyana. So I had to try and find a job while I was going to school. I got a job at a drug store selling ice cream, sandwiches and so on in the little delicatessen section. So I managed to finish my course and got my diploma after some six to eight months.

I came back to New York and started applying for a job, now that I got a diploma. At the first place, I was asked: "What is your experience? None? Sorry, you have to get experience and then come back." Where in the blazes could I get experience if nobody would give me a job? So the next one I went to I said yes, I have six months experience. I had to lie or starve. They said come on and we'll try you out. After working for two or three dry cleaning places I began to think about going back home to Guyana.

One day I read in the newspaper about the Cambridge School of Broadcasting in New York, and I applied. I had accumulated enough money to pay for the tuition and I went to learn about broadcasting, script writing, commercials, techniques for interviewing, and so on. It was a six-month course. After completing that I set sail for home and on my way I stopped in Trinidad. I had a friend Sylvia, who I knew from before, and she arranged for me to stay with her aunt Cecilia Leung. I wanted to spend a few days in Trinidad because the manager of the broadcasting company there was a Guyanese – Gerard DeFreitas. I went to meet him and he explained that Johann Strauss' birthday was coming up shortly. He said, "I want you to write a program, half an hour program." This was a real opportunity for me. So I went to the library to research Johann Strauss, the things he said and things he did. I had to create the program, select the music, write the introductions. The only thing I didn't write was the commercial. I handed it to the station and on the afternoon of the broadcast I sat down with some friends to listen to this program . . . and it was so good, I myself was surprised. Even now I always say that this is one of the best things I ever did, because among the things I did was to have Johann Strauss speaking – he talked about himself and his music and this was done by a German guy with a perfect accent. Everything meshed so beautifully. How do you think I was feeling? Well, up in the air. The next day I went back to Gerard. He said it was all right, it was quite nice but there wasn't any job opening at the moment. I felt used. He knew before I was going to write the program that he didn't have any job to offer me even if I had done the world's best thing. I was so disappointed. He said he would keep in touch but I knew that was the end of the matter because I was not going to stay in Trinidad waiting around. So I told him thank you, and I left. In all my life, even before this incident, I realized that what you want for yourself is not what God wants for you. I believe in God and I trust that whatever I desire, if it is good for me, He would let me have it. My father used to say: "One door shut, another door open."

After returning home, I decided that I would open an advertising agency, because I knew how to write scripts and I felt that I had a good imagination. I always remember Mr. Carrington. He was my mother's friend and advisor. He worked for the lawyers, Cameron and Shepherd. She went and talked to him about my future and explained my plans to start an advertising agency. Carrington thought that it was a good idea, and that broadcasting was doing well in Guyana. He suggested that I call it Ace, ace being the best, the top card. I said that it sounded short and good, and that's how Ace Advertisers came into being.

I started up in the same place at Robb and King Street that my mother had bought with her saved-up money, I think it was $4,000 that she paid. We lived upstairs and my father had the laundry downstairs. So he gave me a quarter of the space – in fact less than a quarter – with my own door and a partition to start up my business. One of my first clients was the well-known cricketer Maurice Green of J.F. Green & Co. He had his office just around the corner in Church Street. Actually, I had gone to him earlier for employment and he had offered me this job to sell Guinness to all the pubs, along with a driver and a car. I did this for a short while. Then when I started the agency, he became my client and I did advertisements for Guinness and various other things for which he was the local distributing agent.

I needed to be creative in the advertising business. I did some commercials, even one for XM rum, although I never used to drink. I called it the "Happy Rum" but with the admonition that "Just enough is good enough." At a later time I had a show during a period when topless females were becoming prominent in America and abroad. I thought that this was a good way to give exposure to a stage show that I was promoting. I placed an advertisement in the papers announcing that a topless female would appear in the show. Shortly after, a policeman came to my office. He told me very sternly that the Commissioner of Police did not approve of such actions and that the show would be stopped. I told him that I understood the situation. But the show went on as planned because the female I had in mind was my three-year old daughter. I had a great laugh over that promotion.

Other advertising opportunities came as a result of a write-up that the newspapers did about me when I returned from abroad, with my qualifications as a broadcaster. I don't know who had done the news item but it came about because I was already a popular figure through my previous activities in football, also known as soccer. I had started playing since I was about 17, while still at St. Stanislaus College. Gussie Resaul, the captain of the Everton team, saw me and got me interested in club football right away. I then formed my own team, Charlton Athletic, with two other friends, two McDavid brothers, who went to school with me. We entered the junior league and we did very well. I was captain for about 10 years straight because they thought that I was the best player. I played inside right – I was a striker. I remember playing against the Artillery Sports Club and scoring three goals in one afternoon and so they started paying attention to me too. I enjoyed playing football and I was invited to play for their senior team, commonly called the Gunners. That was during the war days and it meant that I had to be enrolled in the military, and I have wonderful memories both as player, and later as a referee.

We were not full-time soldiers, we were the auxiliary, on part time duty. Originally we only had to train two afternoons a week. As the war continued, we went and learn how to use the guns, do marching drills and the like. Then we used to guard the bauxite ships. When they arrived in Georgetown we would go on board, check the engine room and the cargo holds. I don't know who they expected would be sabotaging, but we figured we were doing our bit to help the war effort. We also used to guard the powerhouse that supplied electricity to Georgetown. We marched around and were told to watch out for any suspicious activity or people who might want to damage the machinery. Another of our duties was to guard the telegraph company – the wireless telex station at Thomas Lands.[6] Then we had an incident there. When guarding the place we were instructed to stop and challenge anybody entering: "Halt! Who goes there?" The other party would have to state his name and, if you had any doubt, would have to show you some identification. In our company was an unpredictable guy named Claude Vasconcellos. Well, one day, the boss of the telex station arrived in his car and Claude

---

[6] Located just south of the Sea Wall, the telex station utilized three tall masts that served as antennae. The area was a large open field with the rifle range next door.

commanded him to halt, but the driver wouldn't stop. So Claude shouldered his rife and fired . . . and he hit the car, scaring the daylights out of the guy. Poor Vasconcellos, he had to go and explain. He said that the officer who had given him instructions was clear, and the orders were that everyone had to stop. Nobody had said anything about car number 604 having permission to pass. Claude got his moment of glory.

During my service with the Auxiliary I was in Trinidad and one of the first requirements in training was to walk around Trinidad, covering 100 miles in 4 days. Not being a big person in build, and then loaded down with rifle and pack, I didn't give the appearance of being up to the task, and some of my fellow trainees wondered how long I would last. However, I managed just fine while some others, strapping fellows, "fell by the wayside." Subsequently, I was promoted to Lieutenant in the Trinidad Regiment and later appointed Education Officer. I started an 8-page publication entitled "Duck Soup," inspired by the hilarious movie featuring the Marx brothers. The Brigadier saw it, and invited me to publish a regular Army magazine. I answered the call and launched "The Infantry Star" as editor, copywriter, advertising manager, layout designer, etc. I must say that I enjoyed tremendous physical fitness during my army life.

In football, my most memorable moment (outside of my broken cheekbone) was scoring for British Guiana against Suriname. I scored the goal from way out – I took a long shot and the Dutch goalkeeper, Amo, stretched but could not gather the ball. He told me later that he was blinded by the sun, but still congratulated me.

Well, getting back to Ace Advertisers, I began to get clients who wanted their products promoted. I started with J.F. Green & Co. Then Andrew "Chunnie" James was the first one to ask me to do a half-hour radio program for Auto Supplies. I was not an employee at the radio station, I worked for myself, and I was allowed so many commercials per program. I worked on everything to run the program . . . did the introductions, selected the music, and wrote the commercials. The program opened with my reminder: "The clock on the wall says 8:00 and it's time for Tops in Pops."

The radio station at time was called ZFY. It was a private company that was later bought by Overseas Rediffusion Ltd., based in England. Some of the people at ZFY included Lillian Fraser and Olga Lopes. Ulric Gouveia was an independent producer like myself. He had a program and I had a one too. I was also doing spots. I would write the spot and send it to the station and their people would do the broadcast. I just provided the script, and it had to be within their restrictions. They allowed a hundred words for a 30-second spot.

I also got into music – promoting records and making records. I established Ace Records. I used the equipment at the radio station to produce tape recordings and then sent the tapes to Decca, a well-known record company in England. They made the records and sent them to Ace Record Club, which I opened at Robb & King Streets. Record making was another aspect of my life that I enjoyed. In fact, one of the big names was Mighty Sparrow,[7] who first recorded "Jean and Dinah," on the Ace label. This launched his career as a calypsonian. Later Sparrow did another recording of this song in Trinidad but people there seemed to prefer the version I had made.

Then I got involved in show business, with singers and other entertainers when I saw the need for such shows. There were already people doing vaudeville shows, like Sam Chase and Jack Mello; I used to enjoy them so much. They were real down-to-earth, a little bawdy but always a crowd pleaser. So I got into my own shows and I used to travel all over the country, all the way up to Courantyne.[8] By this time, of course, I had an office with several people working for me at Ace Advertisers so I didn't have to be there 100% of the time. I could take a day off to do broadcasting and programs. My best program, that would always be remembered by me and the people involved, was called Gypsy Caravan featuring Mrs. Snodgrass.

It all began when I went to see a little skit performed by Mrs. Ruby Spellen and her friend at a church fair in Kitty.[9] I had known her for some time when she invited me to see the skit. I enjoyed it so much I said to myself, this is ideal – this lady is a natural. That was the birth of her radio character for whom I chose the name Mrs. Snodgrass. I introduced other characters from time to time, like Miss Rosy Cheeks, and other sidekicks to do little things to spice up the show. I had to think of new ideas and jokes and write then into each script. This was a hectic affair. I would often complete it at the last minute because I was doing so many other things. On Tuesday afternoon I would be writing the script and the program would be coming on at 7:30 p.m. We met at the house where Mrs. Snodgrass lived on North Road with her brother, Mr. Rix, of the Real Delight Balata Company. Sometimes there were three, four, or even five people in the cast. Unlike TV where you have to learn the lines by

---

[7] Slinger Francisco was born in Grenada and his family took him to Trinidad when he was one year old. In 1956, at age 20, he recorded "Jean and Dinah" using the name Mighty Sparrow and became perhaps the best-known calypsonian with a singing career spanning several decades.

[8] The easternmost area of Guyana's coastline.

[9] A suburb of Georgetown at that time.

heart, the players were reading from a script, but they still had to know what to do, when to come in, and have the right delivery – expressing surprise, happiness, confusion, whatever – so we had to practice. Generally the cast would meet at 6 o'clock – which was about the time I would be finished writing the script – and practice for an hour or so. Sometimes they would still be practicing when I had to ride my bicycle to the studio three blocks away to start the program with the introductory music. Then Mrs. Snodgrass and her group would come over, sometimes only five minutes before the time to go on air so it was really a touch-and-go business. We had an opening theme, which signaled the arrival of Mrs. Snodgrass. Then, following her theme music, she would come on with her distinctive: "Helloooo." It was a colloquial show with low-brow humor but it was popular. We had a live band with four or five people – piano, guitar, bass, drums, and singer – and there was a guy doing sound effects to create the gypsy setting in which listeners could hear sounds from the outdoors with the fire crackling.

Every week there was something new for Mrs. Mabel Snodgrass and her husband Harry. The show was more popular with women listeners than men because she was the joke-maker and he was the butt of the jokes, most of the time. The women used to tell me that if they were out of the house just before the show came on they would say, "Girl I can't talk any more, I got to run home and catch Mrs. Snodgrass." The situations were usually fairly simple:

Mabel: Well, Harry isn't it nice to go to the countryside and take a walk in the fields?

Harry: Yes, Mabel.

Mabel: Now take a deep breath.

Harry: Yes dear, as soon as we pass this cowshed.

Another show that I was involved with was the Ovaltine Hour. This caused a big falling out between Ulric Gouveia and myself, but we became good friends later. Kenneth Lam's father, M.R. Lam, was the agent for Ovaltine[10] and I suppose he may have regarded me as a promising Chinese talent and so he gave the program to me. Before this it was Uncle Ulric doing the program, and now it became Uncle Vivian. Ulric was doing a good job so naturally he was upset. It was a kids' show with songs, games, quizzes, and such. We also had annual stage shows with Ivy Campbell's Dancing Dolls along with the best of the Ovaltinees. Ovaltine was heavily advertised and M.R. Lam did well with that product.

---

[10] A granular product made with malt, milk and eggs that was promoted as a healthful food. It was typically made into a beverage using milk.

Actually, M.R. Lam gave me another show – The Ovaltine Amateur Hour. We would have people come on air to sing, recite poetry, do a skit, or tell stories. This was done before a live audience and the striking item in the program was the gong. Each participant came up in turn to the microphone to perform and, if the act went well, would be greeted by applause and cheers. However, if it didn't go over well – maybe an unpleasant singing voice, or going off key – the studio audience would begin to groan and mutter and this would soon grow into a clamor for the gong that would bring the act to a crashing halt. Of course, there would also be people among the listening audience at home who would be shouting at their radios for the gong. The person in control of the gong was Harry Mayers, a well-known bandmaster whose orchestra provided the accompaniment. Harry had the onerous task of swinging at the gong when he felt that he had heard quite enough. That was one responsibility I didn't want at all. But Uncle Harry was a musician and knew what he was doing, although at times there were some people who disagreed with his decision to gong or not to gong. Actually, he gonged some people who later went on to become well-known in their own right. One was King Fighter,[11] who became a good calypsonian. I think Lord Canary[12] also got the gong. But that didn't daunt them from pursuing a musical career. I later selected both of them to make records for me. The show was a lot of fun and people took it in good stride. Everyone enjoyed the talent, and enjoyed the gong as well.

You know, the things I used to do, if I were not popular I probably would have been beaten up. I remember we used to arrange dances in low-brow places. Sometimes a fellow would come along with an idea for a dance and I would help to arrange it. One day we were holding a dance at the Labor Union hall at Smyth and D'Urban Streets. A man came to the dance and paid his money. Then he began disputing something and cussing me up and so on. I was standing with the person collecting the money and I had just turned around to look at the complaining guy and he kicked out at me. Well I don't know to this day – I always tell myself this is hereditary, my father's father must have known the art of ju-jitsu or been a kung fu master – I caught his foot, and twisted it and he was down on the floor, wham. Everybody was laughing. The guy got up sheepishly and walked off. From then on, the word spread out: "Don't mess with Vivian Lee." But I was a little skinny guy, no muscular hulk at all.

---

[11] Shirland Wilson switched from the boxing ring to express his talent in song as 'King Fighter' and became a legend among calypsonians.

[12] Malcolm Corrica, 'Lord Canary' was another well-known Guyanese calypsonian.

I also liked ping-pong (table tennis) and I used to go to matches and so on. Eventually I was asked to become president of the British Guiana Table Tennis Association. The previous president wanted to resign and the Association asked me to take over. They were hoping that I would improve their situation using my advertising agency and fund-raising connections. An annual tournament for the Caribbean was played between Trinidad, Barbados, Jamaica and Guyana. The international matches were usually played at Queen's College. The following year after my election as president we were due to go to Jamaica. Fund-raising was mainly by dances but there was a restriction on dances at that time because (I think) of civil disturbances. However, with my usual tendency to take chances I was predicting that the ban would be lifted at the end of July. So I said, OK the first week in August we are going to have a dance. Since people were longing for a "jump-up," I thought that they would be glad to come out and celebrate. But others were concerned that the ban would be extended, determined by the local situation. I said forget that, just go ahead. We rented the Chinese Sports Club. They were glad to rent the hall because nobody was renting at that time. We started advertising. What a crowd we had! I remember Maurice Moore being there and we had so many people attend we didn't have a place to put the money. So I stuffed the money into my pocket and then Maurice Moore, Ecliffe Wharton and myself went to my home with all this money in my pocket. We made a lot of money – enough funds to help the team. I went to Jamaica with them and Maurice went as manager. I think we had a team of five – three boys and two girls. The Harris sisters were among them but we didn't do very well although we enjoyed ourselves.

I was also into music, and I used to play piano a little, having taken lessons from Mr. Percival Loncke. In those days we had to buy sheet music to learn, so I decided we could share since everybody was spending money buying the same thing. I formed the Euterpe Music Club.[13] A few members joined, including Dr. Jerry Manson-Hing, and Mrs. John Martins. We used to meet, talk about music, share music sheets and so on. It didn't last very long because it didn't have many members – just a few months or a year. I was hoping that we would attract some young people but they were not interested. But that was another of my hair-brained schemes.

Finally, I got involved in making a movie "If Wishes were Horses," which had its premiere in 1976. I wrote, produced and directed the

---

[13] Euterpe, Muse of Music, is one of the nine muses of Apollo in Greek mythology.

film.[14] It was a good success in Guyana, we sold out many shows, but it didn't do well outside because it was a product with no big name stars.

Those were some of the things that I was involved with. I tried my hand (and my foot, and my mouth, too) at many things and, all in all, life in Guyana was good to me. Thanks to the wonderful Guyanese people. God bless Guyana.

---

[14] The movie was later made into a video.

CHINESE LESSONS

Irene Akai, née Sue Ping
as told to Trev Sue-A-Quan

The bombs kept raining down, whistling louder and louder as they came closer. I crouched with my schoolmates behind the walls of the classroom that were padded on the outside with piles of sandbags. The school took a direct hit, but it was the dormitory that was demolished. Immediately after came the crash of window panes along with the awful rattling of the building and walls, shaking dust on us as we bunkered down to escape the terror brought by the Japanese bombers. The bombing kept up with regularity, both day and night, accompanied by the noise of the wailing sirens, thunderous bombs, and human cries. The smell of smoke, fuel, gunpowder, and burning flesh wafted through the air.

How could I have ended up in China – in the middle of a war – when I was born half a world away in British Guiana? My father, Sue Ping, had left his native village of Poon Yee in 1900 to seek a better life in the British colony. He settled in New Amsterdam, Berbice County, and there he became known as Benjamin Sue Ping. He worked at shops owned by other Chinese businessmen and later open his own shop. In 1920 he married Adelaide Choong,[1] with whom he had six children, all born in Berbice. Dad's grocery on Main Street was quite successful, but in July 1930 he decided to sell out and take his family to China. He felt it important that his children have a Chinese education and be exposed to Chinese culture. At that time I was seven years old and had gone to school for only one year. We left Georgetown on the *Lady Hawkins*,[2] if I recall correctly, and landed in Halifax, Canada. After going to Vancouver by train, we boarded the *Empress of Japan*,[3] and arrived in Hong Kong three weeks later.

---

[1] Daughter of John Chung-A-Fung, an immigrant from the Hakka village of Kwai Sin, Guangdong Province.

[2] *Lady Hawkins* was later put into war service and sunk on 19 January 1942 by a German U-boat.

[3] *Empress of Japan* was sunk on 9 November 1940 by bombs from German aircraft.

In China we met with Dad's Chinese wife, the one he had left behind, and her two children. Their first child, a son named Yen, was born in 1901, after Dad had already set sail for British Guiana; the second, Fung Sen, was born after he made a brief visit to China in 1918. So there we were, my father with his two wives and eight children. Dad's first wife, whom we called Ma, received us courteously and treated us as her own. Mom was a very easygoing and peaceful person who put her trust in her husband. Her mild temperament was what helped her get through those years in China, because she did not know to speak Chinese, and neither did any of us who were born in British Guiana. Dad built a large two-storey house in Canton, with four big bedrooms upstairs. Dad's eldest son Yen was already married with children and his family lived on the ground floor. Ma's second child, a girl named Fung Sen, also lived on the first floor level, in a room next to the servant's quarters. Over the next few years the family expanded further when Mom gave birth to two other children, while Ma had one more.

Dad was a successful businessman in Canton, dealing in dried seafood and fruits, and was able to build a modern two-level house in his home village. Quite a lot of Chinese did not bother to educate their girl children, but Dad wanted the best training for all of us, daughters included. I attended school in Canton from age seven to eleven and then Dad sent Fung Sen and myself to a boarding school run by New Zealand missionaries, some 10 miles from Canton. We spent four years at the missionary school where we were exposed to Christian festivals, particularly Christmas and Easter. These were occasions filled with fun, but the big celebration was Chinese New Year, a week-long holiday. Then in 1937 the Sino-Japanese conflict became a full-scale war and Canton and its environs became targets for the bombers. The bombing raids went on daily, from 1937 to 1939, and our peaceful and happy school days were severely interrupted. Many of the parents took their children out of school and Dad brought my sister and myself back to Canton so that we could be all together. I then went to Chi Yung High School even though the bombing continued. There were three of us – my sister, a family friend, and myself – who, out of defiance, would sometimes go out at night to buy wonton soup from a small restaurant nearby and sit in the streets in the open air. We felt that it would be all right if a bomb fell on us, because our bellies were full, and we even dared the bombers to do their worst. It may have been just a childish reaction to the terrible destruction going on around us – a gut reaction.

Dad evacuated his family to the countryside but left Fung Sen and me to continue our schooling in Canton, under the care of an old aunt, who would curse furiously when the bombs rained down. Then one day, when we were visiting Mom in the village, Dad told us to get packed, we had to move out right away because Japanese troops were coming. When we left Poon Yee, the objective was to get to Hong Kong, 60 miles away. However, we could not go there directly because Japanese soldiers had effectively cut off that route. We set out on foot with whatever we could carry and for the next few months we fled from village to village, refugees from war. We walked on the country paths and rice field paths, stopping at villages where we were sheltered by friendly locals for a few weeks at a time. Then we would have to flee again as Japanese troops came closer. On the way, we saw others who had left their bedding behind, then their clothing, and possessions, and even their daughters. Dad made sure that we stayed together. Our trek became a long roundabout one to Macao and from there we boarded the boat to Hong Kong, which was not yet caught up in the war.[4] Along with three younger sisters, I was sent to board at Canosian Convent, while Mom and the others found refuge in a bachelor apartment belonging to Jim and Albert Ho-Shing. There were altogether 13 people crowded into that small apartment.

Dad borrowed money to go to British Guiana, departing in January 1939. He arrived with only $5 in his pocket and stayed at the Chinese Association. Because his good principles were well known, he had many friends from before, and was able to get financial and other help from several people, including Alexander Chin (whom Dad had helped when Alex had his own difficulties), Isaac Chin, Charles Yong-Hing, and Victor Fernandes of Fogarty's. They extended credit to Dad to get a wholesale business started at 4A Water and Hope Streets in Georgetown. They told Dad that he could repay them after he was on his feet. Dad then

The Chinese Association, located at Lot 3, Brickdam, opened in 1920. *Public Records.*

cabled Mom to ask her to join him and to bring his sons, because they would be able to help him in running the business. Mom had no intention of leaving her daughters behind. Ma told me that she had found a nice boy for me, but I had no intention of staying there, and

---

[4] The Japanese captured Canton in October 1938; Hong Kong was occupied in December 1941.

Mom sent back a cable: "All, or nothing at all." So Dad had to borrow more money to bring us over. We sailed from Hong Kong to Vancouver aboard the *Empress of Canada*;[5] I believe, and from there we took a train to Montreal, transferred to Halifax and boarded the *Lady Drake*.[6] We arrived in Georgetown in October 1939.

I was 16 at the time and Dad sent me to St. Joseph's High School. Up to that time, my exposure to English studies was during the few months I spent at the Hong Kong convent school. My English was poor. I had to be placed in a class with those who were three years younger than me. I learned a lot of things on my own. I knew the spoken words for a lot of things in English but didn't know how to spell the words until I saw them written down and someone explained what they meant.

The Sue Ping children aboard the *Lady Drake*. Irene is on the right. *Irene Akai.*

The war in Europe affected Dad's business a lot because he relied on imported goods from Canada, England, Argentina, Holland, etc. With a large family to support it was becoming increasingly difficult for him to cope. After two and a half years at St. Joseph's, with fees of $3 due at the end of each month, I decided to quit school to try and help in generating some income for the family. I enrolled in a commercial training school run by Alexander Yhap to learn shorthand and typing. Shorthand was very easy for me because it was a matter of recording the sounds. However, when it came time to put the recorded scripts into English sentences I was at a loss because of my limited ability in English. Because of this, I gave up shorthand and focused on typing. I passed all the stages in the typing examinations, up to the advanced level.

At this time China opened a consulate in Georgetown and my ability with Cantonese plus my increasing knowledge of English landed me a job there. Ismay Fung (who later married John Campbell) was employed as a secretary and I was her assistant, doing typing, preparing invitations to be

---

[5] *Empress of Canada* was sunk on 13 March 1943 by the Italian submarine *Da Vinci*.
[6] *Lady Drake* was sunk on 5 May 1942 by a German U-boat

sent to local guests, and other general jobs. I was in a unique situation because I was perhaps the only young person at the time with knowledge of both Chinese and English – among the local Chinese, those who knew Chinese didn't know English, and those who knew English didn't know Chinese. When the consul received invitations to lunches, dinners, and receptions, I would also be invited to be interpreter.

For a while, I helped to teach Chinese lessons at the Chinese Association after leaving work at the Consulate. These classes had been started by Dr. Ping-Chi Kwong and Ronald C.H. Young, and actively promoted by Marie Evan-Wong. I took over the teaching assignments when these three pioneers went abroad. The classes were intended for local Chinese who had no knowledge of the language of their forefathers. They were third and fourth generation descendants of Chinese immigrants who had arrived during the 19th century. Their parents felt that the ties to China should not be severed and that learning Chinese would be a good way to establish a connection. There were perhaps some 50 children who were enrolled in the classes that ran a couple days a week from about 4 p.m. to 6 p.m. The students sat at long desks and listened to the instruction I gave in conversational Cantonese. There were some simple picture books available with illustrations to make a better impression on the children's minds although they did not take the books home after class. No homework was given, because the focus was on spoken Cantonese rather than the written language, although some basic words were put on the blackboard for them to copy and learn. Conversational Cantonese was quite different from the formal way that it would be written, and it was better that the children learn pronunciation and the tones, rather than having the lessons deal with grammar and structure.

After a while, it was apparent that the children were finding Chinese a difficult language to master, particularly because they did not have people at home who could keep speaking with them in Chinese. So they attended and tried their best in class but then began to drop out one by one until there was not enough showing up at class to continue. The classes had been going for two years or a bit more. One boy who did persist to the end was Pac-hon Chin. He had come from China with his mother when he was a small boy and the early exposure to Chinese as well as his family environment sustained his interest in the Cantonese lessons. He was a brilliant lad and when he did math calculations in his head it was with Chinese numbers rather than English. As a matter of fact, I myself would do the same kind of calculations, using my Chinese mind.

On occasion I would go to see Chinese movies and Pac-hon would also go. The movies were shown at the Olympic cinema on Lombard

Street and the publicity for them would be posted on bulletins at the Chinese Association. Many of them were operas with the male actors wearing flowing gowns, fancy headdress and high platform shoes. They didn't really appeal to me, although I was more accustomed to them when I lived in China.

A group of students who were taught conversational Cantonese by Irene at the Chinese Association. *Irene Akai.*

Yen, my elder brother, had remained in China when we fled Hong Kong, and Dad sponsored him to British Guiana in the mid-1940s. He and his children worked at a shop that Dad opened at Bartica. In 1948, with the war over, Dad decided to send Yen back to China to get the family business re-established. He told me that I should go too. I was 24 years old at the time and knew what was in Dad's mind. I wrote to my boyfriend Ivan Akai, who lived in New Amsterdam, to tell him of this development and immediately he proposed to marry me. Ivan and I had known each other for eight years and we had been writing long letters to each other regularly, maybe twice a week. He played football (soccer) with a New Amsterdam

Irene Sue-Ping.
Irene Akai.

team, and whenever he came to Georgetown for a match, I would go to see him. When Dad received Ivan's offer to marry me, he gave his approval, much to my surprise. Dad explained that he was aware that

Ivan was not from a rich family but that he had good ways – he didn't drink nor gamble. He explained that he himself started as a poor man and there was nothing to prevent Ivan from climbing up later in life. Ivan was much liked by my family and he quit his government job to work at Dad's store.

Dad always maintained close ties to China and his ways were traditional to a large extent. I was expecting that he would want me to have a husband who was fluent in Chinese, or at least knew both English and some Chinese. But he apparently was influenced by other customs – wanting me to have an education, for example. But after Ivan and I got married, Dad did not offer to have us live at his house because the custom in China was that the wife would go to the husband's village. So we rented a room elsewhere to start our married life, and eventually we were able to buy a house of our own.

In one respect Ivan was like Dad – neither felt that his wife should be in the workforce, although I was interested in doing hairdressing. Then one day, Percy Lee died unexpectedly leaving his wife and several children. She was a housewife and the family was left without a source of income. There were four children in our family and I told Ivan that we should try and avoid being left in the same situation. Ivan thought about it for a while and one evening, after returning from a movie, he asked if I was still interested in hairdressing. He had changed his mind, and gave me every support in my hope of going to New York to study. Dad was still opposed to my leaving, but for a different reason – he felt that when I returned he would not be alive. I left in September 1959 and graduated in May 1960. Ivan was scheduled for vacation from his job and joined me for a holiday in North America, but it was cut short when we received a cable that Dad had died. We returned in time for the funeral.

In the mid-1960s I was asked to teach Chinese cooking to a group of people, mainly Chinese women, as part of a fund-raising effort for the United Force political party, headed by Peter d'Aguiar.[7] I had learnt how to cook from watching my mother and I was able to demonstrate how to cook sour-sweet, fried chicken, stir-fried beef, steamed fish and other dishes that utilized Chinese ingredients – foo chook, wanyee, bamboo

---

[7] The two main political parties were the People's Progressive Party (PPP), led by Cheddi Jagan, and the People's National Congress (PNC), headed by Forbes Burnham. These parties drew support mainly from the people of Indian and African ancestry, respectively. Those of other racial backgrounds had divided loyalties. Peter d'Aguiar, of Portuguese heritage, started the United Force party as a conservative alternative to the left-leaning PPP and PNC parties, and drew support from many Portuguese and Chinese, who had become established as the main merchants and businessmen in the colony.

shoots, red dates, etc. The few cooking lessons were held at St. Joseph's
High School and the attendees would afterwards eat the dishes that were
prepared. I was asked to do an advanced cooking class, but I declined
because I was preparing to go to Canada.

Dad would have been pleased to see that I was able to teach Chinese
cooking because he had urged me to master this aspect of Chinese
tradition when I was a teenager. He taught me many lessons in life that
stood me in good stead. As a businessman in Canton he treated people
fairly and with respect, and thus was highly regarded in the community
and in the villages. This was rewarded during the war when others
willingly helped us when we fled from the Japanese bombs and troops.
Then, arriving again in Georgetown in 1939, Dad was helped by several
friends who knew of his principled character. He started from a position
of indebtedness and built his business into a successful operation through
hard work and persistence. These were useful lessons in life. When he
passed away in May 1960, he was about 75 years of age. The funeral
ceremony was held at the Chinese Association with many in attendance.

Drug Store

Harvey Lou-Hing
as told to Trev Sue-A-Quan

Opening a pharmacy, or drug store, was another way that the Chinese took part in the delivery of health care in Guyana. Typically they gained their qualifications as druggists by working for established drug stores and then they branched out on their own.

The first to be active in this field was John Samuel Ho-Yow. He became a sicknurse and dispenser in 1914, and qualified as a chemist and druggist in July 1919. He worked for T.L. Rebitt's Drug Store and, in 1934, set up his own drugstore. In December 1919, James Fung also earned his qualifycations, but then went abroad to gain a degree in dentistry at Chicago College. Solomon Bobb Chan-A-Shing opened his drugstore in 1922 at Queenstown, Essequibo, and became a well-known figure there. Benjamin Philbert Ting-A-Kee and Cyril Augustus Chin became qualified in 1930 and 1933, respectively.

One prominent establishment was Tang's Drug Store, located in the business section of Georgetown. It was owned by Peter "Whitty" Tang, who became registered as a chemist and druggist in December 1939. One month later, Harvey Lou-Hing, joined the list of registered druggists, and followed a similar course as the other Chinese druggists before him, eventually owning his own drugstore.

* * * * * * * *

Harvey Lou-Hing's parents, Edward and Elizabeth Lou-Hing, owned a dry goods shop at La Bonne Intention, East Coast Demerara. Harvey and his twin brother, Clyde, were born in 1915, and were the youngest ones in the family. The boys attended school in Georgetown but had to go and help their parents to sell goods in the shop, especially on busy weekends and holidays. Harvey later lived at LBI, and his parents – or, more likely, his mother – asked the sugar estate managers whether there was a job available. That was how he came to be hired as a sicknurse at the dispensary, which was essentially the estate's hospital. Harvey's duties included going around to hand out medicine to the patients and to assist in caring for their needs. He also learnt to make various medicinal preparations and tonics from the supplies contained in large bottles in the dispensary, as well as finding and counting out the prescribed pills.

This initial exposure to the dispensing of drugs went on for about a year. Harvey then applied to Bookers in Georgetown to obtain more formal training in this field. But this apprenticeship carried no pay. He was assigned to sell medicines at the large outlet owned by Bookers, and working at the dispensary. For five days of the week he worked from 8:00 o'clock to 4:00 o'clock, and on occasion he had to show up on a Saturday. The man in charge of the dispensary showed Harvey how things were run there, and every week there was an hour-long lecture held at the hospital, taught by the manager of the hospital's dispensary. The study course was to provide some basics in science, especially in chemistry. Harvey liked chemistry and was happy to continue pursuing this line of work with Bookers.

The apprenticeship period lasted for three months, and after that Harvey became a paid employee with a salary. His duties required him to sleep at the dispensary every fifth night. There was a room upstairs and a bed was provided, plus tea and biscuits. A watchman was also on the premises and he would call Harvey whenever a customer came to get medicine during the night. After a while Harvey was put in charge of one of Bookers' branch stores, located at Camp and Norton Streets. The drugs and supplies were all provided by Bookers, and Harvey was paid a salary for the management of the store. Then, about 1942, Bookers decided to give up all of their branch stores, selling them off to any interested parties. Harvey felt that he was capable of continuing the business and so he bought the store for twelve thousand dollars, and renamed it Lou-Hing's Drug Store.

The medicines now had to be bought from Bookers at wholesale prices and in the initial stage of operation Harvey employed one person to help with the sales. Because World War II was still ongoing, there were some items that were hard to obtain and he would sell whatever was available until stocks ran out. The popular items were general medicines, such as mercurochrome and tincture of iodine that were used as antiseptic agents for cuts and bruises. Cuts were typically patched up with a wad of cotton wool on which a liberal portion of mercurochrome or iodine was added. The piece of cotton wool would be torn from a tightly-wound roll that was some eight to ten inches long, and held in place over the wound with strips of adhesive plaster. Generally speaking, mercurochrome was preferred by the wounded person – and especially children – because iodine would bring on a distinctly painful experience when it was applied to the cut or bruise. These were the days before Band-Aid strips were invented, and invariably strands from the cotton wool would be come imbedded in the scab that formed over the wound.

Harvey was a part-time doctor of sorts because many people would come by to describe their troubles, and seek an appropriate remedy. If the problem seemed to be more than a minor ailment, they would be asked to go to see the doctor and bring back the prescription. All the customers had to pay for their medicines, since there were no subsidies or rebates available from any government or health-related agencies. Harvey did not encounter cases where people would ask for medicines without paying or for credit. This was because the purchase of necessary drugs was generally regarded as an imperative step in the treatment of medical problems and the patients and their families knew that the money would have to be ready before heading off to the drugstore.

Phensic (a brand of aspirin) was the well-known remedy for aches and pains. Another popular item was Ferrol, a tonic rich with iron and vitamins that was promoted for boosting one's health and immune system. There were not a lot of patent medicines and when a customer wanted a cough syrup, an appropriate mixture would be made up from large bottles containing the essential remedies. Graduated cylinders were used to measure the desired amount of the medicinal concentrate. For small amounts, a V-shaped measuring glass would be employed, while a straight-sided cylinder was used for larger amounts, perhaps several ounces. After pouring the concentrate into a bottle, water or an alcohol solution would be added to fill the bottle. The label of instructions invariably carried the direction to shake well. Bookers made their own brand of cough syrup, called Cure A Cough, and there was also Buckley's cough mixture, but these were less commonly used that the remedies that were freshly brewed in the drug store.

Witch hazel, sold as an ointment in small jars, was commonly used for hemorrhoids as well as a skincare salve. Vaseline petroleum jelly was another product used for skin care, especially for rubbing on babies, and for rashes. Canadian Healing Oil was a popular general-use liniment, good for aches and sprains, rheumatism, and muscle stiffness. Vicks Vapor Rub or Thermogene would be generously rubbed on the chest and back of someone with a heavy chest cough. These various items were commonly found in the homes of most families. Although Tiger Balm could be purchased in Guyana, it was not one of the products available at the Lou-Hing's Drug Store.

Brooks and Ex-Lax were the brand names for laxatives that came in chocolate form. They were sometimes taken away secretly by visiting children (mainly relatives) who had access behind the counter. The children believed they were in for a chocolate treat, not realizing that there would be certain consequences. However, the taste could never match that of real milk chocolate, and the children's interest in the "treat" became a passing episode. Castor oil was another popular item – and definitely not a treat for the children to whom it was generally given to rid their insides of worms, real or perceived. Milk of magnesia was available, as a ready-mixed product.

Lysol disinfectant and washing soda were commonly sold for cleaning homes and shops. Formalin, which is a water-based solution of formaldehyde, was another product used as disinfectant. It was commonly used in hospitals and created the "hospital smell" that pervaded the air. Chloroform was also available for sale but not a big seller because the general public had no ongoing use for such a product.

Bee and wasp stings were usually treated with methylated spirits, although Thermogene would sometimes be pressed into service for such insect bites. Comparable to methylated spirits, supplied in large drums, there was Limacol, made by Bookers. Limacol was a very popular local product, used as a cooling lotion and astringent for fevers and aches as well as a freshener for the face and skin. Bookers also produced a bath soap with the Limacol name and it competed favorably with imported Lever brand soap, and Pears' soap.

The drug store was the place to buy various essences – vanilla, almond, cherry, and so on – to be used in making cakes and pastries. Another food item available was acetic acid. Usually a customer would bring an empty bottle and have it partly filled with acetic acid, which became vinegar when diluted with water. The essences, along with Vaseline, were perhaps the biggest selling products. Harvey eventually converted a section of the store to a grocery. A couple employees, one a Chinese and the other an Indian, were hired to help with the sale of groceries. On sale were flour, rice, saltfish, sardines and other goods commonly found in a grocery.

In 1950 Harvey sold his drugstore, and it became Latchmansingh's Drugstore. Harvey had been attending night school to become trained as a bookkeeper and accountant, and after gaining his qualifying certificate, he decided to give up the drugstore and take up accountancy.

Short Cuts

Compiled by Trev Sue-A-Quan

Mathias Sin-yu Woon was a well-known itinerant barber in Georgetown. Sin-yu was born in 1891 in Stewartville, West Coast Demerara, the son of Simon Woon-A-Fook, an immigrant from China. This account of his activities was compiled from the recollections of family members and various clients of his hair-cutting services.

* * * * * * * *

At one time, Sin-yu Woon tried his hand at gold mining. He went to the goldfields in the interior regions of Guyana, but he was not among those who struck it rich. Whatever he gained was quite small and not enough to support his family. He then dabbled in various other activities, including making bread from his home. The production of home-made bread required him to be working for long hours with a small wood-burning stove in the kitchen. It was a small-scale business and he did not have many customers. This venture also proved to be incapable of providing a decent living.

Sin-yu then took up barbering, although it is not known for certain how he learnt that skill or what caused him to have an interest in it. What is known is that he developed a sizeable clientele among the Chinese families living in Georgetown, and he became a regular feature in their lives. For most families, there was a regular schedule for visits, usually once every two weeks, or sometimes three weeks. However, there were some people that he visited on a weekly basis, one of them being James Sue-A-Quan, proprietor of J.A. Sue-A-Quan's

Sin-yu Woon in the early 1920s. *Barbara Fisher.*

Winery on Robb Street. Uncle Jim, as he was popularly known, liked to have his hair in good order, even though each weekly visit would take away just a small amount of growth.

Sin-yu kept an appointment book in which he could record the families that needed to be served and the times set aside for these visits. But there were also some who came by to his home, on a drop-in basis, although they too would have to make prior arrangements with Sin-yu. One person who came to his home fairly regularly was Frank "Booker" Chan-Choong, who also was an itinerant barber by trade. Booker's aunt married Sin-yu's uncle, so there was a family connection that linked them. Booker was a much younger fellow, and he had a disability – he was dumb, and could emit only basic sounds and grunts. But he knew exactly what he wanted to say, and he used his hands to support the sounds he uttered. Being a longtime companion, Sin-yu could understand exactly what Booker was trying to express, especially by sitting across from him and patiently watching and listening. Sin-yu's mother-in-law also joined in these exchanges and so Booker felt welcome in their home. On many an occasion Booker would be a lunch guest. Perhaps it was through their professional association that Booker and Sin-yu would each be able to get his own hair cut.

There were several characteristics about Sin-yu that became almost trademarks. He used basic hairdressing instruments – none of which was powered by electricity – neatly packed in a rectangular can. There was his special barber's scissors, a long pointed one with an additional semi-circular finger grip attached at the end such that the first and second fingers could come into use when snipping. He also packed another pair of scissors that he used to snip his cigarette when only a short stub remained or if he needed to bring his smoking session to an end. Other items included a tapered barber's comb, soft-hair brush, clipping shears, and a razor. There was also a spray bottle of the type that would be used in bygone days to spray an aerosol of perfume, complete with its rubber squeeze bulb. Finally, there was a tin of talcum powder. Around the tin that housed these tools of the trade, Sin-yu placed the leather strip that was used for keeping the razor sharp. The whole lot was carefully wrapped in the protective cloth which he would use to drape around his clients, and which would be secured by a safety pin at the back of the neck. The parcel of barbering implements was fastened to the carrier of Sin-yu's bicycle, mounted over the rear wheel.

The neatness that Sin-yu showed in carrying around his tools was also evident in the way that he dressed. On his head, a white safari helmet, or cork hat,[1] could be seen. This matched well with the white suit and black

---

[1] The white cork hat was a popular type of headwear that, especially among children, was commonly called a "hug house."

bow-tie that he always wore. Sin-yu donned pant clips[2] to keep the potentially flapping ends of his trousers in place as he rode his bicycle. He also wore silver expandable armbands that kept the cuffs and sleeves of his shirt pulled up, away from the hair clippings.

For young Chinese girls whose parents did not want to deal with the hassle of long tresses, the linzee was the predominant choice, with the hair at the front of the head combed forward and cut straight across at mid-forehead level. The rest of the girl's hair was left to hang straight down and also cut straight across all around at the level of the chin.

Men's hairstyles in those days were rather limited – hair parted on the left, or in the center, or on the right; or else no part at all, with the hair combed back. "Short, sides and back" was the operative phrase. During and

Sharon Lou-Hing with a linzee hairstyle.
Sharon Lou-Hing

after WWII there were some who were influenced by the haircuts displayed by the American military personnel – the crew cut. Among young boys, it was not uncommon for a freshly-cropped head of hair to be greeted with remarks that were sometimes unflattering, such as "calabash cut."[3] Besides the choice of where to part the hair, the boys often groomed themselves to display a muff, with the hair on the non-parted side raised to considerable height. A few puffs of mildly-scented water from the spray bottle were employed to moisten the hair so as to better control the cutting. Sin-yu also shaved beards and stubble without the use of lather – plain water and a very sharp razor were enough. Frequent rhythmic slaps of the razor on the leather strap gave it the needed edge.

The haircutting operations were set up at whatever convenient place was available in the house. It might be the living room, or a hallway, or even the garage that was transformed into the temporary barbershop. There usually would be a specific seat pressed into becoming the client's perch and this could be a stool, straight-back chair, or bench. For young children, a pouffe, or padded footstool, would be placed on the chair to provide additional height. In other households a wooden chair with

---

[2] Narrow metal bands forming an arc of about three quarters of a circle that served as anklets to keep the trouser legs from becoming entangled in the chain or spokes of the bicycle.
[3] Depictive of having a calabash placed on one's head and cutting off any protruding hair.

armrests would serve as a base and a small plank placed on the armrests to provide an elevated platform for the child.

Because Sin-yu had many customers in the Chinese community he got to know the affairs of many families and became the bearer of news, not in the way of gossip (although that cannot be ruled out), but by keeping people up to date on how one family or other was progressing. With those who spoke his dialect he could exchange in a chat but this would not be in any great depth, since, like many second generation Chinese, he was more familiar with English.

The business of barbering kept Sin-yu very busy and he had few recreational activities. It is said that he was very skilled at shooting craps – a master at rolling the dice – but this was not a passion for him. He smoked a lot and rolled his own cigarettes, taking an appropriate amount of filler from a tin of Capstan tobacco, and then carefully trimming off any protruding bits of tobacco using his "smoking scissors." What caught his interest was top-class boxing, and whenever there was a big match scheduled – perhaps Joe Louis in a championship fight – he would go to his radio and scan the short-wave bands to find a station that was broadcasting the fight. But Sin-yu did not keep this enjoyment to himself. For a while Sin-yu lived in a house on D'Urban Street, across the street from the Georgetown Jail. Whenever a boxing match was on, he would turn up the volume on the console so that the sound carried across to the prisoners. Such broadcasts would typically be at nighttime when traffic on the streets was light and the ones in custody would be able to enjoy the blow-by-blow action. They pressed their heads against the bars on the windows and dangled their arms outside. When the fight was over the prisoners would clap their appreciation, shout words of thanks, and engage in a vigorous discussion about the fight, their words carrying some distance in the still of the night.

Sin-yu traveled around Georgetown on his faithful bicycle, setting out early in the morning so as to arrive in time to cut the hair of the various members in the household before they were scheduled to leave for work or school. Appointments were also arranged during a customer's lunch break, after the workday was finished, or on weekends. His bicycle was the means of transportation for his grandchildren. He would carry them, a couple at a time, on the crossbar of the bicycle, but only after he had tied on a cushion to soften the ride for his passengers. Sin-yu covered many miles each week on his rounds and as he grew older he found that the trips were becoming a bit tiring for him. His eldest grandson, Errol Ten-Pow, was in the motorcycle business, and, together with his brother Elson, decided to fit Sin-yu's bicycle with a Velosolex. Invented in France in 1946, the small gasoline-powered motor was mounted above the front wheel. First the bicycle had to reach a suitable speed in the conventional way, by pedaling. Then the drive-wheel on the Velosolex would be brought in contact with the bicycle wheel and this would get the motor started. The motor would then take over and deliver the motive power through the drive-wheel. There were controls for engaging the drive-wheel and for adjusting the speed. The device helped to reduce the expenditure of effort but as time went on, Sin-yu was finding some difficulty managing the controls while maintaining his balance and weaving through traffic. Eventually the Velosolex was removed, and that was about the time that Sin-yu reduced his workload and essentially retired.

RICE GRADER

Sandra Wong-Moon, née Ho-Sing-Loy

Wilfred "Tyer" Ho-Sing-Loy was born on 5 May 1903 in Georgetown, British Guiana, to Henry Ho-Sing-Loy and his wife Sarah (née Wong). Tyer, the eldest of eight children, lived in Georgetown where his father worked as an interpreter for the Immigration Office. Henry was well-known among the Chinese community and helped to form the Chinese Association that was later housed on Brickdam. Wilfred grew up in Uitvlugt and, on 16 June 1937, married Ruby Ming of Plantation Ogle, East Coast Demerara at St. Philips Church, Georgetown. At the time of their wedding, the certificate listed his "rank or profession" as Commission Agent.

Wilfred took his bride to live at 6 McDoom Village, East Bank Demerara, a few miles from the center of Georgetown. He had bought a house there in anticipation of his marriage. This house was huge indeed – it had three big bedrooms, a very large kitchen, dining room and even larger sitting room. Later, he added on to the front of the house to create an office and veranda. The lot was two to three acres in size, and also housed a large chicken coop and run, two guava trees, three or four coconut trees, a genip tree,[1] two simitoo vines,[2] a soursop tree, a star apple tree, a golden apple tree,[3] two or three orange trees, a sapodilla tree,[4] two avocado trees, two plum trees, and a couple mango trees.

A decade after settling in McDoom Village, and after unsuccessfully trying to have children (with a few miscarriages), they adopted me (Sandra) from his youngest brother, Polo, and sister-in-law, Beverly. I

---

[1] A large tree bearing bunches of fruit with a green skin that easily splits away from the fleshy center.

[2] Pale yellow when ripe, this fruit contains a large number of soft, jelly-like beads, each with a seed in the middle. The contents, seeds included, are usually sucked up and swallowed in a batch.

[3] Star apples and golden apples are tropical fruits that are very different from the apples grown in colder climates. A cross section of the star apple shows a star pattern within the circular core; the golden apple has a somewhat tart flavor and a spiny seed.

[4] An oval or egg-shaped fruit with a brown skin. The flesh is very sweet when ripe, and has a somewhat gritty texture.

was born in 1946 and adopted in 1947. From then on, Wilfred and Ruby were Dad and Mum to me. While I cannot remember much before I was about four years old, I do remember my Dad's office downstairs having two large desks, a few chairs and several boxes of papers and samples of things that he imported. I was curious about the various stamps on envelopes and the countries from where they came. It seems that my Dad was an Importer/Exporter of various goods, but I cannot remember what those items were.

Sometime about 1949 Dad started to work at the Rice Marketing Board. We still lived in McDoom Village, and Dad drove to work everyday. I started school in kindergarten at the Anglican Convent of the Good Shepherd in Georgetown, and Dad would take me there in the morning and pick me up after school everyday. He used to take me to his workplace, which was the central marketing agency for all the rice produced in the country. Much of the rice was delivered to the RMB in the form of paddy, i.e. with the husk still on the rice grains, and there was a mill there for removing the husk. I recall seeing several plates of rice on his desk. Samples of rice were usually brought to him on plates, with the raw rice still steaming hot from the mill. He would sniff the aroma from each plate, then let it cool down so that he could feel the texture of the rice with his hand, rubbing the raw grains between his fingers for a minute or two. He would also inspect the color and estimate the proportion of broken or non-uniform grains. Afterwards he would write on a pad and place the "grades" on each plate. I do not know what the grades were, but I presume they were White No. 1, Brown No. 1, etc.[5] I understand that his title was Rice Grading Inspector and I believe he did this job until he retired in 1959 or 1960.

In 1949 or 1950 my grandmother Sarah came to live with us. Grandma Sarah came from Hong Kong, and often told the tale of how she was taken from Hong Kong and ended up in British Guiana. One day, an envoy from a boat that was docked came down their street and invited entire families to a party on the boat. The people were promised lots of food, drink and a good time. Being curious and a little on the hungry side, my grandmother and her brothers pleaded with their parents to attend. So the whole family decided to satisfy their curiosity, and the next day they went on board the boat, where they were able to eat, drink, and listen to "good" music. Before they knew what was happening, the boat had weighed anchor and they were in the middle of the harbor. Many people jumped off the ship and lost their lives. The family decided

[5] The grade of rice determined the amount the Rice Marketing Board would pay to the rice grower.

to stick it out, and after traveling for months they arrived in British Guiana.[6]

My Dad was a very good son. He would come home from work and take care of his mother after the day-nurse left. He would feed her and then take care of her toiletries. She used to smile and tell me he is blessed. She often hid the sweets that he brought for her and then she would give them to me the next day. My aunts Mabel (who married Nathaniel Fung-Kee-Fung), Irene (wife of Dr. Hilton Ho), Flora Barclay, and Eugene would come by to see their mother every week along with their brothers Silas and Polo. Grandma Sarah's nieces, Florence Hing, and Marie Evan-Wong, and sometimes her nephew Leslie Evan-Wong, our family dentist, would pop in from time to time. A couple of times she had problems with her jaw, and Uncle Hilton, who was an eye, nose and throat specialist, came by to help to unlock her jaw. She died in 1952.

In 1956, Dad went on a "world tour" to the Far East and traveled all by himself for around three months. His photograph was featured in Japan in an English-language paper. He was touted to be a representative of the British Guiana Government looking into rice mills for the country. There he made contact with the Sataki Rice Mill Company and became their agent in British Guiana and the West Indies. The first of these rice mills was set up in Windsor Forest at the estate of his brother-in-law, Nathaniel Fung-Kee-Fung, in or around 1957 or 1958. He was known as Uncle A-Hing, most likely from his Chinese given name. His estate was quite large and he raised chickens, pigs and grew a large number of fruit trees for the family's consumption. He also had a dry-goods store in which he stocked bolts of materials for dresses, pants, etc. Sweets, flour, sugar and almost everything needed for the household were the main products. He was also the Justice of the Peace for the Windsor Forest area and many times had to settle disputes among the local people. The second rice mill was set up in Bel Air, at his cousins, the Leungs. Many "rice people" came to see the advanced technology of the Japanese, and some even bought rice mills from my Dad. He later sold his interest in the agency to Mr. F.A. Lewis.

When Dad was a young man he took up the art of wrestling. I have a photo of him posing in his wrestling duds. Dad and his friends, Johnny Ho-A-Shoo, F.A. Lewis, the Chee-A-Tow boys, and his brother Polo used to wrestle in a Chinese group at the Chinese Association. He also did yoga and even into his eighties was capable of standing on his head to

---

[6] The Wong parents, their two boys and a girl, were among the 516 passengers on the *Dartmouth* that set sail on Christmas Eve in 1878 and landed in Georgetown on 17 March 1879. Sarah was about five years old at the time.

demonstrate to my sons. Dad was also an avid tennis player. Mum and Dad went to Georgetown at least once a month to play against Dr. Carlton Fung-Kee-Fung and his wife Eileen in the Georgetown hospital compound. Dad practiced hitting tennis balls against a concrete wall next to our garage. He also held many bridge tournaments at the house. I remember when he came back from the world tour he brought back a mah-jongg set and Aunt Flo Hing came to teach us how to play. He also brought back Japanese chopsticks and we learned to eat with them.

Wilfred Ho-Sing-Loy, the wrestler. *Sandra Wong-Moon*

When Dad's cousin, Marie Evan-Wong, decided she was going to move to London, England, she asked Dad if he wanted to buy her curio business "Shangri-la" from her. Dad bought the store for my Mum and I remember going there after school to help dust and keep the store spick and span. Mum sold Chinese ornaments, pictures, jewelry and anything "Oriental" to those who could afford them. The Governor's wife, Mrs. Renison, was a repeat customer, coming in almost every month for something or other. It was great fun to chat with the many merchants or friends who came in to buy, out of curiosity, or just to "gaff." Shangri-la was next door to the local record store and Mum and I would listen to the latest records of Elvis Presley, Pat Boone, Ricky Nelson, the Platters, Mario Lanza, Lord Kitchener etc., as soon as they arrived. What fun. Of course, we would be their first customers whenever a record went on sale.

It was in 1959 that Dad formed a consortium that went to French Guiana to help develop the rice industry in that country. He sold his home and invested in land and machinery when he settled in Cayenne, the capital of French Guiana, in 1960. I was left at the Convent of the Good Shepherd for a couple of months and then at Uncle Polo and Aunt Bev, as I was in Fourth Form at Bishops High School and wanted to finish high school there. Mum and Dad took Xavier and Eileen Phang (two daughters of Mum's sister Enid) with them as the girls were living with us at the time. This turned out to be a short-lived project because the French Guiana Government, after much red tape and my Dad putting out his money for whatever they "needed" to register the company, buy land and machinery, etc., decided he was not the right person to spearhead the project. His partners were given his holdings and my father literally had to leave that country as fast as he could with no compensation for his investment. He felt he had been robbed by his friends and the French Government, but did not pursue any legal recourse as he felt it would only be throwing good money after bad.

Dad and Mum passed through Georgetown, dropping off Xavier and Eileen so they could travel to their mother Enid in London, England. British Guiana was experiencing some political problems at the time so Dad and Mum moved to Trinidad in 1962 and applied for immigration status to Canada. They received approval in 1963 and after passing the medical examinations, we moved to Vancouver, British Columbia in April 1964.

LAWS AND LOWS

Louis Low
as told to Trev Sue-A-Quan

Archival records show that Law A-un, a 28-year old teacher from the Hakka district of Ka Ying Chow, not far distant from Guangzhou (Canton), embarked on the *Whirlwind* on Christmas Eve of 1859, bound for Georgetown, British Guiana. The arrival of the *Whirlwind* on 11 March 1860 was a significant development in the history of Chinese immigration to the colony because this vessel carried the first Chinese females since Chinese workers began arriving in 1853, and one of the girls aboard this ship later became the wife of Law A-un. He was allotted to Plantation Lusignan, East Coast Demerara, but the manager found him unsuited to manual labor and arranged for him to run a small shop on the estate. He later was involved in various shopkeeping ventures, with differing degrees of success, and in his later years became a catechist at St. Peter's Parish in Essequibo. However, he died only a few months after arriving in Essequibo, on 29 September 1892.

It was not unusual for a Chinese person to choose a different name when his status changed, and Law A-un selected the more auspicious name Lau Shiu-t'ong, portraying his scholarly background. He raised a family of eight children who carried the surname Low. One of the sons, Frederick Orlando Low became the first Chinese lawyer in British Guiana, and a few decades later, his nephew Louis followed in his footsteps in the law profession.[1]

* * * * * * * *

I remember my uncle Frederick Low[2] as a magistrate on West Coast Demerara, in Essequibo, and West Bank Demerara. He was familiarly

---

[1] The Low family surname is pronounced differently depending on the Chinese dialect spoken, and can be written in a number of ways in English. Variations include Law, Lau, Leow, Lieu, Liew, Liu, Lo, Loo, Lou, Louis, Low, Lowe, Lu, Lue, Lui, and Lyew.

[2] Frederick Orlando Low was born on 17 March 1881 at Plantation La Jalousie, West Coast Demerara. After completing seventh standard at school he wanted to become a schoolteacher like his father, but was dissuaded by his family. He was employed by John Ho-A-Shoo, a prominent businessman, and sent to manage a shop at Five Stars on the Barima River that catered to gold and diamond miners in that area. The pork-knockers shopped only on Saturday and this gave F.O. a lot of free time to learn and

known as F.O. Low and assigned to these various judicial areas
depending on the colony's needs. I used to visit him quite a lot.
Magistrates heard both criminal and civil cases and pronounced
judgment without the requirement of a jury. Serious crimes, such as
murder, referred to as indictable offences, would be sent to the Supreme
Court to be tried before a jury. The courthouse for West Bank, Demerara
was located at Vreed-en-Hoop and it was there that F.O. was injured. He
was hearing a case of praedial larceny (i.e. theft of growing vegetables) at
the time, and on a table before the him lay several exhibits relevant to
other cases. The accused was apparently unhappy with how the proceedings were going and was pleading for mercy. Before anyone else
could react, he grabbed an iron bar, one of the exhibits lying on a table
near where F.O. was presiding, and struck the magistrate on the head.
F.O. went out like a light and was taken to the Georgetown Hospital,
where he recovered after a while. It was not the kind of crowning
achievement that F.O. expected from pursuing a law career and
fortunately the injury was not serious. This incident happened some time
in the late 1930s or early 1940s.

There were courthouses located in distant regions and the magistrate
was required to go there when there were cases to be heard. Sometimes
this meant traveling upriver by Government launch, e.g. up the
Demerara River, or Potaro River. At these outlying locations there were
houses provided by the Government for the magistrate.[3]

---

master the skill of shorthand. In January 1902 he resigned his position with Ho-A-
Shoo and joined Hing Cheong & Co in Georgetown. He learnt Latin and French
from private tutors and he found scholarly pursuits more to his liking than being a
clerk. He left his job in June 1902 and opted to read law with S.E. Barnes, a local
solicitor. Not long after, he passed the Cambridge Junior Examinations. His desire to
read for the Bar was supported by Ho-A-Shoo and Chow Wai-hing, owner of Hing
Cheong & Co, who organized fund-raising activities for the promising lad. Several
hundred dollars were raised and F.O. set out for London in April 1904. He was
admitted to Middle Temple and called to the Bar on 1 July 1908 at the age of 27.
[3] F.O. Low was the Returning Officer for the Essequibo River district for a by-
election on 28 May 1934, resulting from the death of the elected representative, the
Hon. E.F. Fredericks. Two persons ran for the vacant seat, Robert V. Evan-Wong, a
merchant by trade, and Alfred R. Crum-Ewing, a manufacturers' representative. On
the day after voting took place, F.O. announced that Evan-Wong had obtained 236
votes while Crum-Ewing garnered 199, with 8 ballots spoilt. Within a few weeks,
Crum-Ewing filed a petition asking that the results should be declared null and void.
He alleged that there was corruption practiced by Evan-Wong's agents and
supporters, specifically Walter Chee-A-Tow, Frederick Sue-A-Quan, Abdool Majeed
Khan, Simon Yhap, Robert Rose Chung, Eric Leung Walker, Issri Persaud, Lilliah,
Ellen Elizabeth Whyte and Kassim Kamal. The petition was heard in the Supreme
Court, with Chief Justice Crean presiding. For the next few months, testimonies were

F.O. left the bench in the early 1940s and practiced law in Georgetown. His first office was on the top floor of the Chinese Association building on Brickdam. The furnishings consisted of a desk, chairs, and cabinets to hold books and clients' legal papers and documents. His clients were mostly Chinese businessmen, but included other nationals as well. The cases were predominantly civil suits. Later he moved to the Wharton Building on Croal Street, and he was still there when I opened my own law practice in 1949, in a room next door. F.O. died on 19 April 1953.

My choice to pursue a career in law was not really influenced by my uncle's achievements, even though he became a well-known figure. After I left school I joined the Public Service as a surveyor's apprentice. I worked with various surveyors and the job took me to several remote areas, such as the Cuyuni River. The surveying crew was a fairly large party including porters for equipment and supplies. During the surveying of one of the lines I almost became lost. I was working with Fred Rodrigues – a tall fellow with a long stride. He moved quite fast and I couldn't keep up with him. I met a junction of some creeks and I went across the wrong one and found myself wandering in the bush for quite a while. Fortunately I had a sense where the camp was. Eventually I found myself at back at our base, but it was completely deserted. After the others did not see me they had set out to look all over the place for me. Later they all came back and found me safely in the camp. After that, I was never left behind.

When we were on these surveying expeditions we wore helmets – the safari-style helmets that we called cork hats. We wrapped long lengths of cloth from our ankles up to our knees, known as puttees, to protect ourselves from snakes and insects. We would encounter all manner of snakes on these outings. One night, a snake, apparently a green parrot snake, made its way inside the tent and was crawling on the roof supports

---

heard about free drinks being provided, drops (free car rides) being offered, along with promises of a feast or two. It would appear that a crowd had gathered at William Sue-A-Quan's rum shop on the morning of election day and some people did indeed get drinks without paying, but William's brother, Frederick, showed the accounting that the drinks were recorded as being on credit, which was a very common practice. Then there were apparently some disgruntled voters who were upset at not getting a drop – the car had run out of gasoline – and asked for a dinner to make up for being made to look like fools. The testimonies were conflicting and confusing and, in the end, the Chief Justice managed to declare the election results void. A new voting date was set for 10 December 1934. Robert V. Evan-Wong and Alfred R. Crum-Ewing again stood for election and each candidate got 199 votes. F.O. Low cast the deciding vote, as allowed by law, in favor of Evan-Wong.

before slithering away. Our tents had open sides and a canvas roof. We slept in hammocks that were hung on the upright posts for the tent, keeping us off the ground where scorpions and other creatures might otherwise reach us. Above each hammock was mosquito netting that provided a cocoon-like shelter. Every morning we had to shake out our clothes and upturn our boots to make sure that no uninvited creatures had taken up residence.

Accompanying the surveying party were some Amerindians who would hunt for us. They were marvelous hunters and fishermen. We would tell them that we wanted fish, and they would go off and bring back fish. Or we might request meat and they would return with it – perhaps a deer or other wild animal. I remember once, when we were up in the Cuyuni, some pork-knockers came to the camp and begged us for food because their supplies had run out. So we gave them a bag or two of flour, each weighing some 90 pounds. These guys just put the bags on their backs and walked off through the highland.

Another assignment in which I assisted was the Bonasika Water Project, for which the surveyor was Walter Ying. That area was very swampy, and when it was time for lunch all we could do was to stand up in the swamp and eat from our lunch carriers; then we carried on with our surveying work. I also did hydrographic surveying in the coastal areas with Sammy Luck and O.K. Yhap. We were taken around by a Government launch from which we would take soundings using a long rope with markings. The main interest for the hydrographic surveys was to show the depth of the water available for boats and to demarcate the coastline.

I did surveying for about five years and felt that it was too tough a life for me, so I decided to do law. I began by reading the relevant materials on my own. The syllabus and law books were available so I knew what needed to be learnt. To get a peaceful surrounding, I used to go to the Botanical Garden during the day to study law there. I studied for about two years and then sat for the first part of the Bar exam, under the supervision of a local representative of the Inns of Court. After I passed Part I of the Bar, I had to go to take the finals in London. I was admitted to Gray's Inn and in June of 1949, I graduated as a Barrister at law. I returned to Guyana right away and was admitted to practice law.

When I was in London, I even gained some experience in the arbitration process. I was staying in a flat for which I felt the rent was too high. I took the matter to Rent Assessment, much to the annoyance of the landlady, and was successful. The rent was reduced and the landlady was mad. When I arrived back to Guyana she actually wrote me demanding money, saying that I damaged her property – various utensils in the house, chairs, and that sort of thing. I ignored her allegations.

After practicing for a while as a private lawyer I did some prosecutions in the Supreme Court in Essequibo. Then I went on the Bench, and my first appointment as magistrate was on the west coast of Berbice in 1957. Not long after I was assigned to New Amsterdam, the capital of Berbice. In the Berbice countryside the population consisted mainly of people of Indian descent, but there were several towns and villages where those of African descent predominated. It is quite likely that my being Chinese played a part in the decision to have me be the magistrate in these areas because it gave the various parties a greater sense of impartiality. I was then assigned to the court in Courantyne, at the eastern end of Berbice County.

My practice consisted of criminal and civil matters before the Supreme and Magistrate Courts – as defense counsel in cases such as murder, serious assaults and other criminal matters before the Supreme Court. I also prosecuted many criminal cases before the Supreme Court and represented clients in civil matters (e.g. divorce and civil claims). In the Magistrates' Courts I defended all manner of summary jurisdiction offences and civil claims.

The jurisdiction of the courts is divided between the Supreme and the Magistrate Courts. The Supreme Court deals with all indictable offences (serious matters as murder, serious assaults, woundings, rape, arson, break and enter, etc.), and civil cases including divorce, and claims amounting to more than $250. The Magistrate Courts have jurisdiction over summary offences, e.g. common assault, trespass, petty thefts, indecent assault, careless driving and other minor offences. The courts also preside over civil actions and debts of $250, rent restrictions, and workmen's compensation. The magistrate would also act as coroner in the event of sudden death. Before an indictable offence is tried before the Supreme Court, a preliminary hearing is heard before the magistrate to ascertain whether there is sufficient evidence to warrant a trial before the Supreme Court. A magistrate is not briefed in advance of cases before the court. The length of a case would depend on the nature of the offence and the amount of witnesses involved. In most criminal cases, defendants are represented by lawyers, while the prosecutor is normally a police officer. In civil cases, the plaintiff and the defendant would normally have lawyers representing their respective clients. In the majority of cases, judgment is pronounced immediately, but sometimes judgment is given at a later date.

There was another, although subsidiary, level in the legal system, administered by Justices of the Peace. J.P.'s were laymen, selected from those in the local area who had established themselves as respected and trustworthy people, perhaps through successful business ventures or land ownership. District Commissioners were also empowered to perform the functions of a Justice of the Peace. Their duties included the witnessing of documents, the signing of warrants, and, in remote areas, the trial of minor offences and civil actions, plus the granting of bail in the absence of a magistrate.

A magistrate does not wear a gown or wig, and evidence is recorded by the magistrate himself, sitting at an elevated desk. Lawyers in the magistrates' courts would normally wear dress suits, preferably dark colors. A witness box is provided, plus seating accommodation for the gallery. In any appearance in the Supreme or Magistrate Courts, the lawyers and anyone attending would rise upon the presiding judge or magistrate entering the courtroom; the lawyers would bow, the judge or magistrate would sit and the lawyers and public would then sit. Court sessions were normally held from Monday to Friday. However, if the list of cases to be heard became too long, a sitting on Saturday would also be held. There would also be some pressure from my superiors if the accused persons could not get their day in court within a reasonable span of time. The Chief Justice at the time was J.A. Luckhoo,[4] who was a very successful trial lawyer. There tended to be a lot of political involvement or implications with many cases, and I had to be careful in exercising good judgment and judicial procedure so that allegations could not be made against me by one party or another. For example, one of the trial lawyers in New Amsterdam was Maurice Clark, of African heritage, who was a friend since our youth, and I was even more strict on him in his presentation of a case than I would be with the Indian lawyers.

Through my many years of experience, I observed that Indians were prone to use the cutlass as a weapon whereas Blacks would resort to fisticuffs and other blunt objects as weapons. In a guilty verdict, a defendant of defendant's lawyer may plead for mercy and sometimes a defendant would shout and curse, but would be in liable to be convicted for being in contempt of court.

On one occasion when I was on West Coast, Berbice, an Indian person was being tried on a criminal matter before me as the presiding magistrate. This person was represented by an Indian lawyer, whom I knew very well. Apparently, this lawyer had informed the accused person that, because of our friendship, the case would be dismissed upon the accused giving him a case of whiskey, apart from the fee charged.

---

[4] Joseph Alexander Luckhoo, at 43 years of age, became the youngest lawyer to be appointed as Chief Justice.

Fortuitously, I convicted the accused of the offence and passed sentence. Sometime after, I found out what took place between the accused and his lawyer from another lawyer. The accused wanted this lawyer to sue his previous lawyer for the return of the case of whiskey.

The post of magistrate carried with it an atmosphere of respect and honor, in addition to the portrayal of sensibility and fair play. The government provided a fully furnished house in the country areas for magistrates. A clerk of court and other staff were made available to perform secretarial services, but we had to take care of our own cook, servant and chauffeur. I would be invited in various social gatherings attended by the elite of the country, and rubbed shoulders with others in high office. Nevertheless, this did not deter me from casually going over to friends and relatives and dropping in for a visit without prior announcement or invitation. After all, there were no laws against that.

Sound Effects

David Foo
as told to Trev Sue-A-Quan

David Foo was born on 5 December 1929 at Uitvlugt, West Coast Demerara to Benjamin Foo. David's great-grandfather immigrated from China as an indentured laborer.

* * * * * * * *

When I was young, my uncle and his friends used to catch wild birds, and this started my fascination with birds. I too learned to catch birds by putting gum on a branch of a tree where the bird was likely to land. The most effective gum was the sap from the breadnut tree – as soon as a bird put its feet on it, it could not escape. In the beginning I would catch grass birds. These were small birds that had no monetary value, but later I caught towa-towa,[1] and that was a bird that could be worth thousands of dollars as a top-grade racer. Training a bird to reach a high grade took patience and skill. It took me many years to learn the secrets, but eventually I became an expert.

My first experience with a towa-towa was when a man gave me one because he felt it was useless. The bird was black in color but the tail feathers were cut up and torn, for some unknown reason. I liked the bird, so I put it in a cage, and then discovered that the bird would fight and bite its own tail. I pulled out all the ripped-up tail feathers, knowing that they would grow back in two to three weeks. I then took the bird for walks, not knowing that it would do good for the bird, because I was still a small boy. But it was through the frequent walks that the bird grew tame and became accustomed to me. Then it started to whistle, and once that happened, a birdman tried his best to get it from me, but I would not let it go.

---

[1] The local name for the pygmy grosbeak, a canary-sized bird with black or brown plumage.

I became very skilled at handling birds and eventually raised them for money. Every Sunday morning I would go to the Green.[2] There, a large crowd of people would gather to see the birds race and some good money could be won or lost from betting on the birds. Actually, it was a singing competition but it was known among the bird enthusiasts as a "race." The objective was to see which bird would first reach the required number of songs, sometimes 25, and quite often, 50. A song was counted from the first sound emitted to the instant the bird stopped, so that if a bird whistled "tweet," then stopped, that would be a song. Some birds would chirp continuously, "tweet-tweet," or "tweet-tweedly-tweet-tweet" but each of these would be considered only one song, because there had to be a definite pause in the singing for the count to register. The counting of the songs was done by experienced birdmen who would look closely at the throat and beak of the bird to detect movement while listening for the song. With his face close to the cage he would call out the number of songs: " . . . 14 – 15 – 16 . . ." At the same time another person would be counting the songs for the competing bird. As soon as the target number was reached there would be great joy and shouting among the supporters of the winning bird. Of course, the losing owner would have to leave with disappointment, maybe to try another day. There would be times when a bird might race vigorously to almost the end: " . . . 48, 49," and then suddenly stop while the other bird slowly picked up the count to overtake the leader, much to the dismay of the owner of the bird that was beaten at the finish.

The arrangement of a race frequently took place before race day. For the novices it might be a dare: "You t'ink you got good bird? Well, I goin' tek you on this Sunday." However, the serious birdmen would be careful in issuing a challenge, just like a promoter for a prizefighting boxer, because there could be much at stake – in reputation and money. The size of the wager would be agreed mutually, let us say $200, and half of it would be put in the hands of a third party as binding money. The rest of the money would have to be brought when the race was going to be run. If a contestant did not appear, the binding money would be lost. Normally there would be two poles set about one foot apart each with a hook at the top. Each bird owner would shield his precious bird from the view of its opponent until the race was called, and then the cages were hung on the poles at the same time. If a bird began singing before the start of the race, those songs did not count. Sometimes when a bird caught sight of its opponent it would start fencing – fluttering its wings

---

[2] Bourda Green is best known as the venue for first-class cricket matches in Georgetown.

and flapping its tail – in an attempt to scare the other one away. The other bird might do the same as well. But when each one realized that the competitor was there to stay, it would settle down and start singing. The race was on in earnest, and the owners would stand nearby, mentally encouraging their respective contestants while closely supervising the count to make sure that no song went undetected or miscounted. The progress of the race was also followed by numerous spectators who might have side bets going, in addition to animated discussion of the track record of a bird, or its trainer. The race was not a continuous session of songs, because the birds would frequently take breaks, sometimes creating a nerve-racking period of silence. If neither bird reached the required number of songs within a certain time, the race was called a draw. I raised a number of champion whistlers and became so good that other people became scared of putting their birds up against mine.

When I was about 16 years old I went to live with my father at Craig, on East Bank Demerara. He was a farmer growing rice and raising cows, and that kind of life did not appeal to me. Then William Sue-A-Quan asked if I would go to help his sons at his shop on Leguan Island. My mother was a friend of William's wife, Johanna, and that's how he got to know about me. The shop at Leguan was located opposite the stelling, and sold liquor and groceries. I worked there for a few years with William's son, Neville. William was getting on to about 60 years of age and after a few years he sold off the business and moved to Georgetown where Johanna ran another family business, the J. SAQ grocery, while the children were attending school in the city. I returned to Craig.

I liked to be outdoors and used to go hunting and trapping to get some nice game to eat. Some animals were known to be very tricky to catch but I found ways to outsmart them. The labba was one of them. I would go to a creek or river to look for cocorite nuts that had fallen and lay submerged in the water. Then when the fruiting season had passed I would use my store of nuts as bait for the animals. My brother Cecil taught me to hunt, and after a while, the student outstripped the teacher. I learned how to scout out the area before I attempted to hunt for any animal. One day, Cecil and his friend Boyo told me that they had stayed up for four nights in a row trying in vain to catch this particular labba. According to them, it might be a voodoo labba because it managed to elude them every time. They showed me the track that the labba followed when it came out to feed at night, as well as the place where they set up their hammocks in the tree to wait for the labba. I soon realized that their hiding place was in direct line of sight when the labba approached. As soon as the labba spotted them, it of course turned tail and ran away. They issued a challenge to me to catch the labba. I was only too happy to oblige.

I resolved there and then to outsmart them, to catch this labba for myself. Without telling Cecil and Boyo, I went to the grocery store and asked the owner to give me a bottle filled with mackerel-pickling brine and salt-beef water. I took this liquid mixture and sprinkled it around the place where Cecil had put the seeds to attract the animal. Labbas are clean animals; they only feed on seeds, cassava, mangoes, and such things. They would never eat meat or anything rank. As soon as a labba smells any foul odor, it would scurry away from the area. I set up my wabani – a small hunting hammock, large enough to fit only one's derriere – higher up in a tree overlooking the path that the labba would follow, and at a location ahead of where Cecil had been placing his bait. I sat without making a sound and waited patiently for the labba to come along for its nightly feeding. When a labba feeds near an area populated by people, it tends to feed about half an hour to one hour before the moon rises. If it were feeding deep in the jungle, away from populated areas, it would feed in the moonlight. Just before 3:00 a.m., I heard the labba coming along the path to feed on the seeds I had laid out for it. I shone my flashlight on the area where the labba was eating. Startled, it turned to the direction of the light. I moved the light to make it go directly into the labba's eyes, and blinded it just long enough for me to squeeze off a shot.

I untied my wabani and descended from the tree carefully. When I got to where the labba lay dead, I saw that it was quite a big one. I estimated it was about 35-40 pounds in weight. I happily stuffed it into my bag, and walked out of the backdam to awaken Cecil and Boyo around 3:00 a.m. They were amazed at my success as they gazed upon this nice fat labba. Cecil exclaimed, "Man, I never saw a hunter like you!" I took the labba home, cut off a sizeable portion and gave it to Boyo for his wife Helen to cook. I returned later in the day to join them in a feast of curried labba, dahl[3] and rice. I also brought a bottle containing some high wine into which I had put small pieces of various body parts of the labba – the ear, whiskers, toenail, liver, and entrails. As we ate and chatted, Cecil, Boyo, and Helen questioned me about my strategy for catching the labba. I took out my bottle of high wine containing the labba parts, and placed it on the table. I admonished them not to touch the bottle or else it would spoil my luck; I wanted them to respect my hunting expertise. Since they had told me that maybe the labba was a voodoo labba, I decided to embellish the story. I told them

---

[3] A dish of creamed yellow split peas.

about the "labba spirit." If I did what the labba spirit wanted, then the labba spirit would give me what I wanted. They cautioned me not to deal with evil spirits. During this entire labba dinner, I could barely keep a straight face. Not only had I outsmarted them and caught the labba, they also believed the story I had made up about the labba spirit!

There was one occasion that my friends told me of a towa-towa that would sing every morning and all their attempts to catch it were unsuccessful. They even dared me to catch it. Then one day they noticed that the towa-towa was singing from a different location and when they turned to look, the singing was coming from my cage. What I had done was to cut back most of the branches on the trees near the ricefield – the ones on which the bird would most likely perch. On the remaining branches that I left standing, I placed the gum. The bird had little choice but to land on my trap. This gum technique was also used to catch larger birds, such as pigeons. However, the trap had to be modified because the pigeons were big enough to be able to free themselves from the gum. I used to set up a stick that was inserted into a bamboo pole. When the pigeon landed there and its feet became stuck it would fly away, but the stick would be pulled out of the bamboo sleeve and weigh the pigeon down so that it could not fly far away.

One day, Neville Sue-A-Quan came to pay me a visit. He wanted to go hunting and I took him to the bush where he shot a big duck. Neville asked me if I would join him in Georgetown to work on a radio store that he and two of his brothers were starting up. Another brother, Edgar, was working for Western Electric in Trinidad, and was familiar with electronics. Edgar had come back for a visit and found that the family's grocery and liquor business was not very prosperous. At the same time he was aware that this might be a good opportunity to become established in a relatively un- developed field of activity in Guyana.

Edgar, eldest of William Sue-A-Quan's six sons.
Ronald Sue-A-Quan

Edgar's youngest brother, William Jr., known as Garbo, was doing radio repairs with Ivan Ten-Pow and liked that sort of work. So the brothers decided to start up their own business in radio repairs and servicing.

The Sue-A-Quan Radio Store on 39 Robb Street was run by three brothers: Jules, Neville, and Garbo. I worked for them as an apprentice, doing various jobs while learning the technology. The area where most of the effort was placed was the manufacture of amplifiers. Jules would be the one working till 2:00 or 3:00 in the morning carrying out experiments and trying to figure out how to make the amplifiers work properly. In those days the big amplifiers had vacuum tubes and utilized both AC and DC power, the source for the latter being a battery. The trick was to get the correct combination of parts and power supplies. I started attending technical school at night and during the day I would help Neville and Garbo to do the wiring for the transformers.

Three Sue-A-Quan brothers operated the radio store in Georgetown. Left to right: 1) Jules, 2) Neville and 3) William Jr. (Garbo). *Margot da Camara.*

After three years, the business started to prosper. There was so much work that we were working night and day making amplifiers and sound systems. Jules and Garbo built the amplifiers while Neville constructed the speakers. All these were made from scratch and we needed to cut, bend and drill sheet metal, punch holes, insert sockets, and wire up the components. The tubes, resistors, capacitors, vibrators and other electronic items were ordered from catalogues. The suppliers were primarily dealers in America and England who had acquired large quantities of army surplus equipment very cheaply and resold them at discount prices. In Georgetown, there was a big store selling radio parts, Alphonso's, but we could get a better price by ordering directly from the dealers abroad. Alphonso's was also used as the benchmark for setting the price of our items. For example, a speaker might be acquired for $10 but if the price at Alphonso's were $80 then the Sue-A-Quan Radio Store would also sell for $80, or close to that price. There was a high mark-up on these radio parts but there were few options for the customer at the time.

The radio store's reputation grew because of the quality of work and products. The sound coming from our amplifier and speaker systems was as good as any from abroad. Various kinds of radio repairs were also performed. In fact, other repair shops used to send transformers to the Sue-A-Quans in order to keep their own workshop and personnel free to do other projects. There was a machine, imported from abroad, which we used for winding transformer coils so it was easy for us to rebuild a faulty transformer. This was a good money-making item because there was minimal expenditure for materials. A customer might go to Bookers for a new transformer and spend $20, for example, but he could also take the old transformer to be repaired at the Sue-A-Quan Radio Store for $10. Then, of course, there were larger transformers that would cost perhaps $40 or $70 to repair, but still less costly than buying a new one. In this way, the Sue-A-Quan Radio Store became the biggest radio repair store in Guyana.

Our technical expertise was second to none in the country. Once, when I was attending technical school, the instructor, Desmond Woo-Sam, posed a question for the class. He explained that he had a set of about six amplifiers that he was building for the government, but was having some problems with humming. After the class, he came and spoke to me, saying that he felt that I could solve the problem because of my experience at the radio store. He invited me to his home where he had big workbench filled with various gadgets and radio parts. I took a look at his design for the transformer and told him that he needed to shield the pre-amp tube – put a can around it – and move it to a different position on the circuit board. He tried my suggestions, and when he tested it for the first time the system worked perfectly. Actually, I knew the solution to the problem from the time he told the class. Desmond had gained his technical training abroad, but theory was one thing, and practice another matter, because the components were the same. With the original layout the pre-amp tube was being affected by the 60-cycle power supply, producing an awful hum. This was the kind of problem that Jules had spent many sleepless nights trying to solve through experiments.

The Sue-A-Quan Radio Store was capable of building transformers and amplifier systems of all sizes, from small ones used in radios, all the way to giant amplifiers for PA systems, jukeboxes, and cinemas. The secret was to correctly match the characteristics of the various components. The radio shop was able to manufacture AC/DC transformer systems that used a 6-volt DC supply from a battery but capable of generating the 350 or even 500 volts needed for the big tubes. The batteries were imported without any liquid in them and we had to make the acid mixture of the correct strength to pour into the cells of the battery. This required some care because when the acid, which we bought locally, was added to the water, a lot of heat was generated in the solution. Pure, distilled water was required, but we used vat water, which was essentially distilled – by Nature.

Jules then became the local agent for Western Electric and one of the contracts was to provide service for the cinemas. When Cinemascope came to Guyana in the mid-1950s, it was Jules' responsibility to install the new speakers that generated the impressive sound effects. Speakers were set up all around the cinema hall such that, for example, a train could be heard approaching from the back and moving to the front of the cinema. Two giant speakers were

Sue-A-Quan's Radio Store on Robb Street. Photo taken in 1988.
Margo da Camara

also set up behind (or, sometimes, next to) the screen, which were capable of really filling the cinema with sound. The effect of switching to Cinemascope was very dramatic because up to that time the cinema screens were relatively small, unchanged since the days of silent movies. Some cinemas were also used for stage performances and whenever a motion picture was shown, the stage curtains would be drawn aside half-way to expose the screen – that was how big the screen was. Then one day, the moviegoers went to the cinema and saw this huge screen stretching from one wall to the other. The impact was tremendous, and the new sound effects were a real blast. All this was set up by Jules and his assistant, named Wharton. The cinema contract kept them very busy as the different cinemas changed to the wide-screen format, not only in Georgetown, but all over the country. They included several cinemas owned and operated by John Choong. Jules then opened up his own business operation on 166 Charlotte Street, called Jules Sue-A-Quan Electronic Services. A large part of the store was set aside for the equipment needed for the cinemas. He had another contract calling for him to service the teletype at *Guiana Graphic*, through which news from abroad was received by the newspaper. Jules asked me to join him in running the Charlotte Street store and a new worker was brought on for the Robb Street radio store that Neville and Garbo continued to operate. Over the years the skill and reputation of the Sue-A-Quan brothers grew. Unfortunately, Jules took ill and he died a few years later in 1963, at age 40. By that time, I had left the employment at Jules' store.

My interest in songbirds continued well into adulthood. I mastered the technique of training the birds to become champions. The key was in communication. God made every creature on Earth, and man can communicate with each one of these creatures. But first it has to get to know you. Here is one example of how I did it. Each day I would take the bird in its cage and put it on the table. Then, with my face pressed close to the cage I would speak to it gently and whistle to it. At first the bird paid no attention and this process went on for a long time. But one day the bird stopped what it was doing and came close by. I looked straight into its eyes and the bird could see its own reflection in my eyes. Then it gave a little chirp. That marked the breakthrough. I gave the bird a name – Black. From then on I would call its name, and even when I was outside the room I could call out "Black," and it would respond "Kweek," indicating that it knew my voice. Then I would whistle to it, many times a day, and when it whistled back, I knew I had established communication.

Training Black for competition came next. Whenever it whistled I would say, "Stop!" Being interrupted by my voice, Black would stop singing. Eventually it got into the habit of stopping after a short song, expecting to hear my voice. In this way the pattern of singing long songs was changed into short bursts. In essence, I was modifying the sound effects, and with that came satisfaction, pride, as well as fortune for me. The next step was to give it exposure to other birds in competition. Eventually, Black rose up in the ranks and became a champion.

Vision and Service

Roy V. Wong

I was born in Georgetown, Guyana. My parents Claude and Helena Wong are the two people who have had the greatest influence on me. My dad was an avid reader and music lover. He was very good with his hands – wood working, repairing our bicycles and broken toys, and even making gadgets that made life easier. My mom was a devout Anglican with a gift of easily making friends and was always sewing, mending, cooking, baking and all the other things a quintessential mother did. They both were compassionate and they instilled in my three sisters and me the virtues of education, honesty, integrity and social consciousness.

I attended Queen's College, and when I was in Form 2 the mathematics teacher, Mr. E.O. Pilgrim, discovered that I could not see the diagrams on the blackboard clearly, so he informed Capt. Nobbs, the principal, who sent a note to my parents advising that I should have my eyes examined. When I got my glasses I found that I could easily see things at a distance that I thought was normal to be blurred, such as house lot numbers across the street. This piqued my interest in vision problems.

After passing the Oxford and Cambridge Joint Board examination, I briefly thought of pharmacy but after a very short period of employment at Bookers Drug Stores I quit and joined the Civil Service as a temporary Class 2 clerk at the Public Works Department. It was quite pleasant working there as the staff members were friendly and helpful. Nevertheless I felt this was not for me so I decided to quit. When I asked Gwen Parris, head of the secretarial pool, to type my resignation, she told me that my permanent appointment had just been approved. This was good news, but I had recently received confirmation of admission to study at the Chicago College of Optometry, and that was where I was going.

On my arrival in Chicago, I was met by a cousin, Delbert Sue-A-Quan, who was studying dentistry at Northwestern University. He thoughtfully arranged for me to stay in the dormitory for a week so he could assist me in getting settled. This was very comforting to me and did a lot to ease the cultural shock. I chose the Chicago College of

Optometry because they offered an accelerated program that allowed one to complete four academic years in three calendar years by not taking summer vacations. It turned out to be a fortunate choice as many of the professors that taught me were on the cutting edge of the evolution of vision care.

Optometry was a young profession evolving and developing as greater emphasis was being placed on the psychology and physiology of vision. These were intoxicatingly exciting times for students – our class in particular was the last of the 4-year program and, as the transition class to the 5-year program, we put in more class room hours than was originally intended as a lot of the new curriculum was introduced into ours. We were inspired as we were going to be the custodians of vision, which is our most dominant sense, indeed it is our survival sense. The curriculum was being extended to prepare the new graduates for the expanded scope of the profession. The USA was where these changes were taking place and it was a hot bed of research and development. The U.K. was following, and as students from all over the world graduated from universities and colleges in the USA and U.K., vision care around the world was evolving to meet the demands being placed on vision in the increasingly information-oriented society.

Contact lenses had also become almost the exclusive preserve of optometry as most of the research and all of the significant developments in the art and science of fitting contact lenses were by optometrists. Probably the most significant development was the microcorneal lens by three optometrists Dickenson, Sohnges and Neill.

As a student, I was inspired to learn as much as possible, hone my clinical skills and be involved in the development of my chosen profession. So I took part in extra curricular activities that would develop other skills. I was a member of the undergraduate Council on Ethics and Professionalism and a member of the Optometric fraternity, Omega Epsilon Phi. Later, when I was elected president, I changed the procedural ritual of pledging towards initiation, to that of the pledges having to perform community service as partial fulfillment towards initiation. It must have been well received as at graduation I was awarded the Outstanding Service Award.

After graduation I took a post-graduate course in contact lenses, returned to Guyana and started my practice. One of the first things I did was pay a courtesy visit to all the practitioners and took the opportunity to invite them to a meeting at my office to discuss the state of the profession and the formation of an association. The meeting went well and resulted in the Guyana Optometric Association being convened and incorporated. I was elected president, Dr. Samuel Blair vice-president, and Dr. Charles Jacobs secretary-treasurer. Later Charles Jacobs put his practice on hold to serve as Finance Minister in the Jagan government.

The Association succeeded in having the old inadequate Opticians Bill repealed and the Optometrists Ordinance of 1956 enacted. This new ordinance reflected the current education and the expanded scope of modern optometry. It also for the first time provided for an optometrist to be a member of the Medical Board, the official body that regulated the health professions. The association from time to time held educational meetings in an effort to bring the older members up to date with the advances occurring in optometry.

Deciding to lead by example, I introduced in my practice a fee structure, charging a fee for the eye examination and vision analysis and a separate fee for eyeglasses, if required. The emphasis was on ocular and visual health. Orthoptics and services for subnormal vision were also available. For a while I was the only one fitting contact lenses in the region, and I had patients who came from Trinidad, Barbados, Antigua and even Jamaica. One case from Antigua was particularly interesting and challenging in that I had to design and fabricate a Galilean telescopic system consisting of contact lenses and eye glasses to provide a magnified virtual erect image to assist him with his severely sub normal vision.

In order to have control over the quality of the prescription eyeglasses that my office dispensed, I decided to set up an optical lab, because, regardless of how thorough and accurate the examination and vision analysis, if the glasses dispensed are not accurate and comfortable to wear, the benefit to the patient would be diminished. A problem emerged while setting up the lab. The cylinder-grinding machine was not producing the desired result. It was a new machine so I checked the installation and carefully followed all the given instructions, but I was still not getting a properly ground lens. I called Fred White of Imperial Optical in Toronto. He identified the problem. The machine was mounted on a wooden stand, which was rocking with the eccentric figure 8 motion of the machine causing a motion loss in the grinding action. Vernon Man-Son-Hing built me a welded metal stand, which we anchored in the concrete floor, and the problem was solved.

All the technicians employed in my lab were young men just out of school and I personally instructed them, making sure that each one learnt all aspects of optical lab work. This proved to be of great benefit to them as, in later years, they did well in optical careers in the USA, Canada and Guyana. Frames, lens blanks, machinery, tools and lab supplies were imported from Germany, France, USA, U.K. and Canada.

In November 1961, I married Phoebe Ngui Kon Sue, and although Phoebe continued to teach at St. Joseph's High school, she still found time to assist me in the business aspect of my practice. After the birth of our first son, Phoebe gave up teaching to be a full time mother and my office manager.

Apart from my practice I participated actively in community service and sports. My main interests and activities were in tennis, table tennis, badminton, karate and basketball. Dr. Tait's house on Murray St. was always buzzing with activities in the arts, music, sports etc., and it was here that basketball in Guyana started. The boys saw a movie of the Harlem Globetrotters and were so impressed by their spectacular ball handling, skill and athleticism that they got a basketball and tried to emulate them. Lawrence and Clairmont Tait, Carl Spence, Ken Corsbie, Mark Matthews, Harry Dyett and others formed two teams, the Ravens and the Panthers, and started playing. Then Jim Chin and I got some of our friends together and formed the Clowns, and competitive basketball started. Soon other teams were formed, including one from the police force and two teams of young Chinese immigrants, a Hakka team and a Punti team. However, soon after they started competing the two teams combined to form a team called the Swans. Eventually, due to business and other commitments, they were unable to field a full team, so the remaining players joined the Clowns. They were a welcome addition, especially Ngui Sam Fat, Ngui Chung Hing and David Liu, who were very athletic and skillful players.

With the growing popularity of the game, we persuaded the Mayor and Town Council to put down a lighted hard court on the Parade Ground at Middle and Carmichael Streets. The Chinese Sports Club graciously allowed the Clowns to practice at its grounds and use it as a home base, and even though the team was very mixed racially, the executive committee approved the building of a lighted hard court. Now with these two venues and, occasionally, the assembly hall at Queen's College, basketball night games attracted huge crowds of spectators. Ladies teams were formed as girls became interested. Some of the people I remember playing key roles in the development of the game were two pastors from the Lutheran Church. Pastor Vossler had played inter-collegiate basketball in the USA and Pastor Hansen, who had a limp, was an experienced referee with a sound knowledge of the rules. We even had the occasional celebrity playing – Sara Lou Harris played with and coached the girl's team, the Clownettes, for a short while.

In table tennis a number of people selflessly gave their time, expertise and facilities encouraging and coaching youngsters in the game. I particularly remember Mrs. Vera Lopes, a champion in her younger days. Vera had a table tennis table at her home and there were always lots of young people playing and being coached by her. I don't think it was actually a club, but it certainly seemed like one as many teams from there were entered in competitions and many champions emerged. Not more than a few blocks away, there was Jimmy Evans doing much the same. There was a friendly rivalry between them to see who produced the best players. Then there was my friend Jerry Wong who worked at Bookers Shipping Department. He was a top class player who always willingly gave much of his time and talent to coaching.

I started karate when I took my three sons to the dojo where Frank Woon-A-Tai, a gifted young karetka, was chief instructor. Frank's ability as an instructor so impressed Archbishop Alan Knight that he made the lawns of Austin House available to him for use as his dojo. After a while the lawns suffered from the repeated pounding of the feet of the karate students as they practiced their katas, kumite and strength building exercises. Frank had every student bring a tuft of grass to try and re-sod the denuded lawn. I am not sure how successful it was with all the various species of grass that the students brought but it certainly was a heroic effort. Frank has since become a seventh dan black belt and is the chief instructor for the Japan Karate Association for Canada and the Caribbean.

My involvement in community service included being a member of the executive board of the Albouystown YMCA, member of the National Sports Council, member of the History and Arts Council, vestry member of St. Saviour's Anglican Church, committee member of Chinese Sports Club, and a member of the Rotary Club of Georgetown. During my year as president of Rotary I initiated the Annual Rotary Lectures, which each year presents a lecture by a distinguished Guyanese. The inaugural lecture was given by Dr. Robert Moore, historian and later High Commissioner to Canada.

After I was in practice a few years, I bought a used Singer sports car. Jim Chin and I drove it to Berbice to visit William Sue Young and we even took it to No.63 beach, which is a long, flat stretch of hard packed sand, and floored it to see how fast it could go. What we discovered from that trip was that the car needed to be overhauled as it was burning more oil than gas. My close friend from school, Neil Savory, used to ride a huge motorcycle and had some experience with motorcycle engines. He offered to help me. Two other friends who played basketball with me on the Clowns team, Stanley Devonish and Dickie Feinmesser, also volunteered to help. None of us however had any experience with motorcar engines but we decided to try anyway and, while we were at it, see if we could improve its performance. We fitted new piston rings, reseated the valves, polished the ports and fitted a home-made straight through exhaust pipe. When we were finished, the car ran well and had an aggressive guttural sound when accelerated. I think we were lucky because all the experienced mechanics we knew were surprised that we were able to even get it to work. They said that it was an overhead camshaft engine, which required specialized knowledge and skill for servicing.

Another of my hobbies started when Alfred Yhap introduced me to the photographic darkroom, the mixing of the chemicals, developing the negatives and making prints. It is still a delightful experience to watch images emerge in the developer. Alfred was a well-known, accomplished, amateur photographer and between him and my friend Chic Young, a part-time professional photographer, they guided me and stoked the fires of my enthusiasm for photography. In a way they contributed to my being awarded an Independence Medal for organizing and presenting a photography exhibition during the independence celebrations.

Commission Agent and Hairdresser

Andy Lee, née Lam

My earliest memories of my grandparents' businesses was of Gramps' commission agency. This was because Grams' section was banned to baby crawlers, being covered with hair, and stink with the lotions and portions used in the name of beauty. We lived in a compound with four houses on Charlotte Street, just within sight of the Law Courts. Grams and Gramps lived in the big house, in front, and right next door to Correia's wine factory from where came the smell of the awful, pungent, molten sealing gunk when the bottles were being sealed. My parents and their children slept in a small house next to the big house. The back houses were rented to the Amins and the Van Sluytmans. Everything happened in the big house. We ate all our meals there and, more often than not, the younger children slept in the big double beds with Grams and Gramps.

Michael Robert "M.R." Lam. *M.R. Lam*

Gramps spent most of his day in a Berbice chair playing the mandolin and hawking and spitting through the window without raising his head. Many a time there would be a shout from the yard because he'd hit somebody or the spittle landed on the saddle or the handle of a bike. His staff would come up to the bedroom to tell him of their progress, notebooks in hand and respect abound. But once the boys got out of sight it was with a shrug of the shoulders and the issue of a few cuss words, because Gramps was never satisfied with their answers. Sometimes he would be presented with a sheet of onionskin[1] with neatly typed rows of figures and he would show that to us and say, "I have to pay all this money! Can you lend me some?" or he would say "Can't pay you 'cause I have to pay this bill." We grandchildren, as well as James Alberga – our cousin who hung out at our house so much that he became one of our brothers – all had "accounts" with him. He "employed" us to pluck out his grey hairs, and with more salt than pepper, his scant mop of

---

[1] Thin translucent paper sheets, frequently used for recording business transactions.

hair was a goldmine to us kids. One cent per hundred! Often when we were counting: 1, 2, 3 . . . 55, 56 . . . he would say "23, 24," and if we weren't concentrating very hard there were many arguments about the number of hairs removed and money owed. I don't remember ever being paid. Maybe my eldest brother Bobby did get his money because he was smarter than the rest of us and Gramps loved his stubbornness. Cary, my second brother, I am sure, was so silly and placid; he was never one for banter and Gramps never bothered to tease him or pay him.

If you ask me seriously, I would say that Gramps never did a stroke of work as work we know it today. He always had time to galavant[2] with us. One day I said that I'd never traveled on a train. Next day he and I went on the ferry and then rode on the West Coast train from Vreed-en-Hoop to the end of the line and back, armed with my favorite egg 'n cheese sandwiches and a bottle of sorrel. I loved the smell of the steam engine and feeling the wind in my face. Gramps used to take us grandchildren everywhere. We toured Bel Air Park[3] when it was being built. We went from Adventure to the Courantyne visiting Chinese families up and down the coast: The Cham-a-Koons and Foos in Essequibo, Stanley Fung wherever he opened surgery on the East Coast, Fung-a-Fats wherever they lived, Chee-a-Tows in Uitvlugt, Kams in Wales, Lams in the Polder, the Sankars on the East Coast. We holidayed at 63 Beach[4] to watch the motorbike races, La Bonne Intention to swim in the black water trench, pick tamarind and ride mules . . . Gramps was absolutely fearless. He took us on the estates right up to the manager's house and asked permission for us to swim in the fancy pools at Blairmont, Diamond, etc. We went in his little Austin with the sky roof. I remember driving through the cane fields, Terry, my third brother, and myself standing with our heads stuck through the roof and wind in our faces until we had to cross over the punt bridge. The car climbed at seemingly a 90° angle and leant over nearly tumbling us all into the trench. I know I sat down quietly after that!

Our houses formed the biggest zoo as well. We were like monkeys. There was nowhere that we did not climb. Gramps used to have the builder come and patch the holes in the roofs of the houses because we used to climb up there and cause the nails to become loose. Mr. Amin complained to Gramps that he never tasted a ripe full-grown mango from his tree in the back yard because as soon as they reached the size of ping-pong ball, we'd eat them. It was a real zoo, in truth – we had dogs,

[2] Galavant: roam or lime leisurely
[3] An affluent housing development on the outskirts of Georgetown.
[4] No. 63 Beach, located in Berbice.

monkeys, birds, peccaries, agoutis, chickens, ducks, pigeons, geese, guinea fowls, and turtles. The compound was our playground. One of the Van Sluytmans' grandchildren was Lloyd Cornelius whose training ground was the yard between the two front houses. From this bat-and ball beginning, Lloyd eventually went on to play First-Class cricket and represented Guyana. All the boys in the compound (the Cornelius lads, Billy Amin, the Lam brothers, and their friends) would play cricket in the yard. Every so often they'd break a window or two, and whenever somebody shouted "run" it wasn't because they "scored," but because something bad happened and they had to scarper. They also used to set off carbide bombs. Pieces of carbide from Uncle Vernon Manson-Hing's car repair shop on South Road were put in an empty tinnin,[5] spat upon, the lid shut tightly, and the bomb shaken and then ignited with a lighted match.[6] One of the Cornelius boys had his thumb blown off by one such bomb.

However, we weren't always the wild bunch. I must have been about seven years old when Gramps (or was it Grams) bought us a second-hand piano and employed Mr. Dummett to teach us the piano, to expose us to "culture." Gramps always bought everything second-hand because he said it was "tried and tested" and he spent quite a few pennies having it tuned up on a regular basis. Bobby and Cary probably learnt to play up to the cream-colored book, and I only got as far as the green book. To say that music lessons were total punishment would be expressing my opinion mildly. One day, Grams and Gramps where having one of their "spates" over Terry. Terry, the Terrible, was always up some mischief or other but was usually defended by one adult or another. This time it was Grams who objected to Terry being smacked by Gramps. It got real heavy and within a matter of seconds they were wrestling around and fell on the piano. The poor piano, infested with wood ants,[7] was reduced to dust and I never had piano lessons after that.

---

[5] Local slang for a tin, or can.

[6] Calcium carbide reacts chemically with water to produce acetylene gas. A tin with a tightly-fitting lid was essential. A hole would be pierced in the bottom of the tin. After the piece(s) of carbide and an appropriate amount of spit were put into the tin, the lid would be replaced tightly, and with a thumb or finger covering the hole, the tin was given a good shake. With the tin held down firmly in a horizontal position with a foot, a lighted match would be brought to the hole at the bottom of the tin. The escaping combustible gas would ignite the explosive mixture inside the tin and cause the lid to blow off with a considerable bang.

[7] Wood ants, or flying termites, would periodically swarm and seek out a new home. After entering the house they would drop their wings and quickly eat their way into furniture and other wooden objects. Imported pianos were favorite targets and after a

The Lam family lived at 160 Charlotte Street. Employees of Katie Lam's salon
stand in front of the common office entrance serving both the commission agency
and salon. The ground-level door on the right leads directly to the hairdressing
room. *M.R. Lam.*

The agency handled Ovaltine, Wrigley's Chewing Gum, drugs from
Jamaica (Dr. Collis Brown's Cure All), cocktail onions and cherries,
Green Giant products, Brunswick Sardines and bloaters [8], and some other
products that I cannot remember. My brothers, Bobby, Cary and Terry,
plus myself, are healthy strong adults today because all through our
childhood we consumed tons of melted Ovaltine and cod liver malt. Our
jaws and teeth can crack any nut, crab shell and bone because of the miles
of chewing gum we pilfered from the sample cupboard. These were the
samples that the salesmen would take on their rounds to offer to
prospective clients, but we were the greatest samplers, by far. Terry once
tried a bottle of pills and I cannot remember if they pumped him out or
caught him just before he ate the whole lot but suffice to say they seemed
to have had no effect on him at all because he is alive and fishing the
fiords of Western Canada today. Terry himself, though, remembers the
incident because we always were able to find the hiding places for the

---

while the wooden frame would become a hollow shell. Creosote and other chemicals
were used to inject into the holes in the wood from where they expelled their
digested pellets, but it was extremely difficult to exterminate the pests.
[8] Bloaters were sides of lightly-salted, sun-dried cod fish dyed golden yellow and
shipped from Nova Scotia. They were soft and fleshy, quite different from the hard,
highly salted, dried fish known as salt fish.

"samples," especially those that looked like Smarties. However, he cannot remember what the pills did to him as we were regularly "washed out" with castor oil and enemas!

Gramps' business section was in the dark side of the "downstairs." It was dark because it was on the western side of the building and too close to Correia's to see the sun. The entrance was wide and there was a counter separating the office from the public. The counter was an important feature of the businesses. It was where Grams and the girls would measure the ornies[9] to be hemmed, market people came to sell or buy products, poor from the Alms house would file past for a weekly "cent," collectors of Ovaltine tops came to exchange them for cups and gifts. Grams stored her boxes of lotions packed in crumbled cork in cupboards under the counter and whenever we opened them, there were always a family of newly-born rats. The office, being our playground, was full of bottles to open, typewriters to destroy, paper on which to scribble, desks and chairs to climb and windows, which, when we clung to them, could swing out into open space. The counter was the focus of my early learning years. It was where I learnt to walk, talk, hide, climb and communicate with just about everybody. When we were really babies, the counter was where they used to lay us down to sleep!

In spite of having to deal with a gaggle of brats, the agency functioned successfully with the help of several employees. There was poor Elsa, the typist, whose job it was to untangle the keys of the typewriter after we "fixed" it for her by plonking our whole body on the keys, thus flipping the arms[10] up as far as they might go, causing them to jam together. Another technique was to manually lift the keys and push them together towards the roller. Then again, we might paint the roller with glue or ink, or rewind the carbon ribbon until it detached itself from the spools, or "ding" the carriage until it fell off. After restoring the typewriter to working order Elsa would then have to smooth out letterheads before typing a letter. Numerous salesmen including my father (Kenneth), Rudy Yan, Brian Chan, Rudolf Lam, Rudy Fung-a-fat and a stream of Indian boys, Cyril, Mohamed, Khan who, to my awareness, were there at our beck and call. The day started with the

---

[9] Ornies, worn by East Indian women, were yard-long lengths of embroidered light muslin cloth.

[10] The typewriter relied on mechanical linkages. When the key for the desired letter was pressed, it caused its corresponding pivoting arm to swing up and strike a carbon ribbon. The mold of the letter at the tip of the arm would create an impression of that letter on the paper, which was held in place behind the carbon ribbon by a platen, or roller. If several keys were pressed at the same time (or the speed of a typist's fingers was too fast) the swinging arms would become entangled.

group gathering to either collect their "order books" and be issued with a list of potential customers wanting to place orders, or to make enquiries as to clients who hadn't been visited in a while. Then they all got on their bikes and disappeared for as long or as short it took them to do their "rounds." Cyril's extra job was to take me to Nursery school at Ursuline Convent on the crossbar of his bike. I preferred Cyril to Mohammed as his bike was the bigger of the two and he didn't ride like a mad man nor bump me up and down with his knee.

Employees pose with Peter and Jackie Lam, grandchildren of M.R. Lam. *M.R. Lam.*

Being a salesman in those times was more like a social event. Dad took me around with him a few times and whilst he was sitting chatting about everything under the sun, I'd be snooping round the shop with full permission from the "boss." A salesman's job in those days was to take note of the shopkeeper's stock and to recommend a new order of goods. A commission agent's job was to employ glib-tongued smart asses who could walk in anywhere with confidence and aplomb. Gramps and Grams, of course, knew all the business people in the country and every night they would meet with a few of them on the Sea Wall for a gaff so that next day Gramps could instruct the boys where to go . . . or admonish them for truculent behavior. Boy, nothing every escaped Gramps' ear.

Orders for each individual customer would be typed on bubble-patterned onionskin paper and dispatched to the manufacturers/suppliers in England, Canada and the USA. The goods are then sent directly to the stores and shops. The only time the agency had sight of the goods coming into the country was when the bloaters bloated or Ovaltine was stored at too high a temperature and had solidified at the bottom of the tin.[11] Tins of solidified Ovaltine, as well as the ones with dents, would be brought home, but the rotten bloaters were thrown away and the shopkeepers would be compensated directly from the manufacturers. I presume Gramps and his team were also involved in chasing up payments

---

[11] The solidified Ovaltine could be identified by shaking the can. Normally, the rustle of the particles of Ovaltine would be heard, but the ones with clumped Ovaltine would produce a clunking sound.

but I never saw Gramps with hard cash except his little flip top change purse filled with coins.

Ovaltine was our main source of income, I think, or indeed it carried the highest profile. Gramps sponsored radio programs, talent contests, sports events (boxing, athletics, cycle racing, soccer matches) and maybe one or two other things on behalf of Ovaltine. We attended the important events and always had the best box[12] in the Globe cinema, choice seats in the sports stadia, and front row seats at the radio station. At these occasions the family was always dressed up to the nines[13]. Gramps wore one of two cream-colored sharkskin long trousers, a white shirt and his only tie with the wheel pattern. Grams wore makeup and one of many outfits she made herself. I was made to dress in lace, and organdie matching everything, which itched and scratched and which gave me a life-long abhorrence to "dressing up." I loved Uncle Vivian's[14] programs the best. I loved the "snow," (chopped white and transparent cellophane paper) that glistened in the spotlights as it floated down to the stage, when the girls dressed as Santa's helpers pranced about on the stage. Desiree Green, a fellow convent girl, was a delight to watch specially since I knew her at school. From time to time, music bands – the Ramblers I remember well – would come to our home to "audition" for the shows. Gramps had little or no control over who would take main stage but it was lovely to be treated to our own personal jamming session. He loved music and I think he would insist on hearing "a bit of music" just for the fun of it.

At sports events – goat racing was Gramps' favorite – we would dole out cups of Ovaltine. Grams and her helpers measured out exact cans of Ovaltine, evap,[15] condensed milk and ice to make a sweeter than necessary mixture of the stuff in enamel buckets. This beverage was served in paper Ovaltine cups along with two Ovaltine biscuits and the many participants at the events would flock for the free offering. It was promotion, after all. Of course, we kids drank and ate the stuff freely and plentifully, proving that it was good after all!

---

[12] In a carry-over from the design of grand opera theatres, "boxes" in the cinema lined the front rim of the balcony area. They were considered to be the best (and most expensive) seats in the cinema and were sectioned off from the rest of the seating area. In local parlance, it was the place from where one could pee on the pit (cheap seating area) below!

[13] "Dressed up to the nines" or Sunday best, or finest clothes.

[14] Vivian Lee, advertiser and broadcaster at the local radio station, was often invited to be the host of various children's programs.

[15] Evaporated milk.

M.R. Lam promoted Ovaltine by sponsoring several different sporting events, although goat racing (left) was his favorite. Katie Lam (right) helped to prepare and offer cups of Ovaltine to the public. *M.R. Lam.*

This Christmas party in 1953, sponsored by Ovaltine, was held at St. Rose's Convent School. *M.R. Lam.*

Being "Ovaltine Lam" was one of the greatest periods of my life. It was a time when any and everything could happen. It was a time when Gramps and Grams used to make things happen and we were never short of interesting things to do. Representatives from the manufacturers came to visit and that meant a tour to visit the customers and hot spots around the country. We went to rehearsals for shows and warm ups for boxing matches. We met the stars of all the shows and sporting events we went to, even the circus whenever it came to town.

I was a good listener in my youth. Grams told me many stories of her childhood and growing up, and how Gramps and herself progressed through their lives. Grams, Katie Theresa Lee, was born to George Alexander Lee and Maria Yee, one of eight children. Maria was half Chinese, half Portuguese and a beautiful woman by all accounts. George, only son of Lee-a-tak and Lo Shee, was born in B.G. Lee-a-tak made a living being a "water man," or manager of a gambling den, in the Chinese business area of Georgetown. Records indicate that they lived at the head of Leopold Street, which was the center of the Chinese community in those days. Lo Shee's first husband was a man named U A-ho, and this marriage produced the U-Mings (Woo-Mings), Hings (M. U. Hing) and Cheongs. In the scramble to escape China 150 years ago, Lo Shee "lost" and left behind another son, and for years mourned for him. After U A-ho's demise, Lo Shee married Lee-a-tak. As the family fortunes increased and the families from Lo Shee's first marriage settled into successful businesses of their own, Lee took his wife, Lo Shee, as well as George, Maria and their family back to China (1901-1906) to look for that lost son. Katie, Rebecca, Vicky, Aldewin where very young, and over the five years when they lived there, they were sent to school and lived ordinary lives. Katie vaguely remembered touring areas of China with her grandfather. She told of watching criminals being beheaded. Convicted men would be carried in baskets hoisted on poles and marched off on the shoulders of bearers. Their last meal was a huge bao (or pao). At the place of execution their hands were tied behind their backs. Then they were made to kneel with head bent forward. The executioner would then wield a huge sword and chop off their heads, which fell into baskets in front of them.

Within a few short years, Lee died. With no real income and money being gambled and smoked away by George, the two women decided to return to B.G. They crossed the Pacific Ocean by boat and the whole of Canada on a train. From Nova Scotia they sailed back to B.G. Grams remembers having a great time on that journey, dancing and playing games with the foreign people. At some place in Canada, she and Becca were made to attend a little Chinese girl's funeral after the priest had heard they were on the train and he wanted the little girl to be buried in the sight of her countrymen.

Back in B.G., Maria and George opened up shops in Beterverwag-ting, and then up the Demerara River, and finally a coffee shop in Le Roy

Street, Georgetown. George didn't mend his ways and the family fortune soon disappeared. Lo Shee died a year after her return to B.G. She is buried in Plaisance. In this time of great hardship, Katie made a commitment to herself and her family never to be poor again – a commitment that she was able to keep to the day she died. She was made of stern stuff, that Katie! Her story restarts when she "spotted" Michael R. Lam one Sunday while promenading in the Botanical Gardens. She fell in love at first sight and decided that that was the man for her. He hadn't a hope of being anything else than Katie's husband. Katie and Michael married and Kenneth, my father, was born not long after – their only child.

Michael and Katie first opened a shop in a backwater, malaria-infested place behind Wales Estate. Katie hated it. They moved into the Polder where Michael and his brother Nathaniel bought another shop. Katie still wasn't satisfied. She went into Georgetown and got a job for Michael with a white commission agency. They moved to D'Urban Street, right opposite the Georgetown jail. Katie opened up a hairdressing salon and a shop and Michael worked in the agency. When the owner of the agency died, Michael bought it and he owned it to the day he died. Katie in the meantime developed and expanded her hairdressing business. She sailed to New York and attended a hairdressing school. Just before I was born in 1946 they moved to Charlotte Street. With the businesses growing and being successful, she brought Kenneth and Viola (my mother) from New Amsterdam, where Kenneth was working for the Civil Service and Viola had opened her own hairdressing business, to work in the family businesses. Dad joined his father in the agency and Mother joined Katie. I was just six months old.

Katie Lam, née Lee.
M.R. Lam.

Grams' salon occupied the other half of the downstairs level at Charlotte Street and was divided from the agency by a three-quarter-height partition with gaps for access to the office. The public entrance was small and opened into a small waiting room which was always filled with Indian women waiting for their long straight tresses to be curled and mangled. There were about six instruments of torture (heating machines). First the hair had to be washed and dried and trimmed. Then the curlers were rolled into neat divisions on the head. A rubber felt-back pad was placed near to the scalp and clipped firmly and tightly by a rubber metal clip holder onto which the iron curlers were slotted in. Then that was covered with a bit of felt and the heating clamps were attached. The perming lotion was overpowering and many women were reduced to tears with the pain and suffering they endured, only to be consoled that they would be beautiful at the end of it all. Many a time I would sit on a windowsill trying to say nice things to these women and feeling the pain.

It was a good business because Grams' salon was always busy and there were always people sitting in the waiting room right up to closing time. At Christmas it was open until midnight. Both Grams and Mother worked very long hours on their feet everyday. We also had a succession of cousins working – Sheila, Dinku and Daphne Lam, Gloria Fung, and a few more who worked there before I was born.

Grams also had a covered-button[16] and buckle service, and an orni hemming business at the back of the house. She imported metal buckles and button tops which were covered with material brought in by the customers. She also had an embroidery machine, which did chain stitches with which she drew patterns in all colors on yards of material supplied by the customers. Most of the customers for this service were of Indian origin. She loved making arty things like artificial flowers, fancy costumes for me to wear at parades (and I always won first prize), slippers, cushion covers – anything that stretched her imagination.

Of the two, Grams was always busy; Gramps seemed to do nothing much. Of the two businesses, well, the agency was the more interesting. Both of my Grandparents were successful in their own right. Grams employed a team of girls, and Gramps had a team of boys. Mix the two and sometimes we were well entertained by the "goings-on at the back stairs." But that's another story. . . .

---

[16] Dome-topped buttons on which the desired fabric can be fitted and fastened with a special base inserted behind the button.

Cookshop, Cakeshop

Helena Yong-Ping and Grace Ten-Pow
as told to Trev Sue-A-Quan

Chinese cooking is generally accepted as one of the fine culinary arts in the world and everywhere that Chinese have gone around the globe they have introduced their style of food to the local community with considerable success. The Chinese in Guyana were known for their operation of two different kinds of eating-houses. One was the Chinese restaurant, typified by small tables, individual chairs, printed menus, tablecloths, place settings, and cutlery. Restaurant dining tended to have an atmosphere of formality, although there were also some that catered to a more casual clientele. The other kind of establishment was the Chinese cookshop, usually located in smaller-sized premises, with benches and long tables, offering a variety of tasty dishes at an economical price. These were the fast-food outlets of the times, in terms of time and money spent. They provided delicious Chinese and local-style fare for the masses, but still appealing to the choosy diner because of convenience and taste.

Running a Chinese cookshop was a long and tedious job. Such cookshop experiences are described by Helena Yong-Ping, née Wong, granddaughter of immigrants who arrived from China on the *Dartmouth* in 1879, with further details provided by her daughter Grace Ten-Pow. Their main cookshop business was located in New Amsterdam. One of the well-known cookshops in Georgetown was run by a Chinese man known as Sheila and accounts of his operations have been compiled from the recollections of several of his customers.

* * * * * * * *

Albert Yong-Ping was born about 1912 to a family of Overseas Chinese living in Vietnam. In the 1930s, when Albert was about 18 years of age, his uncle, Yong Sam-you, who was well established in Guyana, sent for him to work in his grocery. He worked for his uncle in Georgetown for some two years during which time he was given food and board but his wages were kept to repay the passage to Guyana. It was a hard initiation to life in Guyana but Albert did not regret his decision and would later reflect: "British Guiana – good country!" Albert was a small man in stature and was called "Short Man," and "Baby Boy." He, of course, did not know any English when he arrived but he picked it up through dealing with the customers, although he never did learn to read and write in English. His job was to sell to the customers who would point out what they wanted to buy.

Albert next worked as a chef at the Air Base when the Americans were stationed there during the war. He stayed up there during the week and returned to Georgetown for the weekend. He then opened a cookshop in Georgetown – a small place with a few benches and wooden tables. There was no refrigerator at this cookshop, only an icebox. This was literally a box in which ice was placed to provide a cold area for storing meats and vegetables. The menu consisted of pepperpot, curry, cook-up rice, chow mein, low mein,[1] stews, etc., and the cookshop was patronized by workers in the city and fishermen from the wharf. The day started at about 6:00 a.m. when breakfast items were sold and preparations made for lunch. Breakfast included coffee, bread, eggs as well as a local favorite – salt fish, typically served with fried-dough bread, known as "bake." A couple girls were hired to help with the preparation and cooking as well as serving meals. There would be rice to be steamed, stews to be made, broths to be brewed, cook-up to be cooked, and so on, in anticipation of the lunchtime crowd.

In 1944 the Yong-Ping family moved to New Amsterdam, capital of Berbice County, where Albert worked as a chef for a restaurant run by two brothers, Victor and Edgar Ten-Pow. He then opened his own cookshop near Trinity and Main Streets, but in 1946 the family decided to return to Georgetown. There, Albert went into different kind of food service enterprise, a cakeshop (also called "parlor"). The main items were breads and cakes. In reality, these were pastries and baked goods such as tarts, turnovers, buns, and sugar cakes, supplied by bakeries. The shop also offered candies ("sweets"), and beverages, including pop, peanut punch,[2] and mauby.[3] The mauby was home-made and prepared in large

---

[1] Low mein (which rhymes with "chow mein") consists of a bowl of plain noodles upon which the selected items are placed, such as roast pork, sliced beef or chicken, along with vegetables. A thick flavoring broth or soup base is then added to the dish. Chow mein is made with noodles, meat and vegetables cooked together to form a uniform mixture.

[2] A milk-based drink with peanut butter as the main flavoring ingredient.

[3] Mauby is made from the strips of bark from the carob tree. The bark is boiled with sugar (and cinnamon, if desired). Yeast or "stale mauby" is added to initiate the fermentation process. The liquid is poured into suitable containers – bottles, demijohns, buckets – and left for a few days. Mauby produces a considerable head of foam during fermentation. The flavor of mauby is not unlike root beer with a slightly bitter twist.

white buckets, from which the foam would come flowing over the top. With a suitable dipper, a glass of nicely-brewed mauby could be served to the thirsty customer. One of the favorites with the children, especially at lunchtime and after school, was "shave ice." Large blocks of ice were delivered from Wieting & Richter's ice house.[4] The ice was stored in a box and covered with sawdust to act as an insulator from the tropical heat. The shop attendant would brush away the sawdust by hand to expose a clear ice surface. The metal shaver, essentially a empty rectangular box with a blade protruding from the bottom, like that of a carpenter's plane, would be used to fill the shaver with ice shavings. When the shave ice was suitably compacted the flip-top lid of the shaver was opened and the packed ice particles placed in a cup or bowl. The shave ice would then be liberally bathed in a sweet syrup that penetrated through to the middle because of the granular nature of the delicacy. The Yong-Pings made their own syrup from sugar and essence. At the shop there was also a mould that would transform the shaved ice into an ice stick, the local equivalent of a popsicle.

When Helena's mother died in 1954 the Yong-Ping family moved once more to New Amsterdam. Albert started a cookshop, called Kong Tung, in Pitt Street, one of the busy streets in the town. Albert's eldest daughter, Grace was then 11 years old and soon began to take on tasks to help in running the shop. Albert would leave home early in the morning to go to the market to buy fresh vegetables, greens and meat brought in from the countryside. By this time, the hired helper, who lived in a room at the back of the shop, would be up and busy getting the fire going. Then the other staff would arrive to open the cookshop, prepare the ingredients for lunch, get the pot of rice going, and serve breakfast to the early customers. There wasn't any specific item for breakfast per se, and some dishes, for example pepperpot, were known to become "sweeter" when left for a day or two. In fact, one of the favorite breakfast items that Grace enjoyed before going off to school was a belly-full of eggs, rice and pepperpot. There would sometimes be folks who wanted fried eggs or an omelet, while others asked for salt fish and bread, or roast pork and bread. Grace would be the cashier for the breakfast session and her father would return in time for her to get to school at 8:30.

Inside the cookshop was a big table with two rows of benches where the Indian drivers from the Courantyne liked to congregate. Along two walls were double wooden seats, joined back-to-back, that faced onto

---

[4] Karl Wieting and Gustaf Richter established a General Shipping and Commission Agency in 1871. In 1909 a huge ice factory was built and W&R also provided cold storage and warehousing facilities.

tables in booth-style fashion. On the wall was a blackboard displaying the regular menu items and the prices, as well as the "special of the day." The tables were numbered and the waiter, upon serving the customer, would call out: "Table Two has rice and curry," or "Mince and bora for Table Four." The cashier, seated in a caged area, would then jot down the amount to be paid. There was no cash register and accounts had to be carefully kept to comply with the various labor regulations in existence. At the front of the shop was a section where cheese, roast pork, and bread were sold.

Lunch was the biggest meal of the day and by the time the lunch break came around the various pots of prepared dishes would be done and either transferred to large dishes or else the pots themselves would be placed on a counter in the kitchen for the waiters to pick up a helping of the desired dish. The customers were mainly Indians and Blacks and local foods were popular with them including pepperpot, curry, cook-up rice, provision soup,[5] bargee, calaloo,[6] and bora. Among the Chinese-style offerings were chow mein, low mein, and fried rice. These Chinese dishes were made to order because they could be quickly prepared starting from the noodles or rice and adding the various ingredients – meat, vegetables – that were on hand or stored in the refrigerator. Fish and shrimp dishes were prepared on the spot, as well as wonton that had to be folded by hand. Because of the busy lunch period, Grace had to hurry back from school, take her meal quickly, and then help with serving, cashiering, and serving at the front counter, particularly to sell roast pork and bread.

For beverages the customers could purchase lemonade and locally made aerated soft drinks, made by Wieting & Richter, as well as brand-name pop such as Coca-Cola. Heineken beer and the local favorite, pac-pac,[7] were two alcoholic drinks available to go with the meal. The barrel of wine would be rolled outside the shop each morning to leave more room for the dining guests. When pac-pac was ordered the server would take one end of a long flexible tube and insert it into the cask, and then suck quickly on the other end to get the wine flowing by siphon action into a glass or pitcher. Of course, there was no way to prevent the sucker from drawing a little longer or harder on the tube thereby "accidentally" getting some of the wine into the mouth.

---

[5] Made with local root vegetables such as cassava, yam, and eddo along with plantains.
[6] Bargee and calaloo are leafy vegetables similar to spinach.
[7] Pac-pac is a local name for cheap local wine, sold in half-pint bottles or else drawn from a barrel.

The evening meal was not the heavy one and the number of customers were similarly not as many. This allowed Albert to go home at 5 or 6 o'clock while Helena and Grace carried on managing the shop until it closed. The cooked dishes were stored in a safe, essentially an upright cabinet with mesh on the front and sides to allow air to flow through. Sometimes the shop would close at 9:00 p.m. and at other times there would be a few late or lingering customers for whom the cookshop would remain open much later. It was not unusual on occasion for Helena and her daughter to be walking home at almost midnight. It was not every day, though, that Albert got to go home in the early evening. Sometimes there might be a special order for a household gathering or a party, particularly of Chinese food, and he would be able to make dishes with mushrooms, bean curd, bamboo shoots and other ingredients that were typically Chinese. Those who wanted such take-out meals had to provide their own containers, and these might be bowls, basins, calabashes, platters or fine China, depending on the well-being and status of the customers. On occasion the serving plates might be lent out to someone who was familiar to the Yong-Ping family on the understanding that they would be returned the following day.

Besides shopping for fresh supplies every morning Albert was the maker of some of the shop's foods. One such item was dried mustard greens, used for making soups. The greens selected by Albert would be washed and lightly salted then dried in the sun and then rolled up into tight bundles. He also made pepper sauce from grinding fresh peppers and stirring them up into a paste with oil. The bottles of hot pepper sauce were the only things on the tables awaiting the customers in the cookshop. However, preparing these items were not as tiring a process as making lap cheung, the Chinese-style sausage that was used in a number of dishes and soups. The main ingredients were pork, including fatty portions, seasoned with spices and soy sauce, and cut up into small chunks. The pork was obtained from the market or abattoir along with the intestines that had to be thoroughly washed with lime and salt. A funnel was used to stuff the pork filling into the long runners, as the cleaned intestines were called. The packed runner would then be twisted and that point tied with string thereby producing sausage links some six to eight inches in length. Next a cork with four or five pins protruding from it was employed to liberally prick the sausages to allow the pork inside to dry properly. The lap cheung was then hung up outside to dry in the sunshine. They would be dried for as long as necessary to produce the right firm consistency. One important requirement during the drying process was that the lap cheung needed to be watched from time to time, otherwise a link or two, or even the whole length of lap cheung, could be lost to a hungry cat or crow. When such unwelcome would-be pilferers appeared, the Yong-Ping children were quickly dispatched to scare them away.

The most demanding process that took both time and energy was the making of noodles. Working on a long table, the flour, water and eggs had first to be kneaded into a uniform dough. Then Albert would jump the noodles. One end of a long pole, some six inches thick, would be inserted into a slot (looking rather like the stereotypical mouse-hole) in the backing board of the table, against the wall. Then, placing one thigh over the far end of the pole he would hop about on the other leg such that the pile of dough became flattened by the center section of the pole. As the dough became stretched out over the long table the pole would be moved to another mouse-hole slot a short distance away. Eventually a thin sheet of dough would be obtained from repeated jumping, from one end of the table to the other. After a sprinkling with cornstarch to prevent the dough from sticking, the sheet of dough would be rolled up and then Albert would wield the towma, the large traditional Chinese kitchen chopper, quickly slicing across the roll to produce thin coils. These would be shaken to straighten them out into the lengths of noodles and hung on poles above the noodle table to let them dry. For storage the dried noodle strips would be rolled up into a ball. Because of the demand for low mein and chow mein, Albert had to jump the noodles with regularity. In addition, the process was repeated for making wonton skins, or wraps, but instead of rolling up the flattened dough the towma was used to cut square sections from the sheet of dough lying on the table.

Albert also made his own roast pork. Large chunks of pork were cooked in an extra-large wok, implanted into the fireplace, a flat-topped concrete box with several holes for inserting pots. This large cooking pot always stayed on the fireplace and was washed in place. The roast pork was skinless and there was no equipment at the cookhouse to make pork with crispy skin. However, when he was in Georgetown, Albert would sometimes be invited to make roast pork for a banquet or celebration held at the Chinese Association. The Association had a steel barrel – formerly an oil drum – in which charcoal was placed and half a pig hung up to be roasted. This would produce the crispy crackling skin that was a favorite with many Chinese.

The cookshop was open seven days a week although Sunday mornings were devoted to giving the place a good cleaning. With a water hose and hard bristle brushes the concrete floor would be washed and scrubbed. The counters and worktables were scrapped with a metal blade. The place would then be ready for business in the afternoon. The availability of quick-service tasty food at the Kong Tung cookshop attracted the merchants and drivers from the countryside, particularly those of Indian descent. The cookshop was also a popular eating place for New Amsterdam residents and Mr. Kong Tung became known as "a good cookman."

* * * * * * * *

Sheila probably got his name from the sound of his Chinese name, although that real name became a mystery to many once "Sheila" took hold. He was born a few years before World War I and emigrated from China sometime around World War II. His Chinese surname was Loung. Sheila became a well-known figure through his cookshop, Wing Lee, on America Street in Georgetown. The shop was in the middle of a little Chinatown area with various other Chinese-owned businesses in the vicinity. The Chung Wah Club, well known for gambling activities, was located in the upper floor of an adjacent building, and several patrons of the club were also patrons of Sheila's cookshop, where they at least were assured of winning a hearty and delicious meal.

Short and stout in stature, Sheila wore a flour-bag apron while he worked, and as the day went by, the apron collected quite a bit of gravy and other food stains and ingredients from Sheila wiping his hands there before he served customers. The first impression on seeing this slight, apparently grubby, person – plus the fact that he would frequently have a cigarette hanging from his lips – sometimes deterred a potential client or two, even though they were recommended specifically to seek out Wing Lee for delicious food. But those knowledgeable about Sheila's culinary skills were aware that it was the taste of his dishes that really mattered.

Wing Lee was open for lunch and dinner. On going through the 12-foot main door customers were led past the glass counter where pastries such as black-bean cakes (towsa), and collar,[8] as well as soft drinks, were displayed. The dining room was plain in décor – in fact, plain without décor, having blank, dull-colored walls – and it had a few 8' x 3' wooden tables with accompanying benches. But during the lunch period these benches would be filled with people of all complexions enjoying their meals. At the back of the dining area, near the doorway to the kitchen, stood a large glass case poised above a serving counter. Hanging up behind the glass were lap cheung, roast chickens and ducks, plus a side of

---

[8] A sweet pastry item with a filling of grated coconut, shaped into ¾ of a circle, thus the name "collar."

roast pork. On the counter, below the hanging gourmet offerings, were bowls to catch the drippings, and other bowls with fish balls and various sauces. On order, Sheila would deftly slice a portion of roast pork, exactly the amount required. He sliced up the pork himself and, of course, wiped his hands on the apron when he was done. In the kitchen, there was a cutting block for the cooked meat – a cross section of a large tree. Sheila used a towma with a slightly curved blade and, with the front tip of the blade anchored on the block, the handle of the towma would be rocked up and down as the chunk of meat was fed under the knife and become quickly transformed into slices. Over the course of time, the block developed an indentation at the center from the frequent cutting, chopping and scraping that took place on its surface.

Lap cheung and noodles, both being dried by the heat coming from the fireplace, could be seen draped from poles hanging high up in the kitchen. There was a worktable where foods were prepared and dishes placed in transition, and another table for jumping the noodles. Sheila made his own noodles although he trained employees to do the actual jumping. To cut the wonton skins, a long board was used to guide the towma, so as to produce uniform squares. Other employees took care of the fireplace – stoked with wallaba wood – as well as the ever-present pot of soup stock, constantly on the boil. There were some three or four employees working in rotation to fulfill the needs of the busy establishment – cleaning, cooking, serving, and washing the plates, bowls and cutlery in a double sink in the kitchen. Sheila was also involved with these various operations, but was the one to put the finishing touches to the dishes – adding the various meats, vegetables and sauce.

The firewood was stacked up in the backyard of the cookshop, and some 12 feet away was a galvanized sheet metal shed that enclosed the outdoor toilet, used by staff and patrons alike. Another fixture in the backyard was a large tub, available for washing up after a visit to the outdoors, with water flowing constantly from a tap. On occasion there would be a flurry of activity in the backyard, and a quick eye would perceive a cat chasing a rat (or vice versa). Among some in the Chinese community, there was a persistent sentiment that these animals contributed, in part, to the uniqueness of Sheila's delicious cuisine. However, regular customers noted that these outdoor enthusiasts were the same ones they kept seeing time and again, and the rumors remained unsubstantiated. Nevertheless, it was a standing joke that Sheila had a special recipe that other cookshops could not match . . . for reasons unknown.

Low mien, at $1.25 a serving, was perhaps the most recognized and appreciated dish that Sheila created. This consisted of a bowlful of freshly cooked, long, egg noodles topped by four fish balls (or else slices of chicken or pork, as ordered by the customer), a few steamed Chinese greens and a couple ladlefuls of delicious sauce. The sauce he made was one of the secrets to the delicious taste and was based on the flavorful pork drippings that came from roasting the sides of pork. Sheila had a steel barrel for roasting pork and this produced some nice crispy pork. Another favorite with customers were fish balls, made by scraping the flesh of the cuffum fish,[9] seasoning it with green onions, spices and cornstarch, and then taking a small handful at a time and squeezing it into a fish ball. Wonton soup was also high up on the list of favorites for the aficionados of Wing Lee's. Other people recall his noodle soup, or the rice and tasty stew, or the eddo duck, consisting of alternating layers of eddo and duck, steamed to perfection – a Sunday specialty. Sheila had a small stack of paper notepads, no more that a few inches square, on which he wrote the customers' orders in Chinese, and then hung the slips on clothespins that dangled from a wire in the kitchen. The cooking crew did include some black men who worked on general cooking, while the Chinese cooks could presumably read what was inscribed on the order slips.

Sheila's repertoire was not limited to the mien dishes – these just happened to be his specialty. On occasion someone would come by with a turtle and ask Sheila to prepare a nice meal from it. Whether hare or tortoise, it was no contest with Sheila who made equally delicious dishes from these starters. Sheila was also capable of handling local ingredients, such as an iguana, that a sidewalk vendor nearby might have for sale as one of selections of live game and poultry, carried around in a large, shallow woven basket.

Tea was available in the cookshop and soft drinks, such as Pepsi, and beer could be purchased to go with the food. However, those in the know could also obtain a swig of some stronger stuff – served discretely from a teapot . . . and only in the kitchen.

Sheila's low mien gained such a following that even the owners of the neighboring Chin Lee Restaurant would place an order for the delicious dish for lunch, but the order would be conveyed by one of the children who took a note written in Chinese to Sheila's back door.

Sheila was a friendly, affable fellow who spoke broken English. But this did not prevent him from ably communicating his cooking skills to friends. His students became very skilled in the art while learning the names of the Chinese ingredients. Sheila's good friends, including the families of the students, were among those invited to his Christmas

---

[9] A local freshwater fish.

lunch. On Christmas Day, Sheila would host a special lunch for his friends and good patrons. The cookshop was closed but the side door was opened to welcome the invitees. He prepared the best of the best and had ample amounts of top brand liquor (Johnny Walker whiskey, etc.) to go with the fine feast. Sheila would say, "Don't eat rice; that only ten cents a pint!" The banquet was held in the private area of the main dining area and the guests felt privileged to be brought to this inner sanctuary of the Wing Lee establishment.

The Wing Lee cookshop had its heyday in the 1950s and in later years competition arose in the form of other Chinese cookshops and restaurants as well as places offering different styles of cuisine – Creole dishes, fried chicken, and others. Sheila still held his own, but after he contracted tuberculosis he had to relinquish his cookshop duties. When he subsequently died, the city lost a notable figure and an expert in Chinese cooking.

TAKING A COUNT

Rita Launa Graham, née Cheong

My father was the eldest son and I remember everyone calling him by his Chinese name Hing-Co.[1] No one in our family ever called him by his first name Rupert, but we all knew that his birth certificate proclaimed his name to be Rupert Reginald Cheong. He must have had a thing about R since he named all his children with names beginning with an R. Not to show favoritism, our second name started with the initial of our mother's name, Letitia. He was the oldest of seven children, six boys and one girl. I never found out what his father did, since he died at age 40, but I remember my parents telling us that our grandfather Alfred Benjamin Cheong had accompanied my father to my mother's house for my father to ask for her hand in marriage in 1932. I don't remember anything else being said about my grandfather except that he had also been the eldest son of his father. I had always wondered how he died, and years later my father said he had been told that his father died as a result of a sponge being left in his body during an operation.

I was born in the house where we lived on Hadfield Street in Georgetown. It was a typical Guyanese house with three bedrooms, living room, dining room, kitchen and a gallery all on one floor. The bedrooms were huge with double beds in each room. It was a common sight to have a mosquito netting hanging over the bed and a wardrobe and a vanity to hold our clothes and, of course, a clothes-horse. My sister and I shared a bed, while my two brothers shared another bed. The mattresses in those days were filled with coconut fibres, while the pillows were made from chicken feathers that were washed and dried in the sun, with only

Rupert R. Cheong. *Rita Graham.*

---

[1] Co (or Ko) is the Chinese form of address for elder brother.

the soft ends of the feathers selected to be made into a pillow. The house was built on pillars, had windows and jalousies which was typical of the Dutch architecture, skylights on both sides at the top of the house and stairs on the outside. The bedroom windows and the living room windows had shutters that could be propped open with a stick. I remember we had an old iron stove, which stood in the corner of the kitchen but that stove was never used, and instead my mother used a coal pot which had been home-made from pouring cement into a large bucket which had been specially cut out and adapted to the size of the cooking pot. In due time this was replaced by a kerosene stove and eventually a gas stove.[2] We did not have a fridge until I was about 20 years old, and up to that time this necessitated going to the market every day to purchase meat and vegetables and also going to the grocery to buy canned and dry foods.

Our yard was fenced, and there was a concrete bridge joining the driveway to the front entrance at the bottom of the stairs. This bridge was built over a gutter which ran alongside the street and which would disappear under the flood of water whenever the rain fell. As children we delighted in making paper boats and throwing them from the windows overlooking the front of the yard, to watch them sailing along with the current to see whose boat would sail the fastest. There was a huge vat in our backyard that collected rainwater from the eaves trough whenever the rain fell. It was interesting to watch the Health Inspector climbing each month to the opening at the top of the vat to check the purity of the water and then see him insert into the vat live fishes from the container he carried. We understood that these little fishes would eat the larvae of any mosquitoes found in the vat. It was not necessary to have a garage as the car was usually parked under the house. We seemed to have always had a dog and a cat but not really as pets – the purpose of having a dog was to deter would-be robbers by its barking, and the cat was there to catch any mice who dared to enter the house.

I had an idea that my father's parents may have had a bakery since my mother had been given recipes for making Chinese cakes. These had apparently been passed down for generations and my mother ended up with them. I can truly say I have not tasted Chinese cakes better than those made by my mother from these recipes. These were the black-eyed bean pastry cakes (towsa) and the pastry cakes made with nuts called ham-chit-sue and fa-paing. My mother made these cakes once a month to sell to relatives and friends, and on a Friday evening she would start preparing the ingredients. She would have already boiled the black-eyed

---

[2] Petroleum gas was purchased in cylinders delivered to individual households.

beans that made the towsa filling. The peanuts had to be roasted and shelled, and it was our job to grind the nuts with sugar. This was all done by hand with a mill.[3] Our dining room table became an assembly line, with my mother rolling out the pastry and forming the cakes, my sister and I turning the petals on the nut cakes, and then decorating the towsa cakes with a red dot in the center. The pastries were placed on two large baking sheets which had handles at both ends and there they would stay until seven o'clock on Saturday morning, when my brothers, my sister and I each holding one end of the tray, would walk with these large baking sheets (larger than could fit in a regular oven at home) to Fung's bakery, which was not too far from our home, to be baked. The baking sheets held six dozen cakes each. We had to collect the baked goods at about 10:00 a.m. and once we had taken them home, my mother would parcel them off, after which it was our job to deliver them to our relatives and friends who were eagerly awaiting them.

One of the many wedding cakes iced by Rupert Cheong.
Arlene Mittelholzer.

My father had a talent for icing wedding cakes. I remember him mixing the ingredients for the cakes and stirring the mixture in a huge tub. Everything was done by hand as we did not have an electric mixer in those days. The butter and sugar had to be creamed, then the eggs added one by one, and when the consistency was just right the flour was added. Finally the dried fruits (prunes, raisins, currents, mixed peel and cherries) that had been set[4] for about three months with port wine and D'Aguiar's XM rum, were added to the batter. To give the wedding cake its traditional black color, sugar was burnt[5] and stirred into the mixture. It was finally poured into the large baking pans, and these were taken to either Fung's Bakery or La

---

[3] The hand-cranked mill was the time-saving kitchen gadget of the day used mainly for mincing meat.
[4] "To set the fruits" was the expression used for thoroughly infusing the fruits with liquor by letting them soak for an appreciable time.
[5] Brown sugar was heated without other additives in a large pot until it melted and darkened in color. The technique required some skill in judging the correct degree of conversion because overcooking would result in a bitter tasting syrup.

Rose Bakery to be baked, as the pans were too large for a conventional oven. I recall seeing my father preparing the almond paste and finally icing these wedding cakes, which could be two or three tiers high; sometimes the cakes were round, heart-shaped or square. Of course, while he was working on icing the cakes, we were not allowed to be jumping around and making noise, as he had to concentrate on doing a good job. The wedding cakes were always iced in white. It was amazing to watch my father mix the icing sugar, fill the syringe and select the icing tubes for a particular design, then as we watched, he artistically drew the leaves and roses, scalloped edges and cornices all around the cake. Sometimes the decoration called for silver balls to be placed in the icing around the edges and we would eagerly volunteer to do this job. These were really works of art and admired by everyone.

My mother had never worked outside the home and, as was the custom in those days, only the male head of the house was the breadwinner. When we were quite young we had a nanny who took us for walks with the pram, a servant to clean the house and do the marketing and shopping, and another servant to wash and iron the clothes. In those days, the iron was heated on the coal pot, and I remember watching my father's white shirts being ironed after they were washed and starched and hung to dry on the clothesline. I remember my father having a stately old, black, male servant named Cuss whose job it was to clean and polish all the shoes so that they were always clean and shining. I believe he also took care of the maintenance of the yard. Cuss would appear in the morning and would stay until about 7:00 p.m. when he left to go to his own home. Somehow, our fortunes seemed to have changed and one by one these servants disappeared so I can hardly remember when it became my sister's job to go to the market, while it became mine to go to the grocery located just around the corner from where we lived. We eventually got a washer and spin dryer – the height of luxury.

On every second Wednesday morning around 7:00 a.m. our household got ready for a visit by a Chinese barber named Sin-yu Co. My father would have his hair trimmed in the same style he maintained until his death with his hair parted in the middle and the sides and back buzzed short. In all the time I had known my father I had never seen his hair unruly or long. My brothers had to endure having their hair cut as well, and every now and then, my sister and I also had to have our hair cut in that style only seen on little Chinese girls, with a fringe in front (which we called a linzee) and hair trimmed all one length at the sides and at the back. I hated having to have my hair cut as I always felt that he had cut my hair too short.

My father loved to dance, however unfortunately my mother had been brought up in the Brethren Church and their religion forbade dancing, so she never learned to dance. He danced at family weddings and parties we attended, with any lady who was willing to tread the light fantastic. He could also play the piano but played from memory. There was one particular song he knew by heart (I believe it was "Beautiful Dreamer") and whenever he happened to pass by a piano, would play that song. I think his parents had owned a piano, however we did not have one. As far as I was aware, he did not speak Chinese, but he knew how to count in Chinese, and he once sang a Chinese song for us though we had no idea what the words meant. He said his grandmother had taught it to him. As a child I asked him where our family had come from and he guessed that were Punti[6] and had come from Canton, China.

My mother cooked Creole foods, which was a reflection of our Guyanese heritage. One day it would be cook-up rice, another day it would be curry and roti, or pepperpot and rice, or metagee, which consisted of plantains, cassava, eddoes with salt fish. Our main meal was eaten at lunchtime usually at 12:00 noon. On Sundays she would cook Chinese foods, typically chow mein, funcee or wan-yee, and roast chicken and rice. We ate our meals with a spoon and fork. Sometimes if my father was home, he would be the one to slit the throat of the chicken selected for our lunch that day, then the chicken would be placed under a bucket and finally, when all flapping had ceased, the dead chicken would be dunked into hot water and the feathers plucked, to be later cleaned and prepared for making pillows. No part of the chicken was wasted. The head and feet as well as the intestines were cleaned and cooked for dog food, while the heart, liver and gizzard were cooked with the rest of the meat for our lunch.

As children we attended Dolphin's private school on Camp Street. We walked there each day, returned home for lunch, then walked back for the afternoon session. When the school moved further away to Princess Street, it took a longer time to walk, however by that time my brother became the proud owner of a bike. My father bought an American bicycle for my brother when he was about eight years old. It had sturdy fenders on both the back and the front and we all learned to ride on this bike. It was amusing to remember that my brother "towed" us to school on this same bike. My brother Rickford sat on the front

---

[6] Puntis are the original local inhabitants in Guangdong Province as compared to the Hakkas or guest people who migrated into the region from the North at a later period, particularly during the 12th century.

fender, I sat on the cross-bar and my sister Rena sat on the back fender. What a sight that must have been!

We eventually went to St. Andrew's Church of Scotland School where I prepared for the Government County Examinations. Unfortunately, after two tries, I did not win a scholarship and it was time to go to High School. My father enrolled both my brother and I at Central High School, where my sister had attended two years earlier. My brother Renwick, although two years older than myself, did not like school when he was young, so my parents kept him at home until I was ready to go to school, and we were always in the same class together. My father's attitude was that it was a waste to be educating girls as they would soon get married and then all that time and money would be for nothing. I was fortunate to be able to complete high school though my brothers played hokey and never went beyond the third form, although unpaid school fees were a prime reason why they did not attend high school.

I made a lot of friends at High School, mainly Chinese. Their parents had come from China in the 1930s and spoke Chinese at home. Whenever I visited their homes, their mothers and elderly female relatives would speak to me in Chinese, which of course I did not understand, and my friends always had fun telling them that I was a li-ap – an English duck.

I grew up hearing about the deaths of my two eldest brothers who died from diphtheria in 1939. My mother recounted the story countless times to relatives and friends and I heard how they died within one day of each other. Their names were Royce Reginald Cheong and Lytton Rupert Cheong. They were 5 years and 2 ½ years old at that time, my sister Rena was not yet one year old, and my mother was eight months pregnant with my brother Renwick. My parents had been unaware that there was a drain flowing from a dental office next door, which ran right into their yard where the boys played and which carried the bacteria. The whole family had to be inoculated with a series of injections for up to two years after that tragic event.

It was a source of irritation while I was growing up to realize that my brothers did not have to do any housework, it was just not done in those days. My brothers could go out unaccompanied, yet my sister and I had to have our brothers accompany us if we had to go anywhere, or to a party. Being the younger daughter, I enjoyed my childhood even more than my sister who was always kept at home. Because I was born between my two brothers, and had boy cousins who were the same age, I trekked after them, learning to trap lizards,[7] which we placed on ant nests and watched as the ants climbed over and eventually devoured the hapless creatures. Any worms found under large stones suffered the same fate. I became skilled in playing marbles and cricket, traded buttons and hung around with the boys until the year I became eleven. Then I was no longer allowed to play outdoors, but had to learn to behave like a lady. No more whistling while walking on the road, no running down the street, and always being admonished by my mother to walk more ladylike.

Our Phillips radio provided us with home entertainment. We listened to the radio serial, "A man called Sheppard," the spelling bee contests, and the Battle of the Sexes to mention a few, as well as the news and the obituaries at 9:00 p.m. each night. Some of the good times I remember include going on picnics at Hope Beach, near Beterverwagting, where my father would drive over the very narrow bridges spanning the kokers along the Sea Wall before we reached our destination. Only a single car could travel along the road at a time and if we encountered another car coming the other way one car would have to reverse until a wider spot was reached allowing the cars to pass. Hope Beach was sandy and full of shells, which we loved to collect, however we were forbidden to take them into our house, so we always left them behind.[8] Since the beach was located on the north coast of Guyana, the water was always muddy but that did not deter us from playing in the water. I could not swim, however on one occasion my father held me in his arms as the waves crashed over my head and I believe this is the reason why I never learned to swim properly as I hate to have my head under water.

Every Friday night my mother would take us for a walk window-shopping along Water Street. There we would avidly look at all the store windows, especially near Christmas time when the store windows would be specially decorated with toys. If we were lucky, we would stop by Brown Betty, the ice-cream parlor, for an ice-cream cone or banana split. On Saturdays, we walked to the Sea Wall, rested for awhile, and then would stroll from the Fort out along the jetty, and if the tide was out, walk on the beach back to the Band Stand enjoying the cool breeze and the tang of the sea air. Sometimes we were lucky to be driven there by my father, and other times by one of my uncles who went to enjoy the sea breezes. On some of these occasions, the Police Military band would have a concert and everyone would enjoy the lively music being played.

---

[7] A lasso would be formed with the flexible end of stalk of grass and slowly slipped over the neck of the unprepared lizard.
[8] Several Chinese families considered it bad luck to have seashells in the home.

During the August holidays, my mother sometimes took us to spend a bit of vacation time with her half-sister who lived in Coffee Grove, Essequibo. My father would drive the car onto the ferry, behind Stabroek Market, to cross the Demerara River and after we landed at Vreed-en-Hoop, would drive all the way to Parika, where he would see us onto the next steamer. As children we enjoyed the trip, watching the steamer stopping at all the islands, seeing people disembarking, and new passengers coming aboard and then when we finally arrived at Adventure, would still have another hour's journey by car to reach Coffee Grove. It was on one of these trips that we visited the Tapacoma Lake, which was a short distance away. We had heard that the water could be both hot and cold, and only by experiencing it could we truly appreciate this phenomenon.[9]

Every Easter my father took us kite flying on the Sea Wall. My favorite kite was a box kite and we would usually have one or two kites to share among the four of us. Our enjoyment of this occasion was marred by the fact that my father could only spend an hour or two with us, after which it was time for him to return us home, so that he could take his other families to fly their kites.

My father had a school called the B.G. School of Accountancy & Commerce where he taught bookkeeping, shorthand and typewriting. This school was taught in our home and my earliest recollection of our house in Hadfield Street was this big signboard hanging in the front of our house. Classes were held on Monday, Wednesday and Friday each week from 5:00 p.m. to 9:00

Rupert Cheong with six of his children at the B.G. School of Accountancy. *Rita Graham.*

[9] Hot water from a geothermal fissure mixed with the cool lake water so that a person could stand in one place and feel that the water was hot below the waist (or knees) and cold above, and vice versa at another location in the lake. Even by standing at one spot it was possible to experience the temperature of the water changing as different layers of hot or cold water flowed by.

p.m. There were two huge framed certificates hanging on the walls proclaiming that my father had obtained a fellowship and the Commercial Teachers' Diploma from the London Institute of Commerce and could therefore have the letters FCAS and FCI after his name. My father had been educated at Collegiate School in Georgetown and studied at Samson Lee's School of Accountancy which he took over on the latter's death. There were five large tables at which approximately 40 to 50 students sat on benches. These tables were pushed to the side of the wall when not in use, and set up in the gallery and the living room whenever there were classes. When the class was in progress we children were not allowed in the front of the house, but had to stay in the bedrooms or the back part of our house. During this time we ate our dinner and spent the time reading or doing our school homework. My father only taught in the evenings as he had a full time job during the day. He was the local representative of the Institute of Bookkeepers, London, and the Institute of Commerce, Birmingham and whenever it was time for examinations to be held, my father wore his graduate gown and cap with the tassels. It was always a very solemn occasion when he would ring the bell to start the examination and all would be quiet except for the sound of the students writing. After my parents formally separated in about 1958, my father moved his school to his new home at 15 North Road and subsequently he moved to another house at 104 Brickdam.

Empire Garage with its cars for hire.
Rita Graham.

My father seemed to have had a lot of careers in his life. When my parents were first married, he ran a Sunday School to which all his friends and relatives sent their children. He was one of the first persons to own a car and tried his hand at running a hire car service called "Empire Garage" but this business subsequently failed. He employed a chauffeur, however not many people had a telephone in those days, and phone calls were few and far between for someone wanting to hire a car. He worked as an accountant for the Anaconda Gold Mines and that company must have folded as I recall seeing letterheads with that name and ledgers which were stored in our house when I was young. Whether he ever visited that gold mine in the interior is uncertain, but he spoke fondly of a Canadian named George Mott who subsequently returned to Canada when the mine closed down. I recall as a child that our house was filled with other companies' ledgers as people brought their books to be audited by my father, which was supposed to be done during the evenings or at weekends. However, he never seemed to have time to do so resulting in many visits by the business owners to ask when the work would be completed. He worked as the accountant for Bernard & Company, a furniture store, for quite a few years, and then worked for Bookers Shipping. After leaving Bookers, he opened a furniture store where he sold locally-made furniture on Regent Street, but this was not successful and in less than a year, he eventually closed the store. He then went to work for Tangs' Bakery as an accountant. At about this time he became the manager for a musical string band called the Dominators, and was involved in transporting them to and from all their engagements at weekend dances. At the same time he started another business renting folding metal chairs as he found there was a need for this service if the dances were held outdoors or in school halls.

After my grandfather Benjamin died, my father's mother, Elvira, decided to emigrate to Jamaica where her sister lived, and so the entire Cheong family except for my father left the shores of Guyana in 1937 to seek their fortune in Jamaica. My grandmother died in 1941 and my father never saw his brothers and sister until 1970 when for the very first time he left Guyana to visit them in Jamaica. His brothers and sister all married Chinese-Jamaicans and raised their families there. Three of his brothers subsequently emigrated to Canada, where I was fortunate to meet them and their families after 1971.

Since my father's family had all emigrated to Jamaica, we socialized mainly with my mother's family. My mother had three sisters and four brothers and at one period in my life, all the sisters and brothers lived with their children under one roof at the family home at the corner of High & Hadfield Streets opposite the Public Buildings. This house was huge. There were eight bedrooms and each family occupied one bedroom. What always amazed me was the size of the bathroom, which was as big as the largest bedroom and could probably have had more than two dozen people bathing at the same time, if they had so desired.

My maternal grandmother spoke three languages, English, Chinese and Hindi, since her father was Chinese and her mother had come from Madras, India. She called all the granddaughters "Moi," and I recall my mother addressing her older sisters by the word "Chay" before their names.[10] No one else in the family spoke Chinese, however I understand that she used to hold classes to teach English to the new Chinese women

---

[10] In Chinese a younger sister is called Moi and an older sister Chay.

immigrants. When my eldest girl cousin married, her brothers and sister addressed her husband by the name "Chay-foo," and on hearing this, our family also called him "Chay-foo" but we were told that we should not be calling him by this name. It is only now that I realize "Chay-foo" means brother-in-law.

We grew up knowing the Chinese names for certain things (such as foods), parts of the body, bodily functions and so on, but since my parents could not speak Chinese, all identity with our Chinese heritage was lost. Our mother tongue was English and this was the only language spoken in our home. As a child my mother tried to explain to me how my father's relatives were related. However, beyond her immediate family and my father's immediate family it was hard to see the links for more than two generations. My mother tried to impress upon my sister and me that we should be ladylike, that we should learn to sew and play the piano. It had always puzzled me why she should have these expectations for us, as we certainly did not have much money. We made do with whatever we had, sewing our own clothes, or altering clothes from our cousins who had outgrown them. My mother's brothers had done well for themselves and were financially well-off, having worked hard to achieve their successes, and were well regarded in the community.

As children, we rarely saw our father who visited our house only now and then. We dreaded the landlord's visit each month to collect the rent. Eventually the landlord decided to sell the house and my mother's brother Alexander Yhap purchased the house for my mother to continue living there and provided her with a monthly income for living expenses. My father was a busy man and it was only years later that we understood how busy he had been. He had managed to set up four other homes and now had five sets of children. In a small place like Georgetown, it was amazing how he was able to keep these lives separate. Once, I accompanied my father to Miss Daniels, the lady who owned a pastry shop at the corner of Camp and D'Urban Streets. She asked him how many children he had and he told her 24. I have never been able to substantiate these numbers, however I knew that there were six children born to my mother and father. I was aware that his family #2 consisted of seven children (five boys & two girls), family #3 consisted of three children (two boys and one girl), family #4 consisted of three children (two girls and one boy) and finally family #5 consisted of three boys. Over the years I have met some of them. On one occasion when my parents were temporarily separated, my father took my brothers, sister and me for a drive with the children of family #2. At that time only three children had been born, so we grew up knowing about them. I met the children of family #3 when their mother brought them to be enrolled as students at

Central High School where I worked. My father brought the two older children of family #4 to live with us when they were six and four years old, telling my mother that he had severed all ties with their mother and wanted the children to be brought up with us. They lived with us for about three months, after which time they returned to live with their own mother. I recently met one of my half-brothers and in reminiscing – of course his name also started with an "R" – he mentioned how he had met and was attracted to a beautiful girl at a dance only to discover before the evening was over that the girl was his half-sister. He also became acquainted with another half-brother (another "R") through his own sister when they met at a party and they became friends after finding out how they were related.

My father died in November 1976 in an accident on the East Coast road. He had apparently been driving back from Berbice where the band had finished an engagement. He was killed in a head-on crash with one of those huge buses that had strayed on the wrong side of the road at a sharp turn at Mahaica. I once remarked to an elderly acquaintance who had known my father, that I could not understand how he had been able to attract so many women. He thought that my father had lived a full life and had enjoyed every minute of it.

Country Doctor

Trev Sue-A-Quan

Over the ages, medical doctors have been held in high esteem, perhaps mainly because of their training to save life and limb. In the late 19th century, the medical profession appealed to many descendants of Chinese who settled in Guyana, but they could not all achieve the goal of becoming doctors because of the significant cost for medical training. Therefore, only the children from affluent Chinese families could afford the privilege of going abroad to medical college. Among the second generation Chinese, there were Susan and Yit-hoo Ho-A-Shoo, two daughters of a prosperous Chinese immigrant Ho-A-Shoo, who made his fortune opening shops in the interior to provide supplies for the workers in the goldfields. Susan and Yit-hoo attended Edinburgh University, graduating in 1911 and 1916, respectively. Their achievement is more noteworthy because the traditional Chinese attitude towards women – that they should be groomed to become wives and child bearers – still persisted. Another wealthy Chinese immigrant was Ho-A-Hing, and his daughter Martha also chose Edinburgh University for her medical studies. Charles Yow, of the Ng-Yow family, was able to accumulate the necessary funds for his tuition through the family shops operated by his parents and siblings.

All of the above-mentioned doctors practiced their profession in other countries – England, Singapore, and Trinidad. There were several third generation Chinese who became doctors and returned to Guyana. In 1926, Hilton Ho (Ho-A-Kai) gained his degree from London, and Simon "T" Mook-Sang qualified from Edinburgh. Prior to the outbreak of World War II there were Jerry E. Chow, Albert Foo (1933), Maurice O. "Jack" Luck (1933), and Basil Gillette (1936), all graduates from Edinburgh, as well as Arthur Fung (Ireland) and Christian Tjon-A-Man (London).

The duties of a doctor in a city hospital in those days were reasonably similar, regardless of the location or country. The delivery of health care in the rural areas of Guyana had to be adapted to suit the local circumstances. A large area would be the served by a Government Medical Officer (GMO) assigned to that district, and that doctor had to travel around the district to attend to the patients. Sometimes the trip would be by car, and at other times by motor launch, if towns and village upriver needed to be visited. Dr. Mook-Sang was one of the early doctors of Chinese ancestry who served in all three of Guyana's three counties – Berbice, Demerara, and Essequibo. Several other descendants of Chinese immigrants became doctors in the countryside, one of them being Dr. Isaac N. "Dick" Luck, whose activities are described in this account.

* * * * * * *

Isaac Newton "Dick" Luck, the fifth child of J.C. Luck (founder of Central High School), was another one of those who graduated from Edinburgh University. After qualifying in 1950, he returned to Guyana and became a licensed medical practitioner in March 1951. His first appointment was at the Public Hospital Georgetown (PHG) where he practiced general medicine. In the following year, he married my cousin, Patricia Sue-A-Quan. I recall going with Roddy Sue-A-Quan, Pat's younger brother, to scatter rice grains in the apartment in which the

Pat and Dick Luck (1967). *Pat Luck-Williams.*

newlyweds would be living within the PHG compound. This symbolic invitation to a fertile union was perhaps not needed since Dick came from a family of eleven children, and Pat had six siblings. Roddy suggested that we scatter the rice on the bed, the significance of which escaped my eight-year-old mind. It looked rather untidy there, so we ended up leaving a liberal amount of rice under the pillows.

Dr. Luck served in all three counties of Guyana, including at Suddie in Essequibo, Buxton in Demerara, and Port Mourant in Berbice. In 1958, Dick and Pat, now the parents of four children, were stationed at the GMO's quarters at Leonora, West Coast Demerara. Roddy and I went out to stay with them for a while during the school vacations. The living accommodations provided for the resident doctor were ample indeed. On the ground level was

The GMO's residence and clinic at Springlands, Berbice. *Pat Luck-Williams.*

the clinic, consisting of a waiting room, an examination room, the doctor's office, and a dispensary. On the first floor there was a large living room, dining room, bathroom, and kitchen. The bedrooms were on the third floor.

After a day or two, we guests fell into the routine of the doctor's schedule. Early in the morning, I used to go downstairs to pump water up to the storage tank at the top of the house. This provided the building with the water needed for the day. Actually, there was a hired assistant that did the pumping, and it must have amused him to see that I would want to take over this job, with obvious delight to each of us. The pump was attached to the system of water pipes and had the appearance of a disk with an upright handle that, when rocked back and forth in an arc, delivered water to the tank above. The water came from the Public Works distribution network and was frequently tinged with rust. It was used in the bathroom, and for general washing of dishes and clothes, while clear potable water was drawn from a vat in the yard, for cooking and drinking, as well as for final rinsing of bodies and things.

Dr. I.N. "Dick" Luck and eldest son, Ian, in the operating room at Suddie Hospital, Essequibo (1961). *Pat Luck-Williams*

The patients seeking medical attention would usually come with a few supporting members of the family, or friends, and gather in the waiting room. Dr. Dick Luck would see them it turn and prescribe appropriate medicines for their ailments. Since I had an interest in medicine, Dick invited me to watch as he examined the patients and explained their ailments. Most of the cases were relatively minor – colds and fevers, cuts and bruises, sores and stings. On occasion I would help to dress a wound, applying the medication, covering it with gauze, and wrapping the area with bandages or strips of adhesive plaster. Sometimes the problem seemed serious to the anxious patient but, in reality, was simple from the doctor's point of view. One day, a man came to complain about a loss of hearing in one ear that was worsening with time. The doctor checked both ears to see what indications he could find. Then he asked me to get a curved bean-shaped basin and a bowl of warm water, while he explained to the patient that the problem could be fixed. Dr. Dick told the fellow to lie on the examination table, and he had me hold the basin below his bad ear. Dick took up what seemed to be quite an outsized syringe and filled it with water. He then injected the water into the ear and a mass of wax came flowing out as the water swirled around inside to wash the ear. With a restored sense of hearing, the patient beamed with delight as he thanked the doctor for resolving the problem.

On another occasion, a mature lady complained that her breast was swollen and painful. After reviewing her symptoms and making an examination, Dick asked her to lie on the table. He had me retrieve the bean-shaped basin, which I then held against her side, below the troubled breast. Dick cleaned the side of the breast with alcohol and made an incision with a scalpel. An enormous amount of pus oozed from the opening into the basin. It came as quite a surprise to me, but for the knowledgeable doctor it was what he expected. Dick squeezed the affected area to express all of the inflammation. With the application of some medicine and a few stitches, the procedure was completed. Dick then asked me to bandage her up, waving his hand in a circle to indicate a dressing that needed to be wound across her chest area. Here before me, a fifteen-year-old lad, was this grateful lady whose breasts, even after the operation, were well-endowed, and I realized that this situation was more than I could handle. While I was capable of tying bandages to arms or legs, this assignment was a bit beyond my ability. When I balked, Dick realized that his "nurse" was out of his depth. He took over and proceeded to wind the bandages around her body and over her shoulder in a proper manner to give adequate support to her recovering breast.

In general, those that came to the clinic were both capable of making the journey and not willing to wait for the doctor to come by to their homes. The house calls were part of the routine for the doctor, and called "running the district." Once a week the doctor went out in his car to provide medical attention to the people east of Leonora, and on another day a trip along the western route was done. Roddy and I used to go along for the ride after loading up car with the doctor's bag of instruments, along with a box containing various large bottles of medications. As we headed out, we looked out for the white or red flags that were erected along the roadside. The flag-posts were usually no more than a metre (three feet) high and the cloth was whatever was available in the home. Dick explained that the white flags indicated that a visit by the doctor was requested, while a red flag meant that the illness was serious. Dick's routine was to drive to the end of the route while noting where all the flags were posted, but stopping only at the red flags on the outward journey. Then, on the return

Ready to run the district out of Cove & John, East Coast Demerara (1953). *Pat Luck-Williams.*

journey, all the places with white flags would be serviced. In setting up the flags, the determination of what was a serious ailment was of course left to the judgment of the patient and/or family. In most cases, Dick found that the red flags were not indications of urgent medical emergencies – it might be a call for a follow-up visit after surgery at a hospital, or a persistent fever, or a mysterious ailment that the family members themselves could not diagnose. The white flags tended to be raised for minor cases – perhaps it would be to check up on a cold, or sprain, or to learn from the doctor whether a medicine previously prescribed was working, or that the healing process for a wound was proceeding as well as could be expected. With his pleasant disposition, Dr. Dick was good at reassuring the patients. But it sometimes took a bit of searching to find the person needing attention. This was because the flags at the roadside could not show exactly where the intended patient was located. We had to walk among the huts in the village and call out to ask who it was that wanted to see the doctor. Then someone would appear and guide us to the correct home.

When the doctor determined that some medicine was required, he would give instructions to Roddy and myself that a certain mixture should be prepared. We would go to the trunk of the car, which was the mobile dispensary, and use graduated glasses to measure out the prescribed potion. Invariably it was a certain amount of concentrated medicine to which water or an alcohol-based solution was added. The "dispensary" was outfitted with a number of small bottles to hold these medicinal concoctions and Dick would write the appropriate dosage on the label. Many of the patients or the family members would plead for the doctor to prescribe some medicine even though Dick may have determined that the ailment would soon pass without further inter-vention. In those cases Dick would also have us make up a prescription, although that would invariably be a remedy that was more in the nature of a tonic, or even placebo, rather than a specific curative prescription. However, the knowledge of having a medicine on hand was enough to provide a healing effect. The patients were responsible for paying for these various medications and did not always have cash on hand. The doctor would be paid in kind, and he ended up with an adequate supply of eggs, chickens, fruit and vegetables.

If there were a real emergency, some means would be found to rush the patient to the clinic, day or night. Once, in the middle of the night, there was an urgent banging on the door. We arose, quickly got dressed, and opened the clinic. There was a crowd of men who kept pleading for the doctor to save someone. That someone was being supported by two fellows who were essentially dragging him into the clinic. The patient had a dazed look as he was put to sit in a chair. His companions unwrapped a long cloth that was tightly wound around his left hand. The cloth became redder as each coil was removed; it was obvious that the injured man had lost a lot of blood. When the blood-soaked bandage was taken away, an awful gash was exposed – it was between his thumb and first finger and had cut through almost to the point where the bones of these two fingers were joined. Amidst pleas to save the patient, his companions explained that he had been working with a cutlass when the injury was sustained. There were two strips of cloth tied very tightly around the man's forearm, one near the wrist and the other near the elbow. The doctor asked the friends to remove these tourniquets and advised them that these could have caused the man to lose his hand from loss of blood circulation. Dick then washed the wound and determined that, fortunately, there were no major blood vessels or muscles severed. He then injected the area with liberal amounts of local anesthetic and proceeded to stitch the wound. The hand was then bandaged, and a sling made to support the injured hand. Dick comforted the concerned men and thought that he had better administer a sedative to the patient. He asked the companions to pull back the sleeve of the shirt on the injured arm, while he prepared an injection. When Dick came back, he noted that there was a third tourniquet, previously hidden under the sleeve – it was the tightest of the three constrictors.

There was another awakening at the dead of night when the battering on the door sounded really desperate. Outside were a few Indian men who begged for the doctor to see their relative who was dying; she had collapsed and had lost consciousness. All their efforts to revive her were to no avail. Dick packed some supplies into his bag and we drove off at a tear, following the car that led us to the village. In the bedroom a lady lay deathly still. Around her stood several men who, with their backs against the wall, were chanting in an obviously religious fashion to the Superior Being. Dick examined the pupils of the eyes of the stricken woman and showed me how, when he pressed a spot on her arm, the flesh remained indented in dimple-like fashion. Dick called for a bowl of freshly boiled water and the relatives rushed off to comply. He continued his examination as the chants around grew more intense and mournful. In a few minutes, a bowl of hot water was brought in. We looked at it and saw that it was water that was drawn from the tap, because it was rust colored. The doctor asked if there was any clear water and was told that water from the storage tank was available, and some could be collected and boiled. But there was no time to waste – Dick decided to use the rust-colored water to rinse out the syringe. He then filled the syringe with medicine and began injecting it into the patient's arm at a slow rate.

When half of the medication was discharged, the lady's head moved – a slight, barely noticeable motion, but it was observed by all. The chanting immediately stopped and the men placed their hands together and, with palms to their faces, drew their hands downwards from their foreheads to their chests and a collective sigh of relief was emitted. Dick continued to inject the drug until the syringe was empty. The patient's face gave up its stiff appearance and relaxed slightly, although she remained in a drowsy state. Dick explained to the relatives that her condition was serious and he advised that she be taken the next day to the Public Hospital, Georgetown for further examination and treatment. The family offered profuse thanks for rescuing the patient and promised to do the needed follow-up. As we drove back to the clinic, Dick explained that an injection of glucose to counter hypoglycemia can produce one of the most dramatic recoveries for this kind of coma.

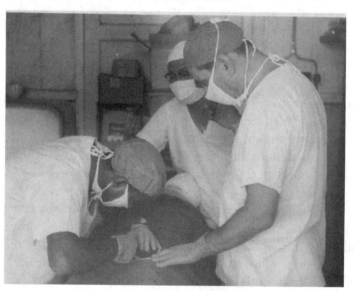

Dr. Dick Luck, wearing spectacles, attending at an operation.
Pat Luck-Williams.

Essentially, the GMO was the general practitioner for the district and major diseases and injuries were referred to the district hospital, or to Georgetown. Relatively speaking, the greatest demand in the countryside for the doctor's services was for the delivery of babies. After labor had commenced, the expectant mother would be brought to the clinic for the final stages of the birthing. Dick felt that the delivery of a baby was one aspect of medical expertise that I need not need to learn, at least not at that time, and I was excluded from the examination room on these occasions. However, while I was not a witness, the birthing process introduced to me to some cultural differences. One day, an expectant Indian mother was brought to the clinic by car. She was well advanced in her labor and within the hour the baby came through. The cry of the just-born infant announced the successful delivery. The male companions, who had brought the mother, perked up and smiled as they heard the cry from within the examination room. A little while later, the baby was brought out to be handed to the doting fellows, and the new mother came walking out by herself, taking slow and measured steps. Dick implored the men to go and help her to the car. A couple of them vocally agreed and took a step in her direction. But then they stopped, and the mother continued to amble her way to the car unassisted. Dick later told me that he had found it was the custom for Indian men to avoid contact with a new mother – and the mother knew that as well.

While birthing was not a part of my learning process, Dick did not hesitate to take me to an autopsy. We drove to the place that autopsies were performed, and entered a stark room with a concrete table in the middle. The table had a slightly raised perimeter to retain any fluids, was gently sloped, and had a hole at the lower end of the table. On this bare platform lay the body of a young Indian girl, not yet a teenager, pale and stiff. Dick explained that she was found in a canal and it was necessary for him to do an examination to officially record the cause of death. He made a long incision across her chest and broke the breastbone to gain access to the lungs. When the lungs were cut, water flowed out. This was the proof of drowning that the doctor was seeking. He put back the body parts in as orderly a fashion as could be expected, and we departed.

Dr. Dick Luck was there for it all – birth to death – and his routines in providing health care to the people in the country in Guyana were typical of the doctors who preceded him, and of those who followed.

Dr. Luck addressing members of the Lions Club at the opening of an Eye Clinic at Skeldon Hospital, Berbice in January 1968. Funds for creating the clinic were raised by the Lions Club. *Pat Luck-Williams.*

Good Sport

Godfrey W. Chin

The cliché, "All work and no play, makes Jack a dull boy" certainly does not apply to the Chinese community in Guyana. By WWII, about 90 years after the first shipment of Chinese indentured laborers arrived, they had entrenched themselves as an integral part of the colony – excelling in commerce and trade (Charles Yong-Hing), education (J.C. Luck, who founded Central High School), medicine (Dr. Buddy Hugh), and law (Charles Fung-a-Fat), to name a few.

The children and grandchildren of the Chinese settlers were now ready to "come out to play," while devoting themselves to the other social and cultural aspects of life available to them in the colony at the time. Although many took up sporting activities as recreational pursuits, only a few excelled at their chosen sport initially, but by the time Guyana gained independence in 1966, the local Chinese had made considerable strides and played a significant part in the national sports scene.

By August 1948, when I started my secondary education at Central High School, the Chinese Association had been built on Brickdam, opposite St. Stanislaus College, and from there, Chinese culture and customs were being preserved and promoted. The Annual Chinese New Year Dinner, held at the Chinese Association, was cosmopolitan in nature with all the local big-wigs in attendance, while the traditional Dragon Dance was a highlight, and a big attraction at festivals and visits by royalty. Notably absent was the traditionally flurry of fireworks and firecrackers, and I always wondered if the taboo was a result of a phobia after the disastrous fire on Lombard Street around 1913.[1]

In 1950, at 13 years of age, I joined Chinese Sports Club (CSC) at Thomas Lands to participate in cricket – Third-Class Rajah and Frank cup competitions, and the two-day Wight Cup tournament. CSC had an informal beginning in 1924 when a few Chinese sports-minded enthusiasts met at the residence of T.M. Chee-A-Tow. In 1929 a group

---

[1] Following the disastrous fire in December 1913, the manufacture of fireworks and firecrackers was prohibited. Importation of these items was granted to the consulate of China for use on special occasions, and not for general use.

of Chinese sportsmen went to Trinidad to compete against their island-based counterparts in a variety of games. The tour was a success and it was agreed that these Goodwill Tours would be held every two years. The need to have appropriately sized grounds to host a visiting Trinidad group was a factor that prompted the Chinese in Guyana to acquire a site in Thomas Lands. Robert V. Evan-Wong was the first president of CSC, holding office from 1931 to 1938. He was succeeded by Stanley E. Lee (1939-40), J.C. Luck (1941-47), James A. Sue-A-Quan (1951-53), and Cyril V. Too-Chung (1954-62).

Having a sports facility alone was not enough to produce top-class athletes. In 1950, the only top-class Chinese sportsman known to me was Rupert Tang Choon,[2] an Inter-Colonial all-rounder from Trinidad, who also played in the regular Goodwill Exchange Matches. Even then, I was too often reminded of the outstanding achievements of our local players, probably designed to inspire newcomers to surpass these performances in the future. My catechisms of good scores included P.W. Lee, 138 (in 1937); C.V. Too-Chung, 106 not out; E.S. Gillette, 101; W.R. Luck, 127 (all in 1939); J. Ho-A-Shoo, 148; L. Ching, 103 not out (1949); and Gary Lee, 178 not out, along with George Fung-On, 118 (in 1952, which was the last occasion of this rivalry). In the eight clashes between 1929 and 1952 the locals shared equal honors with the islanders. At CSC, the star players I sought to emulate at that time included James Chin, Clement Choo-Shee-Nam, W. Lieu, Tit Lee, and Billy Fung-a-Fat. But this cramming must have worked, because, by 1957, CSC was promoted to the newly formed Northcote level, winning on many occasions, and finally to Case Cup, the First-Class level of cricket competition locally. Emerging from their fold was Bud Lee, who could have been a West Indies Sobers – before Garfield came on the scene.[3] Bud was a prolific left-hand opening batsman who relished the fast stuff, and centuries were effortless to him. While attending the University of the West Indies in Jamaica, Bud Lee, Walter Chin and Arnold Gibbons (the Guyanese Trio) started off in the batting order, and when they were done, the team captain often declared, as the score would typically be 300 odd for three. But Bud and Walter preferred to maintain their course in pursuing medical careers – and the West Indies lost a promising potential batting great!

---

[2] Rupert Tang Choon played First-Class cricket from 1934 to 1957 and represented Trinidad & Tobago.
[3] Garfield Sobers, from Barbados, was a legendary cricket player between 1954 and 1974, with all-round ability. He was captain of the West Indies team and set many cricketing records in his career. He was later knighted for his contributions to cricket.

Another great batsman was Albert Choy, whose method for reaching double centuries could be a lesson for many. Add Gary Lee, with his Robert Christiani[4] skill, and Chinese Sports Club (which later became Cosmos) was as fearsome an opponent as any. No wonder, every weekend, hundreds of local cricket fans thronged the CSC pavilion in Thomas Lands to see "the yellow peril in white"[5] bat, bowl, and field. Other outstanding cricketers included Rudy Low, Milton Wong, Hilton Quan, who, in addition to Gary Lee, Bud Lee and Albert Choy, were called up to National Trials. As it turned out, no Chinese played on the Guyana Cricket Team, but there was a Chinese First-Class cricket umpire at Bourda – Wing Gillette. They gained consolation, however, by sharing honors with the formidable East Indian cricket population in the annual Rahaman Cup – East Indians vs. Chinese – which they won on a few occasions. Other outstanding cricket assets include Tunny Low-a-Chee, Michael Akai, Jerry Man-Son-Hing, Terry Solomon, and Richard Chung.

Around 1958, CSC extended the club pavilion, and the next 20 years could truly be called their "Golden Years in Sport." Hockey was resuscitated, and, by 1960, CSC was unbeaten in local competition, winning the Hiram Walker Cup, Dare Shield, and Seven-a-Side event. These trophies were almost regular fixtures in the Club's trophy case, except for the few occasions when arch-rival teams representing Georgetown Cricket Club (GCC) and Georgetown Football Club (GFC) upset the steam-rollers.

It was no surprise that five of the CSC members of that time, together with Vincent P. Chung and Billy Lee (from GFC), formed the nucleus of the British Guiana Team that won the first Caribbean Quadrangular Hockey Championship,[6] held in Trinidad in June 1961. Godfrey Chin was in Goal, with Walter Chin (captain) and V.P. Chung, wing halves, along with "Cha-Cha" John Embleton, center half, forming a Maginot line. With a forward line consisting of brothers Rollo and Gary Lee (inside forwards), Gerald Wong, outside left, with the nippy Eddie Caetano at center-forward, and Norman Wight on right wing, this team was the equivalent of any Dream Team. Raffie Knowles, popular sports writer for the *Trinidad Guardian*, wrote: "On the smooth Queen's Park Oval, it was clip, clip, clip, clip – from Caetano to Gary, over to

---

[4] Robert Christiani, born in Georgetown, played test cricket for the West Indies between 1947 and 1954.
[5] Cricketers traditionally wore white outfits in those days.
[6] The four participating countries were Barbados, British Guiana, Jamaica, and Trinidad.

brother Rollo, occasionally to Wight and Wong on the wings. Nine times into the net, with possibly nineteen chances missed." The razzle-dazzle play almost embarrassed the scoreboard, and at one time it appeared that the first ever double-figure score in Caribbean hockey would be recorded. The reporter concluded that the group from B.G. was "the one team that looked like a team, showed how hockey should be played, and justifiably won the series." From my goal circle I heard the chief groundsman bawling for "a nail and hammer." Jeffrey Lee, still a student at Queen's College, was the seventh Chinese in that contingent.

Walter Chin, temporarily on assignment in Jamaica, returned to Bourda in 1964 representing that island. B.G. won the series, which included six Chinese: Godfrey Chin, Rollo and Gary Lee, and V. P. Chung were the permanent fixtures with newcomers William Lieu and David Cho-Chu. Yet another Chinese descendant, Roger Diyaljee, joined the National Squad for British Guiana to retain their Caribbean title in Jamaica 1965, but lost 1-0 to the All-American Champion, Argentina.

Yours truly, Godfrey Chin represented Guyana on 26 occasions from 1961 to 1975. I was on the President's XI 19 times, took part in two Pan-Am Games, remained unbeaten in three Caribbean Championships (letting in 49 goals, while the forwards up front scored 56). I do not in any way consider myself an outstanding athlete; my prowess was magnified purely because I was very fortunate to play with these resourceful dedicated "Orientals," who used as much brain as brawn on the ball field. I mention this only to accentuate the real impact that Chinese in Guyana played in these sports. I doubt that I would have reached that far in any other community or environment. Hockey clinics were run every Sunday at CSC from 8:00 a.m. to noon, led by Billy and Gary Lee, Walter Chin and Patti Fung-On. They created perhaps the first academy for local sports and it was open to all hockey enthusiasts, Chinese and non-Chinese. Ball control skills were developed by arranging team relay races that weaved past lines of cricket stumps. Shooting, flicking, scoops, reverse-stick strokes, short passes, and penalty corners were rehearsed and drilled. I demonstrated to budding goalkeepers the way to reduce the angle available to the shooter, and how to tackle the opponent as he/she reached the shooting circle. The clinics concluded with a game that tried to highlight these recently-honed skills. The PANAM jet passed overhead every Sunday,[7] perhaps an omen that 80%

[7] Pan American World Airways introduced jet service to Guyana. The jet, departing for Trinidad, would be diverted so as to fly directly over Georgetown, as a promotional scheme.

of these talented Guyanese ballplayers would migrate in the near future. What a loss! The Chinese have undoubtedly flown the Guyana Hockey flag very high!

Patti Fung-on, captain and center half, Donna Tiam-Fook, forward, and goalie Joy Ng Young also led the Women's Hockey Team to major victories.

Facilities facilitate sports achievement, and with the extension of the club's pavilion – a new basketball hard court with lights was built – CSC became a Mecca for the hoop-game, which became popular locally after the 1954 film *Go, Man, Go!*, featuring the Harlem Globetrotters, hit the big screen. A Chinese team, the Clowns, was formed with Gary Lee, Roy Wong and James Pac-Hon Chin (Jim Chin) taking leading roles. The Clowns more than held their own against visiting Surinam and Trinidad teams as well as the hot local squads, including the Panthers, Ravens, and Police. They even formed a Ladies' team, the Clownettes, with Sarah Lou Harris[8] playing!

In the Club's pavilion, Doreen Chow-Wah was mastering ping-pong and emerged a National Champion. She first represented Guyana in 1966 in the Caribbean Championships held in Barbados. She teamed up with Denise Osman and reigned as Caribbean Doubles Champion for quite a while. The nation's table tennis skill rose to a higher level after the Chinese in Taiwan assigned coaches to train the local squads and introduced the devastating "loop." Christopher Chung-Wee became the Men's Champion with this new weapon.

Upstairs in the renovated club, two courts for playing badminton were set up, and while the low ceiling was below the required specifications, south-paw Bud Lee made the National Team with Laurie Lewis and members of the Holder clan. Candy Lee was also a National Star.

On the other racquet court, lawn tennis, Derek Phang won honors at the local and Caribbean level in the 1950s, excelling at the Brandon Tournaments, symbol of Caribbean tennis supremacy. Ian McDonald, who was Derek's doubles partner, considered him to be one of the finest tennis players to emerge from the Caribbean. One little known figure is Gem Hoahing, daughter of New Amsterdam-born merchant, Benjamin Ho-A-Hing. She took up residence in Britain and represented that country at Wimbledon between 1937 and 1961. In 1949, she reached

---

[8] Sarah Lou Harris was one of the top black models in the U.S. and helped to raise the standard of modeling in Guyana. She later married Sir John Carter, who became Guyana's High Commissioner in Britain and Ambassador to the United Nations.

the fourth round in singles competition after defeating the American tennis star, Gussie Moran, although the latter is more remembered that year for introducing a new fashion statement – frilly undergarments – that not only raised many an eyebrow, but also caused gentlemen to drop to the ground . . . in an effort to get more revealing photographs of the lacy display. In 1957, Gem Hoahing again reached the fourth round but was beaten by the number one seed, Althea Gibson, the first black person to play at Wimbledon, who went on to become champion that year. However, Gem remains on the record books of Wimbledon history as being the shortest competitor ever – she was four feet, nine inches tall.

In rifle shooting, Maurice Yong and Bill Ng-A-Fook were excellent sharp-shooters. I recall with pride one Chinese footballer, Vivian Lee, who scored a decisive goal against Surinam. The sole athlete in track and field would be Leslie Chin, a hurdler who raced for B.G. I will never forget the race at GCC, when Olympian Harrison Dillard of the USA reached the hurdles' tape – and strode to the winner's podium ahead of Ken Corsbie and Leslie Chin, in that order. Chinese were never prominent as speedy gazelles. Their skill and success in ball games were due purely to their application and resolve: practice, more practice, and a common sense approach to sport.

Two cyclists who were national level riders were Derrick Ying and "Buckman "Nicholson. Elson and Errol Ten-Pow, were two brothers who owned a motor-cycle shop and relished horse-power, each excelling in his respective class at the Dakota Circuit, at the former airbase built during WWII by U.S. forces.

We must not forget our own Bruce Lee: Charles Woon-a-Tai, Martial Arts Black Belt competitor, who also reached a world standard. Before this one-on-one sport became popular, there were some who engaged in wrestling and boxing, but at a recreational level, although T.M. Chee-A-Tow served as the official timekeeper for boxing matches, while his son, Stanley, officiated inside the ring as Guyana's national boxing referee.

This recap of Chinese on the Guyanese sporting field, would not be complete without my attempt, as is done for many sports, to offer an MVP[9] recognition. Without prejudice, my nominations for the Guyanese Chinese Sports Hall of Fame would be Irwin "Bud" Lee and Gary Lee; for the Chinese ladies: Doreen Chow-Wah and Patti Fung-On.

---

[9] Most Valuable Player.

COMMUNITY SPIRIT

Andy Lee, née Lam
with contributions from Godfrey Chin and Trev Sue-A-Quan

The Church and the Sports Club were the main social institutions of the Chinese community from the 1940s to Independence! St Saviour's in Charlestown was the last and largest of the Chinese churches in B.G. after the Chinese left the canefields and the small villages scattered over the country, migrating to Georgetown, the capital city.

These two institutions could not sustain their activities from only church collections and monthly subscriptions. They were dependent on annual fund-raising events for maintenance and for the purchase of necessary facilities and gear – events which became the highlights in our social calendars. Chinatown Fair was held in October at the Chinese Sports Club, in Thomas Lands. The Chinese Bazaar took place in December.

In the late '50s my father, Kenneth Lam, was one of the main shakers and movers in the planning and implementation of the Chinatown Fair. For months beforehand he would be contacting James Sue-A-Quan, Cicely Ting-A-Kee, and many other members in the Chinese community, to ensure they were ready to run their particular stalls. The Ting-A-Kee and Sue-A-Quan clans were key players because they took on the responsibilities for providing food and drink – key features of the fair.

Preparation for Chinatown Fair began months ahead. It was a 2-day event: Saturday and holiday Monday in the first week of October,[1] Sunday being a respected holy day. There were unwritten rules as to who ran each stall or event. Each committee member had specific spheres of responsibilities but more often than not everyone knew what had to be done. J.A. Sue-A-Quan's Winery always ran the bar and supplied drinks and beverages for the dance that went on to 2:00 a.m. Cicely Ting-a-Kee ran the food stall that was located at the centre of the fairground, within easy reach of the Fair participants.

There were a variety of games of chance and skill, and the average player could come away with several prizes, while filling the cool night air

---

[1] This also generally coincided with the anniversary of the founding of the Republic of China on 10 October (double ten) in 1911, headed by Dr. Sun Yat-sen.

with joyous shouts. Hoop-la, with Gary Lee in charge, was the top attraction, with prizes including bottles of rum, various wines, tins of chocolate, and more, available to be won. Six rings (12-inch inner hoops of an embroidery set) were obtained for 25 cents and the hoop had to encircle the square platform on which the desired prize was placed – just half an inch smaller than the ring itself. Sometimes a purposeful strategy could pay dividends, such as spinning the hoop so that it might twirl around the bottle and work its way around the platform. In some cases the hoop might end up askew on the platform, barely clinging to one or two corners. If the attendant was slow in removing that hoop, this situation might attract a volley of other hoops trying to push down the dangling hoop. Ring-the-Bottle utilized small-sized rings that needed to come to rest around the neck of the bottle. Another variant was Ring-the-Duck, in which a ring was tossed to lasso the duck's neck. The ducks were little yellow plastic ones that bobbed in a trough, with waves created by appropriately stirring the water. Yet another toss-up game was Money-in-the-Saucer, with the contestants trying to make a coin come to rest in a distant saucer.

James Sue-A-Quan's perennial game consisted of a large, vertical, spinning wheel – a solid board with pie-shaped sections of different colours indicating the various brands of wines that his winery produced. There were a several sections indicating "ordinary" wines, i.e. port and ruby wines (locally known as pac-pac), and only one or two sections for the more expensive wines – ginger, orange, cherry, cashew, muscatel. Long metal pins on the outer rim separated the sections and the pointer would click against then as the wheel turned. The heavy board was sent into motion by a push button that activated an electric motor. There were two identical betting boards at the front of the stall, in the left and right corners, and the players would place five-cent pieces on the squares, trying to win a bottle of wine to their taste. The operators – mainly James Sue-A-Quan's son, Roddy, and nephews – had to be vigilant from the time that the bets were called off, because there would always be a few artful dodgers who would either sneak in a late bet, or withdraw a losing coin, or claim ownership to another's winning bet. The many bottles of wine were displayed on a table in front of the spinning wheel, with many more cases stored below.

Dad built a game where a ball was rolled down a sloping platform into holes. You won a prize if you got a certain amount of points, based on the value assigned to each hole. He also built a greyhound racing game. There were six greyhounds of different colours and a set of six dice with corresponding colours was rolled to see the number of spaces each greyhound would advance. Those two were innovative games, never before seen in the country and did indeed generate a lot of money. (Mom and Dad got the inspiration when they went to Europe and saw those games). The various game booths were manned by the younger male members of the club, with the CSC cricket captain and his team playing leading roles.

Roy Wong and Jim Pac-hon Chin organized basketball games and exhibitions on the well-lit hardcourt. These games even included international teams playing against local ones. For those athletes and would-be athletes who wanted a piece of the action, one challenge was to burst the balloons on a wall with an accurate kick of a football, while cricketers needed to bowl and hit the standard wicket a minimum of four times in six tries (a six-ball over). On one occasion a World-Class spinner missed four times out of six – with the gathered crowd cheering as if it were a test match. Ball-throwers had another way to test their arms. The Shy-the-Tins game, ably manned by Godfrey Chin, challenged the competitor to use a maximum of three balls to try and knock down several tins stacked in a pyramid on a distant platform. Over here, there was air rifle shooting and over there, dart throwing.

For those who wanted to literally test the luck of the draw they could try Pull-the-String, where one of several strings would be picked from a bundle, with each string attached at the other end to a prize on the table. This was operated by some of the younger helpers who offered the bundle of strings and distributed the guaranteed prize. However, while a box of candies or an attractive toy might be the coveted prize, there was also a chance that a pencil or pack of cards might be on the end of the chosen string. Other people might try their luck buying one of many tempting gift-wrapped packages, contents unknown, hoping that they picked a winner. Or they could purchase a ticket for the raffle. One year, Mom had a clothes stall where she sold children's clothes and stuffed toys she'd sewn and crocheted over the year.

Prizes for the games were donated by Chinese businesses around town. William Lieu and Jason Fung-On were in charge of the stock and prize room from where stallholders could chose their prizes. At the end of the night the stallholders would turn over their cash boxes – perhaps $200 might be raised from Hoop-La and $125 from Shy-the-Tins.

In addition to the game stalls, there were several individuals of different ethnic backgrounds who were invited to set up small, portable gambling tables. The games utilized dice or playing cards. One of the popular games used several dice, one having regular numbers (one to six), and another with its faces engraved with the symbols for spades, hearts, diamonds and clubs, plus crown and anchor; a third bore other markings, such as circle, square, and star. The dice were placed in a tin by the operator and rattled around before the tin was turned upside down with a thud on the playing board. Bets were open to all comers, children not excluded. These "vendors" were free to set up where they felt they could attract a crowd and worked in the glow of a calcium carbide torch (or two) that emitted a bright white flame along with the distinctive smell of combustion.

A Ferris Wheel such as this was one of the attractions at the Chinatown Fair. *M.R. Lam.*

For the non-gambling types there were donkey rides, the Ferris Wheel, and Merry-Go-Round. Then there was the haunted house – a tent with a dimly-lit, ghoulishly-decorated interior. The carnival atmosphere and variety of amusements at the Chinatown Fair attracted families of all races and places, some coming from the countryside for the big weekend.

Three days before the weekend, normal life in the grounds of the club came to a halt as the stalls had to be constructed on the tennis courts but not on the hallowed hockey and cricket pitch! Stalls were constructed with cheap, bare, wooden planks fastened to Dexion[2] frames and topped with galvanized zinc sheets. Electric wires were strung to carry power to each stall. Strings of multi-coloured lights decorated the Sports Club's clubhouse, perimeter fence and stalls. Areas in the clubhouse and the grounds were secured from the general public; half-drums filled with ice for the drinks delivered. Blueprint plans were checked and re-checked ensuring all the stallholders had all the necessary equipment and space with which to function. The big "game" (La Boule) was set up on the billiard table like a regular casino roulette operation. Richard Chung called out the winning number as the players, three to four rows deep, sought to strike it rich. Everything, especially the entrance gate and perimeter fence had to be strong and tough enough to withstand a stampede of bison because after 9 p.m., when the rag tag Georgetown party-goers of various shades of colour and civility came to attend the dances, it was exactly that.

Saturday started around 11 a.m., when stallholders armed with tons of crepe paper, staple guns, Scotch tape, ladders, chairs and whatever else came to decorate the stalls. The stallholders were free to decorate as they wanted. We children loved this part as we felt we were doing something – wrapping every inch of splintered board in rolls of crepe paper. It was

---

[2] Slotted angle iron lengths that could be linked together with nuts and bolts.

true community spirit because everyone needed a hand and everyone had a free hand somewhere to give. Youngsters would just turn up and got roped in to do something. Every able-bodied person stood a chance of being "invited" to help behind the stalls as well. Auntie Cicely's team was all her children – Margery, Gordon, Jimmy, Robbie, Georgie, and David – along with her nieces and nephews: Jeffrey, Peggy, Nancy and Mary. David DeGroot, Jason Fung-On, and Godfrey Chin assisted everywhere setting up the stalls. C.V. Too-Chung, president of CSC, checked that everything was all right. Signs had to be made. Everything had to be in place for opening of the gates at 4:00 o'clock.

At about 3:00, if we were lucky, we would bike home to bathe and get dressed, only to have to rush back as soon as possible, not wanting to miss a minute of it. The gates were opened promptly at 4:00 o'clock. Chinese families trickled through like sparklers – freshly bathed, dressed and eager to see what's new – and with coconut oil rubbed on their legs. Bete rouche (bête rouge) was a tiny bug that lived in the grass and if you were not properly protected they would crawl up to the warm spots of the body and cause an enticing itch that really made you want to scratch, but, if scratched, turned out into sores. The adults would head straight for the food stall to see "What's for dinner?" and the children scattered in every which way to see what was there for fun and games, and to find their playmates. Young babies and their nannies had their own little favourite benches under the pavilion. Everyone was allowed to play any game, with no discrimination against the young, the aged, the tall or the short, the skilled gamer or the bungler. It was a free for all. It was a time for the whole family to enjoy themselves in the safety of the grounds and among relatives and friends. We were all given "spending money" which, not surprisingly, had to be replenished several times throughout the night.

One of the first activities was the children's fancy dress parade. There were a few judges who took time off from their duties in the stalls plus a sprinkle of an audience cheering on their offspring who paraded their costumes on a stage set near the merry-go-round. In 1956, I wore a kimono, depicting a Japanese girl. Peter, my fourth brother, was dressed as an Indian (war paint and all), while Jackie, my sister, was the Ovaltine Girl – wearing a long dress with an apron, Dutch cap, and carrying a tin of Ovaltine. She was in

Jackie, Andy and Peter Lam taking part in the 1956 fancy dress parade. *M.R. Lam.*

a plaster cast because she had broken her big toe and when she walked, it was budups, budups[3] . . . and we called her that until the cast was taken off some time later! I seem to remember we all won prizes, as did all the participants in the contest. It was a family affair.

From 4:00 - 6:00 it was babies' and teeny tots' time. From dusk to 9:00 it was teenagers' prime time. For the teenaged girls and boys, it was open season, each gal hoping that the guy of her dreams (for that month, at least) would come by and indicate interest by a tap on the shoulder . . . and, of course, she could then choose to demurely display a sufficient degree of disinterest by saying that she was busy at that moment. Yes, games and gamesmanship were the dominant activities.

Auntie Cicely and her team of "Auntie" helpers (Ivy Lee, Thelma Lam, Shirley Manson-Hing, . . .) always made a wide selection of food to sell: chow mein, low mein, black pudding (rice and potato varieties), patties, stuffed eggs, crab backs, souse, fried rice, Chinese roast chicken and pork, won ton soup, pine tarts, pow, towsa, mauby and sorrel. Regular dinner was not cooked at home and we all bought food there, enjoying the festive atmosphere and company. And, if all that food was not enough, there was ice cream topped with flavoured syrups such as lychee. We went for Cyril's ice cream cones[4] filled with vanilla custard or coconut ice cream – as well as a choice of other flavours – straight from the churns.[5] Margery and Auntie Thelma Lam used to fill the cones with one or two scoops and if you begged hard you might get an extra scoop. There was a sugar cotton candy machine near the entrance gate and every youngster had to have a pink sugar cloud on a stick on arrival to the fair.

A Tannoy brand loudspeaker system was wired to cover the whole ground. The Deejay played the latest pop music and golden oldies. The youngsters would pop up at his window requesting their favourite piece and stallholders would ask for an announcement to be made... "Black pudding just arrived. Come and get it." A few times they had to beg the crowds outside to stand back and not to crowd the gate.

After 10:00 p.m., when the dance gate was opened, most of the Chinese families went home and the business of making money was truly on. The La Boule gambling table in the clubhouse was opened and the dance upstairs got into full swing. The hall would be jam-packed with

---

[3] A local slang expression representing the clunking sound.
[4] Bertie Cyril Ng-A-Fook ran a car hire garage and also made ice cream cones using specialized equipment installed at his home. It was a thriving business venture, and Cyril's cones were the popular carriers of ice cream in the country.
[5] Home-made ice cream was produced from special churns (many of them hand-operated).

people who paid a few dollars to do their thing on one of the best dance floors in the city. Tom Charles and the Syncopaters, the top-rated band in the country, played at the dances, with Albert Choy in charge of operations. The calypso beat and rock and roll tunes would send the place shaking as the dancers performed their gyrations, generating much heat in the night. However, they were able to remain cool by enjoying the naturally air-cooled environment, courtesy of the breezes from the nearby Atlantic Ocean wafting through the open louvres. Tables and chairs lined two sides of the dance floor, available for when a temporary break from the revelry was required. From an enclosed booth at the back of the hall, James Sue-A-Quan sold tickets for the various beverages – beer, wine, rum, and other alcoholic drinks. The customers could then collect their chosen intoxicant from the busy attendants at the long counter. This was not a sophisticated bar by any means . . . no martinis, lemon slices, stir sticks, and other extraneous distractions. If someone wanted to have a mixed drink, he did the mixing at his own table.

I remember a lot of the technicalities because my family was very involved with the fair. But every year it was a different "boyfriend"… well, I think that was one of the objects of the fair, wasn't it?

The Chinese Bazaar was held at the Chinese Association in Brickdam. All the proceeds went directly to the upkeep and maintenance of St Saviour's, our church at Broad and Saffon Streets. Again, months before the event, staunch members of the congregation would be busy planning events, preparing/making goodies for sale and, as ever, passing the "begging bowl" around the business community.

One of the main persons involved in the preparations and organization of the Chinese Bazaar was Cicely Ting-A-Kee, head of the Mothers' Union. Auntie Cicely <u>was</u> St. Saviour's. She and one of her sons, Georgie I think, always sat on the left of the aisle around the 4th pew from the altar. She sang the loudest and never wavered from the hymn. She knew all the hymns seemingly without looking at the hymnbook. I was more afraid of her than of Father Stinson, and would get a twinge of guilt on those Sundays when we didn't attend and sped past the church on our way to the Base for a picnic, just as she was singing.[6] Auntie Cicely organized everything. The treats she prepared for the Bazaar were delights that could not be missed. Trays upon trays of crab backs and stuffed eggs – I remember those in particular because they were my favourites. Once again, as with the Fair, we would eat dinner at the Bazaar. Auntie Ivy Lee was always in attendance with Auntie Cicely. I

---

[6] St Saviour's Church was located at the start of the East Bank Demerara road leading to Atkinson Air Field – the Base.

don't know why I remember her more than anyone else, suffice to say that she was always tempting me to buy more! Auntie Cicely was really a staunch member of the church and we all respected her goodness and belief in the community. It was said that the biggest sinners always sat in the front pew, and maybe that is why she never sat there!

The Bazaar was held on a Saturday afternoon in December, which was propitiously timed to make the most of the "giving" season – Christmas! The "wares," crochet doilies, table pieces, little curios and food and drink were laid out on white cloth-covered trestle tables that lined the hall. Chairs and tables were set out in the middle. In contrast to the Chinatown Fair, it was a gentile affair – a time for the ladies, babies, tots and teens of the families to gather. It was mayhem.

One walked up the driveway and bought a ticket at the foot of the double stairway. On the platform at the top, there were always friends who had arrived earlier waiting to see who else was going to turn up. If there were a keen friend waiting, you would then be led to see the best thing or to meet up with the clique of friends already ensconced in a corner. Once the business of buying food, and persuasions to buy unusable curios which might be given away as presents (hoping that you don't inadvertently give it back to the maker), had been done with, the events began. Children's fancy dress parade, teen's dress parade, a recitation or two, a few songs sung by individuals or groups, piano recitals, ballet dancing . . . cultural things, you understand. It was an opportunity for parents to put their children's talents on show, and on stage.

There was an enormous Christmas tree, which touched the ceiling and the pressies[7] were scattered at its foot. Santa Claus was on hand to give the colour coded presents: pink for girls, blue for boys, red for babies . . . that sort of thing. Even if you didn't believe in Santa or didn't want a present, you just had to buy a ticket to shake his hand because it was for the Church. As was the raffle(s)! At every turn, tickets for all manner of things were sold by pretty young girls with demure eyes.

It was most definitely and entirely a uniquely intimate Chinese affair. There were Chinese lanterns and fairy lights everywhere. Almost all the women and girls shook out their cheong sams[8] and embroidered shoes for the occasion. Every female adult was "Auntie" and every male adult was "Uncle." You knew everybody, and everybody knew not only who you were but also ALL of your "business."

---

[7] Presents, in boxes wrapped with decorative paper.
[8] Chinese-style figure-hugging dresses with slit sides cut to mid-thigh level.

PILOTING THE WAY

Bob Chee-A-Tow

In 1865 the *Bucton Castle*, with 353 Chinese passengers, departed from Whampoa, the port facility for Canton (Guangzhou). Among them was Chee A-tow, a 20-year-old pedlar from Poon Yu. He was allotted to Plantation Peter's Hall on the East Bank of the Demerara River. He became known as David Chee-A-Tow and settled on West Coast Demerara where he was a shopkeeper. There he raised a family of 14 children. The eldest of these was Theophilus Milton Chee-A-Tow, who later moved to Georgetown and had a family of 11 children, the eighth one being Ivan Rupert "Vanny" Chee-A-Tow.

* * * * * * * *

My father Ivan was born in 1914 to Grandpa Theo and Grandma Martha Chee-A-Tow in Georgetown, British Guiana. As a young boy, he remembered that his father was fortunate to afford to send his three older brothers to Queen's College but when Ivan became eligible, his father had lost large sums of money through failed investments in the sugar market during the depression years. My dad had to go back to grade school to win a scholarship to gain admission to Queen's. Dad only did three or four years of College before leaving to work for a living.

In the early days, Ivan and his brothers took part in a variety of sports, including boxing, horse riding, tennis, wrestling and gymnastics. He recalled that whilst doing odd jobs on the West Coast he and his buddy Albert Loo were often teased because they were the visible minority among the overwhelming number of other kids of Indian and African origin, but whenever a situation turned physical, he and Albert would beat the daylights out of them.

Later in life, when Ivan was on a tour of duty with the U.S. Army in Guyana, he was piloting a ship up the Demerara River to the U.S. Base Station Atkinson when a soldier on board became drunk and unruly. He had two sailors bring the soldier to him and after an exchange of words, Ivan delivered a right hook that put him to sleep for the rest of the journey. When the ship arrived, he received an apology from the soldier.

Actually, physical contact was sort of a family tradition because Grandpa T.M. was into wrestling and boxing, as well as gymnastics. His home on Brickdam was the gathering place for various Chinese fellows who would meet there to practice and exercise. This budding group of athletes formed the nucleus for the Chinese Sports Club a few years later. T.M. maintained his interest in sports and became the official timekeeper for boxing matches while his son Stanley was the national boxing referee.

Although my father knew how to take care of himself with his fists, his nature was far from a belligerent one. He was helpful to others in whatever capacity he was able. One of my cousins wanted to become a ship's captain and Dad coached him for the examination to obtain his license. He also helped and encouraged a number of young men who worked with him to exceed their expectations, and these men have often demonstrated their gratitude to him for doing this.

Ivan Rupert Chee-A-Tow started his maritime career in 1931 by working as a marine apprentice on schooners that plied between Georgetown and the various islands in the West Indies. On 5 December 1934, he then joined the Transport & Harbours Department as a Marine Apprentice Steamers, working on vessels that sailed up the Demerara and Essequibo Rivers as well as to the North West District. On 18 September 1937 he signed on as a Pilot Apprentice - Harbours. In less than two years later, on 1 July 1938 he became a Pilot's Assistant. On 1 January 1939, the year I was born, he qualified as a 3rd class Pilot - Harbours and by 1 January 1942 he held the position of 2nd Class Pilot - Harbours. As a Government Pilot, he was taken by tug boat to meet the incoming cargo ships out to sea, which he boarded and brought into the harbour.[1]

While he was employed at Transport & Harbours Department and during the outbreak of the 2nd World War, Ivan was seconded to the Royal Navy detachment stationed in Guyana. He was engaged in executing coastal patrols in addition to his piloting duties. At that time the German pocket battleship *Admiral Graf Spee* was creating havoc in the South Atlantic, having sunk several British merchant ships, and one of the assignments was to keep a lookout for the *Graf Spee*.[2] My father recounted that one evening he went out to join a ship, which he was scheduled to pilot, and while he was climbing the ladder the ship was hit by a torpedo. He recalled jumping unto the anchor chain and then

[1] On the mouth of the Demerara River there is a bar that has to be negotiated during a favorable tide.
[2] On 13 December 1939 the *Admiral Graf Spee* was engaged by three British cruisers, *Exeter*, *Ajax*, and *Achilles*, and suffered damages that caused her captain to seek refuge at Montevideo, Uruguay, a neutral country. Given 72 hours to do repairs the ship departed on 17 December, but Capt. Hans Langsdorff scuttled her on leaving Uruguayan national waters, believing that a superior British force was lying in wait.

scrambling to the deck of the tug. That was the last time he saw the cargo ship.

On 31 October 1944 Ivan resigned from T&HD to join the Alcoa Steamship Company of Mobile, Alabama. He operated between Trinidad and Georgetown as a 2nd Officer while one of the ship's officers was in hospital in Georgetown. These trips were of short duration and Dad was not away for any length of time. The War in Europe was still in progress and enemy subs were sighted very frequently just miles from Guyana's Harbour. Apparently his vessel was too small and unimportant to draw hostile action from the U-boats.

It was on 1 July 1945 that Ivan was offered employment with the U.S. Army as Master of the *Gen. R.N. Batchelder*, a large tug. This vessel operated between Georgetown and the U.S. Base at Atkinson Field. At the end of World War II, Ivan began employment with the Marine Canadian Company Sprostons Ltd as Chief Pilot and later Marine Superintendent. He captained a variety of cargo ships as well as the *R.H Carr*, which plied between Georgetown and Wismar, up the Demerara River. In 1952 Ivan was offered a Marine Superintendent position at the British Company Bookers and retired there as Company Director in 1974. At Bookers he was the Chief Pilot and was responsible for the operations of six cargo ships that worked between the West Indian islands and Guyana. Most of the cargo came from Bookers manufacturing businesses.

In our younger days, Dad often took brother Tony and myself to the Sea Wall to go kite flying. We went along three on a bicycle, heading up Camp Street. Later on, in our teenage years, he even invited our school friends to join the family on trips to Buxton beach and Atkinson Air Base for swimming[3] and gymnastics. He himself was fond of swimming and boating.

Throughout his career, my father seemed to have had a good relationship with those he worked with, and I myself recall that on several occasions a number of fellow pilots came over to the house for beverages. Our family was also very friendly with the government Harbourmaster Capt. C.H.Walcott and Booker Brothers' Mervin Matthews. Dad was the first person of Chinese ancestry to be offered the post of Company Director at Bookers. He had piloted the way.

---

[3] The U.S. forces built a large outdoor swimming pool, with diving boards, a shallow section for children, plus changing rooms and showers. It was the first of its kind in the country. After the war, the facility became a popular recreational site for the locals.

FAMILY JEWELS

Mike U-Ming
as told to Trev Sue-A-Quan

In 1861, a family consisting of U A-ho, his wife Lo Shee, and four children arrived in Georgetown aboard the *Chapman* and were allotted to Plantation Ogle on East Coast Demerara. Two of the sons, U-Hing and U-Ming became goldsmiths and jewellers in their adulthood. U-Hing's son, Manuel U-Hing, better known as M.U. Hing, narrowly escaped death in the great fire that consumed the Chinese Quarter in December 1913. As the buildings were burning, looters took the opportunity to relieve the store of much of the jewelry in U-Hing's store. Meanwhile, U-Ming's son, Samuel U-Ming, himself pursued a career as a jeweller. The two families' expertise was handed on to the next generation, with cousins Percy Hing and Samuel U-Ming Jr. joining the jewelry trade.

* * * * * * *

For a while, my dad used to work for R.G. Humphries, the jewellers on Water Street. During that time Uncle Percy also worked at the same company. Sometime around the mid-1950s, Percy Hing and my father decided that they were going to leave R.G. Humphries and start up their own jewelry business. It was located on America Street very close to Water Street, near to Stabroek Market. They shared the premises with an outfit that I think was called New Swiss House, which dealt in watches and clocks – sales & service. The two sections were basically side by side. So, together, the store offered the customers both jewelry and watches/clocks. That carried on for a while and then Percy decided not to continue, I guess after his wife passed away and his son Richard was becoming quite established as a chartered accountant in England. Percy Hing decided to sell out to my dad and move to Jamaica. My dad continued to operate on his own until the riots broke out in 1962 when there was a lot of looting and arson and he never reopened his business there.

A lot of his tools were damaged or stolen by the rioters. The looters would have had little use for the tools; they were on a rampage and just wrecked what they didn't feel like taking. There was a large vault where a lot of stuff was stored and the looters were unable to open or move it, so whatever valuables were in there remained intact. The building was not burned, but some neighboring stores incurred fire and other damage and losses. He decided that, because of the uncertain political and economic climate plus all the civil unrest, the best thing to do would be to send his large young family abroad while he remained to wind up the business affairs.

My father continued to work at home where he kept a duplicate set of tools. In fact a lot of work was being done at home for quite a while. My grandfather, Samuel Sr., lived with us until he passed away in 1955 and he used to help my father and Percy make jewelry at home on a private basis. A workshop had been set up adjacent to the garage and grandfather had his own work desk upstairs. It's interesting the way history has repeated itself, because way back when, my grandfather and M.U. Hing, Percy's father, were also in business together, but I don't know the details.

Samuel U-Ming, Jr. at his polishing machine in the workshop at home. *Mike U-Ming.*

Most of the work was with gold and precious stones. (My dad bought the stones from an outfit that I believe still exists – a company owned by a Polish person, Krakowski.) They did quite a bit of filigree work. I guess the styling would be more East Indian in nature, because of the large Indian community. They made all types of jewelry i.e. rings, earrings, necklaces, bracelets and broaches; people liked to wear broaches in those days. They made a lot of bracelets – those big wide bands that they called slave bands – that were worn at the wrist or clamped on the upper arm.

All of these were made by hand, all the design, the carvings and so on. They were made from beaten gold. The gold would first be milled into 18-carat or 15-carat quality, or whatever was desired. Pure gold is 24-carat and very soft, and it was mixed with an alloy containing mostly copper to produce a much harder product that also was more durable than pure gold. They would have a slab of milled gold, and then put it through special rollers, increasing the pressure to make it flatter and flatter. Then they would cut out a strip and work on that until it was the right size. Some of the slave bands were as much as two inches wide.

My grandfather, up to a few months before he died at almost 80, used to help my dad make various pieces of jewelry. They did a lot of engraving on rings, earrings, bracelets, etc. If a customer wanted something that was heart-shaped, pear-shaped and so on, they could make it from a mould. All of the processing could be done in the workshop at home. There was a gas torch, looking rather like a welder's torch, which they used to melt down gold pieces and remove impurities. In those days you didn't have a source of pressurized fuel gas. You had to keep the pressure up by pumping some bellows with one foot in order to maintain an even flow of the gas into the torch. I don't know what gas it was but when I was a little boy, my father would get us to pump the bellows for him. Chains were made a link at a time and some people ordered some pretty fine chains. It required steady hands and patience to make a chain because the customers wanted each link to be soldered and not just pressed together. They used a type of soft solder to do such welding.

My father did a lot of engraving. He didn't have any formal training, as far as I know, but he was quite artistic. I used to watch him engrave initials and inscriptions on various pieces, and he would be doing it freehand. When he was engraving he would be really focused while he used the engraving tool, the stylus, which was almost like a pen but very sharp. Then there's a polishing and finishing process. Firstly, abrasive material would be used to smooth out the rough spots. They used a lot of emery – very fine. The stuff they used was like sandpaper, but it was the finest grade of sandpaper. After making a ring, for example, they would take a circular tool and wrap this abrasive paper around it and just rub the ring to remove any tiny bumps. Then the jewelry would be polished on a machine with a rotating buffing fabric. There were various solutions to make that gold or silver (he did a lot of silver work too) shiny and smooth. If a piece of jewelry were not finished in the proper way, it would lose its luster very quickly. Some people have jewelry that would stay bright for a very long time, if finished properly.

My father also did silver work and I would say that silver represented 10 to 20% of the business. But gold was the main thing although some customers occasionally wanted platinum or white gold. He could get whatever gemstone you wanted – diamonds, rubies, emeralds, sapphires, and so on, and in whatever size you preferred. They used to carry a stock of precious stones, within a broad price range.

I used to earn a few dollars during holiday time, when I would work at the store. Essentially I would be there to greet customers as they came in because they didn't have a receptionist as such. The watch section was at the front, whereas my dad and his staff would be working at the back. Whenever a prospective customer wanted jewelry the watch guys would have to call my dad from the work area. It helped to have somebody to greet customers and show them items on display. The employees were skilled jewellers. They had tables set up like workstations. Each station was equipped with the necessary tools and adequate lighting. Jewelry manufacture generates a lot of dust and dirt, including gold dust, and they didn't waste that. But, because of the materials they used for finishing and cleaning, it was dirty. They also used a lot of acid – nitric acid – and they couldn't avoid inhaling the fumes, so there was an element of risk involved. They, of course, had the little magnifying glasses – the ones you stick on one eye like a monocle – to have a close look at the stones, diamonds, the work pieces, and so on. When everything was done each piece of jewelry was hallmark stamped stating what carat it was. There were certain standards to maintain according to the British assay regulations. So, if you stamp something 18-carat gold, it better be 18-carat gold. Otherwise you would get a bad name.

Interestingly, quite a number of people would custom order something in those days. They would come in and say they wanted a ring, or a bracelet, and first they would have to decide what carat they wanted, whether it was 9, 12, 15, 18, or something else. They would also have to choose how heavy they wanted it to be, how many grains, pennyweights[1] or whatever. This information would tell how much gold was needed, and then there would be the cost for workmanship. The design was another matter. Generally, the customer would have an image in mind, while some of them just wanted to follow the fashion. Of course, there would be times that they would see the finished product and it would not be what they really wanted. When they came to collect the jewelry they would be very clear about what they wanted, and they would be up front in saying so. It was important to have a happy customer, because you wanted that person to keep coming back. So you

---

[1] One-twentieth of an ounce troy, or 24 grains.

would take it back, and fix it. It made the transaction less profitable but that customer would return. Satisfied customers would then tell their friends.

My grandfather would help with the embossing, in which, for example, initials would be fused onto a piece of jewelry. He also did a lot of engraving on the slave bands. He would draw whatever design the customer wanted – a floral pattern or birds, nothing too exotic. But he would draw this out with a pencil on the gold itself and then proceed to hammer out the design. Despite his age, he had to be accurate or else the thing would have to be redone. He had these little engraving tools and made tiny dots and lines or whatever shape you wanted – flowers with petals, birds, etc. and you could see the feathers in detail. He would be there hammering away for a couple hours at a time, but the constant pounding is what I remember because it was a continuous bang . . . bang . . . bang. He would hammer it on this very hard metal plate. Once the engraving was finished the work had to be smoothed to take out any dents and burrs. After that, the band was bent into the shape of the bracelet.

My grandfather taught us a lot. He taught us to make and fly kites. We made kites of all types – box kites, polygon-shaped with a singing engine,[2] and even fish and butterflies. Of course, he never approved of us putting short tails on the kites to make them zip around wildly. Sometimes we would tie a razor blade to the end of the tail and zip the kite away, trying to cut the strings on other people's kites. But one thing he didn't tolerate was rudeness. We used to get a knuckle on our heads from our grandfather – a sharp rap to penetrate our thick skulls.

Grandfather used to teach us to fish. We used to go fishing a lot in the local trenches, irrigation canals and the seashore. What I remember was, we used to go at the beach . . . the same time that we would go flying kites (and sometimes later on in the year) and we'd go catching crab or sheriga. You had to go with some big tongs or pincers, then take a stick and poke at the holes and drive them out. You had to be very careful how you picked up those little devils because they have sharp claws. This was out on the East Coast, not at far as Ogle, and we would go on the beach when the tide was out. It was a muddy beach with a lot of crab holes. We also used to go catching crab in the dark. It might have been 7:00 or 8:00 at night. We would put a lantern down – a kerosene lamp – and the bundari crabs would just come to the light and we would pick them up and put them in bags or metal drums. We also went on

---

[2] A flap of paper mounted behind a raised triangular section of the kite, that would oscillate rapidly in the wind and generate a loud buzzing or humming sound.

hunting trips on the foreshore and marshy fields. . . to shoot birds, mainly. Then we small fry were the ones who had to go and pick up the birds, slogging through water and mud like retriever dogs. Even so, we thought the experience was such fun, and the birds were a tasty treat.

Even when he was old, my grandfather used to drive the old Austin and he would be the one taking us out to the beach to fly kites. There would be a whole lot of kids piled into that car. But sometimes he would doze off when he driving. He was a hummer – he loved to hum. So there he would be, humming along while he was driving. But once the humming stopped you had to watch out because he probably had fallen asleep at the wheel. It was a family joke, and fortunately nobody got hurt . . . or at least not seriously, because I understand that he once hit a cyclist.

I remember the Chinese Association. I knew that if we were so inclined we could go and learn to speak Cantonese at the Association, something that my father and grandfather tried to get us to do without any success. Both wanted us to go, but my father more than my grandfather even though my father himself couldn't speak Chinese. He just thought it would be nice for us to be able to communicate and as part of our education. Among the children the common attitude was, who wants to learn to speak Chinese anyway? Of course, today I regret it. I guess the Association people would have said, send your children along any time. My dad would urge us and may even have dropped us off in the car a number of times (we had our bicycles and could have gone by ourselves) but we were not interested. On the other hand, my cousins whose father, Cho-Chin, came from China, had the opportunity to speak the language at home with their father.

For me the best time was being a teenager in B.G. It was so carefree. . . a truly fun time. People took the time to be nice to each other, and looked out for each other. If we misbehaved, a neighbor or somebody from several blocks away who knew our parents would bring us home or lodge a complaint with our parents – hey, I saw your son doing so and so down D'Urban Street, or wherever. It was really nice. They cared.

Overseer

Alvin Hugh
as told to Trev Sue-A-Quan

Alvin Hugh, born in 1915, is the grandson of Yu Kong-ku, who according to family legend, was a warlord in China. Yu Kong-ku had four sons, and the second one, Gabriel, married Cecilia Fung, daughter of Fung Pun, an immigrant on the *Whirlwind* in 1860. Gabriel and Cecilia had ten children between 1903 and 1921, Alvin being the eighth child.

* * * * * * * *

I went to school at Queen's College in Georgetown and after completing Third Form I transferred to Central High School, because of financial difficulties at home. I had two brothers who were abroad at university and my father was the only breadwinner. We didn't have enough money to allow me to continue studying, and sometime about 1931 I went to join my father's sawmill at Blake, on the east bank of the Essequibo River, a little way upstream from Parika. The sawmill was essentially a family operation with some twelve employees working for us. The wood and logs came from the upper reaches of the Essequibo River and brought by various suppliers, such as people who held forestry grants, as well as Amerindians who felled trees on land that they owned. We handled all sorts of local wood, including mora, greenheart, purpleheart, crabwood and others.

The trees, trimmed of their branches, typically came to the sawmill by raft. Those logs that were heavier than water, e.g. greenheart, were transported on rafts made of other lighter timber stocks, or else strapped to the outside of a ballahoo. Some of the logs were thirty to forty feet in length and required several people working together to guide them downriver. There was a ramp leading to the river from the sawmill and a steam-powered winch was used to haul the logs to the saw. We would use a circular saw, either 48 or 52 inches in diameter, to square the logs and produce studs, eight or ten feet in length. Sometimes we needed to make larger lumber pieces, perhaps 6 x 6 inches, and 20 or 24 feet in length. These would be needed as supporting beams for buildings. Because of its heavy density and durability, greenheart was used at places where there was extended exposure to water, such as for piles, and in the construction of wharves and stellings.

Squaring a greenheart log. *Crown copyright material.*

Initially we did not have a plane, but we later acquired one to give a nice smooth finish to the boards used for constructing buildings. The shavings from the planing operations were burned along with firewood in the boiler for the steam engine that powered the circular saw. However the sawdust from the cutting accumulated in huge piles at the site because the boiler furnace was not constructed to burn this material. One of the possible uses for sawdust was as insulating material for blocks of ice. There was no ice factory in the Essequibo area, and the only option we had was to use it as a filler for holes and low spots on the site. After the pile of sawdust had grown into an excessively large mound, it was set alight to clear the ground for fresh sawdust.

The pile of sawdust became productive in an unexpected way. Iguanas found the sawdust a wonderful place to make their nests. Digging holes deep into the pile, the iguanas laid eggs and raised their young there. Sometimes I would try putting my hand into the hole to catch an iguana. On several occasions I would end up with a section of the iguana's tail twitching in my hand after the animal had scurried off leaving its tail behind. Eventually, some local residents told me the secret; it was necessary to grab hold of the tip of the tail, the last three to four inches, and then the iguana would be unable to break off its tail. Then, by pulling it out of the hole, the back legs could be grasped, followed by the front legs. The workers would also use this method to get themselves an iguana to eat. The iguana has a small circle on its head and by piercing that spot with a nail or plimpla,[1] the iguana would be killed. Apparently that was a sensitive area, perhaps above the brain. The green skin would be taken off and then the iguana would not be very different in appearance from other kinds of meat. It tasted sweeter than chicken, and when it was done up as a curry it was delicious. But I was able to enjoy iguana only when I was a bachelor because after I got married, my wife Ulex would have none of that in our house.

---

[1] A sharp thorn or pointed tip of a stick or tree branch.

After the logs were cut to the appropriate sizes, they were shipped to our depot at Stewartville, where our residence was also located. We hired punts from a nearby sugar estate to transport the lumber to Uitvlugt, and from there the wood pieces were transferred to dray carts for the last leg of the journey to Stewartville. The haulage was done by individuals who brought their own dray carts or donkey carts for this task. In this way there were several different people gaining earnings from the sawmill operations. The various studs, beams, planks, and so on, were stored in a large shed at the depot with galvanized metal sheets on the roof.

The customers would come to the depot to select the lumber they needed from among the many stacks of different woods, taking the purchases away in whatever means of transportation they had available. The sugar estates bought materials for building houses for their employees, mora being a popular selection for the frames, and crabwood for the walls. Crabwood and silverballi were usually selected for making furniture. Purpleheart, so named from its distinctive purple hue, was preferred by banks as the best material for their long countertops, which, when polished, gave a rich gleaming look. This feature made purpleheart a popular selection for floors also.

After my father died in 1936, I continued to help in running the sawmill operations, but after my mother passed away in 1954, I decided to look for another line of work. Wales sugar estate, owned then by Bookers, was one of the regular customers for the wood products from our sawmill. I told one of the managers of the estate that I was looking for a job. He thought I was joking, but I reassured him that I needed to be involved in something other than the sawmill. The manager recommended me to go to Georgetown to submit an application at the head office for Bookers. As for my qualifications, I explained that I could work well with people and knew how to handle labor relations.

I was rather surprised when I was offered employment at Wales estate because discrimination on the basis of color was an ongoing practice. I credit the manager of the estate for giving me support, because when I started the job in 1955 there were only four people at the senior staff level who were born locally; the rest were British expatriates. I was hired as field assistant in charge of mechanical tillage. My responsibilities were to oversee the tasks in which machinery was used for growing cane. It was an important position in the management of the estate. My appointment did not go over well with the expatriates because it placed me among them as senior staff. They felt that the manager was bringing in some Chinee man above them and their noses, already up in the air, were now put out of joint. The expatriates kept to themselves and did not willingly mix with the locals. The four of us locals consisted of a Portuguese, a

Dougla, a Mulatto[2] and myself, and in this situation, we kept to ourselves. It took some time for the expatriates to realize that we were not inferior to them in ability. Then, they began to talk a bit with us.

Management of the sugar estates was performed by British expatriates. From left to right are an official from the Georgetown head office, a Field Manager, and an Overseer. *Crown copyright material.*

As far as our opinion of the expatriates was concerned, we did not feel that they were the sharpest knives in the drawer. They were sent from England and became senior staff members because of their origin, and they had an obvious resentment of us locals being considered as equals. There was one occasion when I was taken to do estimates for digging a canal. The dragline operations were one aspect of my job, and there was a regular need to dredge or widen canals, as well as to dig new ones. The expatriate whose assignment I was to take over had me join him in inspecting the canal. We had to calculate how many cubic yards of earth needed to be excavated in order to set the price for the dragline operations. He was busily working out the figures when he saw me standing around idle.

"Have you finished, Hugh?" he asked.

"Yes, I'm finished," I replied.

"So how much do you make it?"

I told him the number I had calculated, and he looked at me in wonderment.

"How did you get it?" he queried.

I told him I used this length, that measurement, and whatever distance, and worked out the total. But obviously this was not what had bewildered him.

"How did you finish so quickly, Hugh?"

I had done all the calculations using fractions, but I wasn't going to tell him.

---

[2] A Dougla is a person of mixed African and Indian ancestries; a Mulatto is one with one parent a white person and the other black.

"I did it the short way," I explained, "you were working it out the long way, and I used a short way."

"Whaaaat?" he exclaimed.

Besides digging drains and canals, I would oversee plowing, work involving tractors, and the like. The cane growing period was nine months to a year. During that time the cane would have to be irrigated whenever there was insufficient rainfall. Pumps would be employed to deliver water from the canals. Once the cane was ripe, the leaves would be burned off to clear the overgrowth and drive away rats and snakes. Crews of workers would then come with their cutlasses to harvest the cane. They would cut as close to the ground as possible because the sugar content was highest in the lowest section of the cane stalks. The harvested beds would be replanted. When the yield fell below three tons per acre, these low-yielding sections would be left fallow for three to four months. Laborers were employed to plant the cane. Starting with a long cane stalk the planter would push three eyes[3] of the cane into the soil, almost parallel to the ground, and then chop that portion off. Leaving a short space from the end of the just-planted piece, the next three eyes would be offset to the left. By inserting stalks in this fashion, staggering them left and right, the sowing procedure was almost like sewing. The cane stalks selected for planting were young ones, and each of the eyes would produce a new cane shoot. When a field was being replanting after being left fallow, the soil would be loose and less physical effort would be needed for planting.

There were other jobs that were done manually, such as forking, shoveling, weeding, and manuring. Each of these tasks had a driver in charge and one of his responsibilities was to set a rate for the work to be done. The workers were predominantly East Indians who lived on the estate and worked six days a week. The driver had some flexibility to offer a wage rate that was acceptable to both the management and the workers, since there would be variations in conditions even for the same job category. But, if he tried to go too low he might find himself facing a strike by the workers. On some occasions I was called to be the middleman in the bargaining process. Since my early days on the estate I was well instructed that I had to know exactly what was going to be asked of the workers and be capable of demonstrating the way that the task needed to be done. Otherwise, the workers could argue about the rate offered or else do an ineffective job. The workers were quite cunning, and would try to do the minimal amount of work. For example, they might fork to a very shallow depth, turning only the top few inches of soil. The

---

[3] Nodes on the cane stalk.

overseers were aware of this possibility and carried around long stout sticks to probe into the ground to test how deeply the beds were forked.

Payday for the workers was every Friday. They came and gathered near the window of the pay office. Based on the rate set for each task carried out that week, the management would have the money prepared for distribution. The driver would supervise the payout, calling each worker by number and name to collect his wage. Payment based on a piece rate system was a long established method that had been going on for generations. Later, when Guyana became independent, the government instructed that payment be made for each day worked. Up to that time black workers were hard to come by – they never did weeding when it was a piece rate job – but once a daily rate was established, they came flocking to get work. These workers were quite cunning and would go to hang around in the back dam whenever the opportunity came, knowing that they would be collecting full pay for that day's effort.

The workday started early in the morning when everybody had to show up for orders from the field manager at half-past five, rain or shine, for that day's work. This was essentially an assembly for the staff, and after the orders were given we could go to the mess and get a cup of coffee. By seven or seven-thirty I would be down at the back dam supervising the machinery operations. There was no chance that I could miss getting up because there was a worker assigned to getting everybody awake. He would come by and shout "Boss, boss," and if he heard no response by his second calling, he would take a long pole – one typically used to herd cows – and start up a racket. There was no possibility of missing this wake-up call, be there rain or storm.

Rainy day would of course mean that the roads leading to the back dam would be muddy and I would have to ride a mule to get there. A "bateau boy," assigned to me, would have to run behind the mule, and then hold the animal while I went off to do my work; the distance to the back dam was some three miles. He was also the one who cleaned and polished my boots on Saturdays. On sunny days I would ride my motorcycle to the worksite. The expatriates would have to pedal their bicycles or ride mules to get to where they needed to go.

The senior staff members – the engineer, deputy manager, field manager and the overseers, some 12 to 14 in all – were all provided with housing in the same area of the compound. My family was assigned to a nice three-bedroom house that was formerly built for a very senior person. It was equipped with an oil-fired stove, fridge, and hot and cold running water. An electric boiler provided an ample supply of hot water, which was a definite luxury for tropical Guyana. Electric power was supplied for free and so too were the light bulbs. In this situation the lights under the house were left on, day and night, and if a bulb blew we only needed to call the office and an attendant would be sent to take care of it. He and others also came by regularly to clean the house, polish the floor, and tend the garden. The only person that we hired ourselves was our cook. This comfortable spacious house also came with several items of furnishings, such as a Morris chair,[4] beds, and linen. Then there were some daily supplies that were provided free – soap, kerosene oil for the stove, cow's milk, and, on occasion, fresh vegetables from the manager's garden. Sugar was offered to us at discount price.

The senior staff had access to a launch to take us across to Diamond, on the opposite side of the Demerara River. It ran at regular intervals, but we could also request it for private use for a reasonable fee. We took the launch whenever we needed to go shopping in Georgetown, the ride between Diamond and Georgetown being by taxi or bus. In addition, Wales estate had a bus to take the school children to Georgetown via Vreed-en-Hoop and the ferry. The bus would take the children to the various schools and it would then be stationed at Grove, not far from Diamond. We could take this bus to get to Georgetown if it happened to be available after we crossed the river by launch.

The Hugh family was provided with this spacious house on Wales estate. Photo taken in 1999. *Suying Hugh.*

We had the same vacation leave as the expatriates, namely three months every three years. The passages to go to England or Canada for a family with two children were paid by the company during such leave.

---

[4] Designed by the Englishman William Morris (1834-1896), the Morris chair is a wooden armchair with four holes or slots to hold a crossbar that allowed the hinged back of the chair to be set to an upright or reclining position.

On one occasion we went to London, and walked into the head office for Bookers. We were received courteously and offered tea and biscuits, which we found a pleasant surprise because it required an appointment to see the administrative managers in the Georgetown office.

As a senior staff member, we indeed enjoyed a privileged lifestyle. We even had our own exclusive clubhouse on Wales estate, separate from the clubhouse designated for junior staff, who furthermore did not enjoy the free perks that we seniors received. At our club we could play billiards, table tennis, and darts. There were also tennis courts with balls provided, but we had to get our own rackets. Once a year, the manager would host a dance, and we were entitled to bring two guests. It was a festive occasion with turkey dinner, all the drinks you could imbibe, and, of course, dancing. We enjoyed a life of considerable luxury compared to what the majority of the locals had. To my understanding, I was the only Chinese overseer on a sugar estate at that time.

The senior clubhouse was available for exclusive use by the overseers and senior staff. Photo taken in 1999. *Suying Hugh.*

DISTRICT COMMISSIONER

Lawrence and Esther Yhap
as told to Trev Sue-A-Quan

In the years leading up to Guyana's Independence Day, Lawrence Yhap was a District Commissioner for the colony of British Guiana. There were seven administrative districts along the coastal area of Guyana and he served as D.C. in five of them at various times. As the highest-ranking administrator at the local level, he oversaw the running of the district and represented the interests of the country's government, as well as being the titular representative of Her Majesty Queen Elizabeth II. In a nation comprised of many ethnic peoples striving to become an independent country, the District Commissioner sometimes faced significant challenges in trying to reconcile differing interests – the needs of the local areas and those of the nation, the old ways and the promises of the new ways, as well as the varied perceptions held by fellow countrymen, particularly those of two main racial groups, those of African and of Indian origin. He was thus seen by some people as an example of locally-born emerging leaders, but also regarded by other observers as a remnant of British colonial rule.

In the following story Lawrence Yhap describes his role as District Commissioner, and his wife Esther, whose contributions appear in *italic text*, has nicely filled out the account of their lives as local officials in Guyana.

* * * * * * * *

My grandfather Yhap Young-sau was an immigrant from China. He probably was allotted to work on a sugar estate in Essequibo because his children were born in Anna Regina. My father had a business, what you would call a general store, but a small one. He was the third child and the family was a humble one with no fame or fortune to talk about. I also was born in Anna Regina, in 1919, and was the third and last of his children because he died when I was just eleven months old. My father was an Anglican and my mother a Catholic. We children were baptized as Anglicans, but after our father died we were re-baptized in the Catholic Church. I recall going to a Catholic school in Henrietta not far from our home. After a few years, the family moved to New Amsterdam, the capital of Berbice County, at the other end of the country. This was because my mother's brother Joseph Albert (Bertie) Yip had a business there and Mother thought it would be a better place for our education. I was able to win a County scholarship, good for five years, the first of which was spent at the Canadian Mission School (Berbice High School). Then we moved to Georgetown, the national capital, and I continued my education at St. Stanislaus College, a secondary school for boys run by the Catholic Church. There I graduated with passes at the Cambridge "A" level examinations.

Right after leaving school I was employed in the Civil Service. The office I joined was responsible for licences and the collection of revenues from those licences. There were licences to be issued for buses, vehicles (including bicycles), shops, liquor sales, etc. and the Georgetown office covered a territory from Kitty, at the North-East outskirts of Georgetown, all the way up East Bank Demerara to the bauxite plant at Mackenzie. We had a launch at our disposal to take us to the various local administrative offices where we would carry out audits and make sure that the licences were properly issued and the revenue collected. A report had to be written up for each local authority under the jurisdiction of the Georgetown office to indicate the state of affairs with regard to licences and revenue for that local area. One of my duties was to inspect the liquor shops and check on the strength of the rum offered for sale using a hydrometer. If the rum were found to be diluted, the shop owner would be charged with a fine. The office had a few helpers, called runners, who kept track of the locations of the shops and made a record of those that were already inspected. This helped with our office operations, but it was still a busy time keeping up with the many businesses spread out over a large area.

When it came time to deal with the annual distribution of bicycle licences, the office would be filled with a mad rush of people and I would be writing up licences in a fury. Each licence cost $2 and the individual received a small numbered enamel-plated badge that had to be fixed to the bicycle, typically on the axle of the front wheel, to indicate that it was a licenced bicycle. The colour of the badges was changed from year to year so that it could be easily recognized whether or not the licence was valid. If the police found someone with an unlicensed bicycle a fine could be imposed, or the bicycle seized. The schools helped with processing the bicycle licences by taking on the task of issuing them to the students.

After a couple of years I was assigned to the Springlands office.[1] This appointment was made by the superiors in my office, and I had no choice in the matter. I was just told to report to the Assistant District Commissioner there. The duties were similar to those in Georgetown. I gained more experience at the job and was posted to various stations across the country and promoted to become an ADC. Eventually, I was made a District Commissioner. In the early 1950s I was sent to Leguan

---

[1] Springlands is located at the mouth of the Courantyne River, the waterway that defines the national boundary between Guyana and Surinam.

Island in Essequibo for my first appointment as District Commissioner. After that we moved to East Coast Demerara, next to Fort Wellington in West Coast Berbice, then to Vreed-en-Hoop, West Coast Demerara, and finally to Suddie in Essequibo.

I lived with my grandmother in Georgetown. When I was about 17 years old and attending Charlestown Convent school, I had a good school friend who lived across the street. She had lovely curls and one afternoon I was curling her hair as she sat on the steps of her house. Marjorie Kong lived in the back house on the same lot, and Lawrence, her first cousin, happened to be visiting. When Lawrence appeared at the back step Marjorie, who was on the front step, said to me, "I have a nice boy to introduce you to." Then she called him over and said to him, "I have a nice girl here." A couple days later he asked to visit my house, and so I told my mother and she said to bring him, let him come. Lawrence turned up looking smart and handsome in collar, tie and jacket and from that point on he was stuck. We were married in 1951. Lawrence was presented to the Queen just before independence. He was given a gold inlaid memento. I was presented to the Duke of Edinburgh.

The Queen never attends the celebrations marking a country's independence from Great Britain. She paid a state visit to British Guiana not long before the date set for Guyana's independence – 26 May 1966. I was asked to arrange the local activities for the Queen's visit. I was then in the Ministry of Home Affairs in Georgetown. When I was D.C. in the various districts I used to meet a lot of the fellows in the villages, ex-school masters, and they knew that I had a daughter. They would tell me, look you're moving from district to district and it's not good for this child to be attending one school for a couple of months then moving to another school; it's time you start to think about settling down somewhere. It was then that I applied for a transfer. Whenever we moved from this place to that we had to move the furniture. *While I'm making drapes for one house he might come home to say get ready, get packed. That kind of thing could happen and it didn't happen just once. I became an expert at packing crates of household items.* As a District Commissioner in the countryside there were free quarters provided. If I moved to town, I would have to find my own house, but our daughter's educational needs would be settled. That's why I applied to leave the local districts. I went in

One of the residences of the District Commissioner on East Coast Demerara.
M.R. Lam.

to the ministry and they approved. I transferred to the Ministry of Home Affairs as Assistant Secretary and shortly after came the Queen's visit. This ministry was responsible for her itinerary and that's how I came to be involved right away. Not too long after that came Independence.

I had some prior experience in making similar arrangements for the Princess Royal. I had to write the whole book for the Queen's itinerary, the route and places to be visited, although I did not accompany her. The local committees put in requests to have her pay them a visit and I had to choose the places. She went to the Buxton-BV² area. I had to make certain who was going to be in attendance, and who was to be presented. The same thing had happened with the visit of the Princess Royal. We set out everything, every movement of the cars – so and so would leave in this car, followed by that car, and that sort of thing. *Prior to the Queen's visit her equerry was sent out. Actually the governor should have gone up to meet him at the airbase but he couldn't go, so Lawrence had to go. Of course Lawrence knew the program and he was able to fill in completely. Lawrence took him all around for a preview, and Government House gave a dinner for him. This gentleman mingled a lot and we were all Guyanese, senior officers' wives. He asked who we would like to have come for Independence. Everybody said the Queen. But it was the Duke of Kent who came on her behalf.*

Toward the end of the Queen's visit there was a gathering aboard the Royal Yacht *Britannia* after which the Private Secretary was summoned to enter the State Room. Next came Mr. Douglas, the head of my department. Then suddenly they called me. I didn't know about this beforehand or what was going to happen. Nobody told me what to do in the Queen's presence – kneel down, or bow, or whatever courteous gesture was required. I wasn't told that I would be presented to the Queen, and be given a commemorative gift. I cannot recall now what I did, but the meeting was very brief because she was an hour or so behind schedule in her appointments and had to hurry off to a function at Queen's College.

Shortly after the Queen's visit I made plans to take vacation leave. The Prime Minister's right-hand man came into my office and said that Prime Minister Burnham was aware that I was due for leave, but wanted me to stay on to plan the Independence Celebrations because of the good job I had just done. Now I knew that when the Prime Minister had previously held the office of Mayor of Georgetown,³ his clerk was due for

---

² Buxton and Beterverwagting are two large population centers on East Coast Demerara.
³ Forbes Burnham was elected Mayor of Georgetown in 1963. In the following year he became Prime Minister when his People's National Congress (PNC) party won a majority of seats in the national elections.

leave and the mayor asked the clerk if he would stay on for a few months for a certain project. The clerk replied he already had plans to take his vacation. The mayor told him, in that case go ahead. When the clerk returned he found himself without a job. So I realized that if I took leave it would really be leaving, because I had accumulated one year's amount of vacation time. The Minister of Home Affairs said that the Queen's state visit was one matter, but Independence was our own affair and I could make plans as I saw fit.

It was a challenging task making the arrangements for Independence. *I remember staying up late at night typing up the plans.* For the big Independence dinner I didn't even issue an invitation to myself. I was too busy to attend, but I heard later about it from my colleagues. The gala dinner was held at Queen's College and the dignitaries and other important people were in attendance.

The District Commissioner was a Jack-of-all-trades, master of none. The system in Guyana was different from the system in, I gather, the various British colonies in Africa. In Africa the D.C. was almost like a Prime Minister. He had overall responsibility for everything and he was able to give orders for what he wanted done, and it didn't matter if the person was a professional or other, he had to do it. This was this, and that was that, and whatever he dictated stood. If anybody came to complain, he had the power to decide – he was the boss. The British didn't apply the same system in Guyana. We D.C.'s didn't have that authority. We had a Commissioner of Local Government and a Commissioner of the Interior as the bosses of the District Commissioners and the D.C.'s were just facilitators. The District Engineer was responsible for the public works. Local authorities would have discussions over a project, but when it came to the financing they would come to me. Then I had consult with the relevant engineer to get his advice and recommendation. If anybody wanted to lodge a complaint against the District Engineer I really couldn't do anything, in the sense that I could take the complaint but I wasn't empowered to make a ruling. The engineer had his own chief in the head office, who was superior to him, and complaints had to go to the chief. I couldn't interfere with that sort of thing. So I was more a titular administrative supervisor than a technical director. The New Amsterdam and Georgetown city councils operated as independent bodies and would submit reports for the D.C. to see, but the D.C. could not tell them anything. All the others regions would go through their District Commissioners and reporting had to be done early in the year. The D.C.'s had to see how the projects were progressing and check on whether they were squandering the money or not.

The D.C.'s were chairmen of the committees, and could only give advice. For example, at one time there was a development committee to decide about grants and loans for some places near the Pomeroon River.

Some people owned big estates but they were not developed and the owners asked for help for development. I could get people to tell me what they thought about that, whether it was possible, feasible or not, plus what the engineer must do. *There was a lot of traveling involved.* There was also a committee set up for people seeking help – old age assistance. Each district had a committee consisting of different members from the area representing different interests and the committee would decide on the amounts of the old age pensions, decide on which people could be given assistance from among those who applied for help. Some asked for temporary help and some needed help all the time for their families. There was an immigration section too, with an East Indian fellow who would deal with the people who came from India. *He spoke the language.* If they had conflicts to be settled – family affairs and so on – he would look into it. But he would come and discuss these problems with me. *When people had fights among themselves, they would go to the District Commissioner. It's a good thing we had a peaceful home life.* The D.C. was also a marriage officer who could perform marriages in a civil ceremony. He would preside over the ceremony and the taking of the vows of marriage, but he didn't have the authority to divorce couples.

Some of the typical administrative problems that the D.C. had to deal with were evident when I was posted to West Coast Berbice. We lived about three quarters of a mile east of Hopetown, at Fort Wellington, 52 miles from Georgetown. Hopetown was a place consisting of mainly people of African descent. Near to that was Bush Lot, where many of Indian origin settled.[4] In Guyana there were two administrative systems. One was the elected areas, typically the villages, while the other one, country districts, had appointed members. In the villages, the representatives would be elected, e.g. at Hopetown. In those places that were not organized, they would have their own committee consisting of appointed people. But not all of the villages were organized as local authorities. That is why we attempted to put together smaller units to form a larger one, making it easier for the administration. We would have a meeting with the people in the village and sometimes they didn't want to be associated with the proposed area. Both Hopetown and Bush Lot had reasonably large populations, but could have benefited by joining together; the same thing with Buxton and BV. But each one wanted to retain its own power. Also many of the unorganized areas became hesitant when they heard they would have to start paying taxes after consolidation.

In West Coast Berbice, there were problems with flooding from the sea as well as from the Abary River. Water came in from the sea and the

---

[4] There were at that time nearly equal numbers of ethnic Africans and ethnic Indians in Guyana, each group numbering just over 40% of the population.

properties north of the Public Road were always flooded because sea defenses there were lacking. It was not possible to issue orders to these local authorities to take action. Near to Hopetown and Bush Lot was a small authority, and next to that was a big unorganized area – Trafalgar. The people in Trafalgar wouldn't agree to become a local authority even though they needed protection from flooding. When we went past we would see that the house lots were all flooded and they became dry only when the tide receded. I tried to get them to agree to have a local authority, but without any success. I then heard indirectly that apart from not wanting to pay taxes, they didn't want to become a local authority because at high tide the fish would come rushing up to their doorsteps. At high (spring) tides, we would drive through the floodwater and see people fishing outside their houses. What is more, Bertie Allsopp[5] opened a fish culture station nearby. I had to go often with the overseer to his place. So in addition to the fish right at their door, the people could easily get tilapia, and they wouldn't agree to become a local authority. That's the sort of thing I faced, and then there was the racial thing between Hopetown and Bush Lot. If I said something one way, it would be regarded that I was against them. If I said it with the other slant, then the other side would accuse me.

Another thing was that in a district like at Fort Wellington we had to go somewhere to get things to eat and to purchase. If we went to an Indian shop to buy goods, well that was noted by one group as our favorite place: "Look, he going and buy." If we went to an African place the Indians would call out: "Look, look he going there." Where could we go? As a result I had to sometimes go all the way across the river to New Amsterdam to get things to bring back. Or go to Rosignol.[6] Once there was an Indian fellow who was a member on one of the local boards, and during the rice harvesting season he told us how much a bag of rice would cost. We paid the man. Then people complained that we were taking rice for free: "We saw him put it in the car." *But in fact we were buying broken rice for the dog, which wasn't sold in the shops.*

---

[5] W. Herbert L. "Bertie" Allsopp opened a brackish water fish culture station at Onverwagt for cultivating large shrimp (prawns), coarse shrimp (seabobs) and coastal species, including querriman, mullet, snook, croaker, tarpon (known locally as cuffum), as well as the African tilapia, which he had introduced to Guyana. Bertie progressed to become a noted fisheries expert, a United Nations consultant and Consul General for Ghana in Vancouver, Canada, as a result of his wide knowledge of all sections of that country, having spent seven years in Accra as the UNFAO regional fisheries officer for Africa.

[6] Rosignol was the terminus for the Georgetown – New Amsterdam railway line and located on the west bank of the Berbice River. Travelers then had to take a ferry to reach New Amsterdam, on the east side of the river.

Actually at the beginning of the year when the local authorities were holding their meetings to discuss a proposed budget, the D.C.'s used to attend the meeting and have to preside. The council members would decide to set taxes at 6½%, 5%, 3%, or whatever they felt was needed as a levy to fund what they were going to do. They would then submit their estimate to the D.C.'s office for approval, and he then had to comment on it and decide whether to recommend it or not. For instance, if he thought the taxes being levied were too much for the proposed repairs he could voice his opinion that the taxes were too high. The D.C. would submit that to the Local Government Board and the chairman of that board was the Commissioner of Local Government (the boss for the D.C.'s). On that board were representatives from different parts of the country and from the villages in question. They would go through the estimate along with the comments that the D.C. made. If a local authority applied for a loan or a grant for whatever project it had in mind, the D.C. would have to inspect those works. If it were necessary for an engineer to go with him then he had to tell the engineer. Likewise if it was a health matter the corresponding Public Health officer would go on the inspection tour with the D.C., and give a technical opinion on whether to recommend it or not.

We didn't have any formal connection with the police, only a night watchman. *All the police used to do was to come in the morning, bring the flag, raise it at 6:00 o'clock, and salute it. At 6:00 p.m. they returned to lower the flag.* At one time, Independence, I was in charge of arrangements for the celebrations. I was told that the permits for cars had just come in. This was in order to control the number of cars showing up for the various functions because not any and everybody could be allowed to drive there at will. Then came into my office the superintendent of police in charge of traffic. He told me that the police would be in charge of traffic and should control these permits. I said fine. I gave instructions that the permits be turned over to the officer and that they would become his full responsibility. He took them and left. Shortly after, I was called to a meeting by the Permanent Secretary. Already in attendance was the Chief Superintendent in charge of the whole police force and he was complaining to the Permanent Secretary – he hadn't even asked me anything yet. He was telling the Permanent Secretary that he thought the police should be in charge of these permits. This really surprised me, but I waited until he was finished. I told the Permanent Secretary the permits had arrived but I hadn't even seen them. I then said that the superintendent of traffic came and took the permits, and I had given him instructions to let you know. The Chief Superintendent didn't know that I had already done all that. He thought he was going to lay waste me.[7]

---

[7] To humiliate me.

I was involved with all the meetings and community affairs gatherings as an ex officio leader. For example the Red Cross would write to me through the District Commissioner. I would have to chair the meetings and my official title was "Wife of the District Commissioner." I had a busy life with school fairs, cutting ribbons, handing out end of term certificates, and so on. When I had to raise funds for various causes, say for the Red Cross, I approached the shopkeepers and they never turned me down. They all contributed. And I had to entertain when officials visited. I had a good cook. When the governors came, Lawrence had to get dressed up, usually in a suit, but he had no official uniform. However he had to have a hat, a felt hat, although he never wore it. But he had to have a special hat for the occasion just to carry around; that was part of the dress code.

My mother came to visit us when we lived in Thomas Street, when Lawrence was on a trip to America on a scholarship. I lived opposite the Catholic School and she was going home at about 5:00 p.m. She was walking past the hospital and three sturdy women came down the street with hooked hands shouting "Vote PNC,"[8] and they threw her in the drain. The drain was steep and she broke her shoulder. A man had to come and take her to see Dr. Spencer. At that time she didn't want open her mouth to say how she got there.

We were in Vreed-en-Hoop when the rioting started in 1962.[9] It affected the whole country. As the wife of the District Commissioner, it fell on me to do something and so I organized a committee of 25 to 30 women of different races. We fed 400 to 500 children every day. Late in the evening, after Lawrence had finished his work as D.C., he and I used to go to the various Chinese shops and East Indian shops and they would bring bags of stuff and put it at the back of the car. They didn't want to be seen doing this and didn't want to be complimented, or for it to be known that they were contributing. All this food – rice, potatoes, saltfish, etc. – we didn't want kept at our house because the soldiers used to come through in the night. We lived in the big house on the Vreed-en-Hoop Road, and the local soldiers would come tramping through because it was a Government building. If they found the food they most likely would have eaten it all. We kept quiet and slept with a gun in the bed. I went over to the archdeacon of the Anglican Church, Father L.J. Rowe, who was retired and lived on the premises of the Vreed-en-Hoop Church, St. Aiden's. He said bring the food here. He had a spare room

---

[8] The People's National Congress (PNC), led by Forbes Burnham, was competing with the People's Progressive Party (PPP), led by Cheddi Jagan, in national elections. The former party drew most of its support from the Afro-Guyanese while the latter's following was mainly those of East Indian origin. The PPP won the 1961 general elections under an arrangement for limited self-government of the colony.

[9] There was a strike by Civil Servants in 1962 and then widespread disturbances with political and racial overtones. Troops were dispatched from Britain to help restore order.

at the bottom of the house so we packed all the food there. There was a black man who came to help with the cooking and the East Indians gave big wedding pots, and they set up a fire with all the ladies peeling and chipping up the food.

The Vreed-en-Hoop project went on for several weeks – a daily thing. The children got a good meal, a little bit of everything. My laundry woman – she had three children – said, mistress I got to put in my little bit. She had a boyfriend with a little boat and he used to pick her up the morning at half past three to four outside Vreed-en-Hoop, somewhere there along the riverbank. They would go upriver to where this fellow had a fish place and he used to give us a whole lot of fish, really a lot. Everybody would be sitting under the house cleaning fish – me, and the chauffer, and his wife, and some mothers, and then we would carry it over to this man who would fry it with flour. This was for the Indians in particular, because they didn't eat meat. Once I got a whole lot of chow mein in a parcel and I sent it on ahead before I turned up that morning, and an old lady put on a pot of boiling water and dumped all of it in – we had chow mein soup. They were none the wiser. I enjoyed working with them and being on the committee.

Things were going nicely, and the children would come in at half past eleven and queue up. We had tables and chairs. Then one day, one of the black men who used to help said, "Madam, don't go on the road after this. They are planning to beat you up." Father Rowe said we don't want that to happen. All the stuff was left there and we gradually gave it away parcel piece.[10] We were feeding both races, mostly Blacks, but the Blacks (the adults) wanted to beat me up because I was the wife of the D.C.

The normal age for retirement was 60, but the option was available that you could go at 55. Then the junior staff in the civil service started to complain that if the older ones stayed on to 60, it would take longer for the younger ones to be promoted. So they came to an agreement that the compulsory age for retirement would become 55, with the option to leave at 50. So when my 50th birthday came around in 1969 I decided to apply to emigrate to England and to Canada. At that time our daughter was at the age that if we were to leave things for a year or two she wouldn't have been able to accompany us because she would have been over age. Furthermore, it would have been better for me to make a new start at 50 rather than at 55. By the time the application was arriving in Britain, the approval from Canada had come back. We also left because of the politics in Guyana.

---

[10] Bit by bit, in small amounts.

LIFE ON THE PLANTATION

Jennifer Primrose Foo

Jennifer Primrose Foo was born on 17 May 1958 in Mackenzie, now Linden, Upper Demerara River, to Jamila Shahib Foo and George Lenan Foo, son of Benjamin Foo who was a rice miller and cattle rancher. Jennifer's great-great-grandfather emigrated from China as an indentured laborer.

* * * * * * *

The Idyllic Life

Life in Mackenzie was quite idyllic. Our family lived in an adjoining house located at the corner of Arvida Road and Greenheart Street directly across from the sports stadium. From our front steps, we could see the tennis court, which also doubled as a basketball court. We spent many happy times playing on the tennis court with my mother's younger siblings.

Mom was a pioneer in that she drove the family car, which was quite a novelty in the 1960s as there were very few women drivers in those days. She would have a mishap now and again. One day, she was reversing the car out of the driveway, and ended up way across the street in the ditch against the fence surrounding the tennis court. I was worried about how we would get out of this predicament. Out of the blue, a few Sir Galahads arrived on the scene; they lifted the rear end of the car out of the ditch, and we continued on our merry way. Sometimes Mom took us for drives along the route by the golf course, and the fancy houses for the American and Canadian expatriates who worked at the bauxite company.

My dad was an electrician at the local bauxite mining company called DEMBA (Demerara Bauxite Company). He used to ride a motorbike to work. I was daddy's pet back in those days, and he was my hero. By 1962, my parents had four of the six offspring they would bring forth into the world; the youngest child at that time was the long-awaited son. When we were older, Mom related the story of how we would boldly announce, much to the amusement of our visitors, that we had gotten a new brother who had a "birdie."

At that time, Mackenzie was like any little town in a developed country. We had nicely paved streets, and our lawn was cut by local city employees who used long-handled scythes. We had electricity and flush toilets, and we shopped at Choo-Kang's supermarket for groceries. I remember that Tycoon Choo-Kang was quite taken with me as a child. Whenever he tried to hug me, and I would struggle valiantly to escape until he gave up and let me go.

Mom raised a few Creole hens and a rooster for home use. Beneath the unenclosed area of our house, Dad had built a pen in which there was a small stepladder for the chickens to clamber up and exit into the outdoor fenced-in chicken run. Every morning, Dad let the chickens out into the chicken run. Then we put on our rubber boots, and helped him to wash away the chicken droppings by spraying the concrete floor of the pen with the garden hose.

Sometimes we had fun at the chickens' expense. When we were playing in the yard, we would run toward the chicken run at full speed, and holler loudly as we neared the fence. This tactic scared the living daylights out of the chickens, and they squawked in fright as they scampered away from the fence. But we also liked to pluck blades of grass, and push them through the holes in the chicken wire to feed the chickens. As the sun began to set, we walked around the chicken run making lots of noise to shoo the chickens toward the opening of the pen. One by one, they slowly re-entered the pen where they were locked up for the night.

Sudden Changes

Just after my sixth birthday in 1964, everything seemed to change. We were unable to play outdoors like we usually did. Instead, we were locked up in the house all day, and were allowed to go outside to play only when Dad came home from work in the evenings around 4:30 p.m. At this time, we would watch in amazement as smoke billowed from burning houses on the hillside of Wismar, a town across the Demerara River. I was old enough to comprehend that something bad was going on based upon the adult conversations I overheard. But I was not afraid because Dad, my hero, stood tall and strong.

I remember Dad sitting on the stairs with a metal file, sharpening his cutlass that could not get any sharper. As he sharpened the cutlass, he threw the gauntlet down by boldly declaring, "If anyone touches me or my family, he would surely not live another day." I did not realize that the country was engrossed in major racial disturbances. Dad was not worried about his safety as he is of Chinese ethnicity, and no one bothered him. He was concerned, however, about Mom's safety because she is of East Indian heritage.

My understanding at that tender age was that there was major hatred on the black people's part against East Indians. I did not know why this had happened so suddenly. We had made friends with lots of black children in school, and we had never before experienced this type of racial hatred from anyone. Our black neighbors' children often climbed over the wall, which divided our adjoining verandahs, and came into our house to play.

The adults related horrific stories of how many innocent East Indian men, women, and children were inhumanely tortured, raped, and murdered by black people. When we were older, Dad told us stories of how some East Indian women had been brutally raped by several black men at a time. After the rape was over, soft-drink bottles filled with sand, or broom handles, were shoved into their private parts and caused so much damage, these women were forever unable to bear children.

Since Guyana was still a British colony, soldiers were dispatched from Britain to help to maintain order. I can clearly recall the day when we saw British soldiers going from house to house. When they came to our house and knocked on the door, we were quite apprehensive. Mom went out and spoke to them. They asked her if she wanted to leave Mackenzie. She told them she was okay, and they soon departed.

We could see the police station from our house. Many displaced East Indian people were temporarily housed under the open section of the police station, which was enclosed by a wire fence for their security. They waited there for several days until the ferry returned to take them down the Demerara River to Georgetown. From there, they were scattered to wherever they had other family with whom they could stay. We had some family friends who were housed at the police station. Mom often cooked food, which she gave to the husband (who was black) to take for his wife (an East Indian), and their children.

Auntie Patsy is of Chinese and East Indian heritage. Her husband, Uncle Hassan, is an East Indian. When the disturbances began, she sent her aunt and their three children to Georgetown for safety. I recall her telling my parents that after she and Uncle Hassan had left our house one evening to go home, some black men began to follow them. She was not afraid for herself; she was afraid for Uncle Hassan's safety. She said they started to walk quickly, and tried to dodge the men by cutting through alleyways, and turning down different streets until they arrived safely home.

Plucked from our Idyllic Life

Before we realized what was happening, my parents packed up most of our belongings including the Creole chickens, and we, too, headed down the Demerara River on the steamer *R.H. Carr*. The idyllic life we knew in Mackenzie was over.

We stayed with Dad's brother, Uncle Solomon, at Craig Village on East Bank Demerara. Dad returned to work at Demba. He lived in our house at Mackenzie during the week, and came to visit us on weekends. Mom and her four children slept on one big bed. It was quite a tight squeeze. My brother often cried a lot during the night because he wanted to breastfeed, and sometimes Mom was too exhausted to oblige. I remember one night when she dumped him outside of the mosquito netting to sit on the floor. He cried his little eyes out. I got out of bed, picked him up, and comforted him until he fell asleep.

We never had to sleep with mosquito nets when we lived in Mackenzie. Mosquito nets became a new feature in our life at Craig Village. We had many sores on our bodies, because we scratched wherever the mosquitoes had bitten us. Just when we were getting adjusted to this new life, we moved again – to grandfather Benjie's estate, which Dad had inherited. This estate was located in Friendship Village, three villages farther away from Craig Village. Mom seemed more relaxed after we moved to Friendship. The house had not been properly maintained since grandmother Lucy had passed away. Being the homemaker that she is, Mom wasted no time in making the house more habitable.

It was nice to sleep in our own spacious beds once again. However, we had to get accustomed to a new way of life. Since there was no electricity, we used kerosene lamps. The protective glass chimney of each lamp became black with soot each night. Therefore, we had to make sure we cleaned the chimneys early enough during the day before it began to get dark. Mom cooked on a kerosene stove; no more electric stove. I hated it when the "black pot" (soot) stained my hands and became lodged under my fingernails every time I had to clean that stove. Mom hand-washed our clothes, as we could no longer use our electric washing machine.

Getting accustomed to using an outside latrine was another ordeal altogether. If we needed to relieve ourselves during the night, we used a large potty, which we had to empty first thing in the morning. Mom assigned us new tasks such as scrubbing floors, which required getting down on our hands and knees. As soon as the sun began to set, the evil mosquitoes emerged in droves from their hiding places. Therefore, we lit green mosquito coils that gave off scented smoke, and repelled those pesky insects to some degree until it was time for bed. Sleeping under mosquito nets became a necessity for survival.

When we had company, we used a "gas" lamp, which gave off more light. The lamp burned vaporized kerosene using a special wick. Whenever we lit this lamp, the brilliant light attracted black beetles in droves. I remember screaming in fright the first time a beetle alighted on my hair. To get rid of the beetles, we stuffed them into empty soft-drink bottles. Then we plugged the necks of the bottles with rolled-up pieces of old newspaper, and left the beetles to perish. Another method was to dunk the beetles into a basinful of water, and leave them to drown after we had sealed the top.

We walked around bare-footed outdoors even when the yard became muddy during the rainy season. I do not recall why we did not wear our boots. I hated walking in the mud. Ugh! For much of my younger years, I had "ground itch" between my toes. Yes, life was immensely different.

Growth of Commercial Chicken Farm

Mom began to leave the eggs in the cage to allow the hens to incubate them. The end result was that we got more Creole chickens. Pretty soon, we had a bunch of roosters and hens roaming all over the yard. At feeding time, we shied rice paddy on the ground, and the chickens hungrily gobbled up the feed.

Mom's dad, whom we called Grandfather, and his wife, whom we called Auntie, came to live with us. After a few months had elapsed, they built a house for themselves on the site of an old building, which had collapsed with age. Prior to the construction of the new house, I had heard tales of "Dutchmen" (ghosts) inhabiting the old building. I always made sure I walked as far away as possible whenever I was in the vicinity of the site to avoid those scary Dutchmen.

One day, Mom brought home some newly hatched baby chicks that were clothed in soft, yellow down. Grandfather helped her to build a pen for them. As the chickens grew, beautiful white feathers emerged. As time went by, Mom started to buy more baby chicks. This meant that we had to construct more pens. And thus, a poultry farm grew out of minding a few chickens for our own use.

When the chickens grew to a certain size, we transferred them to another pen because it was time to change the sawdust. We then had the burdensome task of cleaning out the previous pen. The loose sawdust, which covered the concrete floor of the pen, became more and more caked together with chicken droppings as time went by. The compacted sawdust would stick to the concrete floor, and, thus, a lot of "elbow grease" was required to dig it up. We shoveled the old sawdust into empty chicken feed bags. Mom and Grandfather used this waste material as fertilizer whenever they planted vegetables. We then washed the concrete floor using a coconut broom and water mixed with disinfectant to kill any germs. The pen was left to dry naturally in the tropical air.

Mom often took us to the sawmill in Hope Village where we filled burlap bags with the dust that had fallen as lumber was sawn into planks for building houses, etc. I always liked the smell of fresh sawdust. And, of course, the goal was to collect dry rather than soggy sawdust. We often filled the bags almost to the point of overflowing, and dragged them to the rear of our faithful old station wagon. I helped Mom to hoist the heavy bags into the station wagon, and she drove home slowly because of the great weight we were hauling.

We spread the new sawdust on the concrete floor of the air-dried pen. When Mom purchased new baby chicks, we put them into this nice, clean, fresh-smelling pen. We took turns washing and filling the water feeders. Dad manufactured galvanized feeders for the chicken feed that we hooked onto long pieces of sturdy copper wire, which were attached to the rafters the pen. This was purposely done to keep the chickens from knocking them over. At various times during the day, we checked the feeders, and replenished them whenever the feed became low.

The new pen holding the mature chickens contained cages in which the hens could lay their eggs. We filled the cages with dried grass on which the chickens could sit comfortably. The dried grass helped to cushion the eggs, and prevented them from cracking on the wooden bottom of the cage as the eggs plopped out of the chickens. We had to collect the eggs periodically during the day or else they became broken as other hens entered the cages to lay their own eggs.

Occasionally, when it was my turn to pick up eggs, I might notice that a hen was about to lay its egg in the cage. For the heck of it, I would hold my hand out just below the tail feathers, and when the egg emerged, it plopped into my palm. The newly laid egg was moist, but it soon became dry with exposure to the air, as it was still warm from being inside the chicken. Chickens were known to fly up and lay eggs inside the long cylindrical part of the feeders, so I learned to check there for eggs too. When we collected the eggs, we might come across a few that were larger in size than the others. These usually contained two yolks, and Dad called them "double-yolk" eggs. Since the hens were very productive, Mom began to sell cardboard trays of eggs to various grocery stores. However, we always kept the "double-yolk" eggs for our own use.

Mom kept only one or, at most, two roosters in each pen because they fought violently over the hens to protect their territory. There was one particular rooster, which was not my favorite bird at all. This rooster would sneak up behind me whilst I was bent over busily collecting eggs from the cages. Then the critter would squawk loudly, and before I could gather my wits, it would launch itself at me from behind, and spike me with the spur on its leg. I dropped many an egg during these surprise attacks. This belligerent old stalker scratched me so badly one time with its spur, I became afraid to venture into the pen without a big stick. Every time I entered the pen, thereafter, I pointed the stick in the rooster's direction and threatened it in a loud voice; it would scamper away in fright toward the rear of the pen. Yeah, that smart aleck learned not to mess with me, and my big stick!

As time went by, Mom began to buy young chicks with brown and black feathers. They grew up into red-feathered hens that laid brown eggs. So we had both white and brown eggs to sell. After the hens reached a certain age, whereby Mom and Grandfather deemed them past their prime as egg layers, we sold them off individually to customers. But, first, we had to catch the birds. We chased them into a corner of the pen, and grabbed the nearest chicken, holding on tightly as it squawked and fought in a vain attempt to escape. We tied the legs together with twine, and placed the chicken in a sitting position in the pan of the scale to be weighed. Grandfather Benjie's old scale came in quite useful. We used to play with this scale as a toy – placing whatever we could find in the pan on the left, and adding different weights on the right side to balance the scale evenly. Now it was worth its weight in chickens as we charged the customer per pound accordingly.

From Eggs to Plucked Chicken

Mom began to raise other chickens, which she sold either live or plucked. Mom and Grandfather would choose a day just for plucking chickens. Grandfather usually arose very early on that day to light the fires under the two half-drums, which he had filled with water. When the water reached a certain temperature, we went into the pen to catch the chickens, and gave them to Grandfather one by one to be slaughtered. To get ready, Grandfather trapped both of the bird's feet under the ball of his left foot. Next, he grabbed the two wings, pinning them under his right foot. After these steps had been completed, he grabbed the chicken by the neck, and cut its throat with a very sharp knife without severing the head. Since I always wanted to emulate the adults, I once tried to help with the slaughtering. I set up the chicken just the way I had seen Grandfather do it. Then I grabbed the head and was all prepared to slice its neck. The bird began to struggle in protest, and I did not have the heart to take its life. That was the first and last I time I ever attempted to slaughter a chicken.

After Grandfather had sliced the chicken's neck and most of the blood had drained out, he passed the chicken over to us for the next step. I learned to hold the limp chicken by its feet, and submerge it carefully into the boiling water in the drum. The process of soaking the chicken in hot water made it easier to strip off the feathers. After the feathers were removed, I would cut open the chicken just below the breast, thrust my hand inside, and pull out the entrails. I cut the gizzard open, and peeled away the inside membrane along with the undigested feed. I learned to carefully cut the bitter bile duct from the liver without puncturing it. Then I washed the liver, gizzard, heart etc., and inserted them back into the cavity of the chicken. I became quite adept at this procedure as time went by.

My aunt, Angie, taught me how to prepare the guts of the chicken for cooking. First, I squeezed choice lengths of the intestines to empty them of their contents. Next, I took a "pointer" from a coconut broom, used it to pick up a bit of the outer end of gut, and pushed it along the inside of the intestine so as to turn the gut inside out. While the gut was still on the pointer, I ran my thumb and forefinger along its length to clean it some more. Then I took the pointer out, and proceeded to clean another one. After a good amount of guts had been cleaned, I washed them carefully with salt and limejuice. The guts were now ready to be curried. Sounds gross, but they were tasty. Yum, yum!

We had a young dog that liked to eat the entrails of the chickens, and we fed him quite generously. One day, he ate too many of our offerings, and went straight to sleep behind the rear wheel of the station wagon. As Mom was leaving a few hours later to deliver the plucked chickens to the grocery stores, she unknowingly drove over the sleeping dog. By the time we heard the dog yelp, it was too late. It had been crushed to death. Auntie broke down in tears because she had really liked this dog. We were all sad.

Chickens and Ducks

As if it were not busy enough, Mom also began to raise ducks. Uncle Donald's wife had given me a duck as a pet. Mom took the duck to Ma (her mother) who had a drake with which my duck could mate. Soon afterward, we had ducklings, and I became a "grandmother." The ducks grew and multiplied. Mom added some white Moscovy ducks[1] to the mix, and before long, we had lots of ducks in our care. Dad built a pond in which the ducks loved to swim and groom their feathers.

From Chickens and Ducks to Sugar Cane

Uncle Donald was the first one in the family to start growing sugar cane commercially. After a while, Dad decided to get into this business venture too. My parents made arrangements with the sugar estate company in Diamond to have bulldozers sent to grade the land, which was a veritable tropical jungle. Grandfather Benjie had planted orange and cocoa trees while he was alive, and they were pulled down. A dragline also came to dig canals for drainage of excess water, and to allow access for the punts (barges) to take the cane away to the sugar mill.

The main dam, which bordered our property, was accessible by car, and Dad often took us for a drive to check on the progress of the clearing of the land when he came home on weekends. I remember him setting fire to a large pile of uprooted trees to get rid of them. Then a big plough came to till the land. Mom and Grandfather hired workers to do the planting. I liked to watch as they planted the cane. A worker would push a stalk of cane at a shallow angle into the soil, and chop it off just above the "eye," or bud. He continued this process, spacing them about two feet apart, until the whole stalk of cane was used up. I recall being quite impressed by the speed and accuracy of the workers as they systematically wielded their cutlasses.

Before long, the cane sprouted shoots. About three months later, it was necessary to fertilize the cane to ensure that the stalks grew strong and tall. Mom and Dad taught us how to fertilize the cane. The idea was to walk along the path between two rows of cane carrying a bucket filled with fertilizer in one hand. With the free hand, one grabbed a handful of fertilizer from the bucket, and threw it at the base of each cane shoot on the left row, and then the right row (or vice versa) as one progressed

---

[1] Common in tropical regions, Muscovy ducks have less fat layers to protect them from the cold.

along the path. The first round of fertilizer consisted of tiny, round, green pebbles. At about six months, it was time again to fertilize the cane. This time around, fertilizer that resembled large grains of salt was used.

This was all fun – in the beginning. Pretty soon, we grew to hate fertilizing the cane. If we were not careful, we were easily cut from the razor sharp edges of the cane blades. Then when we grabbed the next handful of salty fertilizer, the cuts would burn terribly. One of the side effects of fertilizing cane with bare hands was that our palms became stained from the fertilizer. We would try to scrub them clean; this was an exercise in futility because they remained the same until the old skin had peeled off in due time. To avoid the embarrassment, I hid my stained hands under the desk whenever my school friends came by to chat with me. I envied the carefree life of my citified friends. Yes, those were not fun days at all, lugging heavy buckets of fertilizer in the fields, and fertilizing each cane shoot.

There were times when we had to transport the fertilizer by boat (canoe) because certain parts of the plantation were inaccessible by car. Of course, I wanted to learn how to steer the boat. Mom showed me, but the boat often veered from left to right, and back again, along the canal. Then I devised a plan to sit at the bow of the boat instead of the stern. Whenever the boat headed off course, I learned to use my paddle (oar) to maneuver it back on course. I did eventually learn how to steer the boat from the stern.

On one occasion, Mom had left my sister Colleen and me to unload the heavy bags of fertilizer from the boat while she headed off with a bucketful of fertilizer to fertilize the cane. As I was lifting a bag to hand it over to Colleen, who was standing on the shore, the boat began to drift away from the bank. I grabbed hold of tufts of grass with one hand to pull the boat back in place, while still struggling to maintain my balance as well as my tenuous hold on the bag with the other hand. Unfortunately, the bag slipped and tipped over before Colleen could grab hold of it properly. Some of the fertilizer spilled into the water and other granules fell on shore. We scraped up as much of the fertilizer as we could from the soil. In fear of Mom, we covered up the rest with dried grass.

Mom was no fool. When she returned to get more fertilizer, she discovered our carefully devised plan, and yelled for us to return to the boat. By that time, we had already filled our buckets and had begun to fertilize the cane. As soon as we reached within arm's length, she grabbed both of us, and began to pound on us with her bare hands. This was our punishment for spilling the fertilizer.

Yes, life was not easy growing up on the plantation. There was always work to do. Dad still worked at Demba, and came home only on weekends. As the amount of work on the sugar plantation increased, Mom decided to stop rearing chickens and ducks, with the exception of the few she kept for home consumption. I felt very relieved, because when Mom was busy with the cane business, the burden fell upon me (the oldest child) to feed the chickens, pick up the eggs, and so on.

Adding the Produce Farm

Mom always liked to plant, whether it was flowers, vegetables or whatever caught her fancy. I always called her Mrs. Green Thumb because she could make a rock grow. Mom decided that she wanted to start a farm, and plant vegetables, cassava, eddoes, etc. So she and Grandfather agreed to transform an uncultivated section of the plantation. The soil in this area was loose black soil, which Dad called "pegasse." It was excellent for planting, fertile, and not dense like clay. This land was covered with wild-growing vegetation, so we had to clear it. One day, Mom and Dad loaded all of us into the boat along with cutlasses, an axe, food supplies, etc., and we paddled our way to the new lot. We helped to cut down the smaller trees, while Dad, Grandfather, Auntie, and Mom went after the abundant and taller congo pump trees, which had thick, sturdy trunks.[2] I remember this as being a fun day.

Before we had left home that day, Mom had grated a coconut to which she added water. Then she squeezed the resulting coconut milk from the mixture to create the liquid base for cooking "metagee." She added sliced green plantains, eddoes, chicken (which she had browned at home), and so on. We helped Mom to gather dried twigs and leaves to build a fire. Dad cut two tree branches in a certain way to create forks on one end that were inserted into the handles on either side of the pot; the other end of each branch was anchored in the ground to support the pot above the fire. Then Mom lit the fire, and soon the metagee began to bubble away. We were really hungry by lunchtime. When Mom served up the metagee, it smelled so good. I remember this dish as being the best metagee I have ever eaten in my life. The aroma of the burnt wood had fused together with the flavors of the food, and it was really tasty. We all asked for second helpings.

By day's end, we were totally exhausted as we paddled our way back home. To give us a treat, Dad stopped along the way and took us to pick

---

[2] A tree found in the tropics with leaves that are used as an herbal medicine.

coconuts. Dad made a small circular noose with some rope. He inserted his feet in the loop, and placed his feet on either side of the coconut tree. This caused the loop to become taut and kept his feet from slipping, while providing leverage as he slowly ascended the tree. Dad said the noose was uncomfortable because it put a lot of pressure of the sides of his feet as he climbed the tree. When he reached the point just below where the coconuts were hanging, he began to tug on them with as much force as possible until they became dislodged and dropped to the ground. We were careful to stand at a safe distance away to avoid being clobbered by the falling coconuts. When Dad was finished, we gathered up the coconuts and loaded them into the boat.

After we reached our destination, we chained the boat to a wooden pole, which was anchored on shore. We unloaded the boat, and made several trips to fetch everything home. Thank goodness our house was not far from the canal. Then Dad began to chop open the top part of the coconuts and gave them to us to drink the water. After we had emptied the coconuts, we gave them back to him. He chopped them open so that we could eat the nice, thick meat which we called coconut jelly. We loved adding brown sugar to the coconut jelly before we ate it.

Mom and Grandfather planted plantain and banana trees, eddoes, cassava, pineapples, boulanger, bora, pepper, bagee, and all sorts of vegetables on the farm. I liked going to the farm to help Mom and Grandfather. It delighted me to see how nicely everything looked after all of the produce had been planted. Grandfather had built a log bridge, which extended from the main dam across our canal to the shore of the farm. He anchored two long poles into the center of the canal on either side of the bridge. We would grab hold of the poles, which we used for balance, as we carefully maneuvered our way across the log bridge; the poles followed our progress, arcing their way to the other side of the canal. When we wanted to cross back, we grasped the poles, and treaded along the logs as the poles arced their way back to the point of origin.

Sometimes Mom drove the new mini car on the main dam when she wanted to go to the farm. One day, while I was waiting for her near the car, I heard a noise. When I looked toward the trees in an uncultivated area to the right of the farm, I saw a monkey swinging from branch to branch. It startled a flock of green parrots, which cawed cacophonously as they flew away. I felt thrilled to discover that we had monkeys and parrots on our plantation.

I loved the fresh pineapples Mom brought home from the farm. I learned how to cut the thick peel off the pineapple just the way Dad did in a decorative design, and how to carve the "eyes" out. Then I rubbed salt all over the pineapple before washing it off and cutting it lengthwise into long slices. Sometimes we also ate the hard middle core. The taste of canned pineapple cannot come even close in comparison with fresh pineapple. Mom taught us to grate the pineapples, and cook them with brown sugar to use as filling in the making pine tarts. Needless to say, we ended up with more produce than we could consume. Mom gave some of it away to Ma, Auntie Patsy, and others. Auntie sold the rest of the produce at La Penitence market.

Harvesting the Cane

When the cane was ready to be harvested, Mom drove to the town of Buxton on the East Coast to hire cane cutters. These men were temporarily housed in the old chicken pens, which had been converted into what the cane cutters referred to as their "casa." She also arranged with the sugar mill to have the required number of punts dispatched to our estate to haul the cane away.

Mom and Grandfather would decide which section of the cane field they wanted to harvest first. It was necessary to set fire to the selected area to burn away the dried cane blades and underbrush to provide easy access to the cane roots, and to clear out any snakes. Since burnt cane would ferment rather quickly, it was crucial that Grandfather set fire only to an area that could be harvested in one or two days. Therefore, it was necessary to cut a pathway, which served as a firewall, to prevent the fire from spreading beyond the area that had been selected for harvesting.

The cane leaves and underbrush were burnt prior to harvesting. *Crown copyright material.*

Thick chains with giant hooks on the ends were permanently attached to the front and back of each punt. Ahead of time, Grandfather would tug on one of the chains, and drag the punt along the canal close to where the cane was being cut. Then he placed a plank that extended from the land onto the edge of the punt, thereby forming a bridge. Next, he arranged the two thick unattached chains that always accompanied each punt, at equal distances from the middle and the end of the punt. These chains were laid out so that they ran along the bottom of the barge, and up the sides. The ends of the chains, which also had giants hooks attached to them, were left hanging over the lip of the punt.

Each punt was numbered. An overseer from the sugar mill came during the day to document the number of each punt. Mom or Grandfather also recorded the punt numbers, as well as the names of the cane cutters who had been assigned to each punt. It was customary to have anywhere from two to six cane cutters assigned to every punt. I admired the harvesters at work – they made cane cutting seem so easy. First, a cane cutter would cut off the seared cane blades from the tops of a few stalks of cane. He knotted the ends of the blades together to create a "tie," and placed it flat on the ground. Then he chopped a length of cane at the root, grabbed hold of the severed stalk, sheared off the blades at the top end, and placed the cane crossways on the tie. He continued this

A long, sharp cutlass was used for harvesting the cane. *Crown copyright material.*

process until the bundle of cane had grown to a certain size.

After each worker had cut a number of bundles, he began preparing to transport them to the punt. He first took a long piece of cloth and formed a thick, coiled padding, which he placed on top of his head. In one smooth movement, he bent down, twisted the two ends of the tie around the stalks of cane, and hoisted the bundle onto the padding atop his head. He held on to the ends of the tie with one hand to prevent the cane from slipping out of the bundle as he proceeded toward the punt. He climbed the bridge, and threw the bundle of cane into the punt across the chains. This process continued until the punt was full.

Sometimes the cane cutters filled the punts above the lip. In order to do this, they shoved stalks of cane in an upright position between the inner wall of the punt and the bundles of cane to create an extended barrier around the perimeter of the punt. The cane cutters continued to load the punt, while they carefully monitored how deep the punt had sunk into the water from the weight of the cane. When a punt was full, the chains, which were hanging over the lip of the punt, were hooked together to prevent the cane from tumbling into the water as the punt wound its way to the sugar mill.

Oxen were used on some estates to haul the punts. *Crown copyright material.*

After all the cane in the selected area was cut, a tractor from the sugar mill came in the evening to haul the cane away. The driver of the tractor linked the punts together using the chains that were permanently attached fore and aft on each punt. He then attached the chain on the front of the leading punt to the tractor, and slowly drove out of the estate toward the main canal. After the driver had pulled all of the loaded punts from each estate into the main canal, he connected them together, and hauled the whole lot to the sugar mill.

When a punt arrived at the sugar mill, the chains around the bundles were attached to a crane, and the whole punt-load of cane was hoisted and dropped onto a scale. An employee at the mill recorded the weight of the cane in tons. The cane was then dropped into the cavernous mouth of the mill, where it was ground to a pulp. The resulting cane juice was run off into large vats where it went through further processing to yield crystals of brown sugar.

One week later, Mom or Dad went to the office at the sugar mill to be paid for our cane, which was based on the total tonnage supplied. They were also given the weight that had arrived on each of our assigned punts. Dad manually

Unloading the cane at the sugar mill. *Crown copyright material.*

summed up the total tons of cane that each group of workers had harvested. Then depending on the rate the cane cutters had agreed upon prior to being employed, Dad calculated how much money should be paid to each work group. He further divided up the money equally among the individual members of the group. Dad insisted that Mom learn how to calculate the cane cutters' earnings in the event that he was away from home.

On Vacation in Mackenzie

During breaks from school, Mom would load us up in the station wagon, and drive about two hours to Mackenzie to spend time with Dad. Those were fun times. By now, Dad had been promoted to a supervisor at DEMBA, and he had been given a company jeep to drive. He often took us deep into the jungles near Mackenzie to search for cocorite and couriah. He also brought along a cutlass and a long pole. When Dad located a cocorite or couriah palm, he chopped away the underbrush with the cutlass as he ventured toward to the tree. Since the tree trunk had lots of thorns, Dad could not climb it; neither did he allow us to get anywhere near the tree for fear of the long thorns pricking our feet. He used the pole to jab at the bunch of palm fruits. After a sizable amount of cocorite or couriah had fallen to the ground, Dad collected them and put them in a bag.

Couriah is round in shape and one would have to peel the green or yellow skin to get to the fleshy center. My uncles played marbles with the couriah seeds, and they also made spinning tops from them. Cocorite is oval in shape. I would bite off the protective shell at the top of the cocorite to expose the beginning of the thick brown skin. I then used my teeth to grab hold of and peel away the skin to uncover the pulp inside. The cocorite was now ready to eat. Cocorite pulp is pale peach in color and soft, unlike the barky texture of the owara[3] and couriah. I cannot say that we were tidy when we ate cocorites. We sat on the verandah and spat the skin and the seeds onto the ground below. The yard became quite littered with these remnants. I was always surprised when neither Mom nor Dad admonished us for our untidiness even though the neighbor became quite perturbed.

In Mackenzie, Dad had a Chinese friend named Mr. Lim. When Mr. Lim had gone into partnership with friends to start a Chinese restaurant there, Dad had done all of the electrical wiring for their business. Whenever we went to spend time with Dad at Mackenzie, Mr. Lim invited us to the restaurant for dinner where he always treated us royally by cooking special dishes only for us. I recall once when a patron asked

---

[3] Another common variety of palm fruit with a round seed that was a good substitute for a marble.

Mr. Lim for a dish he had seen on our table. Mr. Lim curtly informed him that it was not on the menu for the public. Also, before Dad came home to Friendship on Friday evenings, it was customary for him to stop by the restaurant to pick up the Chinese food Mr. Lim had cooked especially for us. This was our Friday night treat.

Dad allowed Mr. Lim to live rent-free in our house at Mackenzie. When his oldest daughter, Ming, came from China, she also lived in our house and worked in the restaurant as a cashier. One day, she told us how she used to help her grandparents to plant rice in the fields in China when she was younger. When I related the story to Mom, she promised that if we studied hard, we would get "big office jobs" one day, and our friends, too, would find our story remarkable when we told them how hard we had to work in the cane fields as children.

And Then There was the Milling Factory

After Mr. Lim had dissolved the partnership in the restaurant, he had the idea to mill grains into flour to make porridge. He approached Mom and Dad, and asked them if they wanted to go into partnership with him. They agreed, and before we knew it, one of the old chicken pens had been converted into the factory. Mr. Lim acquired all of the equipment, and Dad did all the electrical wiring (by now we had electricity). Mom was responsible for hiring the workers. She gathered up some unemployed relatives, and pretty soon, we were in business.

Since this new business was primarily Mr. Lim's baby, he called the shots. He decided to mill corn, rice, and plantains. Plantains were expensive, and so green bananas were supplemented. The processing of green plantains and bananas was very involved. Because they had to be hand-peeled, the sap from the skins stained the workers' hands. To lessen this effect, they rubbed coconut oil on their hands before they began peeling. Dad manufactured slicers to cut the plantains and bananas into thin slices. These slices were spread out on large trays to dry in the sun. Mr. Lim purchased a kiln to dry the plantain and banana slices on rainy days. The slices had to be dried to a crisp before they could be ground into flour.

After the grains were milled, we filled plastic bags with the flour, using grandfather Benjie's faithful old scale to obtain the correct weight. Then we had to seal the bags with a sealing machine. We learned to run our fingers inside the top of the bag to clean out the excess flour before inserting that part into the machine; otherwise, the bag would not seal properly. Mr. Lim was in charge of marketing and distribution. He also oversaw the accounting, payroll, and distribution of the profits. It took some trial and error to get the processes to gel into a smooth operation, but after a short while, the business was running like clockwork. We were excited, at first, to help out with this new business venture, but pretty soon it too became a chore.

Then, just about the time that everything was in order and running smoothly, Mom and Dad left for a vacation to the United States. Mom refused to go back to Guyana – to the hard way of life. Dad argued vehemently, but Mom refused to budge. She was determined to remain in order to obtain legal status for the whole family to permanently reside in the United States. The political climate in Guyana had begun to change once again, and Mom was concerned for our future. After three long years, which at times seemed never-ending, my parents finally returned and brought us to live in the United States.

Looking Back

Sometimes when I reflect on my formative years in Guyana, it seems like another life time altogether. Although we had to work hard with my parents on the chicken farm, in the cane fields, and in the factory, we were free to play to our hearts' content at the end of the day when our chores were completed. We did not have to worry about anything because Mom and Dad were always there to take care of our needs.

I will always be grateful that my parents ensured we received the best education they could afford. The sound educational base we received in Guyana has certainly sustained us in our new homeland. And what Mom had predicted many years ago when we were children has come to pass. When our friends observe our achievements, they erroneously assume that we have led a privileged existence all of our lives.

My parents are gone now, but they did have the opportunity to witness the legacy of their sacrifices. While life on the plantation was not easy street, the experience has resulted in hard-working grown-ups of whom my parents were very proud. And, yes, I truly would not trade one day for all the money in the world.

Afterword

The story of the Chinese in Guyana is a continuing one. A large number of the descendants of the immigrants who had arrived from China in the 19th century and the early 20th century became emigrants themselves. They have dispersed to many countries the world over, mainly to the developed nations in Europe and North America. Their encounters as new immigrants represent a new chapter in the lives of the Chinese Guyanese. Some became emotionally and socially detached from Guyana and quickly integrated into the land of their choosing, while others remained connected to the Guyanese lifestyle and culture in which they were raised. As a result, the expectations and experiences of the various individuals differ significantly.

Accounts of the lives of these Chinese Guyanese abroad are being sought in order to present this subsequent phase of the history of the Chinese in Guyana. Readers are kindly invited to submit stories that describe the various activities and experiences of these Chinese in their new homeland. They will be compiled into a collection of short stories that will describe the continuing journey of these people.

For a guideline, the subject persons should have grown up in Guyana and able to describe some of the lifestyle that they left behind. As with any immigrant community, especially one that is more visible than the mainstream population, or speaking a different language (or even a different dialect of English), there would have been challenges along the way in adapting to the new environment. The way that the Chinese Guyanese faced these challenges is the theme of the proposed sequel of this ongoing story.

About the Author

Trevelyan A. Sue-A-Quan was born in November 1943 in Georgetown, Guyana. He is the great-grandson of an indentured labourer who had embarked with his wife and son at Canton. They arrived at Georgetown in February 1874 after 78 days at sea. The family was allotted to La Grange sugar cane plantation on the west bank of the Demerara River.

Many of the second-generation descendants of these Chinese field workers became shopkeepers, including Soo Sam-kuan the author's grandfather. In the process of cultural assimilation his name became transformed into Henry Sue-A-Quan thus initiating the distinctive family surname.

Trev Sue-A-Quan's generation was the one that typified the transition from shopkeeping to professions based on higher education. His brother and sister both graduated from Edinburgh, Scotland and became chief surgeon and mathematician/computer specialist, respectively. Trev attended Queen's College in Georgetown and attained B.Sc. and Ph.D. degrees in Chemical Engineering at the University of Birmingham, England. He immigrated to Canada in 1969 but then pursued a career opportunity with a major oil company in Chicago where he was engaged in research in petroleum processing and fossil fuel utilization. Eight years later Trev headed East — to Beijing, China, becoming Senior Research Engineer at the Coal Science Research Center. He spent five years there and in 1984 returned to Canada with his wife and son. They now make their home in Vancouver.

Trev's interest in the Chinese in Guyana came from a curiosity about the circumstances that caused his great-grandfather to leave his native land. That history was described in his book *Cane Reapers: Chinese Indentured Immigrants in Guyana*, completed in 1999. This collection of stories is a continuation of the saga about the Chinese who migrated to Guyana.

CANE RIPPLES by Trev Sue-A-Quan
is a 6" x 9" book with 352 pages.

ISBN 0-9733557-1-9

Visit the **Chinese in Guyana: Their Roots** website at
www.rootsweb.com/~guycigtr

E-mail: Canereapers@Lycos.com

- -

Name _____

Address _____

_____

_____

Please send _____ copies of *Cane Ripples*
at CAN$25 each   = $_____

Add $10 shipping and handling costs for the first
copy, $2 for each additional copy.   = $_____

Surcharge for shipping outside Canada:
To U.S.A. $4 per copy; Overseas $10 per copy   = $_____

Total payment to Trev Sue-A-Quan   (CAN$)   = $_____

Mail to: Trev Sue-A-Quan,
240 Woodstock Avenue E.
Vancouver, B.C. V5W 1N1
Canada.

Cane Ripples is a sequel to the author's first book, *Cane Reapers*. Check the
website for information about local distributors of these publications.